MALC

THIRD AMERICAN
REVOLUTION

REVOLUTIONARY STUDIES
Series Editor: Paul Le Blanc

MALCOLM X
AND THE
THIRD AMERICAN
REVOLUTION

THE WRITINGS OF
GEORGE BREITMAN

EDITED BY
ANTHONY MARCUS

HB

Humanity
Books

an imprint of Prometheus Books
59 John Glenn Drive, Amherst, New York 14228-2197

Published 2005 by Humanity Books, an imprint of Prometheus Books

Inquiries should be addressed to
Humanities Books
59 John Glenn Drive
Amherst, New York 14228–2197
VOICE: 716–691–0133, ext. 207
FAX: 716–564–2711
WWW.PROMETHEUSBOOKS.COM

09 08 07 06 05   5 4 3 2 1

Library of Congress Cataloging-in-Publication Data

Malcolm X and the Third American Revolution : the writings of George Breitman / edited by Anthony Marcus.
    p. cm. — (Revolutionary studies)
  Includes bibliographical references and index.
  ISBN 1–59102–097–2 (hardcover : alk. paper)
  1. Breitman, George. 2. Communists—United States—Biography. 2. Socialist Workers Party—History. 4. Communism—United States—History. 5. X, Malcolm, 1925–1965. 6. Black nationalism—United States—History. I. Marcus, Anthony, 1963– II. Series.

HX84.B64M35 2005
324.273'7—dc21

2003040634

Printed in the United States on acid-free paper

CONTENTS

II. SOCIALISM

George Breitman on Socialism

III. THE LIFE AND LEGACY OF GEORGE BREITMAN

INTRODUCTION
GEORGE BREITMAN, MALCOLM X, AND THE THIRD AMERICAN REVOLUTION
Anthony Marcus

GEORGE BREITMAN: MARXISM AND MALCOLM X

The legacy of Malcolm X has become big business. There is a Malcolm X movie starring Oscar winner Denzel Washington, a Malcolm X College in Illinois, a Malcolm X Institute of Black Studies in Indiana, Malcolm X memorabilia auctions, and even a United States Postal Service Malcolm X commemorative stamp. At a time when white suburban college freshmen may be sporting Malcolm X pins on their coats, it is difficult to imagine a time, nearly forty years ago, when Malcolm X was seen by most Americans outside the black community as a dangerous extremist who hated white people and advocated violence against them. The *New York Times* editorial on the day after his death described Malcolm X as having a "ruthless and fanatical belief in violence" that had been the cause of his own death. Most of the American Left was not much better than the *Times*, dismissing Malcolm X as a "racist in reverse" and an irresponsible extremist, or simply ignoring him.

This book introduces the life and ideas of George Breitman, a white Trotskyist who was one of the first people outside the black community to recognize the importance of Malcolm X's message to people of all "races." During the last year before Malcolm X was assassinated, Breitman became one of his valued political allies. After Malcolm X's death in February 1965, Breitman helped preserve the legacy of Malcolm X by transcribing, editing, and publishing several volumes of his speeches. Finally, Breitman's own book *The Last Year of Malcolm X: The Evolution of a Revolutionary* remains one of the classic works on Malcolm X.

If Breitman had been merely a "righteous gentile," like Raoul Wallenberg or Oskar Schindler, guided by humanist sentiments, antiracist instincts, or other personal qualities that enabled him to overcome the prejudices of his day, his story would be little more than an interesting moral tale. However, Breitman was acting on more than just personal moral concerns. He was a socialist, guided by the revolutionary Marxist method and principles developed by Leon Trotsky and his Fourth International movement. His education, training, and half century of participation in the political traditions of American Trotskyism ultimately led Breitman and his co-thinkers in the Socialist Workers Party (SWP) to be almost unique among the American Left in their ability and desire to support Malcolm X's turn toward the world revolution. For this reason, Breitman's life and work as a Trotskyist activist and scholar offers a privileged entry point into the political history of race and social justice in twentieth-century America and provides important tools for theorizing about the changes that may take place in twenty-first-century America.

When Breitman died on April 19, 1986, he left behind a monumental legacy in the American Trotskyist movement. One of the founders of the Socialist Workers Party and the leader of its Detroit branch from 1954 until 1967, Breitman edited *Writings of Leon Trotsky*, the definitive fourteen-volume collection of Trotsky's works, along with five other major volumes of Trotsky's writings. In addition to bringing so much of Trotsky's work to the English-speaking world, Breitman wrote hundreds of articles, pamphlets, and flyers explaining society, politics, and history from a Marxist perspective. When, in the 1980s, the Socialist Workers Party turned away from Trotskyism, Breitman led an opposition, eventually being expelled from the Socialist Workers Party and founding a new group, the Fourth Internationalist Tendency.

As Paul Le Blanc points out in his essay in this volume, Breitman educated and inspired three generations of Trotskyist militants through his remarkable ability to give real-life meaning to abstract theoretical debates in social movements. Breitman's work has been read by thousands, if not millions, of readers. At a memorial service held soon after his death in 1986, greetings, speeches, and statements came from friends, followers, and comrades all over the world.

Despite his many accomplishments, his international admirers, and the long list of his titles for sale on Amazon.com, Breitman still remains largely unknown outside the Trotskyist movement. The process by which Breitman came to save Malcolm X's speeches for posterity and make Trotsky's work available and accessible to the English-speaking world remains largely unknown. This book is an attempt to recognize and clarify the political and intellectual vision of one of the rare working-class leaders who could see past American racial divisions and influence the people around him to do the same.

THE TRADITION OF AMERICAN TROTSKYISM

During the process of putting together a book on the life and work of George Breitman, I kept encountering the term "American Trotskyism" in documents, books, and discussions with Breitman's former colleagues. I had often questioned how a political ideology that was above all else internationalist and global in its perspective could possibly boast of an American tradition. The juxtaposition of Trotsky's unyielding criticism of the nationalism of "Stalinist" leadership with the idea of a "tradition" defined by its national boundaries seemed contradictory and somewhat hypocritical. However, as I moved further into the project, it became clearer to me that a tradition of American Trotskyism did in fact exist, and that in many ways its central themes and challenges were embodied in Breitman's work.

Since its start, Trotskyism has never been a centrally coordinated, integrated international movement. It has always existed as an array of national, regional, and international organizations divided and defined by specific national tasks and histories but sharing the same set of revolutionary methods and principles developed in the late 1920s and 1930s by Leon Trotsky and the Left Opposition to Stalin in the Third International. In the United States, Trotskyism has always been defined by the huge challenges facing individuals and organizations attempting to build a revolutionary working-class party in the center of world capitalism, or what has frequently been called "the belly of the beast."

American Trotskyism has struggled with the task of organizing a working class comprised of immigrants from the far corners of the world, raised in the individualist war of neighbor against neighbor for the "American dream," and schooled in the state religion of anticommunism and the militarism upholding America's role as world policeman. Though there are many unique challenges to building a strong, active, and conscious working class in the dominion of the world's wealthiest capitalist class and most powerful state, many are fundamentally similar to those facing Trotskyists in other advanced industrial nations.

American Trotskyists have often taken the lead from their international brethren on such issues as entry into larger reformist political organizations, the struggle against cross-class electoral alliances, bureaucratization of the trade unions, social democratic dogmatism, and the influence of Stalinism on the social movements. However, if there is one critical question that has forced American Marxists to develop their own program, study their own history and society, and lead rather than follow the twists and turns of the world class struggle, it is "the black question." If there is one crucial challenge that has marked the progress of Marxism in the United States and defined the unique theoretical and practical contributions of American Trotskyism, it is the struggle to bridge the deep divide between black and white sections of the American working class.

This divide between black and white has afflicted the American working class since the first color laws were enacted in late-seventeenth-century British North America and has been one of the keys to US capitalism's unprecedented success. It remains one of the primary reasons that the US working class is the least organized, least socially conscious, and most overworked in the advanced industrial world. The lack of an American labor party, comprehensive national healthcare, and many of the other social entitlements that have come to be seen as basic to life in a first-world economy may be partly attributed to this racial divide. In *Das Kapital*, Karl Marx said, "Labor with a white skin cannot emancipate itself when labor with a black skin is branded." This challenge of uniting black and white sections of the US proletariat in defense of their own rights has been a dream of socialists for 150 years.

Attempts to redress black exclusion from "mainstream" history have shown that the leaders of the United States generally have had little trouble bringing blacks and whites together for their own causes. From the murder of the Plains Indians and the charge up San Juan Hill to the ideological and military campaigns against communism in the twentieth century, the American elite have been able to count on blacks and whites working together, though usually in segregated units.

The American working class has rarely been successful at mobilizing black and white together for its interests. In the nearly one and a half centuries since the Thirty-sixth Regiment of Colored Troops led the Union Army into Richmond and conclusively ended slavery in America, the moments when both blacks and whites have been able to join together to fight for their collective liberation have been rare. For Marxists like George Breitman, this collective fight for liberation had been an important part of the First American Revolution of 1776 that ended the British king's rule over what became the United States; it was decisive in the Second American Revolution of 1861–1865 that overthrew the power of slave owners; but it would be central to the future Third American Revolution, which would replace the power of the capitalists with the power of the working-class majority. Breitman's understanding of the importance of black liberation in the process of bringing together the black and white sections of the working-class majority, including his role in helping to shape the brief but promising relationship between Malcolm X and the Socialist Workers Party, was one of the major contribution to American Trotskyism and its struggle to bring about this Third American Revolution.

BREITMAN AND THE BLACK POWER MOVEMENT

In the early 1960s, when few people outside the black community took much notice of the black nationalist religious organization the Nation of Islam (NOI), Breitman was studying its literature and political work. Fueled by his participation in the Socialist Workers Party's debates about the nature of black nationalism (see "How a Minority Can Change Society," "The National Question and the Black Liberation Struggle in the United States," and Malik Miah's essay in this volume) and by his belief in American Trotskyism's unique view, developed in the 1930s by

Trotsky and black revolutionary and intellectual C. L. R. James, that African Americans are potentially the vanguard of the coming third American revolution (i.e., socialist), Breitman set about trying to identify developing political currents in the NOI that might potentially lead to broader social alliances. As he studied, he wrote, presenting his comrades in the SWP with articles, documents, and other materials that explained the problems and prospects involved in working with black nationalists. In 1964 Malcolm X, one of the Nation of Islam's leading members, broke away and formed a black nationalist organization committed to political action involving people of all races. Breitman was ready with an organization that had the knowledge, will, and cadre necessary to explore the potential of this development.

Though the two organizations never concluded an official alliance, during the last year of his life, Malcolm X gave speeches at SWP forums, was interviewed for party publications, and encouraged people to read the publications of the SWP. The Socialist Workers Party gave Malcolm X friendly coverage in its newspaper, the *Militant*, discussed politics with him and his followers, and demonstrated some of the ways that black and white revolutionaries could work toward the same goals within the narrow pathways of the American caste-color system.

Malcolm X's turn to the world revolution was opposed by many of his former colleagues in the Nation of Islam, who saw him as a traitor to his "nation." Breitman also faced criticism and conflict within his organization. There were members of the Socialist Workers Party who rejected the claim that black nationalism was progressive and provided a way forward for the American working class. They argued that black nationalism was not the promised African American vanguard that their movement envisioned and that the revolutionary party should not concede political ground to an ideology based on preserving and reinforcing the divide between the black and white sections of the American working class. Breitman and his co-thinkers struggled to explain why their project did not involve concessions to American racial divisions (see "How a Minority Can Change Society" and "The National Question and the Black Liberation Struggle in the United States," in this volume). While most of the American Left ignored Malcolm X or continued in their view that he was a "racist in reverse," Breitman persisted, leading his party in a project that would prove to be far ahead of its time.

Though Breitman and Malcolm X never actually met—their first meeting had been scheduled for the week after Malcolm X was assassinated—they respected each other and valued one another's opinions as colleagues and fellow revolutionists. Their shared conviction that involvement with the Democratic Party was a dead end, that blacks needed to have their own political organizations before they could make genuinely equal alliances with whites, and that a third American revolution was coming in which black people would play a critical role provided a strong basis for mutually informing (and constructively criticizing) each other's work. As Malcolm X scholar Paul Lee points out in his essay "The Contributions of George Breitman," Malcolm X closely followed Breitman's work during his last year, using it to gain important insights into his own political leadership and the political direction of his organization.[1] Similarly, it is clear from many of the selections in this book that Breitman and the Socialist Workers Party greatly deepened their understanding of the relationship between socialism and black liberation under the tutelage of Malcolm X. Sadly, like so many attempts to bring together black and white radicals, this one was tragically ended by assassination and political intrigue before its possibilities could be fully realized.

Despite being cut short in its first year, the relationship between Malcolm X and the Socialist Workers Party had a powerful impact beyond the small number of people directly involved. Breitman's writings on black liberation and his work as editor of Malcolm X's speeches set the standard for political engagement between the black liberation movement and the socialist movement, providing an example, a social context, and a set of political theories for other largely white Left groups that sought an orientation toward the developing black power movement of the 1960s. Breitman's book *The Last Year of Malcolm X* and his 1964 essay "How a Minority Can Change Society" (reprinted in this volume) introduced a generation of political activists to American Trotskyism's vision of the special role of African Americans as "the very vanguard"[2] of the third American revolution.

THE CONTINUING INFLUENCE OF GEORGE BREITMAN

In the late 1970s, the generation that had come of age amid ghetto riots, antiwar protests, national liberation struggles, and the feminist and antiracist movements matured within a world of recession, "stagflation," austerity, and growing social reaction. The 1980 presidential election that brought Ronald Reagan into the White House marked the beginning of a total war against the 1960s radicalization that Breitman had described as "the biggest, the deepest, the broadest—and therefore the most threatening for the ruling class" in the twentieth century.[3] In 1982, Reagan ordered the Professional Air Traffic Controllers Organization (PATCO) strike broken by the US Army, and the neoconservative movement made great inroads among youth on university campuses. In this period of retreat, many socialists moved to the Right and began to view the Democratic Party as the only viable challenge to the Reagan Revolution. Some even joined the revolution—proclaiming second thoughts about socialism and signing on as advisors, publicists, and staffers for what seemed to be the winning side.

However, many liberals and radicals fought the rightward drift—and one of the most dramatic efforts emerged within the Democratic Party itself. In 1984 and again in 1988, Jesse Jackson made a historic bid to receive the Democratic Party nomination for president. His Rainbow Coalition mobilized a remarkable alliance of civil rights–era black Democratic Party leaders, social movement activists, white trade unionists, and black nationalists, including Louis Farrakhan's Nation of Islam. With a mass electoral base in the black community and support from a wide range of disaffected Democrats, Jackson built (and later dismantled) the Reagan era's broadest and most dynamic working-class movement. The Rainbow Coalition registered millions of first-time voters and brought thousands of new activists into politics.

Breitman, like most Trotskyists, was harshly critical of Jackson's movement, which he correctly predicted would draw thousands of political activists out of the social movements and into what Trotskyists believe is "the graveyard of social movements," the Democratic Party. The rest of the Left was initially ambivalent about Jackson, whom they knew as a relatively conservative minister with a record of opportunism and deep ties to the Democratic Party. However, many leftists ultimately decided to join Jackson's campaign, based partly on the idea that African Americans have a special role in the formation of radical politics—an idea that Breitman had helped popularize in the 1960s and 1970s.

The 1990s was among the most politically somnolent decades of the twentieth century in the United States. With the exception of the popular 1997 Teamster's strike, there was little mass activity to break the consensus of the Clinton years. Clinton started his national political career by marginalizing the black civil rights–era leadership in the Democratic Party. He courted Reagan Democrats in 1992 by publicly disrespecting Jackson in the famous "Sister Soulja" incident and by interrupting the campaign to fly back to Arkansas to oversee the execution of a severely mentally retarded black man, Ricky Ray Rector. Clinton's promise that he could manage African Americans better than George H. W. Bush, whose presidency had been hopelessly compromised by his ineptitude during the riots following the not guilty verdict in the Rodney King police brutality trial, proved true. The low unemployment and expanded economic opportunities of the post–cold war boom led many Americans to "tend their own gardens," play the stock market if they had the funds, and watch the spectacle of their first baby boomer president. Clinton's personal ease with African Americans and perceived sensitivity to their concerns, along with the accelerated growth of the black middle class that Malik Miah notes, contributed to a politically quiet black working class in the 1990s.

However, the new period that opened with the November 2000 elections offers huge political possibilities for the Left. The weakening of the American economy since the George W. Bush inauguration, the contradictions that have emerged from the post–September 11 "war on terror," and other "blowback" from "the short twentieth century" have produced a new global instability that could easily conspire to generate a new radicalization in the American working class. The Clinton-era retirements and purges of civil rights–era black Democrats have left the Democratic Party with a small contingent of young black leaders with little political experience outside the careerism of party life. This vacuum may allow space for a new and vital black radicalism to grow, unfettered by ties to the Democratic Party. Those whom Breitman called "the weakest link in the chain" of American capitalist rule[4] may soon raise new banners and inspire new movements throughout the American political scene. In the meantime, there is no better introduction to the challenges of race in American working-class history than the essays of George Breitman.

NOTES

1. Paul Lee, "The Contributions of George Breitman," *Labor Standard*, 2002, http://www.igc.org/laborstandard/Paul_Lee_on_MX/contributions_of _george_breitman.htm.

2. George Breitman, "How a Minority Can Change Society," p. XXX in this book.

3. George Breitman, "The Current Radicalization Compared with Those of the Past," in *Towards an American Socialist Revolution: A Strategy for the 1970s*, ed. Jack Barnes (New York: Pathfinder Press, 1971).

4. Ibid.

Editorial Note

There are many people who deserve thanks and acknowledgment for helping to finally bring this volume into print. First, I must thank Paul Le Blanc—most authors only dream of finding an editor who is "that good." Steve Bloom provided immense intellectual and technical support. Michael Scott Weinstein, as usual, provided a nice combination of unqualified support and combativeness. The Department of Anthropology and Sociology at La Trobe University; the School of Anthropology, Geography, and Environmental Studies at the University of Melbourne; and the School of International Development at Melbourne University Private all provided institutional and material support. Jo Sanson, as always, was comrade, colleague, companion, and critic all in the best proportions. Ann O'Hear, the first editor at Humanity Books, worked hard to get us past legal and logistic hurdles and Peggy Deemer deserves thanks for bringing us down the final stretch. Finally, and most importantly, none of this would have been possible without the permission of Dorothea Katz Breitman (1914–2004) to reprint her husband's work. Dorothea, a revolutionary Marxist in her own right, was a lifelong companion and comrade to George. Sadly, she did not live to see the publication of this book.

Because this volume is both a living document on social theory and revolutionary methods and a historical collection of the work of one of

America's most important twentieth-century revolutionaries, every attempt has been made to preserve Breitman's original presentation and wording. The notes found in the text are either Breitman's own or ones he approved as part of the publication of his work during his lifetime. Where uncertainty existed owing to the age or quality of a copy, additional copies were found or Breitman's colleagues and collaborators were consulted. The following words, which are part of the special idiom of Trotskyism and Marxism, appear throughout the text:

Fraction—refers to an internal group within a party or organization that takes up a particular area of work, such as "Labor Fraction," "Antiracism Fraction," and so on.

Faction—refers to an internal group within a party or organization that seeks political change in the party and is willing to wage a battle for this change of direction. Factional struggles usually lead to splits.

Entrism—refers to the entry of one political group, a smaller one, into another, a larger one, in order to win it over or break away a section.

Tendency—refers to a politically defined group, usually within a political party or organization, that does not have factional intent but subscribes to a certain political world view that may not be shared by the entire organization.

I

BLACK LIBERATION

CHAPTER 1

GEORGE BREITMAN ON
BLACK LIBERATION
AND MARXISM

Malik Miah

Race relations in the United States at the beginning of the twenty-first century are qualitatively different than they were forty years ago. The adoption of historic civil rights legislation (the 1964 Civil Rights Act and the 1965 Voting Rights Act in particular) formally ended legal segregation in the South and opened a new era in social and class relations. These fundamental changes—a direct by-product of the massive social revolution—led the ruling elite to alter policies. They broke the power of segregationists in the South and allowed African Americans to join the middle class in unprecedented numbers—in professions and jobs long held as white job trusts. Blacks were elected not only as city mayors, state legislators, and members of Congress but also eventually selected to the boards and offices of Fortune 500 companies as well.

Such radical restructuring was something most socialists had not anticipated short of a working-class-led revolution that challenged capitalist rule. Instead, the rulers proved again, as they have done in previous threats to their power, that they could adapt and bend to protect their overall economic interests. They also used brutal force, including assassinations and co-optation. In the middle of the social upheaval of the 1960s, debates were taking place within the black and broader socialist

Malik Miah, a former editor of the *Militant*, has written widely on the black struggle, labor, and international politics. He is an editor of *Against the Current*, a socialist magazine published in Detroit, and a member of the editorial board of *Links*, a Marxist journal published in Sydney, Australia.

movements about how to win full equality for blacks. Some of the most articulate writings were those of George Breitman, a central leader of the Socialist Workers Party (SWP).

A CRITICAL VISIONARY

Breitman, a Caucasian, understood and wrote about the struggles of African Americans better than most black intellectuals. By applying the Marxist method of analysis to the reality of black America, he dissected the African American condition and identified the various forms of struggle. One of his contributions was a sober critique of the strategy of civil disobedience used by a religious-based civil rights leadership. Socialists supported using mass civil disobedience as a tactic to pressure the white ruling class. They did not, however, believe that it was a strategy that could root out racial discrimination, because in their view ending racism required eliminating the capitalist system.

Breitman and the SWP enthusiastically supported the rise of black nationalism. The left wing of the civil rights movement, represented by the Student Nonviolent Coordinating Committee (SNCC) and a new generation of militants in the black ghetto not affiliated with any organization, saw black power and the ideas of Malcolm X, a leader of the National of Islam (NOI) who broke with the NOI in 1964, as the best means of fighting racism. The new militants supported a movement rejecting black capitalism and challenging the ruling elite.

The five essays in this section represent the theoretical foundations of Breitman's analysis and the views of the SWP. The SWP's support of black nationalism, an independent black political party, and of the militancy of Malcolm X (who was assassinated in 1965) made the party unique among the socialist Left.

The SWP correctly recognized black nationalism as a democratic attempt by an oppressed people to end its second-class status by any means necessary. Consistent nationalism, the SWP argued, would lead to clashes with the owners of wealth, divide the oppressors, and lead to alliances among other working people that could cause social rebellions to end capitalist rule. The SWP argued in its resolutions that the struggle for black freedom was a domestic version of the anticolonial revolutionary struggles that had erupted after World War II and saw consistency in Malcolm X's proposal to take the case of black oppression to the United Nations. Vladimir Lenin first explained the socialist understanding of nationalism of the oppressed and its revolutionary dynamic. The theory and SWP practice led a number of blacks in Detroit and other cities to join the SWP and its youth affiliate, the Young Socialist Alliance (YSA).

BREITMAN'S INFLUENCE ON ME

While I was too young to be an activist at the height of the civil rights rebellions of the 1960s, I joined the organized socialist movement in 1969 amid intense debates about how to turn the legal equality on paper into real equality in life. We already knew that ending legal segregation was not the same as having full equality. Racism was institutionalized.

Detroit, my hometown, was a center of the discussions. The black revolutionary workers movement was based in the automobile factories. Black college and high school students were joining militant groups, black nationalist and socialist. The Black Panther Party, which had first formed in Oakland, California, was growing nationally. Our discussions were not about reforming the system but about overthrowing it. We identified as revolutionaries—revolutionary nationalists, revolutionary socialists, Trotskyists, Maoists. It was an exciting time.

The views of the SWP had an impact on many black activists because of the writings of George Breitman and the resolutions adopted by the SWP and the YSA. I, for one, thought Breitman was black, as did many of the new black members in Detroit, because of his insights into the problems of strategy for black liberation. Breitman wrote with a race-neutral and objective style not common among white supporters of black rights. Unlike most white liberals and leftists of the time, he did not lecture to the movement or pretend to be black. He simply wrote what was obvious to everyone and offered an analysis rooted in those conditions. That's why I assumed that Breitman was a black man.

I was pleasantly surprised to learn otherwise. I first met Breitman in 1970 after joining the YSA in 1969. He had lived in Detroit for a number of years, and I had heard about him from local black intellectuals and activists as well as from SWP members. I read his articles and his SWP resolutions, including the 1939 resolution (made a year after the SWP was formed) that said blacks would play a vanguard role in the coming American socialist revolution.

After moving to New York in 1971, I eventually became a central leader of the SWP. Breitman had a big impact on me and other black recruits to the party. He urged us to take a prominent leadership role in the SWP as a whole, not just in its activity among African Americans.

Breitman was the first person to convincingly explain to me the socialist theory of the relationship between class and race. Racism and class exploitation were obvious to me because my father was an immigrant from British-ruled India[1] and an autoworker and my mother lived through the race riots of the 1940s. The 1967 rebellion in Detroit was a vivid memory, too.

Breitman explained how the white auto bosses reaped huge profits from the dual oppression of black and brown workers. He taught me that unless blacks played a vanguard role in the socialist movement, there could not be a successful socialist revolution in the United States. His Americanization of Marxism and the class struggle is one reason I became an internationalist and lifelong socialist.

The first time I had a conflict with other leaders of the SWP was after moving to New York, where I led the SWP's participation in the black freedom struggle. Breitman didn't caution me to hold back. Instead, he urged me and other black leaders to stand up for our beliefs. He said that speaking our minds was the only way to make the SWP stronger. A revolutionary party, he said, is based not only on its ideas and program but also on its leadership. It must reflect the social composition of society. Affirmative action, he said, must apply to multinational, multiethnic revolutionary organizations. It was a radical concept that many SWP leaders gave lip service to at the time but did not really practice. The lesson was important for future clashes I had with the national secretary of the SWP in the late 1980s. It ultimately led to my expulsion from the SWP as the party moved away from its revolutionary origins. Breitman had suffered a similar fate several years earlier.

ROOTS OF RACISM IN AMERICA

The first article by Breitman in this section, "Anti-Negro Prejudice: When It Began, When It Will End," was written in 1954. It offers a Marxist understanding of why African Americans are different from other oppressed ethnic groups. It is valuable reading because many conservatives, especially those in the black middle and upper classes, believe that racism is no longer institutionalized and systematic. The conservative black intellectuals argue that racism is based primarily on the acts of individuals and maybe a few recalcitrant companies that break the law. They say such infractions should not be tolerated but preach that "race" is irrelevant. In California, for example, an early benefactor of affirmative action led the campaign to overturn state affirmative action laws in 1996 and has put an initiative on the ballot to outlaw the collection of data (except by police who apply racial profiling) using race as criteria. These black conservatives see affirmative action programs and other attempts to redress past crimes against African Americans as stigmatizing blacks as "victims." Because they have "made it," they believe that all poor blacks can do the same.

Some may call this progress from the days of Jim Crow legal segregation when racism was integral to big business and government. In reality, the black elite are the modern-day apologists for racial discrimination. These developments reflect a polarization and class division in the black community, which remains overwhelmingly proletarian in composition.

Breitman, of course, was writing at the height of the civil rights rebellions when the changes brought about by the civil rights movement were only on the horizon. But the articles here anticipate and counter many of the arguments of today's black pro-capitalist elements.

ORIGINS OF RACISM

In "Anti-Negro Prejudice,"[2] Breitman explains eloquently that the modern concept of racism is rooted in capitalism. Earlier class societies (feudalism, for instance) did not use skin color to justify slavery or oppression. There had been white slaves in Europe, and slave traders were of all colors and races. "As late as the middle of the fifteenth century," Breitman explains,

> when the West African slave trade to Portugal first began, the rationalization for the enslavement of Negroes was not that they were Negro but that they were not Christian. . . . The invidious connotations of slavery were attached to all slaves, white and Negro. If under these conditions the notion of Negro "inferiority" occurred to anyone, it would have seemed ridiculous on the face of it; at any rate, it could never have received any social acceptance.

The conception of slavery changed when capitalism became the predominant economic system replacing feudalism. It became a big business. "Slavery in the Americas became confined exclusively to Negroes," Breitman continued.

> The Negro was distinguished by his color, and the invidious connotations of slavery could easily be transferred to that; it was inevitable that the theory of Negro "inferiority" and then anti-Negro prejudice should be created, that they should be extended to other nonwhite people who offered the possibility of exploitation, and that they should be spread around the globe.

Breitman explains that the huge profits resulting from discrimination based on race and national origins go beyond class divisions and that the rich will never stop reaping such "awards" willingly. The appearance of an upper-class layer in the black population reflects adjustments made by the ruling class to defuse militancy. It does not change the fact that most African Americans still suffer from racism and exploitation as workers.

DUAL OPPRESSION

Dual oppression—the working-class composition of the black population combined with racial oppression—is the reason that racism can't be eliminated fully under capitalism. In his 1964 article "How a Minority Can Change Society," Breitman explains that social status gives blacks a potentially powerful role in bringing fundamental change. "A minority, properly oriented and led," he explained, "can go much farther than it has thus far gone to make the present system unworkable and intolerable. . . . It consists of making the system so inconvenient and expensive that white people will be forced to ask themselves whether continued discrimination is worthwhile and whether in their own interest they should not help to do away with it altogether."

In "Marxism and the Negro Struggle" (1964), Breitman elaborated on why Marxism is relevant to the fight against racism and capitalism. Harold Cruse, a black academic, had argued that white workers are too conservative to support black militancy and would never change because they benefited from racism. He said Marxism as a theory and program of action was irrelevant to winning black freedom.

Breitman replied that "theory is derived from reality; the more closely a theory corresponds to reality, the better a theory it is." The SWP's analysis of the black condition, he explains, is based on concrete data and changes.

> The Negro struggle in 1964 is not the same thing it was ten or even five years ago—much has changed. . . . The SWP has been studying these changes, trying to understand their causes, find out their direction, and fit their revolutionary aspects into a theory and program of action capable of replacing capitalism with socialism.

The Marxist method is based on studying the facts concretely, Breitman explained. Marxists don't have a preconceived schema into which they fit reality to justify their actions. The relationship of social and class forces must be analyzed, and then and only then is a program of action developed: What demands should be raised? What reforms can be won? These decisions are based on an overall strategic program.

WINNING REFORMS

A false criticism of Marxists is that we analyze only the big picture, not caring for immediate problems or joining the fight for winnable reforms. Breitman answered that reforms are important for socialists but not as an end. Reforms, such as the civil rights laws, were won as a by-product of the struggle for fundamental change. A mass movement, by definition, is an alliance of those who have a goal of immediate reform within the framework of the system with others seeking a revolutionary transformation of the system.

But reforms can be taken back or weakened if a government and state run by working people does not replace the capitalist state. The ruling elite works twenty-four hours a day, seven days a week, to adjust, regroup, and find ways to strengthen its control over the oppressed and exploited. Many of the gains won in the 1960s have been eroded or reversed even though the integration of blacks into the system as junior partners is *permanent* because of the stability it gives the system.

The criticism socialists had of leaders like Martin Luther King Jr. was that King's program, like those of current liberals, accepted the capitalist framework as the way to end racism. Malcolm X, on the other hand, rejected that limited vision, which is why some Marxists were so supportive of Malcolm even while he was a leader of the NOI. He advocated radical changes to the system that would inevitably mean going beyond reforms.

Many black power militants in the 1960s not surprisingly moved from narrow nationalism to revolutionary nationalism and socialism. Breitman's writings were popular among many pan-Africanists and "African socialists," including some who became New Left Maoists. They agreed that militant nationalism was progressive. Yet much of the traditional Marxist Left (with the exception of the SWP) rejected black nationalism and Malcolm X's ideas. The Communist Party (CP) condemned black nationalism, calling it "divisive," a form of "reverse racism," and undermining of black-white unity.

Breitman and the SWP replied that the only effective road to unity between whites (of the dominant oppressor nationality) and blacks (an oppressed nationality) was for whites to give unconditional support to the rights of self-determination and self-organization and to leadership by African Americans.

A QUESTION OF LEADERSHIP

What's needed in the black community is a viable socialist Left and black militant leadership of the Malcolm X variety. Leadership, or more accurately, misleadership, is in the hands of pro-capitalist forces in the community. The primary role of traditional civil rights organizations is to highlight the gap between white and black incomes and other obvious forms of discrimination to win a few more concessions from the white power structure.

The events of September 11, 2001, when a terrorist act in New York City yielded a brutal response by the US government in Afghanistan, led to an unprecedented rise of patriotism in the black communities, reflecting a long-term decline in antigovernment consciousness. This is a big change from the 1960s during the Vietnam War, when the black population was the most antiwar sector of the United States. Even the heavyweight boxer Muhammad Ali refused to go into the army after being drafted, saying, "No Vietnamese ever called me Nigger."

In "The National Question and the Black Liberation Struggle," Breitman outlines a program for black liberation that goes back to the lessons of the 1917 Russian Revolution, which are still valid today despite the demise of the Soviet Union:

> Lenin most clearly and fully recognized the strategical significance of this [the national] question for the revolutionary socialist movement and its vanguard, and worked out a program to deal with its manifold aspects along lines previously projected by Marx and Engels. The principal points of Leninist policy in this field may be summarized as follows: (1) Every nationality has the democratic right to self-determination. (2) Its struggle for this right is just and progressive and must be wholeheartedly supported against the power and privileges of the dominant nation.

No one forty years ago could have guessed that the victory of the civil rights movement would so delay the development of a revolutionary black and working-class leadership. Breitman's understanding of the roots of racism, the role of dual oppression, and the need for an independent black political leadership with a vanguard role makes his writings extremely valuable for today's political activists.

NOTES

1. My father, born in Bengal, worked on British-owned ships during World War II and later was a union organizer in Southeast Asia before jumping ship in California in the late 1940s. After moving to Detroit, he became an active supporter of the national liberation movement in East Pakistan, which became Bangladesh in 1971.

2. The word *Negro* was common at the time. The rise of the black power movement in the late 1960s rejected the word as condescending. *Black* and *African American* are now used interchangeably.

CHAPTER 2

ANTI-NEGRO PREJUDICE

WHEN IT BEGAN, WHEN IT WILL END

(1954)

George Breitman

I t is now common knowledge even among conservative circles in the labor movement that race prejudice benefits the interests of the capitalist class and injures the interests of the working class. What is not well known—it still comes as a surprise to many Marxists—and should be made better known is the fact that race prejudice is a uniquely capitalist phenomenon, which either did not exist or had no perceptible influence in precapitalist society (that is, before the sixteenth century).

Hundreds of modern scholars have traced anti-Negro prejudice (to take the most important and prevalent type of race prejudice in the United States) back to the African slave trade and the slave system that was introduced into the Americas. Those who profited from the enslavement of the Negroes—the slave traders and merchant capitalists first of Europe and then of America, and the slaveholders—required a rationalization and a moral justification for an archaic social institution that obviously flouted the relatively enlightened principles proclaimed by capitalist society in its struggle against feudalism. Rationalizations always become available when powerful economic interests need them (that is how most politicians and preachers, editors, and teachers earn their living) and in this case the theory that Negroes are "inferior" followed closely on the discovery that Negro slavery was exceptionally profitable.

Originally printed in the Spring 1954 issue of the *Fourth International*.

This theory was embraced, fitted out with pseudoscientific trappings and biblical quotations, and trumpeted forth as a truth so self-evident that only madmen or subversives could doubt or deny it. Its influence on the minds of men was great at all levels of society, and undoubtedly aided the slaveholders in retarding the abolition of slavery. But with the growth of the productive forces, economic interests hostile to the slaveholders brought forth new theories and ideas, and challenged the supremacy of the slaveholders on all fronts, including ideology. The ensuing class struggles—between the capitalists, slaves, workers, and farmers on one side and the slaveholders on the other—resulted in the destruction of the slave system.

But if anti-Negro prejudices and ideas arose out of the need to justify and maintain slavery, why didn't they wither away after slavery was abolished? In the first place, ideas, although they must reflect broad material interests before they can achieve wide circulation, can live lives of their own once they are set into motion, and can survive for a time after the disappearance of the conditions that produced them. (It is instructive to note, for example, that Lincoln did not free himself wholly of race prejudice and continued to believe in the "inferiority" of the Negro even while he was engaged in prosecuting the Civil War that abolished the slave system—a striking illustration both of the tendency of ideas to lag behind events and of the primacy of material interest over ideology.)

This is a generalization, however, and does not provide the main explanation for the survival of anti-Negro prejudice after the Civil War. For the striking thing about the Reconstruction period which followed the abolition of slavery was the speed with which old ideas and customs began to change and break up. In the course of a few short years, millions of whites began to recover from the racist poisons to which they had been subjected from their birth, to regard Negroes as equals, and to work together with them amicably, under the protection of the federal government, in the solution of joint problems. The obliteration of anti-Negro prejudice was started in the social revolution that we know by the name of Reconstruction, and it would have been completed if Reconstruction had been permitted to develop further.

But Reconstruction was halted and then strangled—by the capitalists, acting now in alliance with the former slaveholders. No exploiting class lightly discards weapons that can help maintain its rule, and anti-Negro prejudice had already demonstrated its potency as a force to divide, disrupt, and disorient oppressed classes in an exploitative society. After some vacillation and internal struggle that lasted through most of Reconstruction, the capitalist class decided it could make use of anti-Negro prejudice for its own purposes. The capitalists adopted it, nursed it, fed it, gave it new clothing, and infused it with a vigor and an influence it had never commanded before. Anti-Negro prejudice today operates in a different social setting and therefore in a somewhat different form than a century ago, but it was retained after slavery for essentially the same reason that it was introduced under the slave system that developed from the sixteenth century on—for its convenience as an instrument of exploitation; and for that same reason it will not be abandoned by the ruling class of any exploitative society in this country.

But why do we speak of the *introduction* of anti-Negro prejudice in the slave system whose spread coincided with the birth of capitalism? Wasn't there slavery long centuries before capitalism? Didn't race prejudice exist in the earlier slave societies? Why designate race prejudice as a uniquely capitalist phenomenon? A brief look at slavery of both the capitalist and the precapitalist periods can lead us to the answers.

Capitalism, the social system that followed and replaced feudalism, owed its rise to world dominance in part to its revival or expansion of forms of exploitation originally developed in the prefeudal slave societies, and to its adaptation and integration of those forms into the framework of capitalist productive relations. As "the chief momenta of primitive accumulation" through which the early capitalists gathered together the capital necessary to establish and spread the new system, Marx listed "the discovery of gold and silver in America, the extirpation, enslavement, and entombment in mines of the aboriginal population, the beginning of the conquest and looting of the East Indies, the turning of Africa into a warren for the commercial hunting of black skins." The African slave trade and slavery produced fortunes that laid the foundations for the most important of the early industries of capitalism, which in turn served to revolutionize the economy of the whole world.

Thus we see, side by side, in clear operation of the laws of uneven and combined development, archaic prefeudal forms and the most advanced social relations then possible in the postfeudal world. The former were of course in the service of the latter, at least during the first stages of their coexistence. This was not a mere repetition of the slavery of ancient times: one basic economic difference was that the slave system of the Americas produced commodities for the world capitalist market, and was therefore subordinate to and dependent on that market. There were other differences, but here we confine ourselves to the one most relevant to the subject of this article—race relations in the early slave societies.

For the information that follows we are indebted to the writings of an anthropologist and of a sociologist: Ina Corinne Brown, *Socio-Economic Approach to Educational Problems*, 1942, chapter 2 (this government publication, the first volume in the *National Survey of the Higher Education of Negroes* sponsored by the US Office of Education, is now out of print, but the same material is covered in her book, *Race Relations in a Democracy*, 1949, chapter 4); and Oliver C. Cox, *Caste, Class, and Race*, 1948, chapter 16.[1] Dr. Cox's treatment is fuller; he also has been more influenced by Marx.

This is what they write about the ancient Egyptians:

> So many persons assume that racial antipathy is a natural or instinctive reaction that it is important to emphasize the fact that race prejudice such as we know it did not exist before the modern age. To be sure there was group antipathy which those who read history backwards take to be race prejudice, but actually this antipathy had little or nothing to do with color or the other physical differences by which races are distinguished. For example, the ancient Egyptians looked down upon the Negroes to the south of them. They enslaved these Negroes and spoke scornfully of them. Many writers, reading later racial attitudes into the situation, have seen in this scorn a color prejudice. But the Egyptians were just as scornful of the Asiatic sand dwellers, or Troglodytes as Herodotus called them, and of their other neighbors who were as light or lighter than the Egyptians. The Egyptian artists caricature the wretched captives taken in the frequent wars, but they emphasize the hooked noses of the Hittites, the woolen garments of the Hebrews, and the peculiar dress of the Libyans quite as much as the color or the thick lips of the Negroes. That the Egyptians mixed freely with their southern neighbors, either in slavery or out of it, is evidenced by the fact that some of the Pharaohs were obviously Negroid and eventually Egypt was ruled by an Ethiopian dynasty. (Brown 1942)

There seems to be no basis for imputing racial antagonism to the Egyptians, Babylonians, or Persians. (Cox)

On the Greeks:

One frequently finds mention of the scornful way in which Negro slaves were referred to in Greece and Rome, but the fact is that equally scornful remarks were made of the white slaves from the North and the East. There seems to be no evidence that color antipathy was involved, and of the total slave population the Negroes constituted only a minor element. (Brown 1942)

The slave population was enormous, but the slave and the master in Greece were commonly of the same race and there was no occasion to associate any given physical type with the slave status. An opponent of Athenian democracy complained that it was impossible in Athens to distinguish slaves and aliens from citizens because all classes dressed alike and lived in the same way. (Brown 1949)

[W]e do not find race prejudice even in the great Hellenistic empire which extended deeper into the territories of colored people than any other European empire up to the end of the fifteenth century.

The Hellenic Greeks had a cultural, not a racial, standard of belonging, so that their basic division of the peoples of the world were Greeks and barbarians—the barbarians having been all those persons who did not possess the Greek culture, especially its language. . . . The people of the Greek city-states, who founded colonies among the barbarians on the shores of the Black Sea and of the Mediterranean, welcomed those barbarians to the extent that they were able to participate in Greek culture, and intermarried freely with them. The Greeks knew that they had a superior culture to those of the barbarians, but they included Europeans, Africans, and Asiatics in the concept Hellas as these peoples acquired a working knowledge of the Greek culture.

The experience of the later Hellenistic empire of Alexander tended to be the direct contrary of modern racial antagonism. The narrow patriotism of the city-states was given up for a new cosmopolitanism. Every effort was made to assimilate the barbarians to Greek culture, and in the process a new Greco-Oriental culture with a Greco-Oriental ruling class came into being. Alexander himself took a Persian princess for his wife and encouraged his men to intermarry with the native population. In this empire there was an estate, not a racial, distinction between the rulers and the un-Hellenized natives. (Cox)

On the Romans:

In Rome, as in Greece, the slaves did not differ in outward appearance from free men. R. H. Barrow in his study of the Roman slave says that "neither color nor clothing revealed his condition." Slaves of different nationalities intermarried. There was no color barrier. A woman might be despised as a wife because she came from a despised group or because she practiced barbaric rites but not because her skin was darker. Furthermore, as W. W. Buckland points out, "any citizen might conceivably become a slave; almost any slave might become a citizen." (Brown 1949)

In this civilization also we do not find racial antagonism, for the norm of superiority in the Roman system remained a cultural-class attribute. The basic distinction was Roman citizenship, and gradually this was extended to all freeborn persons in the municipalities of the empire. Slaves came from every province, and there was no racial distinction among them. (Cox)

There is really no need to go on quoting. The same general picture is true of all the societies, slave and nonslave, from the Roman Empire down to the discovery of America—in the barbarian invasions into Europe, which led to enslavement of whites, in the reign of the Muslims, in the era of political domination by the Catholic Church. There were divisions, discriminations, and antagonisms of class, cultural, political, and religious character, but none along race or color lines, at least none that have left any serious trace in the historical materials now available. As late as the middle of the fifteenth century, when the West African slave trade to Portugal first began, the rationalization for the enslavement of Negroes was not that they were Negro but that they were not Christian. Those who became Christians were freed, intermarried with the Portuguese, and were accepted as equals in Portugal. Afterward, of course, when the slave trade became a big business, the readiness of a slave to convert to Christianity no longer sufficed to gain his emancipation.

Why did race prejudice develop in the capitalist era when it did not under the earlier slave systems? Without thinking we have in any way exhausted the subject, we make the following suggestion: In previous times the slaves were usually of the same color as their masters; both whites and Negroes were masters and slaves; in the European countries the Negroes formed a minority of the slave population. The invidious connotations of slavery were attached to all slaves, white and Negro. If under these conditions the notion of Negro "inferiority" occurred to anyone, it would have seemed ridiculous on the face of it; at any rate, it could never have received any social acceptance.

But slavery in the Americas became confined exclusively to Negroes.[2] The Negro was distinguished by his color, and the invidious connotations of slavery could easily be transferred to that; it was inevitable that the theory of Negro "inferiority" and then anti-Negro prejudice should be created, that they should be extended to other nonwhite people who offered the possibility of exploitation, and that they should be spread around the globe.

Thus anti-Negro prejudice was not born until after capitalism had come into the world. There are differences of opinion as to the approximate birth date. M. F. Ashley Montagu, discussing the "modern conception of 'race,'" says: "Neither in the ancient world nor in the world up to the latter part of the eighteenth century did there exist any notion corresponding to it. . . . A study of the cultures and literatures of mankind, both ancient and recent, shows us that the conception of natural or biological races of mankind differing from one another mentally as well as physically, is an idea which was not born until the latter part of the eighteenth century," or around the French Revolution (*Man's Most Dangerous Myth: The Fallacy of Race*).

Cox says that if he had to put his finger on the year which marked the beginning of race relations, he would select 1493–94—when the pope granted to Catholic Spain and Portugal jurisdictional control over, and the right to exploit, all of the (predominantly nonwhite) heathen people of the world and their resources. He sees "nascent race prejudice" with the beginning of the slave trade: "Although this peculiar kind of exploitation was then in its incipiency, it had already achieved its significant characteristics." However, he finds that "racial antagonism attained full maturity" only in the second half of the nineteenth century.

Whichever century one chooses, the point is this: Anti-Negro prejudice was originated to justify and preserve a slave-labor system that operated in the interests of capitalism in its preindustrialist stages, and it was retained in slightly modified form by industrial capitalism after slavery became an obstacle to the further development of capitalism and had to be abolished. Few things in the world are more distinctly stamped with the mark of capitalism.

The implications of this fact are so plain that it is no wonder it has received so little attention in the schools and press of a country dominated by capitalists and their apologists. Anti-Negro prejudice arose out of the needs of capitalism, it is a product of capitalism, it belongs to capitalism, and it will die when capitalism dies.

We who are going to participate in the replacement of capitalism by socialism, and who have good reason to be curious about the first stages of socialism because we will be living in them, need have no fear about the possibility of any extended lag with respect to race prejudice. Unlike the capitalist system that dominated this country after the Civil War, the socialist society will be free of all exploitative features; it will have no conceivable use for race prejudice, and it will consciously seek to eradicate it along with all the other props of the old system. That is why race prejudice will wither away when capitalism dies—just as surely as the leaf withers when the tree dies, and not much later.

NOTES

1. Neither of these would claim they were the first to discover this historical information, and it may well be that other scholars unknown to us preceded them in writing about this field in recent years; all we know is that it first came to our attention through their books. Historical material often lies neglected for long periods until current social and political needs reawaken interest in it. These writers were undoubtedly stimulated into a new and more purposeful interest in the subject by the growth of American Negro militancy and colonial independence struggles during the last fifteen to twenty years.

2. Slavery was not confined to Negroes at the beginning. Before the Negro slave population on the plantations, there was the Indian slave and the white indentured servant. But Negro slave labor proved cheaper and was more plentiful than either of these, and eventually they were abandoned. The most satisfactory

study of this question is in the excellent book by Eric Williams, *Capitalism and Slavery*, 1944. Williams writes:

Here, then, is the origin of Negro slavery. The reason was economic, not racial; it had to do not with the color of the laborer, but the cheapness of the labor. As compared with Indian and white labor, Negro slavery was eminently superior. . . . The features of the man, his hair, color and dentrifice, his "subhuman" characteristics so widely pleaded, were only the later rationalizations to justify a simple economic fact: that the colonies needed labor and resorted to Negro labor because it was cheapest and best. This was not a theory, it was a practical conclusion deduced from the personal experience of the planter. He would have gone to the moon, if necessary, for labor. Africa was nearer than the moon, nearer too than the more populous countries of India and China. But their turn was to come.

CHAPTER 3

HOW A MINORITY
CAN CHANGE SOCIETY
(1964)

George Breitman

The year 1963 was the most eventful in the history of the American Negro struggle. As it ended, people all over the country were stopping to assess what had happened, to think over what was done and what was not done, what was accomplished and not accomplished. Clifton DeBerry, the Socialist Workers Party candidate for president this year, had an opportunity at the end of 1963 to make a coast-to-coast tour of most big northern cities and to learn something about the current thinking of Negro militants. He told me one of the things he had observed was the difficulty in getting across the idea about how much the Negro people can do even though they are in a minority, about how much they can do on their own, alone and unaided if necessary. He noticed this difficulty in speaking with Negro trade unionists, but not only them. He felt a lot more attention has to be paid to ways of explaining, in a logical, convincing manner, how much a minority is capable of accomplishing. He felt that misunderstanding on this point is one of the reasons why the idea of an all-black political party has not yet caught on with more Negroes.

Why is it so hard for many Negroes, even militant Negroes, to grasp the full potential of determined minority action? I would say there are three reasons:

First, the teaching, the influence, the propaganda of the whole capi-

---

Originally published in the Spring 1964 issue of the *International Socialist Review*.

talist system from cradle to grave are aimed at brainwashing the people; at convincing them, among other things, that minorities can plead and beg, but cannot do anything significant, cannot accomplish any big changes, until they have the consent of the majority. Above all is this idea burned into the minds and souls of Negroes, whose history is distorted or denied, and who are made to feel not only that they are a minority, but an insignificant minority, who have never amounted to much by themselves and who, without the stern supervision or benign direction of the great white fathers, would hardly know how to flush a toilet. In other words, for Negroes to comprehend how much a minority can do, they must buck everything drilled into them from the beginning of childhood; they virtually have to make a revolution in their thinking.

THE CAPITALIST MINORITY

There is a certain irony in these things taught by the capitalists because the capitalists are a minority themselves—in fact, a much smaller minority than the Negro people. Yet this capitalist minority controls the whole country, lock, stock, and barrel—its wealth, its means of production, its political structure—and therefore is a living refutation of what it tells us about the limits on what a minority can accomplish.

The second reason why it is hard to see the truth about what a minority can do is that the present Negro leadership, almost in its entirety, is enslaved by the ideas promulgated by the capitalist class, repeats and spreads those ideas, and does everything in its power to discourage the mass of the Negro people from taking steps genuinely independent of the white majority.

A third reason is that the radical movement, virtually the whole radical movement with the exception of the Socialist Workers Party, although it approaches questions from a different standpoint than that of the ruling capitalist class, has failed to comprehend the essence of this question, and instead of promoting and encouraging both theoretically and practically an understanding of the dynamics and potential of minority action, in some ways even discourages it. An example is their attitude toward the Freedom Now Party. I do not know of a single organization in this country claiming to be Marxist or socialist or communist that supports the Freedom Now Party, except the Socialist Workers Party. The Communist Party, the Socialist Party, the Socialist Labor Party, the Progressive Labor Movement—all are either flatly opposed to, or feel very uneasy about, the development of an all-black political party independent of the power structure and of the two major parties. And if you trace back the causes, you will find them to be most un-Marxist, unsocialist, and uncommunist failures to grasp the revolutionary implications of the independent struggles of the Negro minority.

I want now to examine some typical arguments by the present Negro leaders against such independent action. When the Freedom Now Party was organized in Michigan a few months ago, the press was very much concerned about it. And every "big name" Negro who came to Detroit for several weeks thereafter was immediately buttonholed by the press and invited to make some statement on, or rather against, the Freedom Now Party. One of these was Rev. Martin Luther King, who obliged with the following statement: "I am opposed to anything or any party that teaches separation of the races because I am for integration. If the party is designed to get more Negroes interested in politics, fine; otherwise I can see no good that can come from an all-black party. One-tenth of the population will never be able to dominate nine-tenths."

In this statement I think Reverend King is guilty of counterposing "separation of the races" and "integration" in a completely false and unwarranted way. The Freedom Now Party does not "teach the separation of the races." It recognizes that this is a society where the races are separated in fact, and attempts to utilize the separation that has been imposed by capitalism in order to change society and do away with the discrimination made by this imposed separation. King is well aware of this. He is a preacher, the head of a church which happens to be all-black. He does not reject or oppose this church because it is all-black. He knows that there is nothing racist about this church being all-black. It is the result of living in a racist society. And he works through this all-black church and tries to build it, at the same time that he advocates integration and seeks to utilize this all-black organization to promote integration.

ALL-BLACK UNITY

Now why can't an all-black party do the same thing that an all-black church does, that is, take advantage of the separation created by this racist society in order to weld together the black victims of racism so that they can work to end racism altogether? Why not? Why is it permissible in King's eyes for Negroes to pray together, but not permissible for them to join together in political action in the way they find most effective for ending their oppression? Shouldn't King, if he is logical and consistent, propose that Negroes give up their all-black churches, too, because they are not integrated? Posed this way, King could reply, "But we have an all-black church because it's the only kind available to us." And the answer of the Freedom Now Party could be, "Yes, and an all-black political party is the only kind available to us that we think has any chance of solving our problems." So King is confusing rather than clarifying the real relation between "separation" and "integration," which are not necessarily opposites at all, since the formation of all-black organizations and institutions may actually be a means of achieving the goal of "integration" instead of being in contradiction to that goal.

King's other remark was even more revealing: "One-tenth of the population will never be able to dominate nine-tenths." Maybe not, although I've already pointed out that the capitalists, a minority of less than 1 percent, dominate the other 99 percent of us. Anyhow, that's not the issue posed by the Freedom Now Party. It is not the Freedom Now Party's goal for the Negro one-tenth to dominate the white nine-tenths. Just the opposite—its goal is to keep the white nine-tenths from dominating and oppressing the black one-tenth. *How* to do this—that's the real difference between King and the Freedom Now Party. Must the minority adapt itself in its methods and tempo to the prejudiced majority, just because it is a majority, and not do certain things because the majority will not like it? Or, can the minority end the domination of the majority by acting with complete independence from the majority ideologically, organizationally, politically— and *only* by acting independently? King prefers not to discuss this real difference. That's why he misrepresents his opponents' position with irrelevant talk about the inability of one-tenth to dominate nine-tenths.

Another noted figure who came to Detroit at that time was A. Philip

Randolph, vice president of the AFL-CIO and president of the Negro American Labor Council. He, too, dutifully came forward with a statement against the Freedom Now Party, from which I'll read just the first two sentences: "Racial isolation in any form cannot register any influence on American political events. It is completely foreign to the political thoughts and actions of America."

It could be pointed out that what Randolph calls "racial isolation," in the form of all-white organizations like the Ku Klux Klan and the White Citizens Council, has registered plenty of influence on American politics. But I think it may be more useful to stress that in his eagerness to damn the Freedom Now Party, Randolph here is really damning himself. By "racial isolation" he means all-black organization for the purpose of ending the isolation foisted on Negroes by a racist society. Randolph is so blinded factionally that he has forgotten his own role, the thing for which he will probably be best remembered; for it so happens that next to Marcus Garvey and Elijah Muhammad, Randolph is the American Negro leader who did the most in this century for what he now calls "racial isolation," that is, all-black organization.

The first March on Washington movement, which Randolph organized in 1941, was all-black, and Randolph was foremost in insisting that it be all-black. Even though it did not materialize as a march, because Randolph yielded to Roosevelt and called it off at the last minute, that first March on Washington movement in 1941 nevertheless accomplished more than the interracial march that took place last August, because it forced Roosevelt to issue the first FEPC [Fair Employment Practice Commission] order, which is more than the 1963 march accomplished. Instead of "isolating" the Negro struggle, I think it can be said that that an all-black organization, small and imperfect though it was, did more to influence American life than any interracial movement has done since.

*   *   *

How do you influence the course of events, anyway? Is it done by strict adherence to the procedures and forms approved by the forces in power, or by following the rules they lay down? All experience, American as well as "foreign," testifies to the contrary. As long as you abide by their rules, either in the way you organize or the way you fight, they know they have little to fear from you and pay you little attention. The only valid test for all-black organizations is this: does it at this time and under these circumstances help or hinder in mobilizing the masses for uncompromising struggle? It doesn't matter if whites, liberal or conservative, don't like it and call it all kinds of names. What counts is what the black masses think about it. If they think it is good, if it enables them more effectively to organize for struggle, then it can have a shattering impact on present-day American society and politics. Influence can be wielded in more ways than one, and that which helps the masses to organize is most "influential" in the long run.

I will cite only one more example of the kind of reasoning employed by Negro opponents of independent minority action. Also attacking the Freedom Now Party was Alex Fuller, vice president of the Detroit AFL-CIO Council. He said:

> We can continue to make gains only by working with people of good will. It is a serious mistake when minority groups, now on the threshold of making tremendous gains for Negroes . . . separate themselves from others who are working for the same objectives. . . . We cannot afford to separate or isolate ourselves. We stand on the side of all democratic-thinking people who believe and advocate first-class citizenship for everyone. We cannot do it alone.

Translated, what Alex Fuller means is this: Negroes can't get anywhere, Negroes can't get anything, unless they remain in the Democratic Party; therefore they must wait until the Democrats are ready. But the truth is somewhat different. Negroes will never get first-class citizenship in a thousand years so long as their political power remains tucked away in the vest pocket of the Democratic Party. If they have to depend on and wait for the Democrats or the Republicans, and similar "people of good will," their children and their children's children will never know the taste of freedom.

Nobody in his right mind wants to separate "from others who are working for the same objectives," but it is a lie to pretend that the Democratic Party, any more than the Republican Party, has the "same objectives" as the Negro people. If that were the case, the present massive Negro revolt would have no purpose or meaning. The objective of the major parties is to quiet the Negroes with a few token concessions, while the objective of the Negro people is freedom.

Surely there's a difference here, and it is just this big difference that separates Negroes from Fuller's "democratic-thinking people." Negroes want freedom now, and "democratic-thinking people" want them to have it later. The only way Negroes can prevent "separation" from the liberals on this issue is to give in to them and let them decide when and where and how much freedom Negroes shall have. That's what Alex Fuller and the other Negro leaders have done and what they want the Negro people to do or keep on doing. But the tendency favoring the Freedom Now Party has decided that a hundred years of political dependence on these democratic-thinking people of good will is enough, because such dependence, far from bringing them to "the threshold of tremendous gains," will lead only to another hundred years of the same. They have made their declaration of political independence, and now they are striking out on their own, determined to use their political power for themselves first, last, and all the time.

THE NEGRO MINORITY

Before proceeding to our examination from a Marxist point of view of how much and not how little a minority can do, I should make clear that I am not talking about just any minority, but about a minority with certain characteristics, certain features, and a certain history. And also, yes, I am talking about a minority of a certain size. Let me get the size question out of the way first.

Obviously, not every minority is big enough to do the things I am talking about. Size is important, too. If there were only 2 or 3 million Negroes in this country, which is approaching a population of 200 million, they could not accomplish what a minority of 20 million can. But 20 million is a big force, big enough to tear things up, big enough and weighty enough to appreciably affect the course of events. After all, how many countries in the world, not only the new ones in Africa and Asia but also the old ones in Europe and the Americas, have a population of 20 million? Out of more than one hundred countries, not more than twenty-five at the most, so that around three-quarters of the countries in the world are smaller in population than the Negro people of the United States.

Size and relative weight are not the only important factors to be considered. A minority of even 40 million cannot do much if satisfied with its conditions or indifferent and apathetic about them. As important as size, or more important, in deciding what a minority can do are social, economic, political, historical, and psychological factors.

What I am trying to say is that what a minority can do depends on whether or not it is oppressed and exploited because of some minority trait or feature, is separated out by society for special inferior status, is denied equal treatment, opportunity, and rights; whether or not it is at the bottom of the social ladder so that when it rises it shakes the whole structure; whether or not it is a part of the most productive and potentially most powerful force in the modern world, the working class, and yet at the same time is denied the full benefits of membership in that class; whether or not the oppressive and exploitative society in which it exists is stable or in crisis, challenged on all sides, and therefore no longer able to maintain the status quo; whether or not this minority believes that it can take advantage of the crisis of society; whether or not it is affected by and responds to the great tides of change and revolution sweeping the globe and has a sense of kinship and solidarity with the masses rising up and changing the rest of the world; whether or not its oppression tends to knit it together for common action and goals; whether or not it is compact and so situated geographically that it can act with maximum cohesiveness and impact; whether or not it has learned to see through the brainwashing which the ruling class uses to keep this minority in subjugation; whether or not it has lost patience as well as respect for the majority; whether or not it sees any further reason to continue believing in promises or in gradualism; whether or not it has the capacity to free itself from the influence of conservative leaders who have always held it back and to replace them with more militant and revolutionary leaders; whether or not it realizes it never has made any gains except by fighting for them; whether or not it has the capacity to defend itself against terror and violence; whether or not it is developing a militant and radical consciousness, ideology, philosophy, and methodology of its own that can motivate and spark sustained, audacious, and independent struggle.

In short, I am talking about characteristics that fit the American Negro people or which they are in the process of acquiring at an extremely rapid rate. Of the many things such a minority can do, I shall now list some, not necessarily in the order of their importance.

WHAT A MINORITY CAN DO

1. It can force serious concessions from the ruling class. Anyone who expects the capitalist class to grant full and genuine equality to the Negro people is going to be sadly disappointed because equality is simply not compatible with, or possible under, a social system of the type that we have in the United States today. But that is no reason for Negroes to stop trying to get whatever they can squeeze out of the ruling class until the time comes when it can be deposed. Militant struggle can force the present ruling class to lift some of the existing racial restrictions and barriers in the form of more rights, more jobs, better jobs, better schools, better housing, less police brutality, and a greater measure of formal equality before the law. Negroes will not settle for such partial gains and concessions, but they would be fools not to fight for them and take them and utilize them to press for other and more fundamental changes.

2. A minority, properly oriented and led, can go much further than it has thus far gone to make the present system unworkable and intolerable. Bayard Rustin calls this "social dislocation" (and warns against its "limitations"). Rev. Albert Cleage, chairman of the Freedom Now Party in Michigan, calls it "a strategy of chaos" (and urges its application be expanded). Others give it the name of "mass civil disobedience." Whatever you call it, it has barely been utilized in America up to now. It consists of making the system so inconvenient and expensive that white people will be forced to ask themselves whether continued discrimination is worthwhile and whether in their own interest they should not help to do away with it altogether.

It means lying down, interposing your bodies on the airport runways, on the expressways, at the plant gate, at the school entrance, at the bank, at the points of production, and the points of distribution, and the points of transportation, and throwing a monkey wrench into the wheels of the system, attempting to paralyze it, to bring it to a stop. It means saying: "If we Negroes can't have decent and equal schools, then let's not have any schools. If we can't have jobs and job equality, then let no one be able to work. If we can't vote, then let no one be able to vote. If we can't belong to the unions as equals, then we don't care what happens to the unions." It means carrying the principle of the sit-down strike, which stops production, much further and into entirely new areas of social life.

I say that this has hardly been exercised as a full-scale weapon of the Negro minority, but I have no doubt that it will be. Already some members of the Student Nonviolent Coordinating Committee, headed by Diane Nash Bevel, have proposed such action and have had it rejected by moderate leaders like Reverend King, who *talks* about civil disobedience but is mortally afraid of really unleashing it without restriction on a mass scale. The sit-ins, the lie-ins, the wade-ins, etc., were just a small, faint, preliminary version of what is still to come in a giant size and to the accompaniment of deep social convulsions and conflicts. To avoid misunderstanding, let me say that what I am talking about here is not pacifism but an all-out struggle, which will be the equivalent of a general strike when it reaches full flower. And a general strike usually tends to pose questions about who shall have power in the land.

3. A minority can, merely by carrying through its fight for democratic rights without compromise, help to educate and radicalize the American people, especially the youth in whose hands the future lies. In fact, it is already doing so. You in this audience of young socialists and young radicals know better than anyone else how profoundly your thinking about the whole world has been influenced by the Negro struggle; how their fight for equality enabled you to see through the official myths about "democracy" and "the free world," to understand the brute reality of the capitalist power structure, to reach new conclusions about capitalism and socialism. Not only the Cuban revolution, not only the danger of atomic war, but something much closer to home, the Negro revolt, has helped to educate or reeducate you, to shed the blinders of liberalism, and to persuade you to dedicate your lives to the fight for a better world. In this respect you are not so much unique as early, because the deepening struggle of the Negro minority will have similarly healthy effects on other young people and on some of the not completely hopeless older people as well.

POWER OF EXAMPLE

4. A minority not only can educate other forces but can set them into motion, too. It can stimulate them to fight for their own needs and interests through the power of example as well as the power of pressure. You heard one illustration of the power of example this morning—the report

about the rent strike which began among Negroes in Harlem and is now spreading to some white sections of the population in other parts of New York City. Another small but striking example occurred in Detroit last summer. A militant Negro demonstration in front of police headquarters, to protest the police shooting of a young Negro woman in the back, came to the very brink of a physical clash. That was a Saturday, and it was followed two days later, on Monday, by another demonstration at another police station, near which cops had shot a young white man in the back. This second demonstration, involving mainly young whites, *raised the same slogans as the first* and culminated in a pitched battle with the cops after the youths had thrown rocks and bottles at them. Not long ago I noticed a small newspaper item about some airline strike pickets who had been picketing up and down outside the Newark terminal for a long time, with little public attention paid to their grievances. One day they suddenly decided to go inside the terminal and demonstrate there, which was prohibited by an injunction. Quickly arrested, they were asked what had got into them. Their explanation was that they had seen that Negroes were able to get action by sit-ins and by going places where they weren't supposed to, so they thought it was a good idea to do the same.

These are all small-scale illustrations, but bigger and better ones are in the offing. The rulers of this country are well aware of the stimulation-and-contagion effects of militant Negro struggle. That is one reason why they want to stop it before it goes too far, and explains the hasty turnabout that induced the previously indifferent Kennedy administration to suddenly introduce civil rights legislation last year.

5. A determined minority can also divide the majority, can actually split it up at decisive moments and junctures. This, of course, is one of the best ways of reducing the disadvantages of being a numerical minority, because it drastically changes the odds against the minority. The Socialist Workers Party's 1963 convention resolution[1] showed how this process has operated historically. If our analysis and theory are correct, this isn't a matter of history only, but of the present and the future. Let me refer briefly to the Civil War as an example of the process which can split the majority.

The Civil War was not just a conflict between abstract and impersonal forces, between Northern capitalism and Southern slavery; it was a struggle between classes and living people. No one played a greater role in stimulating and progressively resolving that conflict than the slaves and ex-slaves. Again and again in the three decades before the Civil War, the rulers of the North and the South decided to avoid a final showdown by compromising over the slave question. Great hopes were raised and brilliant reputations were made overnight by these eminently "reasonable" negotiations and agreements reached over the bargaining table in Congress and then enacted into law. But the slaves were not consulted about these great compromises. They would not have consented to them anyway, because they left the condition of the slave unchanged, that is, intolerable. So the slaves continued their own independent efforts to become free, just as if these great compromise agreements had never existed.

HOW SLAVES FOUGHT

They continued, just as before, or more so, to run away by the thousands and tens of thousands, to commit sabotage and arson, and to engage in various forms of civil disobedience, self-defense, and insurrection. These independent actions of the slaves helped to prevent the compromises from working and to stimulate the birth and growth of abolitionism among whites, who threw their weight onto the scales against further compromise. Thus the slaves reopened and widened the gap between the South and the North every time the great compromise statesmen tried to close it.

By acting in every way they could to defend and liberate themselves, the slaves drove a wedge between the slaveholders and those who wanted to compromise with the slaveholders. By acting in self-interest, and alone when they had to, the slaves divided the whites politically and morally and deepened the divisions to the breaking point. That, above everything else, is what made the struggle irrepressible, constantly widened the breach and deepened the division among the whites, and led inexorably to civil warfare. And then, at the crucial moment, after the outbreak of the war the rulers on both sides had tried so hard to avert, the Negroes pressured the Northern government into accepting a revolutionary emancipation policy and completed the process by providing what the reluctant Lincoln later admitted was the military balance of power in the war itself. All this happened without a conscious plan, you might say instinctively. Imagine what will happen when the Negro militants absorb this lesson from history and then consciously work out a strategy to fully utilize this process that is set in motion by the elemental desire of the masses to be free!

We can expect, we can be certain, that the deepening of the Negro struggle for equality will have similarly divisive effects on the white majority in our own time. The majority is not homogeneous anyway; it is strained and torn and in conflict over a thousand questions of policy and class interest. A skillful leadership of the Negro minority will know how to pick the right place to drive new wedges, to deepen already existing and potential differences among the whites, to sharpen their conflicts, to set them fighting each other, and, in the process, as the SWP 1963 convention resolution also says, to find mutually beneficial alliances with those classes and forces whose interests are closer to those of the Negroes against those forces that are most hostile to the Negroes.

Under certain conditions, therefore, a minority, just by fighting for its own rights, can divide the majority into two or more minorities locked in combat with each other. This in turn can result in bringing to power a different kind of majority, not based on color, in which the original minority can take a leading part.

Those who confine themselves to scratching the surface can see only the limitations of being a minority, which leads to lamentation, pessimism, and self-induced paralysis or subservience. But when we examine the situation in all of its complex and contradictory reality, probing it deeper and from all sides; when we study majority-minority relations in motion as well as when they are standing still; when we perceive that the majority has problems too, and weaknesses, and many points at which it is vulnerable and susceptible to successful attack, and that these majority problems and weaknesses are becoming more acute than ever before, then we find, not just limitations for the minority, but also infinitely varied and promising openings and opportunities for transforming, transcending, and overcoming limitations.

POLITICAL POWER

6. The Negro minority is also in a position to upset the whole political structure of this country—just by "going it alone" in politics, just by the decisions Negroes make about how to use their own votes and their own

minority political strength. Our 1963 convention resolution explored this question, too, before the present Freedom Now Party was started, but it bears restatement because it is such an effective refutation of black liberals who contend the Negro is politically impotent and "destined to fail" if he acts on his own in politics.

Negroes can form their own party. Negroes can run their own candidates against the Democrats and Republicans. Negroes, because they are already a majority in many districts, thanks to the segregated housing system that jams them tightly together in the big-city ghettos, can, right now or any time they form their own party, elect dozens of black candidates to Congress from these districts and hundreds of state and local representatives. In this way they can get representatives in public office who will be responsible and accountable to the Negro community instead of to the corrupt major party machines. And since this bloc of black representatives will not be small, it will enable them to hold and wield a certain legislative balance of power and to compel bigger concessions from the power structure than the tokens and crumbs they are now thrown; all of this, you notice, without any drastic change yet in political relations—just by taking advantage of the political and electoral conditions created by segregation, by refusing to vote Democratic or Republican, by voting black. This would mark a real advance, at least in the number and quality of Negro representatives in office, but that would be only a part of the result of independent political action.

By forming their own party, Negroes can paralyze the Democratic Party and rock the whole political structure to its foundations. Without Negro votes, the bell will toll the doom of the Democratic Party. Without Negro votes, the Democratic coalition with the labor movement will be undermined and destroyed. Without Negro votes for that coalition, the unions will be forced to reconsider their political orientation, and this will encourage and strengthen the union forces who will eventually form an independent labor party. Without Negro votes, the present two-party system will pass from the scene and be replaced by something different, out of which Negroes may be able to acquire new and more reliable allies than up to now. And all of this can be accomplished by the simple device of forming a Negro party and running independent Negro candidates. Really, when you think about the potential, you can almost pity the ignorance of those Negro leaders who preach that Negroes are incapable of any political role other than tagging along behind the liberals.

7. The last on my partial list of things the Negro minority can do should be of special interest to another and smaller minority—socialists, white and Negro. I am convinced that if other Negroes, not yet socialist, are not so concerned with this point now, they will be later, as their continuing political experience draws it to their attention. At any rate, my point is that the Negro people, although a minority, can, with consistently revolutionary leadership, lead the American working class in the revolution that will abolish capitalism.

We have long held the view that while the Negro struggle is the struggle of an oppressed minority for democratic rights, for equality, it tends, because the masters of this country are both unwilling and unable to grant equality, to become part of the general movement of the exploited and oppressed to abolish capitalism and proceed toward socialism. In this tendency to pass over from democratic to socialist goals, to pass beyond the capitalist framework that now envelops it, the Negro struggle is similar to the colonial struggles, which also take off from democratic aims, such as independence and self-government, but find themselves unable to attain those democratic aims until they wrench the capitalist boot from off their neck. The Chinese call this process "the uninterrupted revolution," and Leon Trotsky called it "the permanent revolution." But that is not what I am discussing here. What I am talking about now is something else—the capacity of the Negro people to lead the working-class revolution to replace capitalism with socialism.

ROLE OF MAJORITY

To grasp this idea, we must rid our minds of the conception that any social revolution in general or any working-class revolution in particular has to be led by a majority. I will try to illustrate this by going back to the first victorious workers' revolution, the Russian Revolution of 1917. It was victorious because it had the *support* of a majority of the Russian people. But it was not led by any class, or by any vanguard of a class, that comprised the majority of the population. It was a revolution *supported by the majority*, and it could not have succeeded without that majority support, but it was *led by a party that represented a class that was a minority of the country*.

We call it, and it was, a working-class revolution. But out of 150 million people in Russia in 1917, the workers were a small minority. There were probably no more than 10 million workers, and that included agricultural workers, some of whom were workers only part of the time. Counting their families, they made up about 15 or 16 percent of the total population. Yet this class, with a proper leadership in the form of Lenin's Bolshevik Party, was able to lead a revolution that abolished capitalism in Russia.

This is one of the things that befuddled and ruined the Mensheviks, the Social Democrats, and other white liberals of that day. As they understood Marx's analysis of the conditions needed for social revolution, it could not take place and should not even be attempted until the country was industrialized to the point where the working class was a majority of the population, as in England then or in the United States today. And if it was attempted before the workers were a majority of the population, it was, according to these people, bound to fail. And they were so sure the Russian Revolution was not according to either Hoyle or Marx that most of them pitched in and did their utmost to make it fail.

NEED FOR ALLIES

But they misunderstood Marx and Marxism, as fortunately Lenin, Trotsky, and others did not. A socialist revolution can be led by the working class even when the working class is a minority, provided that working-class minority can get an alliance with, and support from, other noncapitalist forces and classes in the country. In Russia this meant an alliance with the peasants, who constituted around 75 percent of the country. The working-class minority was able to lead the Russian Revolution and lead it to victory, not only because it took advantage of the crisis of the capitalist class in war, not only because it had a qualified leadership, but also because it worked out an effective alliance with the most oppressed sections of the peasants.

This alliance was designed to meet the most pressing demands of the peasants, but it did not make any concessions to them about the need to throw the capitalists out of power; and it was based, first of all, on the needs and interests of the working-class minority, because the workers were the backbone of the revolution, the most revolutionary force in the country.

Now why, in discussing the American revolution of the 1960s and 1970s, have I gone all the way back to 1917 and far-off Russia? I did so because I thought it would throw light on the distinction between the *making* of a revolution and the *leading* of a revolution, on the leading role that a minority can play, on how dogma can blind you to the leading role of a minority, and on how the successful leadership of a working-class revolution by a minority class depends partly on its ability to make alliances with other exploited classes and groups. I know I am not proving anything about America by this reference to Russia, but perhaps it can help us to look at the role of revolutionary minorities in a fresh way.

The working-class revolution has to be led by workers through their independent party, or parties, or councils. That's one of the things Marx taught us. But Marx never said anything about the revolution having to be led by white workers. He only said by workers—by the most revolutionary workers. The Negroes in this country are a racial minority, but that is only one of their aspects. It would be truly fatal to forget their other primary aspect, namely, that in their overwhelming majority they are proletarian in composition. In fact, Negroes are more proletarian than whites in this country. Negroes are an important section of the working class as well as a racial minority. Unless we are blind, we must see that they are at present and will probably remain the most radicalized section of the working class, the section of the working class that has the most to gain and nothing to lose from social revolution. If this is true, then why should it be so hard, when we are discussing what a radical minority of the working class can do, to conceive of the possibility that it may lead the rest of the working class and its allies in the revolution that will abolish capitalism?

As a matter of fact, that is just what Leon Trotsky, who did so much to rescue authentic Marxism for my generation and yours, was trying to teach us twenty-five years ago when we set out to reach a correct and revolutionary analysis of the Negro struggle. Things were different in 1933, before the CIO, and in 1939, long before the current radicalization of the Negro people. But let me read you some things Trotsky told us in the 1930s[2] and see if they do not apply with even greater validity and relevance to the changed conditions of the 1960s. My first quotation is from a discussion in Turkey between Trotsky and an American, thirty-one years ago, at the depth of the depression and before the CIO was formed. English was not Trotsky's native tongue, and his English was not too good, but his ideas were. He was talking, in 1933, about what would happen when a mass radicalization began in America, and he said:

> I believe that by the unheard-of political and theoretical backwardness and the unheard-of economic advance the awakening of the working class will proceed quite rapidly. The old ideological covering will burst, all questions will emerge at once, and since the country is so economically mature, the adaptation of the political and theoretical to the economic level will be achieved very rapidly. It is then possible that the Negroes will become the most advanced section. We have already a similar example in Russia. The Russians were the European Negroes. It is very possible that the Negroes also through self-determination will proceed to the proletarian dictatorship in a couple of gigantic strides, ahead of the great bloc of white workers. They will then furnish the vanguard. I am absolutely sure that they will in any case fight better than the white workers. That, however, can happen only if the Communist Party carries on an uncompromising merciless struggle not against the supposed national prepossessions of the Negroes but against the colossal prejudices of the white workers and gives it no concession whatever.

That was 1933. Six years later, in 1939, Trotsky discussed the Negro struggle with another delegation from the United States, and, touching on the conditions that make workers conservative or radical, he said:

> If the workers' aristocracy is the basis of opportunism, one of the sources of adaptation to capitalist society, then the most oppressed and discriminated against are the most dynamic milieu of the working class. We must say to the conscious elements of the Negroes that they are convoked by the historic development to become a vanguard of the working class. What serves as a brake on the higher strata? It is the privileges, the comforts that hinder them from becoming revolutionists. It does not exist for the Negroes. What can transform a certain stratum, make it more capable of courage and sacrifice? It is concentrated in the Negroes. If it happens that we in the SWP are not able to find a road to this stratum, then we are not worthy at all. The permanent revolution and all the rest would be only a lie.

Let me repeat just three of those statements now: It is "*possible that the Negroes will become the most advanced section.*" It is possible that the Negroes "*will proceed to the proletarian dictatorship . . . ahead of the great bloc of white workers.*" "*(T)he Negroes . . . are convoked by the historic development to become a vanguard of the working class.*" What Trotsky was trying to get us to understand twenty-five and thirty years ago, it is plain, was the possibility that the Negroes could lead the working-class revolution. Our party tried to understand this and to express it in the very first resolution on the Negro struggle it ever adopted, which made it the first party ever to put this idea forward. Let me read the first two sentences of that resolution, which is reprinted in full in *Documents on the Negro Struggle*, and which was adopted by the Socialist Workers Party convention in 1939:

> The American Negroes, for centuries the most oppressed section of American society and the most discriminated against, are potentially the most revolutionary element of the population. They are designated by their whole historical past to be, under adequate leadership, the very vanguard of the proletarian revolution.

So what I have been trying to say, in stating that the black minority can lead the white majority of the working class in the coming social revolution, is not really new, because the Socialist Workers Party explicitly stated that concept in a formal convention resolution in 1939, before most of the people in this hall were born.

Then why does it seem new to many of us? Because, I am sorry to say, there can be a big gap between accepting or even repeating an idea in a general way as logically correct, and grasping in all of its concreteness a profound truth that flies in the face of all prevailing opinion and prejudice, absorbing it and making it a part of you, a central part of your thought and your action. There is also a considerable difference between accepting a general proposition that may turn out to be correct at some indefinite future time and accepting it as a possibility, or even a probability, that can have the most far-reaching consequences for you right now or in the near future.

Although in 1939 we accepted the idea that the Negro minority can lead the working-class revolution and readily adopted that as the official position of the Socialist Workers Party, the truth is that it was only a surface acceptance and adoption. We were not yet ready, despite what we put in our resolution, to fully understand what Trotsky was trying to get us to see. And six or seven weeks after our 1939 convention adopted this resolution, J. R. Johnson,[3] the chairman of our party's committee on Negro work at that time, who had been under Trotsky's influence the chief author of the resolution, wrote in our paper an article referring to the resolution. Johnson said that while the idea in the resolution was correct, and while "the place of the Negro is in the very front," nevertheless the formulation in the resolution was an "overstatement." Instead of saying that the Negroes are destined to be "the very vanguard," he wrote, it would have been more correct to say that they are destined to be "in the very vanguard." This was a real weakening of the idea Trotsky had tried to persuade us of. Although it left the Socialist Workers Party with the most advanced position on the Negro struggle, it was a definite step backward.

But now, with Trotsky long dead, I think we are able to return to that original unweakened idea and see it in an entirely different light—not as an overstatement, but as a cold, hard, factually correct appraisal of a vital possibility that can crucially affect the future of all Americans. Because what Trotsky could not teach us completely we have now been able to learn from the actual development of the Negro struggle itself right before our own eyes these last two or three years. What we were not advanced enough in the 1930s to accept as theory, we are now able to apprehend as concrete current event. Because the fact is that the Negroes are already a vanguard. They are already out in front of most white workers. They are more radicalized than the white workers. They are more ready to fight and to sacrifice and die in order to change this system.

And so today many of us, I am sure, will be able to grasp and act on the concept of Negroes as leaders of the workers' revolution not just as a possibility but as a probability. I shall not try, because that is a job for the whole movement, to work out or complete everything that flows from this concept, except to say that much does, and that all of it seems to me a cause for optimism. Nor shall I try here to discuss the kind of alliance I think the Negro vanguard of the working-class revolution will have to effect with the advanced section of the white workers if the revolution is to be led to success, except to say that I do not think it can be an alliance that will make concessions in principle to the white allies of the Negroes, any more than the revolutionary vanguard in Russia sacrificed any principles in their alliance with the peasants. Instead, I shall conclude, with much left hanging, by saying that if the ideas in this talk are correct, if the concepts about what a minority can do will be of practical and theoretical benefit in advancing the Negro struggle for freedom, then what they demonstrate is the validity and even the indispensability of Marxism to Negro revolutionists, whether or not they belong to the Socialist Workers Party.

NOTES

1. *Freedom Now: The New Stage in the Struggle for Negro Emancipation* (New York: Pioneer Publishers, 1963).

2. *Leon Trotsky on Black Nationalism and Self-Determination* (New York: Merit Publishers, 1967), p. 95c.

3. The party name of Trinidadian-born intellectual C. L. R. James.

CHAPTER 4

MARXISM AND THE
NEGRO STRUGGLE
(1964)

Harold Cruse

PART I

When the Socialist Workers Party (Trotskyist) announced in the *New York Times*, January 14, that it had nominated a Negro, Clifton DeBerry, to run for president, it allowed us the opportunity to discuss in depth a question that has long been agitating many individuals, friends and foes, concerning the relationship of Marxism to the Negro movement in America today. We emphasize "today" because some years ago it was impossible to be objective about this inasmuch as the Marxist movement as represented by the Communist Party was so indissolubly linked with practically everything Negroes attempted to do that it was impossible not to find a Communist or two under the bed if one looked earnestly enough. Hence, some very relevant issues about Marxism were distorted and confused by a barrage of heated denials and accusations about the "Red Menace."

Today, the relationship between the Negro movement and the Marxist movement has gone through a succession of qualitative changes on both sides. Today the Negro movement has developed to its highest level of

---

"Marxism and the Negro," by Harold Cruse, first appeared as a two-part article in the May and June issues of the *Liberator*. George Breitman responded in a five-part series entitled "Marxism and the Negro Struggle," which was printed during August and September 1964 in the SWP's weekly newspaper, the *Militant*.

organizational scope and programmatic independence in this century. In the meantime, the dominant trend in American Marxism, the Communist Party, has declined to the low status of a weak, ineffectual sect creating a vacuum in "revolutionary" politics which the Trotskyists are desperately trying to fill. But the eclipse of Communist Party Marxism went hand in hand with the decline of labor union radicalism in America. White labor (as differentiated from black labor) went conservative, pro-capitalist, and strongly anti-Negro. This created a serious and a practically insoluble dilemma for the Marxist movement because the theory and practice of revolutionary Marxism in America is based on the assumption that white labor, both organized and unorganized, must be a radical, anticapitalist force in America and must form an "alliance" with Negroes for the liberation of both labor and the Negro from capitalist exploitation. No matter what the facts of life reveal to the contrary, no matter what the Marxists say or do in terms of momentary "tactics," this is what the Marxists believe, and must believe, or cease functioning as a Marxist tendency. For Karl Marx's dictum on this question was that "labor cannot emancipate itself in the white skin where in the black it is branded." Today, the Trotskyists consider themselves to be the most "orthodox" of Marxists.

The fact that white labor in America today is clearly unsympathetic to the "emancipation" of either Negro workers, or the "petit bourgeois" Negroes, or the "intellectuals," as the Marxists are fond of citing, poses, as was said, a serious dilemma for the revolutionary Marxists. On the other hand, the Negro movement's rise to the ascendancy as a radical force in America completely upsets Marxian theory and forces the Marxists to adopt momentary tactics which they do not essentially believe in. In short, they become opportunistic. Here we refer to the white Marxists, the black ones are another question which is currently personified in the case of DeBerry. However, the realities in America today force the Marxists to deal with the Negro movement as the de facto radical force, but this does not hide the fact that the Marxist movement is in a serious crisis. Moreover, the greater the Negro movement becomes as an independent force, the more the Marxists must strive to ally themselves with the Negro movement, but the deeper does the crisis become for the Marxist movement itself. For the "alliance" it attempts to forge with the Negro must be one where the Marxists dominate in order not to be absorbed. This "alliance" is meant to build the Marxist party, not the Negro movement, in order to rescue the Marxists from their own crisis. In the Fall 1963 issue of the *International Socialist Review*, the Trotskyists, in discussing the Freedom Now "movement," said:

The present tasks of the SWP in connection with the Negro struggle for liberation are . . .

(4) To expand and strengthen the party's cadre and forces in the Negro organizations and the civil rights movements, by: (a) recruiting revolutionary Negroes and helping to train them for leadership in the party and mass movements.

Elsewhere the Trotskyists said:

In the same way the influence of the colonial revolution . . . upon vanguard elements of the Negro movement has helped prepare the emergence of a new radical left wing. In all these cases, it is the task of revolutionary Marxists to seek to win the best elements of this newly emerging vanguard to Trotskyism.

However, the *real* issue at stake here is: Who is destined to be the dominant and decisive radical force in America—black radicals or white radicals? And this is a question that will and must be settled outside the scope of any existing "theory," Marxian or otherwise, because there is no "theory" that covers this development. Such an American theory (if it is ever written down) will have to come from blacks. Hence, we have the most unprecedented situation yet seen in the Western world—a Marxist movement with a time-honored social theory which does not work out in life with a mass following, and a viable Negro movement of masses in movement which is stymied because it has no social theory or program to take it further. World historical trends have brought both the old Marxist tradition and the new Negro movement face to face on either side of a profound impasse. The Trotskyists, being the most astute of all Marxists, attempt to bridge the chasm by nominating a Negro for president! But this desperate gesture cannot cure the Marxian crisis by enlisting the Negro potential. Moreover, it is not the right remedy for what really ails the Negro movement at this juncture. It is the same thing as offering an impoverished man with a wife and ten kids a Palm Beach vacation with some political VIPs and all the trimmings just "to get away from it all." What'll happen to the man's family? These are some of the reasons why the SWP's presidential announcement caused so much confusion, anger, and suspicion within the ranks of the Freedom Now Party movement concerning "white radical influence." For DeBerry also linked himself with the Freedom Now Party without the party's permission to do so—a well-known Marxian type of maneuver in Negro affairs.

As the Negro movement stops and gropes about for its methods of entering its next stage, this question of Marxism's influence will keep bobbing up in different situations. Hence, it is necessary for black radical "thinkers" (as opposed to the "strugglers" or "street-men" as some proudly call themselves) to get a clearer understanding of why the Marxists act the way they do and why they are in a crisis. The Negro movement is also in a crisis despite its late achievements—a crisis which is linked to world developments broader than our own problems and with roots in events which predate us.

The crisis of Marxism in Europe and North America has its roots in the confused events of the Russian Revolution of 1917. In the case of the Socialist Workers Party, it was Leon Trotsky, its guiding revolutionary thinker, who first said that a socialist revolution was even possible in Russia. This was in 1905 when none of the Russian Marxists agreed to that possibility (not even Lenin). Trotsky was denounced as a ridiculous visionary for saying this but later won other Russian Marxists over to his thinking. Thus Trotsky was actually the *theoretical* father of the Russian Revolution and Lenin was the chief architect and leader.

Marxism, as Marx himself developed it, did not foresee or predict a "socialist revolution" in a backward agrarian country such as Russia. According to Marx, the revolution he predicted had to come about in a highly industrialized nation which had necessarily created a large, industrial class of workers, well-organized and well-trained in the production skills of capitalist industry. The capitalist class of owners would get richer and more compact due to monopoly growths, and the working class would get poorer and poorer to the point where they would revolt and overturn the system and expropriate the owners. Recognizing full well that they were revising the original view of Marx, both Trotsky and Lenin then agreed that if a socialist revolution was possible in Russia—a large agrarian country with only a small degree of industrial development—

then this revolution could not stand alone. It would have to be supported by simultaneous revolutions in the advanced nations of western Europe.

But such did not happen. There was a revolution in Russia, but it had to stand alone because supporting revolutions elsewhere did not succeed. The result was that the most important single event of the twentieth century was transformed into its gravest tragedy. Moreover, it put the Marxist parties in western Europe, the United States, etc., in a serious dilemma—a dilemma which over the years has deepened into a series of crises. This is because every social revolution that has taken place since the Russian Revolution has also developed out of industrially backward, agrarian, semi-colonial, or colonial conditions while the working classes of the advanced white nations became more and more conservative, pro-capitalist, and *pro-imperialist*. Moreover, the very fact that the world revolutionary initiative had passed from white nations of the capitalist world to *nonwhite nations* of the colonial and semicolonial world introduced another factor in revolutionary politics, the racial factor, which the Western Marxists never admitted should be a factor of any importance at all. Workers, in their opinion, regardless of race and national differences, should all think alike on the question of capitalism and imperialism. The Trotskyists still function under this grand illusion. This is why Clifton DeBerry, in the Socialist Workers Party's announcement, had to project his support of the Freedom Now Party on the basis that it is "a step toward independent political action by *labor* and Negroes." By this he means *white labor* and Negroes (emphasis ours [Cruse's]). But the leaders of the Freedom Now Party never made any such pronouncement. The Freedom Now Party is a step toward *independent black political* action. Clearly, the Trotskyists do not really want this. Because Marxism is in a crisis in America, they must attempt to project the idea of the Freedom Now Party in their own Marxian image, with the old worn-out, discredited theme of Negro-Labor unity.

The Trotskyist theoreticians realize very well that a truly independent black political party which functions irrespective of what white labor does or does not do will further deepen the already serious crisis of Marxist creed in the West. It could show that Marxian ideas about capitalism in advanced countries are not to be taken seriously. A whole raft of Marxian formulations would be further called into question. In any event, none of this would be the fault of the Negro. Rather, it would be the fault of the Marxists for being dishonest with themselves and misleading generation after generation of innocents about the true nature of the Russian Revolution. What was this revolution? How did it really occur and why? What did it achieve? The Communists and the Trotskyists, twin branches of the same withering tree trunk of Western Marxism, have been attacking and accusing each other over these questions for almost forty years. Why?

Let the Trotskyists tell it—it was because Stalin and the bureaucracy "distorted" and "betrayed" the "socialist revolution." But the Trotskyists have only inherited a problem in socialist theory and practice that Trotsky made for himself. Who was it but Trotsky himself who first claimed that such a revolution was possible? All the facts reveal that Trotsky got the very kind of revolution he actually made and deserved and then disowned it because it wasn't really "socialist." He accused the Stalin bureaucracy of "terrorism," of "smothering democracy," of "suppressing the opposition," of taking away the political power of the workers' soviets (councils). But it was Trotsky himself who set such precedents by ordering the brutal suppression of the Kronstadt sailors' revolt of 1921 long before the Stalin bureaucracy set in.

The Russian Revolution logically turned out just the way it had to, considering how and where it was achieved and what the social objectives were it set for itself. Trotsky helped formulate these objectives. Nothing was betrayed—it was the Russian revolutionaries who "betrayed" themselves, and the Russian masses suffered. After Trotsky's revolution it was imperative that the Communists industrialize a backward country in as short a time as possible because there can be no socialism until there is enough of an industrial base to socialize (i.e., nationalize). Hence, all the political conflicts between Russian factions centered around the great, pressing problem thrust on them by their own revolutionary seizure of power: how to plan and administer nationalized property, most of which had to be built before it could be administered. This was no ordinary task and the nature of the revolution itself brought to the fore just the type of individuals needed to perform the operation—Stalin and his Stalinists, single-minded, dictatorial, brutal, and practical. Not the Trotsky type at all. Trotsky opposed this natural trend of his own revolution and was expelled from Russia.

According to a strict interpretation of Marxian formulations, Trotsky tampered very loosely with Marxian "laws" and reaped the whirlwind. This premise of course absolves Marx of responsibility for the tragic, antisocialist aspects of the Russian Revolution. The intent is to argue that if

Marx was right about the workings of "historical laws" and Trotsky was a Marxist, then something was wrong about Marx's "historical law" formulations. Either this, or Trotsky was a Marxist who gravely misinterpreted the functioning of Marxian laws. But it was Marx himself who insisted: "One thing is certain: I am not a Marxist." Meaning what? Are we to take it to mean that because his prophecies about advanced capitalist societies, the white nations, did not materialize that we are entitled to say that Marx was wrong because he himself failed to properly interpret the very laws he is credited with being the first to discover? If this is the case, then we have a strong premise for taking Marx at his own word. If he himself admits he was not a "Marxist," then who was really a Marxist after he passed away? Whose claim to be a Marxist must anyone take seriously?

We pose these questions because the Trotskyist nomination of DeBerry for president grows out of the Marxists' belief that the "historical laws" have preordained the Negro movement in America to be used as a kind of transitional social phase leading to the "Marxian revolution." In this instance we are to suppose that the Trotskyists are applying the "methods and principles of historical materialism," that is, the "laws" correctly "before the fact." But even to grant the Marxists, for the sake of argument, the validity of their own Marxian premises, we have to say that their application of the "method" is no more "Marxian" than others that failed to bring, in their opinion, "Marxian" results. This might surprise or even shock the Trotskyists, coming as it does from non-Marxist radicals of the Negro movement. However, it is not that we are prejudiced against "Marxism" per se. We study Marxism just like we study objectively all social science schools of thought which claim to be "scientific." What we strenuously object to are the "methods" that the Marxists use.

Fundamental to all Marxist formulations is the *dialectical method of theory and practice.* Marx made it amply clear that his method was dialectical; hence, any approach to social life which is not dialectical cannot be Marxian. We would tend to agree with many, such as the late C. Wright Mills, who said of Marx, "His *method* is a signal and lasting contribution to the best sociological ways of reflection and inquiry available" (emphasis ours). We make a distinction here between Marx's original *method* and the *applications* of his latter-day disciples. We reject these findings precisely because they are not, in our opinion, arrived at by the dialectical method of reflection and inquiry.

How did Marx arrive at his conclusions about the role of the working class in capitalist society? Through the application of one of his prime laws of dialectics: *the law of the unity and conflict of opposites.* In dialectical processes social phenomena, for example, classes, ideas, institutions, etc., are not static, but go through constant development and changes. Capitalistic production creates capitalists and workers (opposites) who come into conflict because their class interests are not identical. Capitalists exploit workers by not paying them their full labor value. Capitalists seek the highest rate of profit through intensified exploitation of the working class. The conflict of interests generates "class struggle," for example, strikes. Marx observed that the basis of class struggle lies in a "contradiction" between the methods of production and the "social relations" of production (private property). These "contradictions" can be resolved only by a social revolution wherein the working class overthrows or otherwise expropriates the capitalists. This description of dialectics, while simplified, explains why Marxists have considered it to be the historic role of the working class in capitalist societies to usher in the socialist era.

However, Marx came to these conclusions about the working class in Europe over a hundred years ago, and these predictions still have not been borne out in the advanced capitalist societies of western Europe and North America. Yet, it must be stated that according to his own dialectical premise of analysis, Marx had every right to make such predictions. All the evidence abounding in the social and political life of Europe in Marx's time pointed to revolution. Moreover, the failure of the social revolution to materialize in the advanced capitalist countries does not at all invalidate Marx's dialectical method. What does become invalid is the subsequent "application" of the dialectical method by the followers of Marx in the twentieth century. We say this because if one accepts the premise of dialectics, then we accept the view that everything in social life is constantly changing, coming into existence, and passing away. But, if this dialectical premise is "truth," then why is it assumed that everything in society is subject to the processes of change *except the historical role of the working class in advanced capitalist nations*? Why is this white European, North American labor movement itself exempt from dialectical change in terms of class position, ideology, consciousness, etc., and in terms of what other groups, or classes, this labor movement fights, supports, or compromises with in the "class struggle"? Has it not become abundantly clear that the white labor movement in the advanced capitalist countries has, indeed, abandoned the Marxian "historical role" assigned to it? Do we not have the right to claim, then, that European and American Marxists who still hew to this "white working class" line are practicing *mechanistic materialism* rather than *dialectical materialism*?

PART II

Classical Marxism rejects all forms of mechanistic materialism because it "denies any genuine evolution in the sense of the emergence of new forms and new qualities of new things." Hence, the very premise of dialectical thinking demands, in this instance, an admission that "new forms of social consciousness" can develop within capitalist societies which are of more political relevance than even the "social consciousness" of the conservatized labor movement. Any other conclusion than this is manifestly antidialectical. Hence, fundamental to the crisis in all the schools of Western Marxism of the advanced capitalist countries (the white nations) is the crisis that has long gripped the philosophical system of thought, the "kernel" around which the entire political, economic, cultural, theoretical, and programmatic structure of Marxism must hinge. It is a crisis of dialectical materialism which was conceived by Marx as a method which had to comprehend the reality of the world, but is no longer able to do so. The reality of world revolutionary events is running far ahead of Marxian theory.

In 1939, when the European white working class was armed to the teeth along the borderlines of their nations ready to spread war and mayhem against themselves all over Europe, and half the world, Trotsky, writing about Marxism in the United States, could say with the most lofty detachment: "By the example and with the aid of the advanced nations the backward nations will also be carried away into the mainstream of socialism."

Here is expressed in the most graphic manner the supreme illusions of the Western (or in Trotsky's case) the "Westernized" white Marxist. They cannot let go of the *idée fixe* of the white working class "saving" the world's humanity. Rooted in their preconceived notions, their undialectical ideas, is the deeply ingrained "white nation ideal." Hence, "socialism" becomes like "capitalism" a white-nation conception, the great "white working-class" prerogative. Thus, the "white man's burden" shifts from the capitalist's missionaries to the socialist's revolutionaries whose duty to history is to lift the "backward" peoples from their ignominious state to socialist civilization even if the whites have to postpone this elevation abroad until they have managed to achieve it at home. But in so doing, the white Marxists' dialectical conceptions of world developments become a distorted image of the reality that is taking place before their very eyes.

Hence, the dialectical analyses that Marxists project concerning world developments are, in truth, mechanistically gross distortions of the original dialectical methods of Marx, who was essentially true to his method for his own time and circumstances. It was not the fault of Marx that the world changes, for this was already explicit in dialectics. But the distortions of today's Western Marxism lie in the fact that Marxists treat dialectical materialism only from the standpoint of how the impersonal productive forces develop, how the material forces evolve in society and bring about class relationships, or cause human society to go through stages from feudalism to capitalism. Or further, how capitalism penetrates the underdeveloped world and brings the latter into the capitalistic network, etc. But Marx pointed out that "in the social production which men carry on they enter into definite relations that are indispensable and *independent* of their will" (emphasis ours).

Which means that men are subject to the blind forces of the laws of social production unless they become "socially conscious" of what is happening to them. But how men become socially conscious is a problem of the *theory of knowledge and reflection* which is an inseparable category in the dialectical method of social inquiry. If men did not comprehend the nature of material forces, they could not be able to intervene into the process of these forces in order to shape events, that is, to control blind forces. Thus, men, or classes, or groups, or even nations, could not assume the task of "revolutionizing" societies unless they are positioned to do so and also have the necessary consciousness to shape events. In this regard, social developments can position certain classes to shape events, give them the potential, yet such classes remain without the consciousness or the will to make history.

But there are always other classes and it is the implied function of dialectics to correctly perceive what classes are being brought to the forefront of social consciousness by "blind" material forces. This class will become the social force chosen by "historical laws" for historical roles rather than preconceived classes that history has left behind. Lenin dealt most thoroughly with how men or classes receive their sense perceptions of the real world, but Marxists today bypass this aspect of dialectics because they believe the social role of the "proletariat" alone settles this question for all time.

White Marxists have tried to make world reality fit their dialectical pre-conceptions, but world developments require that dialectical conceptions embrace world reality. But such conceptions cannot come from the minds of Western Marxists whose philosophical views have become provincially rooted in the crisis-reality of the Western world and cannot transcend the conceptual limitations of that world. They talk "revolution" but revolution is being made by others. Hence, world social developments run ahead of the world social theory. [William F.] Warde says that the principles of historical materialism are applicable everywhere "provided they are applied with full consideration of the facts in each case." But the question Warde does not discuss is: "Who is to determine this? Those who are making the world revolution or those in the West whose 'dialectical' views are anchored down to the lethargy of the white working class?" [William F. Warde was a pen name of SWP intellectual George Novack.]

The Marxian theory of knowledge (dialectics) implies that if the "backward peoples" of the world are carrying themselves into the "mainstream of socialism" instead of being led there by the "aid of the advanced nations" as Trotsky saw it, then the "backward peoples" must replace the white working class as the "chosen people" of the dialectical functionings of world society. Hence, if "historical science" or "dialectics" is to be considered really scientific, it must be developed and verified in life by the inclusion of the social experiences, the history, the ideas and political philosophies, the points of view of the backward peoples. In short, it is the social reflections of backward peoples that count today the world over. For it is their social consciousness that is determining which way history is moving. Hence, dialectical materialism is no longer the "philosophy of the proletariat" (i.e., the European proletariat) as the Western Marxists would have it.

It is the fate of the Marxists to be imprisoned within their illusions, and that is the source of their crisis. They cannot deal with the race question in America in terms of their dialectical method except superficially, which they must attempt to conceal by all too obvious practices of political expediency, such as the DeBerry nomination. This must, of necessity, bring them into serious conflict with the Negro movement itself. For the Negro movement has its spiritual affinities not with the white working class of America whose status vis-à-vis American capitalism is qualitatively different from Negroes'. White labor's heyday is behind them in the history of the 1930s. The American Negroes' movement is currently a semicolonial revolt which is more inspired by events outside America than within it. We can much better explain the Negro movement's relationship to world developments today by quoting Leopold Sedar Senghor, president of the African republic of Senegal, from his pamphlet on African Socialism:

> We are not communists. . . .
>
> The paradox of socialistic construction in communist countries in the Soviet Union is that it increasingly resembles capitalistic construction in the United States of America. . . . And it has less art and freedom of thought.
>
> But a third revolution is taking place, as a reaction against capitalistic and communistic materialism, and which will integrate moral, if not religious, values with the political and economic contributions of the two great revolutions. In this revolution the colored peoples, including Negro Africans, must play their part, they must bring their contribution to the construction of the new planetary civilization.

Of the Negro American in this "third revolution," Senghor quotes Paul Morand as saying: "The Negroes have rendered an enormous service to America. But for them one might have thought that men could not live without a bank account and a bathtub."

*   *   *

The living facts of the world revolution today are more persuasive than any revolutionary theory that ever came out of western Europe since the death of Marx. We do not hold Marx accountable for any deviations or distortions that either history or men have imposed to detract from his doctrine. He was a towering product of his times, and his conclusions about the society of men tore away the veil that hid the profound forces that moved societies. However, his forecasts have been negated by the very dialectical process he himself revealed. Yet, to say, nay insist, that history should act just the way Marx thought it would is to do an injustice to a great thinker and imply, thereby, that dialectics is a philosophical fraud as many have tried to do (even some who called themselves "Marxists"). But neither history nor dialectics, which is history's inner clockworks, stand still. Neither is history prone to bestow special historical prerogatives on any special class of people forever. It is the peculiar juxtaposition of time, place, and social circumstances which decides who is going to play the role of prime movers of history. Hence, we can well understand Marx's own assertion "I am not a Marxist." It would have been a historical tribute to Marx's self-effacement if Leon Trotsky had admitted: "Though I played fast and loose with Marx's laws, I am no dialectician."

Hence, in America today the Socialist Workers Party must strive to conceal the theoretical bankruptcy of Western Marxism by the highly questionable political strategy of entering into political competition with a Negro political party (which is not even established) by using a Negro candidate for high office. Some capitalists trying to cash in and exploit the Negro economic market could not have been more crass and opportunistic. But what is revealed here that is more striking than mere crassness is the unreality that hovers around much of what American Marxists do. Basic to all is the Marxist illusions about the "working class–socialist myth" as concerns the Russian experience. For the Trotskyists to be forced to let go of this dead issue would be to force the admission that the Trotskyist Fourth International is and always has been rather utopian. For after the seizure of power in Russia by the Bolsheviks and the creation of soviets, the problem became more Kantian than Marxian. The Marxist revolutionary idealists assumed that Marxist elites once in power would act in accordance with the Kantian "categorical imperative" and perform their functions according to an ethical code of "right conduct." This has been and always will be a problem of revolutions.

However, the hard American realities and the Negro movement force the Trotskyists to push all these issues that once agitated the international revolutionaries years ago into the background, depart from the book, and play it pragmatically by jumping on the bandwagon of the black political party idea. But this cannot work. The Freedom Now Party will not be used to save the Marxist tradition in America from its own illusions about the nature of a social reality today. The problem of Clifton DeBerry's role as a

Negro Marxist of the Western mold is a contradictory thing that cannot be solved within the context of the political, social, and cultural philosophy which the Freedom Now Party will attempt to mold. In view of what Leopold Senghor says on the matter of communism, an American Negro Marxist becomes a rather misplaced figure in the real scheme of things. And his position is made all the more ridiculous if he is involved politically in beating the "dead horse" issue of Stalinism versus Trotskyism. What can this really matter to the "third world" in view of the fact that Russia's place and impact on the twentieth-century revolution is established and well known? Trotskyists in the West have been reduced to the role of ferreting out Stalinist vestiges in world revolutionary currents, analyzing the "distortions" of revolutions already made, projecting an ideal of the "socialist revolution" that has never been seen or experienced, while rehashing Trotsky's theory of "permanent revolution"—an undialectical concept because everything, including revolutions, is a process of change and developments. Trotskyists are the "purists" of the Marxist camp—astute, analytical, and possessed with the insight to refine, from their own point of view, every aspect of historical materialism. But they cannot escape the theoretical net of the crisis of Marxism in the West. Hence, Clifton DeBerry becomes a mere pawn whom the Trotskyists can attempt to foist on the black political party wearing a king's crown that is much oversized.

The Negro movement possesses inner qualities of different degrees of nationalism and integrationism whose economic, political, cultural, and psychological implications are too much for Marxian theory today. To attempt to confuse these unknown qualities with the white labor mystique of the Marxian Left would be to disrupt the natural development of the Freedom Now Party [and] confuse the real native issues of the Negro with the unreal and irrelevant view of the Marxists concerning American realities. Such intrusions will be fought with every weapon at the FNP's disposal.

The Freedom Now Party is predicated on the idea of achieving independent black political power in the United States through economic, cultural, and administrative approaches. In this fashion, the Negro movement in America becomes aligned with the real nature of the world developments involving nonwhite peoples. In this realignment of world social forces, the reality is that white capitalist nations, including all the different classes within these nations, from upper bourgeoisie to lower proletariat, have become, in fact, bourgeois and relative middle-class strata vis-à-vis the nonwhite peoples who have become, in fact, the "world proletarians." This is the real outcome of "dialectical" processes in our age. If world unity of different peoples is ever to be achieved within a democratic framework, this unity must be sought along the paths of "social consciousness" that clearly reveal future possibilities rather than the "dead ends" of the past that we have encountered before in radical politics.

MARXISM AND THE NEGRO STRUGGLE
Reply by George Breitman

WHAT MARXISM IS AND HOW IT DEVELOPS

The Negro movement continues to unfold with ever-increasing scope and power, but, like most mass movements, empirically—feeling its way along through experiment, trial and error. It is working out its positions, policies, and orientation step by step under the press of immediate necessity.

Since the system against which it is rebelling is capitalist, its policies are becoming more and more anticapitalist, implicitly for the most part, but explicitly, too. But the most advanced elements of the movement (radical and nationalist) have not yet projected or adopted a clear-cut ideology or a comprehensive program of social revolution based on a thorough examination of US monopoly capitalism and the ways and means to end its domination.

Need for Theory

The need is felt for the movement to broaden its perspectives and formulate a fundamental theory for its action. Some Negro intellectuals are trying to fill this need. Inevitably, this begins with analysis and critique of existing theories. Having rejected liberalism, that is, liberal capitalism, behind which Lyndon Johnson, Walter Reuther, Roy Wilkins, James Farmer, and Martin Luther King are all united, the Negro intellectuals are faced with the task of defining their attitude to Marxism, the theory and practice of scientific, revolutionary socialism.

Marxists can only welcome the most searching examination and criticism by black radicals. The one thing we ask is that Marxism be discussed as it really is, and not as one of the many straw men substituted for it through malice or ignorance in this country, where the misrepresentation of Marxism is a national industry.

This elementary condition for fruitful discussion is not met in Harold Cruse's article on "Marxism and the Negro" in the May and June issues of the *Liberator*. Primarily a polemic against the Socialist Workers Party, this article is designed to support Cruse's thesis that Marxism is unrealistic, unable to adjust to revolutionary reality, dominated by "white" thinking, and intent on exploiting and dominating the Negro movement. Cruse's depiction of Marxism is on a higher level than one finds in most of the capitalist press, but it, too, suffers from many errors and distortions. We shall start with his conception of Marxism in general.

Estimate of Marx

Cruse tips his hat to Marx, acknowledging that he was a great thinker, whose dialectical materialist method of analysis vastly expanded the world's knowledge about society. But he can find nothing positive or creditable to say about twentieth-century Marxists. He accuses them of merely repeating what Marx said, of being inflexible, of clinging to outdated ideas and failing to adjust to changed conditions. Simultaneously, he accuses them of the opposite fault—of not repeating what Marx said, of being too flexible, of deviating from Marx so much that they don't really deserve to be called Marxists.

Heads I win, tails you lose: When modern Marxists repeat what Marx said, they are parrots, and when they don't repeat what he said, they are not Marxists. Let us take up first the second of these charges—"deviation."

As a theory Marxism began with Marx, but it did not end with him. If it had, if Marxism was only what Marx discovered and formulated a century or more ago, it would have no claim whatever to being called scientific; it would be classified now as some kind of dogma or cult, and the world would have stopped debating about it long ago. Marx developed his theory and worked out some of its laws on the basis of the knowledge and conditions of his time. His theory would indeed be useless today if other thinkers, using his method, had not added to it and brought it up to date in the light of subsequent knowledge, different conditions, and new experiences.

Cruse criticizes the twentieth-century Marxists for adding to what Marx started, adapting his ideas to conditions that did not exist in his day, and applying his theory in circumstances it was impossible for Marx or any other human being of that time to foresee. This would make sense only if one expected a theory to have magic qualities: to be full grown and fully developed at birth, to apply to all times and places in the same way, to be perfect, unimprovable. No one makes such demands of other theories and sciences. Modern evolution is not, cannot be, the same thing as the findings of Darwin a century ago, but it stems from them, it is an extension of them. Similarly with Marxism.

"Deviations from Marx"

Cruse would probably concur with these remarks as a generalization, saying that what he is talking against are not extensions of Marx's theory, but deviations from it—deviations so great that they have thrown Marxism into a hopeless and insoluble crisis. We can better understand what he means by deviations from Marxism, and therefore what he means by Marxism, when we turn to the only example he gives of such deviation: the Russian Revolution of 1917. (As will soon be seen, the role of Marxism in the Russian Revolution sheds important light on the real relationship between Marxism and the Negro struggle.)

The chief deviator, says Cruse, was Leon Trotsky,

> who first said that a socialist revolution was even possible in Russia. This was in 1905 when none of the Russian Marxists agreed to that possibility (not even Lenin). Trotsky was denounced as a ridiculous visionary for saying this but later won other Russian Marxists over to his thinking. . . .

Serious Dilemma?

> Marxism, as Marx himself developed it, did not foresee or predict a "socialist revolution" in a backward agrarian country such as Russia. According to Marx, the revolution he predicted had to come about in a highly

industrialized nation which had necessarily created a large industrial class of workers . . . [who] would revolt and expropriate the owners. . . .

[The Russian Revolution] put the Marxist parties in western Europe, the United States, etc., in a serious dilemma—a dilemma which over the years has deepened into a series of crises. This is because every social revolution that has taken place since the Russian Revolution has also developed out of industrially backward, agrarian, semicolonial, or colonial conditions. . . .

According to a strict interpretation of Marxian formulations, Trotsky tampered very loosely with Marxian "laws" and reaped the whirlwind.

It is true that Marx expected the working-class revolution against capitalism to begin in the industrially advanced countries, and it is also true that it began in a backward, semicolonial country. But neither fact invalidates Marxism or convicts Lenin and Trotsky of "tampering" with Marxism. On the contrary, the overthrow of capitalism in Russia signaled the beginning of the end of capitalism as the dominant world system and therefore was, in fact, the first major confirmation of Marx's theory.

The time sequence of revolutions expected by Marx was shown to be faulty or outdated, but that was a minor thing compared to the fact that the working-class revolution predicted by Marx actually took place, that the workers decisively demonstrated their ability to take power away from the capitalists, that a gaping wound was torn in the side of world capitalism.

A crisis? Yes, the Russian Revolution produced a crisis all right—for capitalism and imperialism, a crisis that still haunts them. For despite the subsequent degeneration of the Soviet Union during decades of isolation, the Russian Revolution has been an example for the oppressed masses in many lands and has inspired successful revolutions against capitalism and imperialism by other colonial and semicolonial countries. Some more "crises of Marxism" like that and world capitalism will be finished.

Lenin and Trotsky were, unlike Marx, able to see the possibility of the revolution occurring first in an industrially backward country because they lived later and, "standing on his shoulders," were able to see farther. Much happened to change the world during the third of a century between Marx's death and the Russian Revolution. That was the period when capitalism definitively passed beyond the industrial stage and entered its monopoly stage (imperialism).

Monopoly Capitalism

Marx had shown that capitalism was inevitably moving in the direction of monopoly, but he did not live to see it arrive there. The imperialist conquest of the world, the final subjugation and division of Asia and Africa by the advanced capitalist powers, created a new situation. They lodged new and deeper contradictions in the capitalist system—and opened new opportunities for the revolutionary opponents of that system.

In this situation Lenin and Trotsky applied the method they had acquired from Marx. Lenin's theory of imperialism, its corollary insights into colonialism and nationalism, and Trotsky's theory of permanent revolution added new and indispensable features to the body of Marxist thought. They revealed weaknesses in the capitalist structure that had not existed or had not been visible in the mid-nineteenth century: Imperialism would break first at its weakest link, the ruling classes in industrially backward countries would not be able to put up as much resistance to revolution as their stronger brothers.

Prime Example

Applied to Russia and acted on, these additions to Marxist theory resulted in one-sixth of the world being torn out of the capitalist stranglehold. How can one ask for a more magnificent example of the creative application of Marxism to a specific country and a specific set of problems and relationships? What Cruse calls "tampering" is Marxist theory enriched and made concrete under special and unique conditions. Marxism would be dead today if not for those additions.

When Cruse sees deviations because Lenin and Trotsky did not merely repeat what Marx had said, he shows an inability or unwillingness to recognize important features of Marxism—its richness, its variety, its ability to cope with changing situations, its unfinishedness. Marxism is not only what Marx worked out a century ago, nor only what Lenin and Trotsky added when they applied Marx's method to the conditions of their time, but also what subsequent Marxists did, do, and will do as they apply this theory to other situations, including some that do not even exist yet.

Marxism is a theory in the process of development, which grows in power and scope as it is applied to specific situations and to new conditions. It developed when Lenin and Trotsky applied it to the specific conditions of Russia in the epoch of imperialism ("Russianized" it). It developed further when the Socialist Workers Party applied it to the specific conditions of America ("Americanized" it). And it continues to develop as the SWP applies it to the specific conditions of the Negro community in the United States ("Afro-Americanizes" it, as the SWP put in the 1963 convention resolution, *Freedom Now: The New Stage in the Struggle for Negro Emancipation*).

Based on Reality

Theory is derived from reality; the more closely a theory corresponds to reality, the better a theory it is. Marx studied the conditions and struggles of the west European workers, learned from them, and incorporated those lessons in his theory. Lenin and Trotsky did the same with the Russian workers and peasants. And from its inception the Socialist Workers Party has been doing this with the conditions and struggles of the American Negro people, which have always been unique in many respects. Embodied in its theory and program are many lessons learned from the Negro struggle, and from the ideas, feelings, and outlook of the masses in the black ghetto.

Nor is that all. The Negro struggle in 1964 is not the same thing it was ten or even five years ago—much has changed. Speaking at a recent Freedom Now Party rally in Detroit, state chairman Albert B. Cleage noted: "Everywhere the black man's whole conception of himself, of his struggle has changed. You may not know the day you started thinking differently but it has changed" (*Illustrated News*, June 29). With the change of the black man's conception of himself and his struggle have come many other changes—in goals, strategy, tactics—even changes in the way certain words are defined.

The SWP has been studying these changes, trying to understand their causes, find out their direction, and fit their revolutionary aspects into a theory and program of action capable of replacing capitalism with socialism. It has been listening to and learning from non-Marxist figures—such as Malcolm X, Reverend Cleage, William Worthy, Jesse Gray, Daniel Watts, James Baldwin, the exiled Robert F. Williams and Julian Mayfield, even Harold Cruse sometimes—who to one degree or another express the thinking, feeling, and aspirations of the black ghetto which, as Robert Vernon recently pointed out, is "more solidly working class and revolutionary in outlook than the trade unions, or anything else in America today." From these studies and from its own participation in the struggle, the SWP in the last year or two has developed a number of ideas—Marxist ideas—about black nationalism, separatism, independent black political action, the Negro's relation to the capitalists, to the white workers, etc. Whether these ideas are perfect or less than perfect, whether they are complete or only beginnings toward a more complete grasp of reality, no one can deny that they do grapple with vital questions concerning the Negro people and their allies. Certainly no other party in this country has done more than the SWP along these lines.

A Straw Man

The most discouraging thing about Cruse's article is not that he rejects Marxism, but that he deliberately refuses to confront or even mention what the SWP thinks, says, and stands for. Preferring to construct a straw man that even a mental flyweight can demolish, he simply ignores what the Marxists actually advocate and propose. For example, the SWP is the only organization claiming to be Marxist in this country which says that black nationalism is progressive and offers it support and collaboration. Isn't it strange that Cruse can find no space for this fact in an article about the SWP and the Negro movement? Or would stating such a fact undermine the whole structure of his polemic?

In some cases where the SWP position is widely known, Cruse accuses the SWP of saying things it doesn't really believe in, but he is always careful not to inform his readers just what those things are so that they can make their own judgment. He never offers evidence of the alleged insincerity, merely asserting that Marxists cannot believe the unstated things they claim to believe because then they would have to give up Marxism (at any rate, Cruse's version of Marxism). Of the SWP's pioneering effort to Afro-Americanize Marxism, which should be of some interest to readers of an article called "Marxism and the Negro," he never gives the slightest hint or notice.

This may be one way to "win" a debate, or to create and strengthen prejudices against Marxism. But it's a poor way to educate black militants, or anyone else, about Marxism, or anything else. Cruse has the right not to discuss what the SWP really stands for, but an article about the SWP is a strange place to be exercising that right.

THE COLONIAL REVOLUTION IN TODAY'S WORLD

The main revolution in the world is the colonial revolution, says Harold Cruse in his article, "Marxism and the Negro" (*Liberator*, May and June). And the main trouble with even "the most astute" Marxists of the Socialist Workers Party and the Fourth International, he contends, is that they do not and cannot understand or recognize this.

The reason why they cannot understand this, Cruse says, is that they are obsessed and blinded by Karl Marx's outdated idea that the workers in the industrially advanced countries are the principal or only revolutionary force in the world.

The result, he says, is that Marxists take a paternalistic attitude toward the (colored) colonial parts of the world, believing that their emancipation must wait until the (white) workers of the industrially advanced countries make their own revolution, after which they will "lead" the colonial people to their freedom. An additional result is that Marxism is obsolete and the Marxists in a crisis which they cannot resolve.

Those are Cruse's charges. Now let's turn to the facts.

It is a matter of record, which anyone who reads can check for himself, that the Socialist Workers Party and the Fourth International believe and assert that the colonial struggle is the center of the world revolution today and has been since 1949.

For evidence, we cite one of many documents, *Dynamics of World Revolution Today*, a resolution adopted by the Fourth International at its Reunification Congress in June 1963 and printed in *International Socialist Review*, Fall 1963 (available from Pioneer Publishers as a pamphlet).

This resolution states very plainly that the principal center of the world revolution shifted to the colonial world beginning with the triumph of the Chinese Revolution, and explains why this happened, what its effects have been, what the problems of the colonial revolution are, and how these problems can be overcome.

This position is so well known that when Mikhail Suslov, Soviet ideological hatchet man, made a speech last April trying to discredit the Chinese leadership, he said:

> Does anyone think perhaps that the Chinese theory making the regions of Asia, Africa, and Latin America the "principal zone of the storms of the world revolution" represents something original? No, this is the repetition almost word for word of one of the principal theses of current Trotskyism. One can read in the decision of the so-called Fourth International (Trotskyist): "As a result of the successive failures of the two major revolutionary waves of 1919–23 and 1943–48—and of the minor one of 1934–37—the main center of the world revolution shifted for a time to the colonial world." Here is where the source of the political wisdom of the Chinese leadership must be sought.

Not only is this fact refuting Cruse's contention well known, but it is well known to Cruse, too! We can state this categorically because Cruse himself quotes in his article a short passage from this same resolution, *Dynamics of World Revolution Today*. (It is a passage urging revolutionary Marxists to recruit black radicals influenced by the colonial revolution.)

Why does Cruse do this? Why does he misrepresent the SWP's position on the colonial revolution? We can only conclude that he finds it easier to argue against positions that the SWP does not hold than against those it does hold.

The facts are similarly damaging to Cruse's charge that Marxists ("Western" or "Westernized" or white) have a paternalistic attitude toward the colonial (colored) people. The only example he offers, Leon Trotsky, is about the worst he could pick.

Cruse's sole piece of "evidence" is a sentence in the last paragraph of Trotsky's pamphlet, *Marxism in the United States*. This was written in 1939, shortly before World War II, which Trotsky thought would surely provoke revolutionary outbursts in both Europe and its colonies. Once the socialist revolution began, he wrote, it would spread rapidly from country to country, and "by the example and with the aid of the advanced nations, the backward nations will also be carried away into the main stream of socialism." He was referring here to all industrially backward countries, including those in eastern Europe as well as the colored countries.

Socialism Messianic?

Cruse, however, considers this sentence "proof" that Marxists have a "lofty detachment" toward the colored people, that Marxist socialism is a messianic "white-nation conception," that revolutionary socialists deem it their "duty to history . . . to lift the 'backward' peoples from their ignominious state to socialist civilization even if the whites have to postpone this elevation abroad until they have managed to achieve it at home." Quite a big indictment to spin out of that little sentence.

But it simply doesn't stand up. Far from believing that workers in capitalist countries are the only revolutionary force, Trotsky insisted many times that "the decisive word in the development of humanity" belongs to "the oppressed colored races" (1932). He repeatedly expressed the view that "the movement of the colored races against their imperialist oppressors is one of the most important and powerful movements against the existing order and therefore calls for the complete, unconditional, and unlimited support on the part of the proletariat of the white race" (1937). This was long before the current colonial upsurge, and it is in this spirit that both the Socialist Workers Party and the Fourth International have always been guided.

In May 1940, a year after the sentence cited by Cruse, when World War II had already begun, the Fourth International held an emergency conference where it adopted a manifesto on "The Imperialist War and the Proletarian Revolution," which was supported by the SWP. Trotsky wrote this document, and since he was assassinated a few months later, it represents his final, mature, considered judgment on the question.

It could almost have been written as an answer to Cruse's claim that Marxists think the colonial people should wait for, depend on, or trot humbly behind the industrially advanced countries. After urging the colonial masses to take advantage of the war crisis in order to break free from their imperialist masters and urging the workers in the imperialist countries to support the colonial revolt, Trotsky explicitly stated:

No Need to Wait

The perspective of the permanent revolution in no case signifies that the backward countries must await the signal from the advanced ones, or that the colonial peoples should patiently wait for the proletariat of the metropolitan centers to free them. Help comes to him who helps himself. Workers must develop the revolutionary struggle in every country, colonial or imperialist, where favorable conditions have been established, and through this set an example for the workers of other countries.

So the SWP considers the colonial revolution foremost today, like Cruse, and supports it "completely and unconditionally," also like Cruse. Having disposed of differences invented or exaggerated by Cruse, we can now turn to some real differences.

Cruse holds that the colonial revolutionary movement is the only important one; that no other revolutionary movement or tendency today means anything; that how the world goes and how history is made will be determined entirely by the colonial (colored) revolution against the imperialist (white-controlled) countries.

The SWP's world outlook is far less simple because the actual situation is much more complex. It sees the fate of the world being decided by the combined operation of three factors: 1. The colonial struggle against imperialism, which is today the central and most active revolutionary sphere. 2. The struggle for political revolution in the workers states, involving the ouster of the privileged bureaucratic caste that is now dominant and the restoration of workers democracy. 3. The struggle for social revolution in the imperialist states, involving the end of capitalist rule and its replacement by the rule of revolutionary workers and their allies.

To the SWP these three spheres of the world revolution are intimately connected and interdependent. Although they develop unevenly, they reinforce and strengthen each other. Victories for one benefit the others, and vice versa. A correct strategy for the world revolution, which alone can permanently guarantee the gains won in each of these spheres, requires a realistic appraisal of their potentials, limitations, and interrelationships. (Such an appraisal is brilliantly supplied in the already mentioned resolution, *Dynamics of World Revolution Today*.)

Absurd Illusion?

Cruse regards the very idea of workers revolution in the capitalist countries as an absurd and harmful illusion; he appears much surer of this than the capitalists. For him class struggle between workers and capitalists is meaningless or irrelevant. He lumps together all the antagonistic classes in these countries as if they were one harmonious family (except the Negro people in the United States, whom he considers a part of the world-wide colonial revolution). He has nothing to say about developments inside the workers states. (Since he says Stalin was the type of leader "needed" in the earlier days of the Soviet Union, he may also think the Soviet workers "need" the Khrushchev type today.)

What leads Cruse to thus exaggerate the strength of the enemy and shut his eyes to the possibility of aid from allies inside the capitalist and workers states? These and related errors flow from his method, which sees only things-as-they-are, fixed and frozen, rather than as a process replete with contradictions, reversals, and change (despite all his talk about dialectics).

The class struggle in the capitalist countries is at an ebb? Then it will always be this way! The workers are conservative, apathetic, hogtied by the capitalists and their labor lieutenants? Then it will always be this way!

This is the same way most people viewed the colonial revolution twenty-five years ago, and the Negro struggle ten years ago, when the conditions for today's upsurge were still maturing beneath the surface. The Cruses of that day, prisoners of outward appearances, could also only sigh: It will always be this way! It is not a mode of thought helpful to people who want to prepare for revolutions.

The colonial revolution has made great advances and it will make more. But these advances have not got rid of imperialism, especially on its home grounds. Yet the continued existence of imperialism, with its preponderant economic and military strength, is the main deterrent to further, deeper, and faster revolutionary gains in the colonial sphere.

The converse is also true. The abolition of capitalism in the imperialist centers and its replacement by workers states will open new avenues for the colonial revolution. It will bring invaluable economic aid to the colonial revolutions, enabling them to curb or prevent bureaucratism, limitations of workers' rights, and other deformations that breed in the soil of economic backwardness and poverty.

A crucial question for revolutionists everywhere therefore is how to achieve the abolition of capitalism in the imperialist sphere. Must it wait, as Cruse's position implies, until the colonial countries are strong enough to defeat their imperialist foes in direct military combat? And will the imperialists wait until that occurs without launching their own offensive first, including the H-bomb?

Or are there forces inside the imperialist countries that can be welded together into a revolutionary movement capable of disarming the capitalists, throwing them out of power, and joining in fraternal collaboration with the colonial revolutionists?

As Clifton DeBerry, Socialist Workers Party candidate for president, wrote in an answer to Cruse (which the *Liberator* invited but has not printed yet), the policy Cruse counterposes to Marxism "would in fact leave the colonial peoples subject to an unending threat of imperialist attack."

Hit at Root

The job of ending this threat cannot be done by the colonial revolution alone. "That job has to be done within imperialism's home base," said DeBerry. "It calls for a revolutionary struggle by the workers, nonwhite and white combined, to abolish the capitalist system from which imperialism springs."

The same error is committed by Cruse when he tries to define the nature of the Negro struggle. To him it is, purely and simply, "a semicolonial revolt, which is more inspired by events outside America than within it."

While we question the last part of that statement, we agree that the Negro struggle definitely has many characteristics of a semicolonial revolt, and believe it is to Cruse's credit that he has been one of the foremost propagandists of this idea. (He probably will not be pleased by our assertion that this idea can be traced back to the Marxist Lenin, who was the first, to our knowledge, to include the American Negroes among the oppressed national minorities, nationalities, and nations of the world; but it is true.)

People unfamiliar with this idea may be able to grasp it by asking themselves: Suppose the Negro people, instead of being scattered throughout the country, were concentrated in one section of the United States, or in one area outside the United States. And suppose that they were dominated by the same forces that now dominate them, and that they were treated, or mistreated, in exactly the same way they are now—denied equal rights, confined to the worst jobs, paid less, unemployed more, etc. Wouldn't it be plain then that they are subjected to a colonial-type oppression?

Not Only Aspect

But while this is one major aspect of the Negro struggle, it is not the only one. Cruse oversimplifies this question, as he does on the world scale with the colonial revolution. Here he reminds us of those blind men, each of whom touched a different part of an elephant—tusk, leg, trunk, and so on—and mistakenly thought they understood the whole reality of the elephant.

The aspect of the Negro struggle that Cruse shuts his eyes to is its class aspect. Negroes are exploited not only because of their color, but also because of the class to which they belong in their great majority. They are a part of the working class, the most exploited part, the most proletarian part, and whatever hurts the workers as a class hurts them, too—usually first and always hardest.

To ignore the dual and combined character of the Negro struggle is to blind oneself to the dual sources of its full potential. As both a racial-national and class struggle, it is fed and powered by the two most explosive fuels in modern society. These are the sources of its dynamism, and although race and class operate unequally and unevenly at different times, they are both sources that will contribute to the victory of the Negro struggle.

Any theory which does not recognize and combine both these aspects will prove fatally defective. The early American socialists, who saw only the class aspect, are an object lesson in how badly astray you can be led by a one-sided grasp of the dual character of the Negro struggle. Cruse is making a similar mistake in the other direction. The Marxist attempt at a synthesis is the most enlightening so far. If it is not yet fully or adequately worked out, then it ought to be—by black radicals as well as the SWP—because it points in the right direction.

THE ROLE OF THE WHITE WORKERS

Can Marxism be of help to black radicals in working out a program capable of winning freedom for the Negro people? The Socialist Workers Party says yes. Harold Cruse says no (*Liberator*, May and June). This is a question each person can check for himself by finding out what the Marxists say and do. Especially what they say and do about the nature of the society we live in (capitalism), its strengths and weaknesses, and the relations its ruling class has with other forces at home and abroad.

The Socialist Workers Party says that American capitalism is a sick and unjust system, which has seen its best days and is slated to be replaced by a new, socialist system. This change will not be imposed by some force outside this country, although outside pressures will help, but will be brought about by internal forces, by classes and groups here inside the United States, rebelling against capitalist domination and mismanagement.

One of the major internal weaknesses that will bring about the downfall of capitalism is its racism. The capitalists have no intention of abolishing racism, which benefits them politically by keeping the workers divided and economically by keeping down the wages of all workers.

It is doubtful that the capitalists could abolish racism even if they wanted to, but nobody has to lose sleep over that question because they don't want to. The most they will grant are mild concessions and very gradual reforms (like the 1964 civil rights law) that may eventually make the South like the North, where racism is still supreme, despite all the laws, commissions, and constitutional provisions.

Reforms will not end racism, now or a hundred years from now. Rocking the boat is needed to get concessions, but it is not enough to get equality. We need a new captain; we also need a new boat. There are only two ways to achieve Negro equality. One is through a socialist revolution that will end capitalist rule. The other is through leaving this country, separating from it to form a new nation or to migrate to a country free of racism. Neither way is easy.

But is a socialist revolution possible? The answer would probably be no if racism were the only evil bred by capitalism. It isn't. Capitalism spawns many other evils, which it would take a book to list. The most prominent—and they all generate opposition to capitalist rule—are unemployment, poverty, insecurity, thought control, the growth of ultra-right reaction, and the danger of a war that may wipe out humanity.

Nothing to Lose

These evils, which are inherent in capitalism, create the conditions for an anticapitalist movement which, properly led, can oust the bankers and corporation executives and four-star generals and white supremacists now in control. The members of this movement will come from the classes and groups that have the most to gain and the least to lose from profound and far-reaching change: revolutionary workers, young—

"Wait! Now wait just a minute," interrupts Harold Cruse, who has been sitting by impatiently up to now. And he launches into his attack on the idea that the workers can play a revolutionary role in this country. His position is substantially this:

There was a period of labor radicalism in the 1930s but it has declined and ended. White workers have become conservative, pro-capitalist, and hostile or indifferent to the Negro. There was a time when it seemed reasonable to expect that they would usher in socialism, but it's too late now. The only ones capable of revolutionary action in this country are the black people.

Labor Mystique?

Then, turning to the theme of his *Liberator* article, he lets the Marxists have it. They are so obsessed by this "working class–socialist myth," this "grand illusion," this "white labor mystique," that they have lost touch with reality and are virtually out of this world. He says:

> [T]he theory and practice of revolutionary Marxism in America is based on the assumption that white labor, both organized and unorganized, must be a radical, anticapitalist force in America and must form an "alliance" with Negroes for the liberation of both labor and the Negro from capitalist exploitation. No matter what the facts of life reveal to the contrary, no matter what the Marxists say or do in terms of momentary "tactics," this is what the Marxists believe, and must believe, or cease functioning as a Marxist tendency.

If this means what it says, it certainly is a poor argument. When a man insists something "must be," and it obviously isn't, then everybody concludes that man is some kind of a nut, and everybody is right. But if he's obviously a nut, why spend so much space and time refuting him?

The truth is that the Socialist Workers Party does not believe the workers must be radical and anticapitalist. We are well aware that the overwhelming majority of white workers in this country today are not radical, thanks to capitalist brainwashing, relative prosperity, treacherous labor leadership, and political immaturity. That is why socialism in general, and our party in particular, is not stronger and better able to back up the Negro struggle. What we believe is that the workers must become radical if they are to solve their problems, and that they will become radical under certain conditions and at certain times. "Must become" is a different horse from "must be."

Not Inevitable

Marxists have never believed that the workers in capitalist countries must be or have been radical all the time. We do not idealize the workers, knowing full well and from painful experience that they can be and often are infected, corrupted, demoralized, exhausted, and disoriented. Their radicalism waxes and wanes, rises and sinks, depending on their conditions, leadership, and level of consciousness. (Isn't this also true of the Negro masses?)

The American working class has not been radical during most of its existence. Even when it was more radical than today, during the 1930s and 1940s, it never reached the point of breaking with the politics of the capitalists whom it was battling on the picket lines and creating its own, noncapitalist, political party. The most radical sector of the working class today, the black workers in the ghetto, wasn't always as radical as it is now.

Socialists believe that the working class can become revolutionary—not always, but sometimes. And that on such an occasion, which does not occur all the time or last forever, it can, in cooperation with other noncapitalist forces, and with consistently revolutionary leadership, abolish the system that breeds racism, poverty, regimentation, and war. The question of leadership is crucial precisely because such opportunities do not knock at the door often, or for long.

Our assumption, therefore, unlike the one Cruse imputes to us, is not that the working class can or will be radical all of the time or most of the time, but that the conditions created by capitalism must radicalize it some of the time, and that even though revolutionary situations occur rarely, one can be turned into a successful conquest of power. As the Cuban experience demonstrates, a successful revolution can then quickly alter conditions enough so that the revolutionary consciousness and will of most of the workers will remain high and become permanent.

Cruse does not consider such a working-class revolution possible, like most Americans, or even New Left professors like C. Wright Mills. With other sophisticated opponents of Marxism, he lives in a world that is changing with dizzying speed, but he thinks everything is going to change except the workers. Talk about a grand illusion! Even the most ignorant capitalist knows better than that. That's why they distort the teachings of Marxism and try to isolate and suppress socialist ideas and movements.

The future of this country will be determined in large part by the relations among its three major forces: the capitalists, the white workers, and the Negro people (mostly workers, too). At present the capitalists dominate and have the support of most white workers. Cruse thinks this is going to last forever. It won't, because of the internal contradictions of this system.

The central contradiction is the material readiness of our society for socialism and the ideological and political uneasiness of the white workers to fight for it. Tied up with this is another acute contradiction— the readiness of the Negroes to fight for jobs and justice by the most militant means and the uneasiness of organized labor and the white workers as a whole to support the black people.

From our analysis of the social structure, we conclude that the contradiction prevailing between white workers and Negroes is not absolute, but relative; not permanent, but transitory. The alienation between them is no more enduring than the political and ideological partnership between the white workers and their bosses.

Can Narrow Gap

In fact, these two states are interconnected. Any deepening of antagonism between the white workers and the ruling class, any cutting of ties between them, any opening or widening of breaches between them, objectively sets the stage for a lessening of the antagonism and a narrowing of the great gap between the Negro movement and the white workers.

The outlook of white workers is going to be altered from two directions. One is from the independent struggle of the Negroes, which tends to upset the status quo and introduce unsettling elements into class relations. The disrupted patterns of politics in this election year testify to the power of the independent Negro struggle to disarrange and overturn customary modes of thought and action. Is there any reason to think that white workers will not also be shaken up and divided, and some of them torn out of their ruts, as the Negro struggle continues to develop and explode?

The other and more basic modifying factor comes directly from the operation of the capitalist system itself. In the next decade automation will create vast armies of unemployed and undermine the security of all workers, even those of high seniority, skill, and privilege. America's share of the world market will be shrunk by the colonial revolution and competition from other capitalist countries, and this will drive the capitalists to attack the wage rates and living standards of the employed workers.

Isn't this certain to provoke anticapitalist sentiments and attitudes, not only among the youth and unemployed, but also among unionists still on the job? Won't such radicalization make white workers more susceptible to suggestions of joint action with the Negro movement? Won't the possibility be opened for a change in the present situation, for united action by the two anticapitalist movements against the upholders of the system responsible for their common insecurity and misery?

We hope that what we have just written will not be distorted. It is a perspective to be worked for, not an existing reality. We do not think the achievement of joint action will be easy or quick. We are not suggesting that the Negroes should wait until the white workers are ready for collaboration, before they build their own movement, with its own leaders, ideology, and program. We are not proposing, and we do not favor, any alliance where the white workers call the shots and the Negroes comply.

We are talking about an alliance of equals. An alliance with radicalized, not conservative, white workers. An alliance against all capitalist parties, not one behind the Democratic Party. Therefore what we are talking about is the future (less distant than it may appear on the surface) and not today. We concur 100 percent with the decision of militant Negroes to concentrate on building their own movement and working out tactics based first of all on the situation as it is today.

Coming Changes

What we add is that it will not remain as it is today. A correct overall strategy has to take that into account, too, be prepared for the changes coming, and promote them. For they will benefit Negroes as much as white workers.

The SWP's 1963 convention resolution (*Freedom Now: The New Stage in the Struggle for Negro Emancipation*) stated that the first stage of the alliance we foresee and predict will very likely be the knitting of ties between the black vanguard and the revolutionary socialist vanguard. We continue to seek such ties. We are on the side of the Negroes wherever they clash with prejudiced and privileged white workers. We support and work with black radicals even though they have crossed off the white workers forever as any help to their struggle.

We feel no inconsistency in doing so because we are confident their own experience will teach them, as it will teach white workers, that collaboration between both camps is ultimately indispensable if the power structure is to be toppled and not simply shaken and renovated. Experience will prove that the monopolists cannot be dislodged from their seats of power except by a transformation of the relations among the three main forces—a dialectical transformation of the capitalist–white worker partnership into a Negro–white worker alliance against the capitalist regime.

THE NEED AND RESULT OF INDEPENDENCE

A program to win the Negro struggle for equality must be based on a correct analysis of its main features. Among these are its independence, its vanguard role, and its need for independent political action. We shall compare the Socialist Workers Party positions on these questions with what Harold Cruse claims are its positions (in *Liberator*, May and June).

Cruse says the growing independence of the Negro movement produces a crisis for Marxists: "The greater the Negro movement becomes as an independent force . . . the deeper does the crisis become for the Marxist movement itself. For the 'alliance' it attempts to forge with the Negro must be one where the Marxists dominate."

But facts are stubborn things, and the record bulges with facts refuting Cruse's claim that the SWP is opposed to the independence of the Negro movement from the labor movement, or from anything else, including the SWP itself. Throughout its entire existence the SWP has thought, said, and argued just the opposite. It was the first radical organization in this country to assert the correctness and necessity of Negro independence.

As long ago as 1939, when the SWP was only a year old, it declared in a unanimously adopted convention resolution: "The awakening political consciousness of the Negro not unnaturally takes the form of a desire for independent action uncontrolled by whites. The Negroes have long felt and more than ever feel today the urge to create their own organizations under their own leaders and thus assert, not only in theory but in action, their claim to complete equality with other American citizens. Such a desire is legitimate and must be vigorously supported" (*Documents on the Negro Struggle*, Pioneer Publishers).

The SWP has never wavered in this position in the twenty-five years since then, as an examination of its latest (1963) convention resolution will prove. It states that "the liberation of the Negro people requires that the Negroes organize themselves independently, and control their own struggle, and not permit it to be subordinated to any other consideration or interest" (*Freedom Now: The New Stage in the Struggle for Negro Emancipation*).

Why do genuine Marxists take this position? Why do we advocate that the Negro movement must be independent, even of the SWP? Because the history of Negro oppression in this country has been such that the more independent the Negro movement becomes, the more revolutionary it becomes. And the more revolutionary the Negro movement becomes, the better it is for all revolutionists, white and black. The radicalization of the Negroes cannot help but to stimulate radicalization among whites, too.

Contrary to J. Edgar Hoover—or to Harold Cruse—we Marxists have no interest whatever in "dominating" the Negro movement. Our aim is to influence the Negro movement, as it is to influence the labor and any other progressive movement, and we make no secret of that. We do so by offering it our revolutionary ideas, which the participants in the Negro movement of course can freely accept or reject in accord with their own estimate of what they need and want.

We believe that the sooner the Negro movement becomes completely "undominated" (that is, the sooner it becomes completely independent and revolutionary), the sooner it will approach and accept the ideas and policies that the Marxists have reached; and that the process of ever-growing independence will in the end inevitably lead it, as the result of its own experiences, toward close collaboration with other revolutionary forces, including the SWP. That kind of fraternal relation, rather than domination, is the only one worth having, and it is the only one we seek.

One of the more astonishing statements in Cruse's article is that "the Negro movement's rise to the ascendancy as a radical force in America completely upsets Marxian theory" and therefore deepens the alleged crisis of Marxism.

We can only wonder what "Marxian theory" Cruse is talking about. Since he insists, wrongly, on identifying the Communist Party and the Socialist Workers Party as "twin branches of the same withering tree trunk of Western Marxism," despite the irreconcilable differences between them, maybe he is thinking about some kind of "Marxian theory" coming from the Communist Party. It certainly is not and never has been any theory of the SWP, which is the target of his present polemic.

Permanent Revolution

Our theory has been strikingly confirmed by "the Negro movement's rise to the ascendancy as a radical force." For Leon Trotsky, making use of the Marxist conception of the permanent revolution, predicted more than thirty years ago that the Negroes could become "the most advanced section" of the working class, that they could reach revolutionary consciousness ahead of the white workers, that they could become the revolutionary vanguard. Twenty-five years ago the SWP adopted a convention resolution declaring that the Negroes were destined to become "the very vanguard of the proletarian revolution" (*Documents on the Negro Struggle*).

So the Marxist theory which Cruse tries to discredit foresaw the radicalization of the Negro movement (not in all its detail, but in its general sweep) long before it happened, when the empiricists of that day and others stupefied by the status quo could not even dream of such a development.

Moreover, the SWP not only predicted that the Negro movement would become the radical vanguard, but advocated it, and worked for it, and exults now that it is happening. Why in the world then should we feel that our theory has been upset? Why should the confirmation of our theory by real life throw us into a crisis? If only all our theories could be "upset" this way! The truth, once again, is the opposite of what Cruse says, and happens in this case to be an especially good reason for black radicals to become better acquainted with the Marxist method and program.

When we say that Negroes will play a vanguard role, Cruse tries to confuse what we mean, and to imply a manipulative motive; by attributing to us the "belief that the 'historical laws' have preordained the Negro movement in America to be used as a kind of transitional social phase leading to the 'Marxian revolution.'"

If he will be so kind, we would like to state our position ourselves, minus the slanted terms he prefers. We do not know of any "Marxian revolution," with or without quotation marks, and that is not what we advocate. The American revolution will be a social revolution—that is, it will remove the present ruling class from political power and reconstruct society on new, nonexploitative foundations.

Nor do we consider the Negro movement to be any kind of "phase," transitional or otherwise. We expect it to be an integral part of the revolution, before, during, and after the winning of power, until it, the Negro movement, is satisfied that racism is abolished beyond the possibility of return.

Vanguard Position

What we think is this: Historical conditions, yes "laws," have placed the Negro movement in a vanguard position—in the leadership of the mass struggle to change society socially, politically, and economically. Its radicalization marks the opening stage of the revolution that will accomplish these changes. As this revolution continues and develops, the whole political structure will begin to come apart, and other forces will be drawn into the revolution, for and against. Which side wins will depend on which draws the strongest support from the as-yet uncommitted and inactive majority.

Cruse's snide implication that the Marxists plan to "use" the Negro movement and then cast it aside has no basis at all. We have said a thousand times what we said in our 1963 convention resolution: "The SWP believes and acts on the belief that the working class cannot achieve its aims without the Negro people achieving theirs. The American revolution for a socialist democracy cannot succeed unless it is based on an equal and mutually acceptable partnership between the working class and the Negro people."

This is our perspective, openly stated. It does not involve subordination of the Negro movement "to any other consideration or interest." It does not involve the slightest infringement on the independence of the Negro movement, which at all times must be led by its own representatives and animated by its own goals. We do not believe that this perspective is inconsistent with what black radicals want, if what they want is revolution. If we're wrong, we'd like to be shown.

In the light of what has already been said, Cruse's distortions about the SWP's attitude to the Freedom Now Party can be handled rather briefly. His four charges, somewhat contradictory, are: (1) We don't believe in or want a truly independent black political party. (2) We engage in maneuvers against the Freedom Now Party. (3) We compete with the FNP, even before it is established, by running a Negro candidate for president in 1964 (Clifton DeBerry). (4) We disrupt the FNP's development.

The SWP's well-known position in favor of Negro independence of course applies with full force to black political action. For many years we have endorsed and supported independent Negro candidates running against the capitalist party candidates. To support such candidates when they band together in a party of their own, and to defend their right to do so in their own way, is only an extension of our long-held position, and comes almost automatically for us.

Every politically informed person in the country knows this. The anti-Marxist writers Tom Kahn and August Meier (in *New Politics*, Spring 1964) have even said that the all-Negro Freedom Now Party idea "was originally projected by the predominantly white Trotskyites and for some months received its chief organizational support from them."

This is untrue. The SWP's 1963 convention resolution endorsing "the idea of a Negro party, a civil-rights party or an equal-rights party" specifically noted that the idea had been raised in previous years by Adam Clayton Powell and the *Liberator*, and early in 1963 by Elijah Muhammad and William Worthy. We would be glad to claim credit for conceiving the idea, but it would be dishonest to do so. What we can claim credit for is having publicly supported the idea of an independent black party before anyone had taken organizational steps to create one.

But if we did that, then why, even before the new party has been established nationally and on a stable basis, would we rush to "compete" with it? Cruse calls us "astute." But what's astute about encouraging the formation of another party if your first response, before it has even been assembled, is to compete with it? The charge is ridiculous on the face of it.

There isn't the faintest trace of "competition with the FNP" in Clifton DeBerry's presidential candidacy, except inside Cruse's head. When DeBerry was nominated by the SWP, it was perfectly plain that the FNP would not be able to run a presidential campaign in this, its first year of existence. Moreover, DeBerry, every chance he gets, expresses his and the SWP's complete support for the effort to create a mass, independent FNP. (And gets criticized by Cruse for doing so. What is DeBerry supposed to do: keep silent—or oppose it?)

Michigan Ballot

The FNP has won a statewide place on the ballot only in Michigan. There, the day after the FNP filed its petitions last spring, the SWP, which had filed its own petitions and won ballot rights in 1963, publicly stated that it was in the campaign to fight the Democrats and Republicans: "We are not campaigning against the Freedom Now Party, which in our view has valuable contributions to make to the electoral struggle for a world free of oppression and exploitation. We welcome its entry into the election campaign, and hope it will get a fair hearing from whites as well as Negroes." As proof that this is not just talk, the Michigan SWP is not running against, and is endorsing, the FNP candidates in every Michigan district where they have the slightest chance of being elected.

Clifton DeBerry has already refuted the "maneuver" charge. The claim that he "linked himself with the Freedom Now Party without the party's permission to do so" rests in its entirety on the fact that DeBerry, without ever pretending to be a spokesman of the FNP, expresses support for the FNP and urges black militants to help build it. Any expectation or demand that DeBerry has to get permission from the FNP, or the Democratic Party, or the Republican Party, before he expresses his political views about them, is—what shall we say?—slightly fantastic.

The "disruption" charge is equally baseless. DeBerry and the SWP are said to be "disrupting" the development of the FNP because when they discuss the FNP's meaning and effects, "they must attempt to project the idea of the Freedom Now Party in their own Marxian image, with the old worn-out, discredited theme of Negro-Labor unity."

What this means is that DeBerry and the SWP discuss the significance of the FNP as Marxists. But what's wrong with that? Does it stop other people from discussing it from whatever angle they wish? Does it interfere with Cruse's right to discuss it as an anti-Marxist? Or the right of any FNP member to discuss it as he pleases? How is DeBerry's exercise of his right to express his opinion, whether the opinion is right or wrong, "disruptive" to the FNP's development?

The whole charge is further exploded when we observe that Cruse bases it exclusively on a *New York Times* report that had DeBerry saying he supports the FNP as "a step toward independent political action by labor and Negroes." Twisting this a little, Cruse paints this as opposition to the FNP:

> The Trotskyist theoreticians realize very well that a truly independent black political party which functions irrespective of what white labor does and does not do will further deepen the already serious crisis of Marxist creed in the West. It could show that Marxian ideas about capitalism in advanced countries are not to be taken seriously.

Even if DeBerry said it the way the *Times* reported (a "step to independent political action by labor and Negroes") rather than the other way around ("by Negroes and labor"), Cruse knows very well what is meant: that DeBerry and the SWP believe that a mass black party, by upsetting and then destroying the Democratic-labor-Negro coalition, will give impetus to the formation of an independent labor party, too.

And what's so terrible, worn-out, or discredited about such a prediction? Does Cruse think that the stimulation of an independent labor party by the growth of a mass FNP would be bad? Then let him argue that. Does he think it impossible? Then let him argue that. And let him not substitute for such arguments, which would be fruitful, his unfounded claim that we cannot be for a truly independent black party because it would deepen "the crisis of Marxism."

The only crisis it would deepen would be the crisis of capitalist politics, the crisis of the Democrats, the labor bureaucrats, the liberals, the Negro gradualists—which is precisely one of the reasons we are so strongly for it. And by the way, aren't the breakup of the two-party system and the radicalization of American politics high on the list of "Marxian ideas about capitalism"?

RELATIONS BETWEEN
WHITE AND BLACK RADICALS

Marxism so far has done more than any other theory to shed light on the nature of the Negro struggle and the direction in which it is moving. Since Marx, it has illuminated the economic roots of racism, and the workings of the capitalist power structure which oppresses the Negro people and must be toppled if their oppression is to end. Since Lenin and Trotsky, it has clarified and shown the progressiveness of the nationalist and racial aspects of the Negro movement. And in our time the Socialist Workers Party is working hard to understand and explain current trends and to combine them into a realistic program for emancipation.

Harold Cruse (*Liberator*, May and June) accuses us of harboring a "white labor mystique," which it was not hard for us to disprove because we are against mystiques of any kind or color. In the same breath he creates a mystique of his own when he speaks of the "unknown qualities" of the Negro movement, as though they somehow defy rational and scientific analysis.

In our 1963 convention resolution, which Cruse persistently refuses to confront, we have made an analysis of the very qualities he calls unknown (separatism, assimilationism, nationalism, self-determination, independence, etc.). Our analysis may not be perfect or complete, but it has already proved fruitful. Further progress can be made by testing, deepening, and extending this analysis, not by labeling the conditions it studies unknown and implying they are unknowable.

Historical Science

In another place, Cruse says that "if 'historical science' or 'dialectics' is to be considered really scientific it must be developed and verified in life by the inclusion of the social experiences, the history, the ideas and political philosophies, the points of view of the backward peoples" (among whom he includes the American Negroes)—Well, that's what we've been saying, too, before Cruse did. That's just what we've been trying to do when we undertake to Afro-Americanize Marxism. Robert Vernon's writings on the black ghetto in the *Militant* are a striking example of the value of this approach.

But when we do it, Cruse refuses to even comment on the result. We hope that other black radicals, who don't have any anti-Marxist axes to grind, will become acquainted with our work in this field and join in on it.

While we recommend Marxism as the best theory now available and defend it against Cruse's type of attack, we know that no theory, not even the best, is perfect. That would mean knowing everything about a given situation, which is impossible. No theory automatically provides all the answers; that takes work. No one gains access to the answers merely by adopting a theory, or by saying I am a Marxist, or a black nationalist, or any other *ist*.

Even the best theory in the world does not safeguard anyone or any movement against making mistakes and lagging behind changes in reality. The question is whether their theory enables them to avoid fatal mistakes, whether it enables them to learn from mistakes, correct them, and avoid repeating them. In this respect, too, the Marxist record is superior to others.

Years of isolation and attack by backsliders and refugees from Marxism as well as by capitalist spokesmen, and the need to stand firm against them, have unfortunately tended to create the impression that Marxists are rigid people who think they know it all: "Here is a finished science with all the answers worked out; sit down and study it." But this is not the case, and mature Marxists do not think it is.

We don't have all the answers. We think we have the method for finding them, and we have no patent on that. In seeking the answers and using the method to find them, we urgently need and want the active collaboration and aid of those who have most to gain from revolution, the people who are least privileged and least corrupted by this society—the black masses and the radical thinkers who most authentically represent them. We think Cruse's article does harm because it tries through misrepresentation of Marxism to discourage this collaboration.

"White" Theory?

Another impression which we hope to dispel is that Marxism is a "white" theory and philosophy. We know it isn't, but that's how it looks today to many black people, especially in this country, who are justifiably suspicious of white ideas and influences because they are usually oppressive to

Negroes. Cruse tries to fan this suspicion against Marxists in order to prevent a fair examination of our ideas.

It is true that Marx was classified as a white, and that the early development of the Marxist movement occurred mainly among white people in the advanced capitalist countries. But Marxism is, and is meant to be, a tool and weapon for the revolutionists of all races, and should not be rejected out of hand any more than a gun should be rejected by black rebels in South Africa merely because it was manufactured by white workers.

In any case, things have changed since Marx's time, and in the world today the millions of nonwhites who consider themselves Marxists and supporters of Marxism outnumber their white co-thinkers. As Clifton DeBerry asked, in an article which the *Liberator* asked him to write but has not printed, "[I]f Marxism is white, Western, and obsolete as Cruse contends, how can he account for the fact that from China to Cuba, where capitalism has been abolished by mass revolution, this was done under the banner of Marxism? How does he explain the fact that socialism is becoming the most popular mass creed in almost all the countries and continents where colored peoples are fighting for freedom?"

Because Cruse considers the American Negro struggle a semicolonial revolt, DeBerry asked further: "If Marxism has been so helpful and correct as a guide in the fight against imperialism and white supremacy in the colonial world, what prevents this method from being equally useful in the Freedom Now struggle here in the heartland of imperialism and white supremacy?"

Cruse says that "the real issue is: Who is destined to be the dominant and decisive radical force in America—black radicals or white radicals?" We don't see that as the real issue at all. Far more important is the question of how black and white radicals can pool their forces to promote their common aims against their common enemies.

Black Leadership

Cruse's assumption here is that Marxists are opposed to black leadership, but it simply isn't so. We don't care what the color of the leadership of the coming American revolution may be—only that it be a leadership with a correct program and be capable of guiding the masses to the abolition of capitalism.

We expect that such a leadership will include members of all races in this country, whether they are organized in a single revolutionary party or an alliance of such parties; that Negroes will contribute more than their proportionate share to this leadership; and that they may well be a majority. In any case, it is absolutely certain that the struggle of the Negroes today, in the revolution that is coming, and afterward, will be led by Negroes.

When we say black and white radicals have common aims and therefore should be able to work together, we do not mean to minimize the differences that do exist between many black radicals and the Socialist Workers Party. Besides our differences over the future role of the white workers, there are three others that should get mention here.

A weakness of some Negro intellectuals, like Cruse, is that they proceed with their analyses and arrive at their conclusions by assuming the indefinite perpetuation of the present conditions of the struggle and of the relations of social forces on a national and world scale. They do not see further than the initiating stages of the Third American Revolution.

They are empirical in their reasoning—a method consistent with liberalism and reformism, but inconsistent with a thoroughly revolutionary outlook. This method is faulty and can be fatal because it leaves its practitioners unprepared for sharp turns and liable to be caught by surprise. This is one reason for their rejection of Marxism, which views all things in their contradictory development.

Basic Perspective

Another difference Marxists have with some black radicals concerns a basic perspective. As we have said, we believe that Negroes will not achieve equality or freedom in a capitalist America; they will get it through socialist revolution or through separation or migration. This flows from our analysis of American capitalism in its monopoly stage and from our analysis of the combined national-proletarian character of the Negro question.

What about those who see only one side of this dual character, only the national-racial side and not the proletarian? (Let us call them pure-and-simple nationalists, to distinguish them from black nationalists with a broader view, including socialist-nationalists.) Some of them think Negro equality can be won in this country without abolishing capitalist rule; others leave this open as a possibility. Neither, in our opinion, has thought the question through.

If the capitalists can give employment, education, housing, and an end to police brutality, segregation, and discrimination to twenty million Negroes, at the bottom of the social structure, then American capitalism would have succeeded in eliminating the most fundamental and urgent economic and social evils of our time. This would even enable it, some would even say entitle it, to endure indefinitely.

Reformist Line

Acceptance of such a possibility, or even a half-hope of it, implies the adoption of a nonrevolutionary perspective and a reformist line of thought. It then would not be necessary to wage an uncompromising struggle for basic change in the power structure and in social relations. It would be enough for the crew to rock the boat so as to exert pressure on the captain—instead of organizing a mutiny to get rid of the captain and his slave ship.

A pure-and-simple nationalist outlook, which ignores the working-class element of the Negro struggle and its dynamics, that is, its implicitly anticapitalist tendencies, runs the risk of being derailed at some point along the way because it fails to foresee the direction of the mass movement, both black and white, and the kind of resistance it must encounter from the capitalists. Negroes will play a leading role in any anticapitalist revolution in this country, but it will not be successful if they are the only anticapitalist force involved.

A third difference exists between us and those like Cruse who assume that not only the ideas and attitudes of white workers, but the ideas and attitudes of militant Negroes, will remain substantially unchanged. They underrate, even exclude, the influence of socialist ideas as formulated by Marxism in the coming stages of the fight for freedom.

There are actually three components, very unequally developed at this point, at work in the Negro movement: its proletarian composition, its nationalism, and its socialism. The first two are already obvious; the third is still largely latent although distinctly implicit in its orientation in practice. The socialist element is small and embryonic at present, just as the conscious and avowed socialists are few. Will it remain this way?

Those black nationalists who slight the socialist element inherent in their movement commit an error comparable to those who today slight black nationalism. Here the colonial revolution they feel kinship with has something to teach them. Cuba and Algeria have recently shown how a nationalist, democratic, revolutionary mass movement can, through conclusions derived from direct experience in struggle with imperialism and its agents, grow over into a consciously socialist movement, party, and government.

We believe that this dynamic of the permanent revolution will be operative in the evolution of American black nationalism, too. The further it goes in a revolutionary and anticapitalist direction, the closer it comes to socialist and Marxist policies, methods, and outlook. We can be all the more confident of this because black nationalism in this country is far more urban and proletarian than rural and peasant.

A final point: despite differences and the critical exchange of views, black radicals and Marxists are both engaged in finding the solutions to the evils bred by capitalism. These specific answers are not given in any books. But Marxism is our method and it is too useful for us to surrender it until we can be shown a better one.

Let the non-Marxist black theoreticians try other methods and let's compare the results. Whatever they come up with that is good and useful we shall gladly adopt, as we have done in the past. There is plenty of room in Marxist theory to accommodate and incorporate everything progressive that develops out of the theory and practice of the Negro revolt. At the same time we believe the non-Marxist nationalists should try to think out their positions to the end and state them plainly, so that everybody can check and learn from the conclusions of both their tendency and ours as the struggle moves from one stage to the next.

While awaiting such tests, we proceed in the conviction that Marxism is relevant to the Negro struggle; that Marxists have much to learn from the black working-class ghetto that can make their theory more effective and complete; that black radicals have much to learn from Marxism that can be used to formulate a program to win freedom for the Negro people; that non-Marxist black radicals and white and black Marxists have so many things in common that they can and should work together in as many areas as possible, despite their differences; and that their common needs and further experience will bring them closer together and into genuine collaboration before, during, and after the coming American revolution.

CHAPTER 5

MALCOLM X

THE MAN AND HIS IDEAS

(1965)

George Breitman

I t is still painful to speak of the death of Malcolm X. It is probably
too soon to appraise him adequately. It will take time before we can
do him justice, before we can see him in his full stature. It is painful
because with him gone, we momentarily feel smaller, weaker, more vulnerable.

Our sense of loss is for his family, for the movement he was building,
for the Negro people, for the revolutionary cause as a whole. There is also
something in us that cries out against the fact that he was cut down in his
prime, still a young man, before he had made his full contributions to the
struggle, before he had accomplished everything he was capable of
accomplishing for human emancipation.

I was still a young man twenty-five years ago when another great revolutionary was assassinated—Leon Trotsky. Perhaps I did not fully
realize how much his leadership, advice, and political wisdom would be
missed, and probably I was under the influence of the belief common
among young people that to show certain kinds of strong emotion is a
sign of weakness. Anyhow, I did not cry when Trotsky was killed, but I
could not help crying when Malcolm was killed.

It was not because I considered Malcolm the greater of the two men.

This speech was given at a meeting of the Friday Night Socialist Forum at Eugene V. Debs Hall,
Detroit, on March 5, 1965, twelve days after Malcolm's assassination. The text was first printed in
the *Militant*, March 22 and 29, 1965.

One reason for the difference was the realization that Malcolm, at the age of thirty-nine, was still in the process of reaching his full height, still in the process of working out his program, still in the early stage of building a new movement—whereas Trotsky, at the age of sixty, had already reached full maturity, had already worked out his main ideas and his program, and left behind him the solid foundations of a movement that could not be destroyed by war, by persecution from both the Allied and Axis powers, or by cold war reaction and witch-hunts.

But while it is painful to speak of Malcolm, and not yet possible to see him in full perspective, we are able even now to begin to make an appraisal of his ideas, and of how he came to the ideas that constitute his heritage. When we do this, we must try to put emotion aside, or to bring it under control. That is what Malcolm urged when he spoke here in Detroit three weeks ago—that we learn to think clearly about the struggle and the ways the power structure seeks to curb and sidetrack the struggle; that we think clearly and rely on reason and learn how to see through trickery.

Malcolm Little's mother was born as the result of her mother's rape by a white man in the West Indies. When Malcolm was four, the house where he and his family lived was burned down by Ku Kluxers. When he was six, his father met a violent death, and he and his family always believed his father had been lynched.

The family was broken up. Young Malcolm lived in state institutions and boarding homes. He got high marks at the grade school in Mason, Michigan. Then, at the age of fifteen, he became a dropout. He went to live with his sister in Boston, and went to work at the kinds of jobs available to Negro youth—shoeshine boy, soda jerk, hotel busboy, member of a dining car crew on trains traveling to New York, restaurant waiter in Harlem. There he drifted into the degrading life of the underworld—gambling, drugs, hustling, burglary. You can find it all described in his autobiography, up to and including his arrest for burglary, conviction, and sentencing to ten years in prison. That was in 1946, when he was not quite twenty-one, the age of many of you in this audience.

What were his ideas then? That life is a jungle, where the fiercest survive—by fleecing the weak and defenseless; where each man looks out for number one, which can only be done by accepting the jungle code. "The main thing you got to remember is that everything in the world is a hustle," he was told by the friend who helped him get his first job.

Although his father had been an admirer of Marcus Garvey, feelings of race pride did not exist in the young man with the zoot suit; he tried to straighten his hair in emulation of white men, who, as he later said, had taught him what he knew and instilled in him the values of racist white society. I think you can find thousands of youngsters in today's ghetto like twenty-one-year-old Malcolm Little in 1946.

Prison is hell. Prison is also a place where you can think, where some important decisions have been made. Eugene V. Debs, after whom this meeting hall is named, was converted to socialism while he was in prison in 1895. Prison was where Malcolm underwent a conversion that literally transformed his whole life.

By letters and visits from members of his family, he was introduced to the Nation of Islam, headed by Elijah Muhammad. This American religious sect, popularly known as the Black Muslims, worships Allah and practices some rituals of the orthodox Muslim religion, with certain variations of its own, especially in the sphere of race.

It teaches that original man, when the world was a paradise, was black, and that white man is a degenerate and inferior offshoot, destined to rule the world for 6,000 years and then be destroyed. The 6,000-year period is now ending, and black people can save themselves from the coming catastrophe only by withdrawing, by separating, from the white man and following Muhammad, the messenger of Allah.

From a scientific standpoint, Black Muslim mythology is no more and no less fantastic or bizarre than other religions. But the Black Muslims are a *movement* as well as a religious group, providing a kind of haven and hope and salvation for outcasts, encouragement at self-reform, brotherhood, and solidarity against a cruel and oppressive world.

I am not going to go into detail about the Black Muslims; you can find plenty about it in writing. The point is that Malcolm experienced a genuine religious conversion in prison, believing that Elijah Muhammad was a holy man and that the Nation of Islam provided a path of salvation not only for him but for his people.

While in prison this dropout after the eighth grade began to educate himself and learn how to speak and debate, so that he could participate more effectively in the movement after he got out. Not knowing how else to proceed, he started with a dictionary, copying into a tablet words beginning with "A" that might be helpful. He was astonished to find so many

"A" words, filling a tablet with them alone. He went through to "Z," and then, he writes, "for the first time, I could pick up a book and actually understand what the book was saying." The story speaks volumes about the quality of education in Michigan—and the United States.

From then until he left prison, he spent all the time he could in the library, "picking up some more books." Within a few years he was to become the most respected debater in the country, taking on one and all—politicians, college professors, journalists, anyone, black or white, bold enough to meet him.

There are tremendous reservoirs of talent and even genius locked up in the black ghettos and white slums, among the masses—which can be set free and put to work when they acquire hope and purpose.

After six years in prison, when Malcolm was twenty-seven, he won a parole by getting a job with his oldest brother, Wilfred, as a furniture salesman in the Detroit ghetto. That was the spring of 1952. Later that year he traveled to Chicago to hear Elijah Muhammad, and he met him. He was accepted into the movement and given the name of Malcolm X. He volunteered his organizing services in Detroit, and did so well that he was made assistant minister of the Detroit mosque, after the membership had tripled.

At the end of 1953 he went to Chicago to live with Muhammad and be trained by him for some months. Muhammad sent him to Philadelphia, which had no mosque; in less than three months a mosque had been formed. He was obviously a man of unusual talent, energy, and devotion. Muhammad picked him to head the movement in New York, and he went back to Harlem in 1954, before he was thirty years old. In a few short years his work helped to transform the Black Muslims from a virtually unnoticed to a nationally known organization; and he himself had become one of the country's most noted figures, one of the most desired speakers on the nation's campuses, and the object of admiration by the most militant youth.

*   *   *

Before proceeding chronologically, I want to say a few words about Malcolm as a public speaker. I am not an expert in this field and I hope somebody who is will make a study of it. There is certainly plenty of material, thanks to the fact that many of his talks were taped and are readily available.

His speaking style was unique—plain, direct as an arrow, devoid of flowery trimming. He used metaphors and figures of speech that were lean and simple, rooted in the ordinary daily experience of his audiences. He knew what the masses think and how they feel, their strengths and weaknesses. He reached right into their minds and hearts without wasting a word; and he never tried to flatter them. Despite an extraordinary ability to move and arouse his listeners, his main appeal was to reason, not to emotion.

This is true even about speeches where he was presenting ideas that he abandoned in the last year of his life, such as the last great speech he made as a Black Muslim—his speech to the Grass Roots Conference in Detroit in November 1963, which is available from the Afro-American Broadcasting and Recording Company. It is one of his best speeches—although, I repeat, it does not reflect his thinking at the end—and worth listening and relistening to, because of the qualities I have been trying to pinpoint. Because his main appeal was to reason, he was the very opposite of a demagogue, the very opposite of what the kept press called him.

It was also a style very different from Elijah Muhammad's. I don't mean only that Malcolm commanded the weapons of wit and humor, which are alien to Muhammad. Muhammad's appeal was to faith, to authority (divine authority), to the hereafter; Malcolm's appeal was to reason, to logic; it dealt with the real and the present, even when he was expounding Muhammad's line. To be able to listen to Muhammad for any length of time you had to be a believer, convinced in advance, while Malcolm seemed to achieve his greatest success with non-Muslims.

These few remarks about Malcolm as a speaker are admittedly inadequate; I make them only in the hope of interesting someone more qualified than I to study and write about it. I wanted only to convey the idea that there rarely has been a man in America better able to communicate ideas to the most oppressed people; and that this was not just a matter of technique, which can be learned and applied in any situation by almost anybody, but that it was the rare case of a man in closest communion with the oppressed, able to speak to them because he spoke for them, because he identified himself with them, an authentic expression of their yearning for freedom, a true product of their growth in the same way that Lenin was a product of the Russian people.

*   *   *

We come now to the end of the second period of Malcolm's life, 1963, and the split with Muhammad, which was consummated in March 1964. The year 1963 was a year of stirring and movement in the Negro struggle, with hundreds of thousands in the streets; the year that the struggle moved from the South to the northern ghettos, where the Black Muslims were strongest. It was not yet a revolution, but a prelude to revolutionary struggles. This was the situation that sharpened a dilemma and then produced a crisis in the Black Muslims.

By their militant stance, they had helped to push other Negro organizations to the Left. This was their positive contribution. But they were on the sidelines of the struggle, not participants. They talked in angry tones, but did nothing when non-Muslim Negroes were under attack. They were separated not only from whites but from Negro militants.

Among the members, younger and less conservative than in the pre-Malcolm period, signs could be detected of a desire to get into the battle, to pass from propaganda to action. Muhammad tried to allay the ferment; one example was his call, at the organization's national convention in February 1963, for independent black political action. But he soon pulled back from this and other moves that might have drawn the Black Muslims out of their abstentionism. When the Freedom Now Party was started six months later, he refused to endorse it or let the members join.

The occasion for the split was a remark made by Malcolm after John F. Kennedy's death in November 1963, followed by Muhammad's silencing of Malcolm with a virtual suspension that was deliberately intended to be humiliating. But this was only the occasion, not the cause. The basic factor behind the split was the growth of militancy and mass action in the Negro community, and the different ways in which the two main tendencies in the Black Muslims wanted to respond to the masses knocking on the doors of their mosques.

There is an instructive relation between the way Malcolm came into the Black Muslims and the way he left. He turned to them from a state of isolation, not only the physical isolation of prison, but an alienation from society generally and from his own people as well. His years in the Black Muslims had been good for the organization, and they were good for him. He had traveled all over the country as Muhammad's chief troubleshooter, and he knew the ghetto nationally as no one else did. His vision had broadened, his interests had widened.

He entered the Black Muslims because he was alone and lost, and he left, you could say, because now he was in closest touch with the Negro people, attuned to their needs and wants more than the Black Muslims were or wanted him to be; because he was becoming the spokesman of a growing multitude looking for a new road; because he had found a new role, or rather because a new role had been thrust upon him, which his whole life's experience told him he had to accept, however difficult it would be.

It could not have been an easy decision. Consider the circumstances: thirty-eight years old; a wife and several dependent children; a secure post, relatively well paid, home provided, car provided, expenses; great prestige; a position in an organization second in authority to a man in his late sixties who was not in good health. Some men in his place would have taken the easy way—keep quiet, do as you are told, stay out of the line of fire, mend your fences, and wait. That's the American way—in business, government, church, fraternal, and labor circles.

But Malcolm was not that kind of man. He had been disturbed to see that Muhammad and some of his ministers were, like other preachers of puritanism, not living in accord with the strict puritanical code they pre-scribed for the rank-and-file Black Muslims. He tried to overlook things like this—his eyes were mainly turned to the outside world of the broad Negro struggle. He was not the only minister who knew that new, bolder, and more active policies were needed if the Black Muslims were to ful-fill their real responsibilities to the Negro people. But the other ministers who recognized the need for change—they played it safe. They weren't Malcolm X.

Malcolm had what can be called a second rebirth early in 1964 when he decided his place was with the Negro masses more than with Muhammad's organization. As a Black Muslim leader, he had rejected corrupt American society. Now he passed from merely rejecting it (a neg-ative, passive position) to rebelling against it and organizing to change it (a positive, active position). That was the essence of the change.

Some ultraleftists in the Negro community did not understand this and talked condescendingly about Malcolm's becoming "weak" or "soft." But the American ruling class and its spokesmen understood what was hap-pening, and they were more hostile to him after the split than before. And they had greater reason to hate and fear him after he set out to build a new movement. That is why, as George Novack puts it, he "was crucified by the paid press long before he was martyred by the assassin's bullets."

We have heard the expression, "the new Malcolm X." It is appropriate in some ways, misleading in others. Some of his ideas did change starting last March, but others did not. Let us at least mention those that did not change before examining those that did:

> That Negroes can get their freedom only by fighting for it;
> That the government is a racist government and is not going to grant freedom;
> That gradualism, the program of the liberals, white and black, is not the road to equality;
> That Uncle Toms must be exposed and opposed;
> That Negroes must rely on themselves and control their own struggle;
> That Negroes must determine their own strategy and tactics;
> That Negroes must select their own leaders.

—These are ideas that Malcolm believed before he left the Black Muslims and that he still believed the day he died.

*   *   *

In approaching the immensely difficult and exhausting job of building a new movement, in opposition to new as well as old enemies—a task which radicals should best be able to understand and sympathize with—Malcolm showed from the start that he did not want merely a replica of the Black Muslim structure plus some modifications in policy. He wanted a different kind of organization, with a different kind of relation between the leaders and ranks.

The Black Muslims built everything around a mystique of leadership, faith in and submission to a divine, all-wise chief. That Malcolm wanted something radically different could be seen from the statement he made at his first press conference after the split. He denied that he was "expert in any particular field." He called for help in the form of ideas and suggestions from all quarters, especially students, white or black.

He not only accepted advice, but sought it. He not only invited criticism, but welcomed it. I am aware of one such case personally. I never met Malcolm or saw him in person, but I wrote many articles about him, most of them supporting and defending him. It was typical of him, I think, that the only one of these articles about which he sent me a message of appreciation was one that was most critical of some implications in a speech he had made.

When he read something useful or pertinent to the problems of his organization, he would go out of his way to get copies for his fellow leaders so that they could read and think about it and develop informed and collective attitudes. On the day he was killed, he was scheduled to present for discussion his ideas on the program of the Organization of Afro-American Unity. It is plain that he was trying to build a far more democratic organization and a far more collective leadership than the Black Muslims ever dreamed of. This is evident also from the fact that he did not fear to associate with radicals and refused to bar them from the organization, despite the discontent of some of the more conservative members.

Malcolm's courage was not only physical, but intellectual. We can appreciate its magnitude only if we fully understand the degree of his dependence on and subordination to Muhammad before the split. For more than twelve years, for most of his adult life, he had been to Muhammad like a son to a father—no, more than that, for few sons are so voluntarily and so long obedient. And then, with very little advance notice, he was on his own. Three days before his death he told a *New York Times* interviewer: "I was the spokesman for the Black Muslims. I believed in Elijah Muhammad more strongly than the Christians do in Jesus. I believed in him so strongly that my mind, my body, my voice functioned 100 percent for him and the movement. My belief led others to believe." In contrast, he continued, "I feel like a man who has been asleep somewhat and under someone else's control. I feel what I'm thinking and saying now is for myself. Before, it was for and by the guidance of Elijah Muhammad. Now I think with my own mind, sir."

To think with his own mind—that is what all the forces at the command of the ruling class in this country are organized to discourage and prevent the Negro from doing. You need intellectual as well as physical courage to think and say things for yourself, to think new thoughts, to search out ideas that have been forbidden by the ruling class, to seek them among the Mau Mau in Kenya or the Simbas in the Congo. That is the true mark of an open, honest, and free mind—and of a revolutionary leader.

Malcolm remained a believer in Islam after the split with Muhammad, but it was in the official and orthodox Islam he saw during his trip to Mecca last year. He praised Muhammad even as he left his organization, thinking or hoping that friction with the Black Muslims could be avoided while he turned his attention to the broad Negro struggle. With the advantage of hindsight, we can see this hope was unfounded. An independent movement of the Malcolm X type was a threat to every vested interest in the country, every privileged hierarchy. And it did not take long for Muhammad to launch ruthless and slanderous attacks designed to isolate Malcolm, because he feared that otherwise he would be deserted by his own members. Perhaps Malcolm might still be alive if he had realized from the start how much he imperiled the status quo, and had acted and prepared differently. This we don't know, can't know.

Malcolm believed in black unity after as well as before the split. But as a Black Muslim, what he meant and had to mean was black unity under the leadership and control of Muhammad, and with unquestioning acceptance of his religious dogmas and discipline. The kind of black unity Malcolm sought after the split was the unity of all Negroes, whatever their religions, whatever their philosophies, so long as they were ready to fight for freedom.

It was a movement away from religious sectarianism toward nonsectarian mass action. But this aim could not be fulfilled by his first organizational step at the time of the split—the founding of the Muslim Mosque, Incorporated. As a religious organization, it would obviously be limited in its appeal. Malcolm soon corrected this by forming the broad Organization of Afro-American Unity. The selection of a religious group first showed how closely he was tied to his past even one year ago; the addition of the OAAU not many weeks later showed how rapidly he was able to transcend the limitations carried over from his past.

*   *   *

We must spend some time on the issue of self-defense, or, as the press called it, "violence." We have to spend it, although the truth is so obvious, because the press centered their attacks around this issue.

Malcolm always was for self-defense—in his teens, when he was part of the underworld; when he was a Black Muslim; and in his last year. In each of these three periods, however, the idea had a different content for him. The Black Muslims say you have the right to defend yourself when attacked, and that this right is granted by Allah and his messenger. Malcolm validated the right on political and constitutional grounds; he brought it down from heaven to earth. The Black Muslims defend themselves, but Malcolm went further and said all Negroes should defend themselves; with him the right became specific, concrete, and practical. The difference was apparent when Muhammad's first attack on Malcolm revolved around Malcolm's advocacy of defensive rifle clubs.

Seeing many students in the audience, I shall try to convey my point this way. Let me suggest that one or several of you prepare a research paper on the subject: "How the Press Reported Malcolm X's Views on Violence." It would be very enlightening. It would give you insight, through one example, of the way 99 percent of the American people get the "information" on the basis of which they form their ideas. It would illuminate more than the single example; it would reveal some basic features of American society as a whole and how it is controlled through propaganda posing as news or fact.

As a model for such a research paper on Malcolm and violence, I recommend a recent book called *A Curtain of Ignorance* by Felix Greene, a journalist familiar with China. What it does is compare the facts about China with what the American press has been writing about China for the past fifteen years. The result is devastating. I will read but one example.

In 1963 Mao Tse-tung issued, at the suggestion of Robert F. Williams, a statement on racial discrimination in the United States. The key sentence said: "I call upon the workers, peasants, revolutionary intellectuals, enlightened elements of the bourgeoisie, and other enlightened persons of all colors—white, black, yellow, brown, etc.—to unite to oppose racial discrimination practiced by US imperialism and to support the American Negroes in their struggle against racial discrimination."

Here is how the *Christian Century* (and many other publications in this country) described that statement: "A summons to colored peoples to unite in war against the white race was issued from Peking in the name of Mao Tse-tung. His call for worldwide racial war reflects a degree of hate and desperation which can only be described as psychotic."

The writer of my proposed research paper will find Greene's book useful because *exactly* the same method was used with Malcolm's statements on violence. And its use was no more accidental in one case than in the other.

Those of you who heard Malcolm know that he did not advocate violence; he advocated that Negroes defend themselves when attacked. He said it a hundred times, he said it a thousand times. He said that he was opposed to violence and wanted to stop it, and that Negroes could contribute to stopping it by letting the attackers know they would defend themselves. He could have said it a million times and the readers of the American press still would not have known the truth.

Take the *New York Times*. This is supposed to be the best daily paper in the country, in the world. Urbane, sophisticated, liberal on certain civil liberties and civil rights questions. But it hated Malcolm with a fury I cannot recollect it showing to anyone else in the thirty years I have been reading it. The mask slipped the day Malcolm was killed, and the ugly face of American capitalism showed through in the editorial that appeared the next morning. There is a Latin saying: *Speak nothing but good about the dead.* The *Times*'s approach to Malcolm was: *Speak nothing good about the dead, and if you must, twist it to make it look bad.*

"He was a case history, as well as an extraordinary and twisted man, turning many true gifts to evil purpose," says the *Times* editorial. ("Case history" and "twisted" is their way of saying Malcolm was mentally unbalanced. So he was insane, and evil to boot.)

". . . his ruthless and fanatical belief in violence . . . marked him for fame, and for a violent end." (So his alleged belief is linked to his death, in some kind of cause-and-effect relation; he was responsible for his own murder.)

". . . he did not seek to fit into society or into the life of his own people. . . . The world he saw through those horn-rimmed glasses of his was distorted and dark. But he made it darker still with his exaltation of fanaticism. Yesterday someone came out of that darkness that he spawned and killed him." (The darkness that he spawned! So Malcolm was not only mad and evil; he also possessed magical power—he made himself look like 39, but he must have been at least 350 years old to have "spawned" racial violence.) The editorial concludes with the magnanimous concession that the murder "demands an investigation." Not because it was a criminal act but because it "could easily touch off a war of vengeance of the kind he himself fomented."

Now why is this? Suppose that I, a so-called white man, or any white person, went downtown and stood on a box and said, "White people should defend themselves when attacked." Would I be branded an advocate of violence, a racist, or a fanatic? No, the worst I would be called would be a nut.

And if a white person got up there after me and said, "White people should defend their interests when they are attacked in Cuba or Vietnam by sending invasion armies or bombers," would the press condemn him as a fomenter of violence, or a racist fanatic? No, some would say, "Of course, it goes without saying," and others would declare, "That man belongs in the White House." The White House, not the nuthouse.

What is the difference? The difference is that black people, not whites, are being attacked or are subject to attack. And the very thought of someone encouraging Negroes to defend themselves makes the apologists for American racism see red, or black. So much so that they can hardly work up the pretense that they are in any way unhappy about Malcolm's murder. This difference shows beyond doubt how permeated with racism this country and its press are. The only other country in the world with such phobias and psychoses is South Africa.

It is too bad that so much time has to be spent explaining such obvious truths, because Malcolm's stand on this issue was not the central part of his philosophy—just the most controversial. It was an indispensable part of his program, for how can anyone expect to win freedom unless he is willing to defend his person, rights, and property against violence designed to terrorize and silence him? But it was not a central part, and is not, by itself, the solution to the Negro's problems. Even when Negroes organize for self-defense, as they should and inevitably will, they will still not be free, because inequality is built into this society, in every warp and woof; the system itself exudes and perpetuates inequality.

*　　*　　*

Next is the question of race. Here Malcolm made a very pronounced change in his thinking. Partly through the influence of Islam, a religion which views and treats all races alike, and partly through his contact with revolutionaries in many countries, he threw overboard the whole Black Muslim mythology about superior and inferior races and its doctrine about inherent evil and degeneracy in a white skin.

Repudiating racism in all forms, he resolved to judge men and movements on the basis of their deeds, not their color or race. Deeds, not words; and he was pretty shrewd about distinguishing between the two, as in the case of white liberals (or black liberals, for that matter). He developed a historical approach to racism. He knew American whites had been conditioned, miseducated, and infected on race worse than most European whites, for example, and he remained more on guard with Americans. He distinguished in a similar way between the older and younger white generations in America.

When Young Socialist Alliance leaders interviewed him and asked what he considered to be the cause of race prejudice, he didn't give anything resembling the Black Muslim position. "Ignorance and greed," he replied. A scientific socialist of any race might turn the three words around, saying "greed and ignorance," and might expand on the theme at greater length, but would not say anything essentially different. "You can't have capitalism without racism," he said on an earlier occasion.

*   *   *

Malcolm had been abroad before his break with Muhammad, but only briefly, carrying out assignments for Muhammad, not on his own. But after the break in 1964 he traveled to and through Africa and the Mideast twice, spending almost half of his remaining life abroad—studying, searching, discussing, learning, seeking help and giving it. And when he returned he was not just a sympathizer of the colonial revolution but a staunch internationalist, on the side of the oppressed and exploited masses of the world against their oppressors and exploiters—whose central fountainhead he recognized to be US imperialism, the dominant force in what he called the international power structure. No one in the world denounced the US role in the Congo more forcefully and effectively.

One purpose of his trips was of course to mobilize African support behind the project to put the US government on trial in the United Nations for the continued oppression of American Negroes, with which he had limited success. But the State Department credited him, or rather blamed him, for a good part of the strong stand against US imperialism taken by African nations in the United Nations at the time of the latest atrocities in the Congo. As he knew, the CIA and similar agencies take an interest in what the State Department doesn't like.

Those who heard him in Detroit the week before his murder knew about his hope to unite the many millions of the oppressed in Latin America and the Caribbean together with their Afro-American brothers and sisters against their common exploiter.

So he was simultaneously broadening his horizons and zeroing in on American imperialism—this product of the segregated, locked-in ghetto who broke through and over the walls of national boundary and race to become an internationalist; this internationalist who admired John Killens's definition of a patriot: "Dignity was his country, Manhood was his government, and Freedom was his land."

*   *   *

In the area of political action Malcolm was also far ahead of the Black Muslims. That didn't take much doing, since they abstain from politics. He favored Negroes' organizing politically and running and electing their own candidates, and driving out of office black stooges of the major parties. He participated in a Harlem conference on independent political action two months before his death.

But his position on politics was largely general. He said he found some good in what the Freedom Now Party was doing, and while he was in Africa last summer, he briefly gave consideration to an offer that he run on the Michigan FNP ticket for the US Senate; he decided instead to remain in Africa longer. However, he never affiliated with the FNP, for reasons not discussed publicly; maybe he thought the FNP was premature or launched without sufficient groundwork on too narrow a basis.

While his thinking on politics was still in a process of development, and uncompleted, there was nothing general or tentative about his attitude to the capitalist parties and the two-party system. To him they were both enemies of the Negro people, currently as well as historically, and neither merited an iota of support from Negroes. He had nothing but contempt for the Communist Party's support of Johnson in 1964. While he did not endorse Clifton DeBerry, the Socialist Workers Party candidate for president, he did attack both of DeBerry's major opponents; and in his own way made it easier for DeBerry to get a hearing from Harlem audiences, thus indicating a measure of sympathy. He said he would be willing under certain conditions to consider running as an independent candidate for mayor of New York against the Democratic and Republican candidates in 1965. In terms of the political spectrum, he stood on the radical side, although he had not reached strong conclusions about *how* to organize independent black political power.

The speech Malcolm had started to make when he was shot down was to deal with the program of the Organization of Afro-American Unity, and of the militant black movement generally. We know that he had been thinking about the question of "alliances," the question of the independent Negro movement's relations with other forces in this country, and that he had circulated among other OAAU leaders literature dealing with some aspects of this subject.

Even if we did not know that, it would be logical to assume that he would touch on this question, because no organization defines itself and clarifies its own program and perspectives without simultaneously defining its relations to its enemies and its friends, present or potential. Now we may never know where his thinking had led him on this point, and can only speculate. But even speculation can be oriented by some definite facts.

At his first press conference last March, Malcolm had this to say on the question of alliances: "Whites can help us, but they can't join us. There can be no black-white unity until there is first some black unity. There can be no workers' solidarity until there is first some racial solidarity. We cannot think of uniting with others until we have first united among ourselves."

This, as I pointed out at that time, is not the statement of a man claiming that black and white working-class solidarity is unnecessary, or that it is impossible. On the contrary, it is the statement of a man explaining one of the conditions through which workers' solidarity may be achieved on a broad and durable basis. And if I may quote myself for one more sentence, I noted: "Revolutionary socialists will certainly agree [with Malcolm] that a meaningful and mutually beneficial labor-Negro alliance will not be forged until the Negro people are organized independently and strongly enough, numerically and ideologically, to assure that their interests cannot be subordinated or sold out by the other partner or partners in any alliance."

The subject must have come up often during his subsequent travels abroad, where his ideas were strongly influenced during his last year. But he stuck to his position. When he spoke at a Militant Labor Forum in New York last May, he said: "In my recent travels into the African countries and others, it was impressed upon me the importance of having a working unity among all peoples, black as well as white. But the only way this is going to be brought about is the Negroes have to be in unity first."

So far as I have been able to learn, that remained Malcolm's position to the end. He was not opposed to alliances with other forces, including labor, provided they were the right kinds of alliances and provided the Negro part of the alliance was independently organized, so that it could guard against betrayal by being able to pull out of any alliance that went bad.

There is no doubt whatever in my mind that Malcolm would have favored an independent mass black movement making alliances with a radicalized mass labor movement when conditions produced two such components for an alliance. I have no doubt about it because he was willing, even now, in the absence of two such mass movements, to collaborate with radical whites under certain conditions. A man willing to collaborate with numerically weak radical forces, as I will try to show Malcolm was, would have to be out of his mind not to collaborate with mass radical forces. And whatever the *New York Times* and *Muhammad Speaks* say, Malcolm was not out of his mind.

* * *

Next let us consider briefly Malcolm's attitudes to capitalism and socialism. In an interview with the *Young Socialist*[1] he stated: "It is impossible for capitalism to survive, primarily because the system of capitalism needs some blood to suck. Capitalism used to be like an eagle, but now it's more like a vulture and can only suck the blood of the helpless. As the nations of the world free themselves, then capitalism has less and less victims, less to suck, and it becomes weaker and weaker. It's only a matter of time in my opinion before it will collapse completely." Marxists might question whether capitalism will collapse, or have to be collapsed, but who can question that in his last months Malcolm was taking an unequivocally anticapitalist position?

Malcolm did not learn about socialism by reading Marx, but he managed to learn about it anyway. He learned about it from the colonial revolution, especially its pro-socialist contingent. He had discussions with Castro and Che Guevara and Algerian socialists and socialists in Ghana, Guinea, Zanzibar, and elsewhere, including the United States. When he was asked last May at the Militant Labor Forum what kind of political system he wanted, he said:

> I don't know. But I'm flexible. As was stated earlier, all of the countries that are emerging today from under the shackles of colonialism are turning toward socialism. I don't think it's an accident. Most of the countries that were colonial powers were capitalist countries and the last bulwark of capitalism today is America and it's impossible for a white person today to believe in capitalism and not believe in racism. You can't have capitalism without racism. And if you find a person without racism and you happen to get that person into conversation and they have a philosophy that makes you sure they don't have this racism in their outlook, usually they're socialists or their political philosophy is socialism.

Clifton DeBerry was sitting on the same platform and took the floor to comment on when and where flexibility was correct: in tactics, yes, but not in relation to the principle that the capitalist system and capitalist parties are enemies of freedom, justice, and equality. To which Malcolm replied: "And that's the most intelligent answer I've ever heard on that question." So I think it fair to say that the legacy of Malcolm is not only plainly anticapitalist but also pro-socialist. I do not say he was a Marxist—he wasn't—and we can only guess if in his further evolution he would have become one, as Castro did in his later development. But that clearly can be reckoned as a possibility.

A few words about Malcolm's relations with the revolutionary socialists, the Socialist Workers Party and the Young Socialist Alliance: The record is plain about our attitude to Malcolm. We regarded him as one of the most gifted and important leaders of the struggle while he was still a Black Muslim. When he started his own movement, we called it a momentous development that might turn the struggle onto the road to victory, and publicly pledged our aid in the job he was undertaking. For this we got abuse and condemnation from so-called radicals and liberals; our white members were called "white black nationalists" and other names because we supported Malcolm's movement. All this was long before he had said a single word favorable to socialism, and when the image of him in most so-called radical minds was of a man who would rather die than have anything to do with whites, even revolutionary whites.

On the other side was Malcolm's attitude to us. As a Black Muslim he used to buy the *Militant* when it was sold outside his rallies. He later said that even then he urged Negroes to read it. Less than a month after his break with Muhammad, he spoke at the Militant Labor Forum in New York and publicly praised the *Militant* for telling the truth and wished it success. He spoke for the Militant Labor Forum another two times during the next nine months, after each of his trips abroad. He wasn't even scheduled to speak the second time: his secretary, James Shabazz, was to be part of a panel, but Malcolm phoned and asked if he would be acceptable in James Shabazz's place, and of course he was.

At most of the OAAU rallies he would put in a plug for the *Militant*, without any solicitation on our part. He smoothed the way for it to be sold at Harlem stands and shops. In January, when he gave his interview to the *Young Socialist*, he discussed with the YSA leaders the probability of his making a tour of the nation's campuses in collaboration with the YSA later this year. He would almost surely have spoken here at Debs Hall for the Friday Night Socialist Forum while making that tour. Black SWP and YSA members were welcome to join his organization; whites associated with the *Militant* were welcome to attend OAAU rallies.

So our relations were friendly and mutually helpful—on our part, because we believed that he and we were on the same side in the struggle, had the same enemies, and were traveling in the same direction. In our 1963 convention resolution, the Socialist Workers Party had stated that black nationalism and revolutionary socialism "are not only compatible but complementary forces, that should be welded closely together in thought and action." We predicted that would happen, and so far as Malcolm and we were concerned, it was beginning to happen.

On his part, I think, collaboration was taking place because he felt that we, unlike the liberals, unlike the Communist Party, unlike the Socialist Party, unlike most white radicals, did not want to subordinate his movement or the Negro struggle generally to the government, to the Democratic Party, to the American labor bureaucrats, to the privileged bureaucrats in noncapitalist countries, or to anyone else; and that we did and do want the Negro movement to attain full independence of program and action and to develop uninterruptedly in an uncompromisingly militant direction along the lines that best suit its needs.

Once Malcolm was convinced of that, and of our sincerity, as evidenced by our readiness to stick by our principles, however unpopular they might be, there was no bar to our collaboration. I want to stress that he would have taken this attitude to any militant group, even nonsocialist, provided it was, in its own way, independent of the government and opposed to racism.

*   *   *

Let us now conclude this discussion of Malcolm's ideas during the last year of his life by examining his positions on black nationalism and separatism. This is important because some political opponents of Malcolm already are circulating distorted stories about him, alleging that he was on the verge of quitting his movement, going over to his opponents, etc. And important also because there may be some ambiguity about his relation to black nationalism as a result of a statement in his interview in the current issue of the *Young Socialist*.

Black nationalism and separatism are not the same thing, though unfortunately they are often confused. Separatism is a tendency favoring the withdrawal of Negroes into a separate black nation, either in America or in Africa. Black nationalism is a tendency for Negroes to unite as a group, as a people, in organizations that are Negro-led and Negro-controlled, and sometimes all-black, in order to fight for their freedom. Black nationalism, as it now exists, does not imply any position on the question of a separate nation in the future, for or against. So you can be a black nationalist without being a separatist, although all separatists are black nationalists. You will find a much better and longer analysis of this greatly misunderstood distinction in the Socialist Workers Party's 1963 convention resolution, *Freedom Now: The New Stage in the Struggle for Negro Emancipation* (distributed by Pathfinder Press).

When Malcolm was a Black Muslim, he was of course a separatist. At his first press conference after leaving the Black Muslims last March, he said he was out to build a black nationalist movement, and the major stress was on black nationalism. But he also had a few words to say about separatism. He said he still thought separation was "the best solution"; previously he would have said the *only* solution. "But," he continued, "separation back to Africa is still a long-range program, and while it is yet to materialize, 22 million of our people who are still here in America need better food, clothing, housing, education, and jobs *right now*" (his emphasis).

At the time I took this to be a declaration of his intention to build a black nationalist movement that would attempt to unite the Negro people in a fight for immediate needs, while at the same time continuing to hold up separation as a nation as an ultimate objective, and to make propaganda for it accordingly. But I was obviously wrong, because after that statement last March I cannot find any place where Malcolm advocated a separate nation. And on May 21, a few hours after returning from his first trip to Africa, when he was asked at a press conference if he thought Negroes should return to Africa, he said he thought they should stay and fight in the United States for what is rightfully theirs.

Perhaps he thought a separate nation, while desirable, was so far off there was no use talking about it. Perhaps he thought it was a divisive issue impeding black unity. Or perhaps he no longer thought it desirable. In any case, he stopped being a separatist at the time of his break with the Black Muslims, or soon after.

What about his position on black nationalism? Everyone called him a nationalist, friend and foe, and there was no question about it until a few weeks ago. Then he was asked, in the *Young Socialist* interview, "How do you define black nationalism, with which you have been identified?"

He began his answer by saying, "I used to define black nationalism as the idea that the black man should control the economy of his community, the politics of his community, and so forth." That is, he used to define it in the traditional way, as I tried to do a few minutes ago.

The second paragraph of Malcolm's reply, which you can read for yourselves in the *Young Socialist*, relates a discussion he had with a white Algerian revolutionary he met in Ghana last May who sought to convince Malcolm that his self-designation as a black nationalist tended to alienate people "who were true revolutionaries dedicated to overturning the system of exploitation that exists on this earth by any means necessary." His third and final paragraph was:

> So, I had to do a lot of thinking and reappraising of my definition of black nationalism. Can we sum up the solution to the problems confronting our people as black nationalism? And if you notice, I haven't been using the expression for several months. But I still would be hard pressed to give a specific definition of the overall philosophy which I think is necessary for the liberation of the black people in this country.

Please notice: He was reappraising his *definition* of black nationalism and wondering if it can be *summed up* as the solution; he had stopped using the term, but he had not yet been able to find another definition for the philosophy necessary for black liberation. Now let me offer what I think is the explanation for all this.

Malcolm had been a black nationalist—it was the starting point for all his thinking, the source of his strength and dynamism. And he remained a black nationalist to his last hour, however uncertain he was about what to *call* himself or the program he was trying to formulate. It would be a bad mistake to mix up what he was with what he thought might be a better name for what he was.

The most urgent need of the Negro people is still the mobilization and unification of the Negro masses into an independent movement to fight for their freedom. Black nationalism is still highly progressive because it contributes to that process and to the creation of that kind of movement. But black nationalism is a means, not the end; it is a means, but not the only means; it is probably an indispensable means toward the solution, but it is not the whole solution. It helps to build an independent movement, but it does not necessarily provide the program that will lead such a movement to victory.

In a series of articles in the *Militant* last year, I tried to clarify some questions about black nationalism by noting that there are at least two types of black nationalist. One is the pure-and-simple black nationalist. He is concerned exclusively or primarily with the internal problems of the Negro community, with organizing it, helping it to control the economy of the community, the politics of the community, etc. He is not so concerned with the problems of the total American society, or with the nature of the total society within which the Negro community exists. He has no theory or program for changing that society; for him that's the white man's problem.

Now Malcolm was not that kind of black nationalist, or if he was a year ago, he did not remain that. As he discussed with people in Africa, in the Near East, at the United Nations, and in the United States, as he studied and thought and learned, he began to become a black nationalist plus. Plus what? I have already given you many quotations from his speeches and interviews showing that as he studied the economy, the nature of the political and social system of American capitalism, as he developed greater and keener understanding of how this system functions and how the ruling class rules and how racism is a component and instrument of that rule, he came more and more to the conclusion that not only must the Negro control his own community, but radical changes have to be made in the society as a whole if the Negroes are to achieve their freedom.

Black nationalism, yes. But the solution cannot be *summed up* as only black nationalism. Needed is black nationalism plus fundamental social change; black nationalism plus the transformation of the entire society. Whatever difficulty Malcolm may have had in finding the right name, what he was becoming was black nationalist plus revolutionist. (The *Young Socialist* interview shows that he had great respect for that word.)

There are really only three ways in which it is possible to think of the Negro people getting freedom and equality. One way (notice I said to *think* about getting freedom) is through gradualism; peaceful reform; a little bit now and a little bit more ten years from now. Not Freedom Now, but Freedom Later, which for purposes of Negroes now alive, means Freedom Never. This is the program of Lyndon Johnson, Reuther, King, Wilkins, and Rustin. Malcolm, as we know, flatly rejected this approach.

The second way is through separation, through migration to Africa, or through obtaining part of what is now the United States. Malcolm, as I indicated, had turned away from this approach, whatever his reasons may have been for doing so.

The third way—and I repeat there are only these three ways, there are no others—is through the revolutionary reorganization of society, by basically changing the economy, political structure, laws, and educational system, and by replacing the present capitalist ruling class with a new government instituted by the forces that are opposed to racism and determined to uproot it.

From the quotations I read you before on what Malcolm was saying about capitalism and socialism and racism, it is clear that Malcolm tended to favor this third approach, or at least had his eyes turned in that direction. He wasn't sure *if* it could be done, and he wasn't sure *how* it could be done, but he was thinking about it and how it fitted into the program and activity of the Organization of Afro-American Unity.

This, I believe, correctly explains his uncertainty about what to call himself. He was a black nationalist plus, a black nationalist plus a social revolutionist, or in the process of becoming one.

Socialists should be the last to be surprised at such development. We have for some time been stressing the tendency of nationalism to grow over into and become merged with socialism; we have seen just that transformation occur in Cuba with Castro and his movement, which began as nationalist. We have argued against many opponents that the logical outcome of black nationalism in a country like ours is to reach the most advanced, most radical social and political conclusions. That is why we have advocated and predicted that black nationalists and revolutionary socialists can, should, and will find ways of working together.

Malcolm's uncertainty about the right name arises from the fact that he was doing something new—he was on the road to a synthesis of black nationalism and socialism that would be fitting for the scene and acceptable to the masses in the black ghetto. He did not complete the synthesis before he was murdered. It remains for others to complete what he was beginning.

Now he is dead, taken from us in what might been the most important and fruitful year of his life.

Let us not deceive ourselves. It was a stunning blow, as Frank Lovell said at last week's memorial of the Afro-American Broadcasting Company, a stunning blow to the Negro people and to those Americans who want to eradicate the system that breeds racism. Men like Malcolm do not appear often or in great numbers. The enemies of human progress benefit from his death. The fighters for human progress are weakened and hurt by it.

But a stunning blow to the struggle does not destroy the struggle. Malcolm will not easily be replaced. But he will be replaced. The capitalist system breeds not only racism but rebels against racism, especially among the youth. Malcolm cannot be replaced overnight, but meanwhile we all can and should strive harder, work harder, fight harder, unite more closely to try to fill the gap left by the death of this man we loved, and give help and encouragement to those destined to replace him.

NOTE

1. This interview, held on January 18, 1965, and published in the *Young Socialist* (March–April 1965), has been reprinted in *By Any Means Necessary* (New York: Pathfinder Press, 1970).

CHAPTER 6

THE NATIONAL QUESTION
AND THE
BLACK LIBERATION STRUGGLE
IN THE UNITED STATES
(1968)

George Breitman

The Bolsheviks were enabled to conquer and hold power because, among other things, they had a well-grounded view of the national question and knew how to apply it under the specific circumstances of the Russian Revolution. The great value of this asset can be properly estimated when it is remembered that no other party of the prewar social democracy, from the right wing through the center to the left-Polish tendency of Rosa Luxemburg, held a correct position in theory or practice on this crucial problem.

The Leninist teachings on the national question have become an integral part of the theory of permanent revolution in the epoch of imperialism and the transition to socialism. Owing to the extremely uneven development of world society since the bourgeois revolutions completed their progressive work, there are very few thoroughly homogeneous states under capitalist rule. Most of them contain oppressed nationalities within their borders or under their domination which yearn to throw off their bondage to an alien power and achieve self-determination as a free and independent people.

The national question, which first exhibited its irrepressible explosive force during World War I and the Russian Revolution, has since become of prime importance in the world revolutionary process. The urge of the

---

Originally published as a pamphlet (New York: Merit Publishers, 1968).

colonial and semicolonial countries in the grip of the imperialist powers to assert their claims to independence has been intensified to the maximum by the liberation struggles in Asia, Africa, the Middle East, and Latin America over the past two decades.

Lenin most clearly and fully recognized the strategical significance of this question for the revolutionary socialist movement and its vanguard, and worked out a program to deal with its manifold aspects along lines previously projected by Marx and Engels. The principal points of Leninist policy in this field may be summarized as follows:

1. Every nationality has the democratic right to self-determination.
2. Its struggle for this right is just and progressive and must be wholeheartedly supported against the power and privileges of the dominant nation.
3. The popular nationalist movement has every right to separation from the ruling nation and establishment of independent nationhood if it so chooses.
4. It retains this right even in relation to a workers' state of which it may be a part.
5. In the interests of socialism and democracy, the representatives of the revolutionary proletariat are duty-bound to be exceedingly sensitive to the feelings and demands of a hereditarily oppressed people, to accord them every possibility of developing their own capacities in their own way and under their own direction, and to lean over backward in removing any grounds for the perpetuation or revival of chauvinist or supremacist attitudes against them, so that genuine relations of equality and fraternity between the respective nations can be fostered and achieved.
6. At the same time, the Bolsheviks insisted upon the necessity for workers of different nationalities who must conduct the struggle against a centralized capitalist state to unite voluntarily in a single centralized party.

These teachings on the progressive historical significance of the struggle of oppressed nationalities and the attitude to be taken toward them, which were first validated by the victory of the Russian Revolution, have since spread throughout the world. They have found fresh confirmation in the liberation struggles of the colonial and semicolonial countries that have featured the world revolution since the end of the Second World War.

Paradoxically, these national movements have not been confined to the underdeveloped peoples of the third world. They have also sprung up within the most advanced industrialized states such as Belgium, Canada, and the United States, not to speak of the resistance of the workers' states in Eastern Europe against domination by the Kremlin. The most momentous of these movements in the capitalist lands is the liberation struggle of the more than 22 million Afro-Americans.

Although their movement for self-determination springs from the racism and disabilities they suffer under the white-supremacist monopolist regime in the United States, it has been fed and fostered by the example of the colonial revolutions, which have in turn found inspiration in the October revolution. It is immediately and consciously connected with the ongoing efforts of the peoples on the African continent to cast off foreign domination and take charge of their own affairs. In this sense, the struggle of the black masses for emancipation and equality on North American soil today is linked with the revolutions of the oppressed nationalities arising from the October revolution and the ideas of the Bolsheviks on this question, which have sunk so deeply into the minds of oppressed peoples everywhere over the past half century. We shall indicate later on how these ideas were transmitted to the American revolutionists and applied to the complex problems presented by the black liberation struggle.

*   *   *

The massive uprisings of Afro-Americans in Newark, Detroit, and scores of other cities during the summer of 1967 have focused world attention upon the black liberation struggle in the United States. What is the nature of this movement, what are its principal problems and its prospects?

Even though most of its leaders and participants do not yet think in such terms, the black revolts should be viewed within the dynamics of the unfolding socialist revolution in the United States. The strivings for equality and freedom by 22 million black people directly oppressed by the foremost capitalist power are more than justified on their own account. But the fact that this part of the population almost all belongs to the working class and is largely located in the core of the country's biggest cities, including its national capital, gives exceptional importance to its increasingly bitter and violent collisions with the American ruling class. As the uprisings certify, black people constitute the most combative and advanced section of the anti-capitalist forces within the heartland of world imperialism.

The vanguard role of the black liberation fighters in the United States is akin to the leading role of the insurgent colonial masses at this point in the progress of the world revolution. Their attacks upon the white capitalist power structure deal staggering blows to US imperialism on its home grounds, just as the resistance of the Cuban, Vietnamese, and other freedom fighters is checking its aggressive designs on the international arena. These interlocking struggles reciprocally strengthen one another as they weaken the chief imperialist adversary. This interconnection is more and more explicitly recognized by the leading spokesmen and among the ranks of both sectors of the anti-imperialist camp.

The black liberation struggle in the United States has a two-sided character. Most liberals and many pseudo-Marxists go astray by failing to understand its duality. As the drive of an oppressed racial minority bent on self-determination, freedom, and human rights, it is first of all a popular movement with a nationalist and democratic mainspring. But it is much more than that. The Afro-American struggle is not a peasant movement for agrarian reform in a backward country. It is the upheaval of superexploited workers crowded into city slums who are victims of intolerable conditions of life and labor in the richest and most advanced capitalism. They constitute the backbone of the industrial reserve army of US monopoly capitalism.

This combined character of their struggle, which is both national-democratic in its demands and proletarian-socialist in tendency, endows it with doubly explosive force. The black rebels are so many time bombs planted in the vital centers of the capitalist colossus.

The struggle for emancipation has deep historical roots in the colonial slave system of the Americas, the southern cotton kingdom, and the Civil War and Reconstruction of the nineteenth century. The last formally emancipated the black chattels but did not give them elementary bourgeois rights on an equal footing with the rest of the American nation. The nationalist feelings and features of their struggle today have antecedents in Marcus Garvey's movement during the 1920s.

The modern phases of the struggle began with the 1954 US Supreme Court decision prohibiting segregation in the public schools and the 1955 bus boycott in Montgomery, Alabama, the original capital of the Confederacy. This was the citywide mass action that launched the civil rights movement and propelled Rev. Martin Luther King into the spotlight.

In the thirteen years since then, the struggle has gone through two main stages of development. The first period, from 1954 to 1965, was on an extremely elementary level, corresponding to the inexperience and illusions of the Afro-Americans newly entering upon the path of mass struggle. The movement was centered in the South, the most retarded section of the country, rather than in the metropolitan North and West. The avowed objective was integration into white society with full civil rights, which meant elimination of the more flagrant legal and social abuses inflicted by official racism. Court and legislative challenges, backed up by nonviolent civil disobedience to put pressure on the authorities, were the principal means of action advocated and practiced by its moderate middle-class leadership (the National Association for the Advancement of Colored People, the Southern Christian Leadership Conference, the Congress of Racial Equality). Even the student youth from the southern black campuses who launched the Student Nonviolent Coordinating Committee (SNCC) in 1960 and engaged in sit-ins and other forms of direct action were partisans of this method and outlook.

The high points of this phase were the massive August 1963 outpouring at Washington, the Mississippi Freedom Summer of 1964, and the march from Selma to Montgomery in 1965. It succeeded in focusing national and international attention on the racial conflict in the United States, impelled the Kennedy and Johnson administrations to pay lip service to the complaints of the black population, and forced Congress to pass several civil rights bills. Neither these measures nor Johnson's trumpeted "war on poverty" removed or alleviated the most burning grievances; they did not end discrimination or police brutality or give jobs, adequate education, housing, and other essentials to the black community. The liberals' policy of reliance upon pressuring capitalist politicians or pleading with them was stigmatized as "tokenism" and condemned by the more militant spokesmen for the race.

The discrediting of this course and the widespread disillusionment with its meager results ushered in the second stage of the struggle. This was announced by the 1964 outburst in Harlem, followed by the explosions in Watts in 1965 and in Newark and Detroit in 1967. This increasingly aggressive phase of the black revolt has far from run its course. It is marked by growing rejection of the goal of assimilation into white capitalist society and its culture and equally vigorous assertion of the right to self-determination of Afro-Americans—a demand formulated in the slogan: black control of black communities.

Although these black power trends are nationwide, embracing South, North, and West, they are most pronounced and powerful in the northern urban ghettos. The leadership comes largely from young people who are not simply militant but revolutionary in temper and outlook. These fiery rebels scoff at pacifist principles and consciously act according to the maxim popularized by Malcolm X: Freedom by any means necessary.

The representative figures of these consecutive stages are Martin Luther King and Malcolm X. Dr. King is the American Gandhi, a middle-class leader aspiring to achieve equality for black Americans through the acquisition of civil rights by peaceful, legal, and electoral means. While they are not averse to exerting limited forms of mass pressure, he and his associates plead tearfully with the powers-that-be to heed the just claims of the black minority and redress their grievances lest they push beyond the framework of the established order.

As a recipient of the Nobel Peace Prize, King is honored by official white society as well as by many blacks. The Democratic administrations have turned to him at critical moments to restrain aroused black communities, just as he looks to them to relieve the conditions of the restless Afro-Americans. While King retains a measure of popularity and esteem among middle-class elements, his influence has steadily waned as his tactics have failed to deliver the goods. Today he has largely forfeited whatever authority he had over the discontented urban masses.

These ghetto dwellers have instinctively absorbed and acted upon many of the teachings of Malcolm X in the last and most productive year of his life. The key ideas he advanced include black leadership of black people, summarized in the slogan "black power"; self-defense; black pride and solidarity; identification with Africa and the colonial liberation struggles; intransigent opposition to the white capitalist power structure and its twin parties; opposition to all imperialist interventions against colored peoples; collaboration after their own unification with those militant whites who, following the example of John Brown, are ready to do more than talk about fighting racial injustice and social inequality.

The martyred Malcolm is the ideological guide and inspirer of the black radicals. He is the hero of the youthful rebels who are in the forefront of the liberation ranks and spearhead the street actions in the cities and the demonstrations on the campuses. His autobiography and speeches are required reading for young radicals, black and white.

Malcolm was the herald of the black nationalist ferment in the black community. This nationalism is the product of the system of racism, segregation, and discrimination which has been an integral part of American capitalist civilization from its birth and which, despite lavish promises, has not been essentially mitigated in recent decades. The growing consciousness among Afro-Americans of their status as a distinctive group with its own interests and objectives has been intensified by the independence struggles in Africa and the colonial revolution and sharpened by the glaring and growing contrast between their own conditions and those of white Americans. The ghettos serve to unite them physically, economically, psychologically, and culturally.

At the present point, black nationalism is more of a mood than an organized force. It is highly diversified in its manifestations, which range all the way from advocacy of a separate nation to searches for the special values of "negritude," from proponents of black business ownership to revolutionary disciples of the Malcolm X school and black Marxists.

There are quite a few "Marxists" in the United States and other countries who misjudge the nature of the nationalist sentiments among Afro-Americans and fail to grasp their highly progressive character and revolutionary thrust. The aspiration of 22 million blacks to decide their own destiny is in itself just and democratic. But there is more to the matter than that.

Its assertion in practice keeps bringing them into headlong conflict with US capitalist society and its state apparatus, which will not and cannot satisfy their economic, social, legal, political, and cultural demands. The irrepressible opposition of the insurgent black masses has objectively become the most upsetting and radicalizing factor in American life. This is recognized by the politicians and press when they speak of "the racial issue" as the most important and urgent in the United States today.

The other side of the dual nature of the freedom movement makes it all the more menacing to the capitalist regime. This rebellious social force, striving for equality and human rights, is at the same time an indispensable part of the working class reacting against excessive exploitation. Its black nationalism is indissolubly fused with its proletarian situation, no matter how little or how much this or that individual realizes the fact Afro-American resistance and rebelliousness willy-nilly becomes the most violent and matured expression of anticapitalist opposition within the United States.

Black nationalism is often confused with separatism, though the two are not identical. Separatism is only one facet, one trend, and as yet a minor one, in the broad and agitated stream of Afro-American nationalism. It is an ultimate option which has yet to be adopted by the black masses. Whether or not they will ever choose to exercise their right to territorial division and autonomy depends upon the further development of American history.

At the present juncture most politically conscious radical black nationalists call for "black power," interpreted as control over their own communities. Some go further. The Conference on Black Power, held at Newark immediately after the uprising there, enthusiastically adopted a resolution proposing the initiation of "a national dialogue on the desirability of partitioning the United States into two separate and independent nations, one to be a homeland for white Americans and the other to be a homeland for black Americans." As the mood of the ghetto dwellers hardens and hopes for solving their problems under the existing system dwindle, they can raise more determined cries for separatism than this mild proposal for discussion.

The ghetto uprisings, which have extended from Birmingham, the principal industrial center of the South, in 1963 to scores of cities from coast to coast in 1967, must be considered as the most aggressive manifestations of black nationalism to date. These revolts are rehearsals for further encounters that will be better prepared, on a larger scale, and not so quickly suppressed. The basic causes of the upheavals are racial segregation and injustice; rent gouging; price extortion; substandard housing in dirty slums; inferior and racist education; bad or nonexistent health and recreational facilities; lack of job opportunities and widespread unemployment, especially among the youth; and a general alienation from a society whose ideology and culture are openly or subtly racist (which explains the beginnings of radicalization even among middle-class people, intellectuals, and students who can escape the slums). In almost every instance they were touched off by acts of police harassment. The anger and frustration produced by these conditions have been inflamed by the Vietnam War, which has caused the slashing of antipoverty and welfare appropriations by the White House and Congress and the drafting of disproportionate numbers of Afro-Americans for military service.

Despite the frantic and fruitless hunt for culprits and scapegoats on the part of the authorities and witch-hunters, these actions were not planned or directed by any organization. They were spontaneously provoked by the unrestrainable rage against their misery and mistreatment seething throughout all black communities. Their anger was vented in the first place against their most obvious oppressors, the agents of "law and order," and the merchants who fleece them in their neighborhoods.

These counterattacks against the racist system and its armed defenders demonstrated a high degree of unity and solidarity in the black community. The ghetto dwellers were elated at the opportunity to strike back at their enemies and exploiters and retaliate for the countless indignities heaped upon them. One of the most noteworthy features of the actions was the leading role of the young people. Unlike their more conservative elders, these new-breed rebels have been brought up in the atmosphere of the colonial revolution, the resurgence of Africa, the awakening of the black masses, and the freedom movement that has been advancing since 1954. They are imbued with a revolutionary ardor which makes them willing to sacrifice their lives in the cause of black liberation.

These street mobilizations, which assumed forms of armed warfare in numerous places, testify to the revolutionary propulsion behind the movement which has only begun to display its creative power.

Despite its vast promise, the movement at its present stage is subjected to heavy handicaps which hold back its progress. Its activities are spasmodic, uncentralized, and localized. They need to be unified, better coordinated, and more consciously and systematically directed on a national scale. Unfortunately, the movement does not yet have any authoritative leadership with a program capable of welding militant cadres together and helping them organize the masses.

The main defect of the liberation forces is the absence of an independent black political party, no matter what its name, which could mobilize and lead the people against the two capitalist parties, both on the electoral field and in mass actions against the evils of the system they uphold and administer. Ninety-five percent of the black voters cast their ballots for Johnson in 1964, and the two black mayors first elected in the big American cities in 1967 ran as Democrats.

Most of the moderate leaders seek to keep the black people shackled to the Democratic or Republican machines. But even the most defiant black power spokesmen have yet to grasp or state the necessity for breaking completely and conclusively with capitalist politics and moving ahead to genuinely independent, all-black political organization and action. Many of them try to evade the crucial problems posed by politics on the grounds that electoral efforts are worthless or harmful diversions from more effective forms of direct action.

These apolitical opponents of an independent black party do not yet understand the great benefits such an enterprise can bring in arousing, enlightening, educating, organizing, and uniting the Afro-American masses and providing a vehicle for the idealism of militant black youth. It is, indeed, the best available way to realize the popular slogan of black power they champion.

They hesitate to advocate this proposal because, among other reasons, they envisage a new black political organization as a duplicate of the existing vote-catching machines that they rightly despise and reject. They do not see that such a party can be—and under pressure from its constituents would have to become—the leader and organizer of mass actions as well as an electoral apparatus. It would not only seek to elect its own candidates to office but could participate in every area of struggle that affected the welfare of black people: rent strikes, boycotts, fights for jobs and control of schools, and against police brutality and military interventions against their colonial brothers. It could inscribe on its banner Malcolm X's motto: "Freedom by any means necessary."

The establishment of such a party would not only add a powerful arm to the Afro-American struggle, enabling its members to speak in a single voice and make alliances on an equal basis with other oppositional forces. It could shake and break up the two-party system that has long ensured the stability of monopolist domination in the United States. Such a shattering of the established political structure would immensely accelerate the regrouping of class forces on American soil.

In the first flush of their drive toward self-determination, carried away by the surge of the urban uprisings and in justifiable revulsion against the institutions and practices of the white-supremacist system, some of the finest militants shy away from any type of political organization. They believe that it is totally incompatible with direct mass action. They hastily and uncritically transfer tactics and techniques which have proved applicable in the Chinese, Cuban, and Vietnamese liberation struggles to the far more complex circumstances of combating and defeating the ruling class in the stronghold of world capitalism. They categorically counterpose armed struggle, and more narrowly guerrilla warfare, in the cities to mass political organization as the sole indicated and effective mode of revolutionary action.

They also proceed on the mistaken assumption that electoral and parliamentary action is outmoded or has been bypassed and believe that armed struggle alone is on the agenda. They overlook the meaning of the fact that in 1967, after the uprisings, black voters turned out in great numbers to nominate and elect black mayors in Gary and Cleveland, even on Democratic tickets. In certain electoral districts the black candidates received all the votes. Moreover, they offer the black communities no alternative to the Democratic or Republican candidates in the 1968 presidential campaign.

In their exclusive preoccupation with armed struggle and associated forms of direct action, however legitimate that may be, the ultraleft militants fail to come to grips with the most pressing problem of the present hour in the struggle for emancipation. That is the barely begun task of organizing, unifying into a cohesive force, and educating the millions of blacks who must shoulder the colossal assignment of overturning white supremacy and radically transforming capitalist America. This prolonged and difficult job cannot be impatiently waved aside or skipped over by those who aspire to lead the black revolution.

The most agonizing contradiction in the present situation is the readiness of the black masses for the most vigorous actions against their oppression by the racist capitalist system and the inertia and apathy of the white workers. The deep prejudices among the white workers and the alienation between them and the black communities is the baneful heritage of four centuries of white supremacy and racism; of a consistent policy of dissension and disunity between black and white, inculcated and enforced by the possessors of power, property, and propaganda; of a cor-

rupt and conservatized union bureaucracy which shamefully discrimi-
nates against black workers; and of the materially privileged position and
general political and ideological backwardness of the more favored elements of the working class.

These adverse circumstances compel the black resistance fighters to
combat the plutocracy single-handed without support, and even with a certain measure of hostility, from the main body of the working class. Common
action between the black masses and the white workers is indispensable for
any successful long-term effort to abolish American capitalism. But that
requires prior organization of the black masses on the one hand and a resurgence of labor militancy on the other. Neither of these prerequisites for
cooperation against their joint exploiters has yet come into existence.

This is not surprising or unprecedented. The various forces called
upon to make a social revolution rarely move onto the field of battle all at
once, or at an even rate. In the United States today the blacks are far out
in front while the white workers lag very far in the rear. This irregular
development of the anticapitalist struggle creates excruciating problems
for both black and white revolutionists.

Their difficulties are great. But they are more than matched by the
perplexing problems facing the monopolist rulers of the United States in
dealing with the black liberation movement. For a decade the deluded
decision makers at Washington thought they could dispose of the
demands of black people by big promises and small concessions. This has
not worked and the moderate leaders they counted on to hold the insur-
gency in check have been used up. The revolts in the cities multiply, grow
in intensity and ferocity, and become ever harder to bring under control.
What are the rulers of America to do in so serious a social crisis?

Although their previous policy is manifestly bankrupt, they have still
to elaborate and adopt a different line of policy to handle the new situation. They have not shrunk from using police, state troops, and federal
paratroopers to put down the uprisings with savage vindictiveness. At the
same time neither Congress nor the president is able or willing to take the
steps required to wipe out the injustices that provoked the uprisings.

The high and mighty possessors of power are obviously uncertain how
to proceed. They are caught in a tortuous dilemma. They need social peace
and stability at home to pursue their imperialist adventures abroad unim-
peded and to present an attractive image to the rest of "the free world." Yet

they have been no more successful in pacifying the Afro-Americans than they have in breaking the will of the Vietnamese to be free.

They can either continue the course of conciliation and concessions interspersed with punitive measures, which has proved ineffective over the past decade, or embark upon outright repression. Neither alternative is satisfactory or workable. If the richest capitalist country on earth could not remove or even alleviate the grievances of 22 million Afro-Americans during six years of the biggest boom in its history, can it muster the means to do so under less propitious economic circumstances in the years ahead?

There remain the "extreme solutions" of apartheid on the South African model or genocide. Many Afro-Americans anticipate and dread this eventuality, which spurs them to fight all the more uncompromisingly for their rights and lives. The imperialists who dropped atom bombs on Japan, and napalm and antipersonnel bombs on women and children in Vietnam, are fully capable of the worst atrocities. But for the time being they are restrained from resorting to the most extreme measures by powerful considerations of international diplomacy and public opinion and by fear of dangerous domestic consequences.

It would be risky and costly to try and crush the determined resistance to such a Hitlerite course that is bound to be put up by the millions of blacks concentrated in the major population centers of the country. Such a cruel and bloody racial and civil war would entail the abolition of democracy and the attempted damping of some form of military dictatorship on the whole American nation. A counterrevolutionary move along such lines would arouse resistance from other sections of the people and have incalculable consequences.

No matter from what angle it is approached, the confrontation between the black insurgents and the white-supremacist capitalist regime is fraught with immense revolutionary perspectives.

In an article published in on the fiftieth anniversary of the October revolution, President Ho Chi Minh stated that "complete victory can be won by the national liberation revolution only when it develops into socialist revolution." This theorem of the permanent revolution applies with full force to the black liberation struggle in the United States because of the proletarian composition of the black population, their economic role under monopoly capitalism, and the impact of the lessons absorbed from the colonial revolutions.

Up to now the movement has unfolded along nationalist-democratic lines. But, like the Chinese, Cuban, Vietnamese, and similar revolutions, it has an inherent and irresistible tendency to break through the narrow confines of pure and simple nationalism and acquire a more and more pronounced anticapitalist and anti-imperialist cutting edge. The fundamental problems of jobs, housing, education, and foreign policy confronting the movement are social, economic, and political in character and require a transformation of class relations for their solution.

This logic of revolutionary and progressive nationalism in the imperialist era has already manifested itself in the black liberation movement. Its most advanced leaders and conscious fighters have begun to embrace the internationalist spirit and class-struggle concepts of Marxian socialism. Malcolm X was the great pioneer who initiated a process of evolution from black nationalism toward socialism and internationalism. His ideas have been taken up since his death and carried forward by certain SNCC and CORE leaders, among others. The speeches of Stokely Carmichael at the OLAS [Organization of Latin American States] Conference at Havana and his subsequent tour of the capitals of the third world betoken a rapprochement between the adherents of the most combative black nationalism and the positions of revolutionary socialism. This alignment is bound to become closer as the struggle against "Uncle Sham" intensifies on all fronts.

The Socialist Workers Party was the first radical tendency in the United States to recognize the full import of the black liberation movement and the revolutionary implications of black nationalism. It has been among their sturdiest and most consistent, though not uncritical, supporters at all stages of their development. This was acknowledged by Malcolm X and evidenced in his friendly attitude toward the Socialist Workers Party, which has been most instrumental in popularizing his views. The Socialist Workers Party seeks to reinforce collaboration on all levels between black militants and revolutionary socialists in order to further the aims of the black liberation struggle and prepare the vanguards of both the black masses and white workers for united action, in combat to the end, against the racist profiteers.

The Socialist Workers Party has derived its understanding and orientation on this key problem of the American revolution from the teachings of Lenin and Trotsky. In the ideologically primitive period before World

War I and the Russian Revolution, even those American socialists who had shaken off racial prejudice did not recognize the special place and great importance of the doubly exploited black people in the revolutionary process. They submerged the distinctive claims of the blacks in a single undifferentiated struggle of the working class as a whole against the capitalist system.

The thinking of the pioneer American Communists on this matter was profoundly transformed when they learned about the Leninist ideas on the revolutionary-democratic dynamism of the national question and the Bolshevik strategy for liberation of the oppressed nationalities. Their understanding was enhanced as they later assimilated the theory of the permanent revolution.

During his last exile, from 1929 to 1940, Trotsky, the creator of that theory, transmitted to his American followers a deeper understanding of the progressive nature of the black struggle for self-determination. His program called for its unconditional support from all genuine revolutionists. He perspicaciously forecast that black Americans, as the most dynamic segment of the working class and the most capable of revolutionary courage and sacrifice, were destined to become its vanguard.

This method of approach has guided the subsequent major resolutions of the Socialist Workers Party which have analyzed the dominant features of the successive stages of the struggle from 1939 to 1967. The publications containing their conclusions have had a broad circulation and considerable influence upon black and white radicals over the past decade.

The 1967 uprisings were a milestone in the black liberation struggle. They unmistakably marked its transition from reformism to revolutionism, from petitioning, praying, and relying upon the promises of glib capitalist politicians to the most aggressive and advanced forms of direct action. There will be no turning back along this road.

The black liberation struggle in America has likewise become a component part of the world revolution and is bound to become an ever-more-powerful factor in its development because of its presence in the entrails of the imperialist monster. It acts as a mighty and unmanageable force, upsetting the equilibrium of monopoly capitalism, challenging its domination at home, and setting examples which can prod other oppositional elements of American society into action.

What are its prospects of victory? Liberals and skeptics of all varieties insistently point out that the minority status of the Afro-Americans, who compose only one-ninth of the population, dooms to defeat any far-reaching revolutionary objectives. The odds against them are overwhelming, they say.

These faint hearts overlook a number of considerations. First of all, the 22 million blacks are a unique minority. They compose the largest, most compact and influential sector of the urban population. They are already more than half the residents of the national capital and by 1970 ten of the biggest northern cities are expected to have black majorities. They are not only rooted in the heart of the metropolitan centers but also in the basic industries, transportation, and the service trades.

In the second place, they have powerful allies abroad in the colonial lands, the workers' states, and among progressive-minded people the world over, who sympathize with their strivings for equality and emancipation. They also have domestic supporters among the rebel youth. Finally, their isolation on the home front can be overcome once a sizable segment of white workers shakes off its lethargy and moves in an anticapitalist direction.

The Afro-American resisters have embarked upon the most formidable revolutionary undertaking of our time: a mortal contest with the world's strongest capitalist regime in its own citadel. That victory will not come easily or immediately. A costly, bloody, and prolonged conflict, which will hold many surprising twists and turns, looms ahead. The American Marxists are committed to do all in their power to aid and speed that victory as an inseparable part of the socialist revolution in their country.

II

SOCIALISM

CHAPTER 7

GEORGE BREITMAN AND THE MARXIST METHOD

Steve Bloom

I remember a conversation I had once with George Breitman. I wanted to consult him about an article and said that I would particularly value his critical comments because I knew he was a student of Marxist philosophy. Breitman replied that he wasn't a student of Marxist philosophy. In fact, he did not think he understood abstract philosophical questions very well at all.

This surprised me because Breitman's own writings and speeches meticulously adhered to the Marxist method of thought known as "historical materialism." But his comment brings home an important point: the best way to understand Marxism is not through abstract philosophical writings, but to look at how Marxists actually write about both contemporary situations and history. Clearly Breitman absorbed what he needed to know through reading and listening to individuals like Leon Trotsky, Jim Cannon, and others. Readers of this book should prepare themselves to receive a similar education.

Steve Bloom, who first joined the Trotsykist movement in 1968, has served as National Administrative Secretary of the Fourth International Tendency and as managing editor of the *Bulletin in Defense of Marxism*. His writing has appeared in the *Militant*, the *International Socialist Review*, and *Against the Current*, as well as in many other publications.

SOME ESSENTIALS
OF THE MARXIST METHOD

Breitman develops several essential elements of a Marxist method.

First, he never treats social or political phenomena as static, frozen in a moment of time. He always asks: Where did this come from? How is it evolving? There can be no understanding of the present without also understanding this process by which things come into being and pass into the future.

Second, social phenomena have roots both in the material conditions of society and in the ideas and actions of human beings. The material conditions create the context within which human beings act. They limit the potentials for effective action. But human action can be, and often is, decisive in shaping the course history actually takes. (This is a central theme of "The Rocky Road to the Fourth International.")

Third, every social phenomenon, and even every individual human being, is a complex of contradictory elements and tendencies, pulling in different directions. It is inadequate to merely appreciate the sum of these different elements, the surface appearance that the casual observer will see. Real understanding requires us to take the thing apart and understand it in terms of its component parts—at the same time as we appreciate the dynamic interactions between those parts that create the whole. If we do this, opportunities for action can sometimes be found by focusing on specific elements.

Also in this context, genuine Marxists reject the common idea that there are all-knowing leaders who should be followed without question. Leaders are human beings, which means they are fallible. Good revolutionary leaders have the ability to educate and explain things in a way that will help others to understand, and thereby act through conviction rather than through blind faith. They likewise learn new things themselves, through interactions with the world, with other leaders, and with rank-and-file activists.

There is also no such thing as a party that never makes mistakes. What revolutionaries need is a party that can recognize mistakes when they happen and, through a process of discussion and debate, figure out how to correct mistakes before serious or irreparable damage is done.

Lessons that revolutionaries learn for themselves in this way, through struggling with the world and with each other, will be understood much more profoundly than lessons absorbed passively, through reading history or listening to theoretical lectures—important as historical and theoretical study may be.

Fourth, all contemporary events will be both similar to and different from events that have occurred historically. Stressing either the similarities or the differences, without taking the other into account, will inevitably lead to a false appreciation of what is happening.

Fifth, the difference between words and actions is crucial. All individuals and organizations should be measured *primarily* by their actions when words say one thing and actions tell us something else.

Sixth, Marxists base their opinions on facts—verifiable through historical and contemporary records. Breitman, in writings here and elsewhere, tells us more than once how he came to new conclusions as the result of reading documents he hadn't seen before.

Seventh, Breitman offers readers one of the best short explanations of what we call "the transitional method" that I have ever read. This is a key to understanding the entire programmatic framework of revolutionary Marxism (here contrasted to a more sectarian kind of practice):

> It seems to be the difference between the approach of narrow propagandism and the approach of revolutionary activism. In the first case you write an article explaining "the Marxian principles on war" and hand it out to those who are interested in such matters; you won't affect many people that way, but you have done your duty and presumably can sleep well. In the second case you intervene in the class struggle, helping to set masses into motion against the ruling class or to provide bridges for those in motion from the elementary, one-sided, and illusory conceptions they start out with toward better, more realistic, and more revolutionary concepts about capitalism and war and how to fight them.

Breitman's talk on "The Liberating Influence of the Transitional Program," from which this passage is taken, develops that idea considerably.

Finally, even three pieces that seem rather simple and straightforward, "The Trenton Siege by the Army of Unoccupation," "Wartime Crimes of Big Business," and "Should Progressives Work in the Democratic Party?" offer an underlying dialectical theme: the difference between the form of seemingly "democratic" institutions (legislatures and political parties) and the reality of these institutions as masks behind which the ruling class takes care of business for itself.

POLITICAL CONTEXT

Something should be said about the political context of the 1930s and 1940s—the period covered in much of the material reprinted in this section. Breitman asserts that these years were part of "the most eventful four decades in revolutionary history" (see "The Liberating Influence of the Transitional Program: Three Talks" in this volume), which strikes me as somewhat startling, yet indisputably true. And this truth helps explain why it remains essential, even today, to study the experience of working-class struggle and bureaucratic betrayal during these years, seeking to learn its lessons.

The Trotskyist movement arose in reaction to the consolidation of Stalinist rule in the Soviet Union during the 1920s. Despite myths to the contrary, the Russian Revolution of 1917 was at first a gigantic experiment in democracy. Power in the former tsarist empire was transferred to mass assemblies of workers' and soldiers' delegates—called soviets. Delegates to these assemblies were easily recalled if they did not properly represent their constituents. Within these soviets only Lenin's Bolshevik Party was willing to both call for, and fight for, Soviet power. That is why, in the period leading up to the October revolution, the Bolsheviks gained an overwhelming majority.

After the insurrection, the Bolsheviks attempted to maintain a genuine coalition with other Soviet parties. But with the outbreak of civil war less than a year later, two developments made a multiparty, democratic Soviet government impossible to consolidate. First, with so much energy and attention directed toward defending the revolution militarily, the soviets lost their character as mass democratic institutions. The Soviet experiment became increasingly dependent on the Bolsheviks *as a party apparatus,* rather than as the genuinely elected representative of rank-and-file workers, soldiers, and peasants. Second, most of the non-Bolshevik elements that had been active in the soviets began collaborating with the counterrevolution.

This period had three other effects on the new Soviet Republic that enabled Stalin to consolidate his dictatorial rule. The most revolutionary working-class elements, both within the Bolshevik Party and within the mass movement, rushed to the front lines in the civil war. Consequently, they were absent from political battles for a crucial period and were killed in disproportionate numbers by the White armies. Also, the Bolsheviks, as the ruling party, began to attract more opportunistic elements into its ranks. Because the new government was desperate for experienced administrators, many of these individuals quickly gained positions of authority. Finally, the civil war destroyed even the minimal economic infrastructure that the new Soviet government had inherited from the tsarist regime. Life in the USSR became a daily struggle for mere survival. Many people starved. Under these circumstances there was tremendous pressure, even on honest revolutionary elements, to use positions of authority to guarantee that at least they and their families would have something to eat. And thus a significant number of Bolshevik administrators were gradually transformed into Bolshevik bureaucrats. It was this bureaucratic layer—both old Bolsheviks who had lost their revolutionary spirit and new Bolsheviks who had joined the party for opportunistic reasons—that provided the power base for Stalin's rise.

Even with this support, however, Stalin had to engage in massive repression to break the revolutionary spirit among the masses and of those old Bolsheviks who did not succumb to the inducements of bureaucratic life. This accounts for the massive expansion of internal police security measures and the creation of the Russian Gulag—where literally millions of honest fighters were killed.

There was, likewise, a massive purge of the old guard of the Bolshevik Party. The entire central committee of the party that made the revolution was murdered by Stalin, with the exception of Stalin himself and Lenin, who died from a stroke (precipitated by a failed assassination attempt). Breitman refers to two important events that were part of this process: the murder of Trotsky, in exile in Mexico, by a hired Stalinist assassin in 1940, and the infamous "Moscow Trials" that began in 1936. During these proceedings, many revolutionary leaders "confessed" to the fantastic frame-up charge that they had become spies and saboteurs in the pay of the imperialist powers.

Of course, none of these Stalinist crimes were openly carried out in the name of consolidating a counterrevolutionary bureaucratic dictatorship. The world was told that this was the continuation of Leninism, of Bolshevism, and of proletarian revolution. And because most of the world did not know any better, that was generally believed to be true. Stalin was looked to by many honest activists for leadership during these years, and he took full advantage of that fact. He knew that a genuine working-class revolutionary upsurge in Europe would doom his regime because it would inspire the workers of the Soviet Union to reassert their democratic control over the Soviet government. At the same time, Stalin and his bureaucratic followers had a stake in the maintenance of the Soviet economic system, which was the source of the wealth they were exploiting for their own personal enrichment.

The result was a foreign policy that thwarted revolution in Europe while hiding behind a smokescreen of revolutionary verbiage, which fooled many. The goal was simply to maintain the USSR with its bureaucratic regime intact. During the late 1920s and early 1930s Stalin declared that the world was ripe for revolution everywhere and that communist parties should be engaged in sustained insurrectionary politics. All other working-class parties were declared objective agents of imperialism—what the Stalinists called "social fascists." There was, supposedly, no real difference between fascism and bourgeois democracy. "Revolutionary" politics was thus reduced to a caricatured, full-scale political war between capitalism and communism, with no mediating factors.

This policy, known as "Third Period Communism," resulted in a series of ultraleft misadventures by communist parties around the world. And it was directly responsible for the victory of fascism in Germany—when the Communist Party (CP) refused to join the Socialist Party (SP) in a united front to combat the rise of Hitler to power. Between them, the German CP and SP organized a majority of the German working class and could have stopped fascism in its tracks had they combined forces. But the policies of the Stalinists kept the German workers divided and permitted the Nazis to take power without a struggle.

Eventually, the rising fascist threat in Europe, created in part by the very policies Stalin was following, began to pose its own dangers to the Soviet Union. Stalin then made a sharp turn. No longer were fascism and bourgeois democracy evil twins. Now the task of the workers was to defend bourgeois democracy, in alliance with the "peace-loving" and "democratic" pro-capitalist forces. Once again, however, the idea of genuine working-class revolution was nowhere to be found.

The classic disaster of this "popular front" period was the civil war in Spain. Here the masses rose up in an insurrectionary struggle. But the Communist Party refused to help lead the workers to take power and create a socialist government. Instead the Stalinists insisted that the goal must be restricted to a "popular front," which would defend capitalist property relations so as not to alienate "democratic" allies. Trotsky warned that Spanish capitalists and the "capitalist democracies" (Britain, France, and the United States) would prefer a fascist victory (aided by Mussolini and Hitler) over a republic based on even a hobbled working-class radicalism. This proved true, and despite a heroic struggle by revolutionary elements in the civil war, the Spanish republic was defeated.

This cycle—revolutionary upsurge, the failure of that upsurge to result in a genuine victory for socialism, and the reconsolidation of capitalist rule (often in its most repressive, fascist form) as a result—was repeated in country after country in Europe and elsewhere during the 1920s and 1930s. Trotsky concluded that the central problem of the human race could be boiled down to a "crisis of revolutionary leadership." The thought was simple, and to anyone versed in revolutionary socialist theory, unassailable: the masses were demonstrating, periodically and repeatedly, that they were ready to make a socialist revolution. They were blocked time after time because their leaders—either Stalinists or social democrats—had a different political agenda. What was needed was the recreation of the missing element: genuinely revolutionary parties that could rally the masses in opposition to both Stalinism and social democracy.

And yet, faced with the overwhelming material advantages that the Soviet government had at its disposal—both to distort Bolshevik teachings to the advantage of the Stalinists and to vilify and even murder genuine revolutionaries—the Trotskyist movement never managed to consolidate more than a relative handful of dedicated activists during this period. This is the political backdrop for much of the historical discussion presented here by George Breitman.

Finally, let us look briefly at one event, within the Trotskyist movement itself, that is referred to a number of times in the following pages. One of Trotsky's political conclusions was to call for a defense of the historic gains of the October revolution (the planned Soviet economy) while steadfastly opposing the Stalinist dictatorship. In a war between the Soviet Union and imperialism, the Trotskyist movement was pledged to fight for the victory of the USSR, despite the bureaucracy, just as workers should fight to defend a bureaucratized trade union under attack by the bosses.

As the United States began to prepare for its entry into World War II, a group arose in the Socialist Workers Party, the US wing of the international Trotskyist movement, that began to question Trotsky's viewpoint on this question. There is no room here for a description or assessment of the factional struggle that developed as a result. But the reader should be aware that a split occurred in 1940, with the opposition—led politically by James Burnham and Max Shachtman—breaking away to form a new political organization called the Workers Party.

This split was extremely deep and bitter on both sides. Trotsky and the SWP asserted that it was a split between the proletarian revolutionary elements, who had remained in the SWP, and the party's former "petty-bourgeois" wing. That assessment remained unchanged in the party during subsequent years and constitutes a basic assumption that Breitman merely mentions in the talks and articles in this section.

It is one of the minor ironies of history that I—still a firm (if critical) believer in the revolutionary tradition of Leon Trotsky, James P. Cannon, the SWP of George Breitman, and the Fourth International—find myself, as this essay is written, outside of the SWP, which has degenerated considerably from the group that once defended that tradition, and in a relatively new revolutionary socialist organization called Solidarity, founded in 1986 through a fusion of forces, including some who continue to identify with the historical tradition of Max Shachtman and the Workers Party. Once again I do not have the space here for an extensive discussion of how various political groups evolved to the point where such a unification became possible. I cite the fact only so that readers will, once again, be conscious of the dialectic through which politics and history unfold in ways that constantly surprise and confound the expectations of revolutionaries.

CHAPTER 8

THE TRENTON SIEGE BY THE ARMY OF UNOCCUPATION (1936)

George Breitman

INTRODUCTION

A number of weeks ago a committee of the Workers Alliance of Essex County, New Jersey, called at a relief station in Newark and straightened out a case that had come up the day before, and then, while they were waiting for a clerk to attend to a food order they had succeeded in winning for a widow and two children, they listened to the words of the supervisor of the station. One remark she made struck them rather forcibly, raising, as it did, a thought they had never taken into consideration: "You'd be surprised," she said, "to learn how many people, people with education and intelligence and means, are altogether ignorant of the true state of affairs of the relief problem. The vast majority of those with whom I talk think that all you have to do is go out and get a job—just like that. It takes something like the siege you put on down there in Trenton, something like that mock session, to shake them out of their smugness and complacency."

The Trenton Siege by the Army of Unoccupation was first published in 1936 by the Workers Alliance. It was reprinted after fifty years by the Fourth Internationalist Tendency (FIT), the group that Breitman helped found after his 1984 expulsion from the SWP. This reprint of his Depression-era pamphlet was published shortly after his death and is being presented here with the original 1936 introduction.

This is true. The chief function the Army of Unoccupation fulfilled at Trenton was an educational one. It brought before the eyes of the general public of the state and the nation, of the middleman, taxpayer and citizen, in such dramatic form and in such sharp relief that they could not be ignored, the true conditions of the unemployed and relief clients of the state; it made clear to them that the unemployed workers of the state were not as well off and not as well taken care of as they had been led to fondly imagine by certain politicians, moneyed interests, and newspapers; and it drove home to them the sobering conclusion that the unemployed, if trifled with too long and too often, if compelled to undergo added hunger and suffering, if neglected and kicked about still further, were a force to be considered seriously and dealt with carefully, were a force that would not forever remain silent and inactive, would not forever continue to turn the other cheek.

But infinitely more important than even this was the effect that it made and was bound to make on the unemployed workers themselves. It taught them a lesson of immeasurable value, and it drew for them in bold and striking colors a picture that will not soon be forgotten. First, it exposed definitely and finally the true nature of the old party "statesmen" whom the workers had elected to sit in the Trenton State House to legislate for them, revealing them as calloused and hardened politicians who showed interest in the relief situation only insofar as it affected their personal political careers, their pocketbooks, and the financial groups whose interests really concerned them. No unemployed or employed worker who had followed the events with any attention could fail to understand now that the capitalist parties and the capitalist politicians, like the system that breeds them, have nothing to offer them but added misery, exploitation, and suffering; no worker could suffer any longer under the illusion that he could gain anything from these cynical, brutally indifferent representatives of finance capital, these stupid, selfish tools of the ruling class, who played and still play with human lives, human souls, human values, as your baby might play, let us say, with a kitten, except that they do it deliberately, consciously; no worker could expect, after this, anything from them save what could be wrested from them by hard, militant, well-organized struggle; and no worker could believe, after witnessing the very revealing sight of the two parties on the surface, bitterly antagonistic to each other, in reality, sharing not one fundamental difference in policy or principle uniting to wage a common fight against the unemployed, that he could gain anything for himself and his class except by uniting with his natural economic allies into an organization that would unitedly fight their battles.

And the second and the chief lesson of the Trenton siege, in connection with this last point, is not that it pointed merely the general direction the unemployed must follow, but that it left the advanced sections of the unemployed no alternative than to organize, and it left them no other organization they could enter, if they were effectively to fight to maintain the low and miserable standard of living they now "enjoyed," let alone if they were to raise that standard, than the Workers Alliance of America.

The Workers Alliance is a nationwide, nonpartisan organization of unemployed and relief workers, dedicated to winning for the workers of the city and soil adequate cash relief, unemployment insurance at the expense of the government and employers, jobs for all the unemployed at union wages, and "the establishment of a new social order in which planned production according to need will replace the present chaotic system of production for profit, a social system which will provide security, justice, happiness, and plenty for all" (*Declaration of Principles*). It is open to all workers "regardless of race, creed, color, sex, nationality, or political belief" who are willing to abide by its principles and rules. In its few short years of existence it has already ably demonstrated its strength, its potential influence, and its material value to both the organized and unorganized unemployed of the country. It has waged an aggressive war against all attempts of the administration to slash to the bone the few crumbs of relief that were being given out. It has in a good many states forced the WPA administration to raise wages, to reduce hours, to pay union wages, to cease discrimination against organized workers. It has, just a few months ago, feeling the need for unity of the unemployed, united with other national, state, and local unemployed organizations, building a stronger front against the common enemy on a common program, bringing together to lead the unemployed the best, the most experienced, and the most determined men in the American labor movement. And, to come closer to home, it was the Workers Alliance of New Jersey that led the unemployed in their siege of the State House, and their fight since then to return the relief administration to state and federal control.

The conclusion you must reach, I repeat to the unemployed and WPA

workers, is inescapable: With the state of affairs every day growing darker
as the two old parties play football as a coming attraction to the elections,
with us as the football; with the belts about the bellies of the unemployed
every day being drawn tighter as the administration "experiments" on us
to determine just how little can be spent on us and yet keep us half alive;
with the need for a stronger and larger organization to fight back becoming
every day more apparent; in your own interests, in the interests of your
family and your class, you must join the Workers Alliance, build it, and
fight our battles with it and through it! Building the Workers Alliance
means fighting for bread, clothing, and shelter for your children!

And it is to help to build it by telling the true story of the Trenton
siege, the circumstances surrounding it, leading up to it, and resulting
from it, the victories we gained and the mistakes we made, that this little
pamphlet has been written. Its style is simple and appealing to workers, it
is brief, it is informative, it has been issued at the cheapest price possible,
and it must he gotten into the hands of every unemployed and WPA
worker in the country. By seeing to it that it receives wide distribution, we
are seeing to it that the Workers Alliance is built. Writing it and printing
it were acts calculated to build the Workers Alliance. Circulating it among
as many people as possible, therefore, becomes the duty of every member
of the Workers Alliance.

John Spain Jr.
Trenton, New Jersey, July 5, 1936

RELIEF: HOOVER'S TO ROOSEVELT'S AND BACK AGAIN

The beginning of the depression is usually set at the end of October 1929.
It didn't, of course, affect the average worker at once, and it wasn't until
1930 and 1931 that the total of unemployed began to rise into truly staggering numbers. The various municipal governments had charge of the
relief problem, and we can all remember how they managed it. Who,
indeed, can forget the breadlines that decorated the country, the stories of
men and women begging to be arrested so that they could have food (of
a sort) and shelter, the pompous declarations of the politicians that the

depression was a temporary thing, and that in no time "prosperity" would be back, and therefore it would be a mistake to "pamper" the unemployed, to "rob" them of their initiative as the dole had "robbed" the English workers of theirs, to break down that good old 100 percent American individualism that bosses like to see their workers imbued with, and thus "delay" the return of "good times"?

Well, in short enough time, about the end of 1931, the municipalities came out with the not so surprising statement that they couldn't carry the relief burden any longer, that they would require federal aid or they would be faced with bankruptcy and the unemployed with complete starvation. Then it was, when there was no other way out, that the government took over relief.

A few years more passed, and it was 1936. Roosevelt, who was going to take care of the "forgotten man," had succeeded in taking care of the big business man, had succeeded in stabilizing business without making any similar success in solving the unemployment problem; even his own New Deal statisticians had to admit recently that if business were restored to its 1929, predepression production level, there would still remain 20 percent of the employable workers for whom employment could not be found, that is, the advances in industrial efficiency since 1920 would still leave between eight and ten million workers capable of working who would never be able to get a job again under the present system. The poor unemployed worker was still out in the cold, still "forgotten."

That, however, didn't make a particle of difference to the bankers, the corporations, and the other heavy financial interests (of both the Democratic and Republican Parties), and they began to howl to the moon that the administration was sending the country to the dogs by spending "so much money" on "chiselers." . . . And what does Roosevelt, the "people's friend" do now? What does he want to do? It's an election year, and he wants to get elected. He can't antagonize the small businessman, he knows, or he's done for—and he isn't in the White House for his health, you know. It isn't long before the order goes out to cut out federal relief, turn it back to the states, and if they can't manage it, or if they don't want to manage it, let them turn it back to the municipalities: the treasury can't stand it, the rich are complaining too much, and so on. Yes, that's how he solves the relief problem—by shoving it off on the municipalities which have admitted they can't handle it, and, to make things still worse for them, by giving orders to fire 700,000 WPA workers by July 1. Everyone's satisfied, he mutters, and now we can get back to the business of preparing for the next war by spending more on armament this year than in any since the last war. Everyone's satisfied now, of course, everyone but the unemployed. But the unemployed—what the hell, they don't count, they won't protest, why, they're so worn out and tired and weary and undernourished from the diet they've "enjoyed" under the ERA [Emergency Relief Act] that they haven't even got the energy to say boo. Why, most of them haven't even got the energy to go to the polls and vote, so to hell with 'em.

NEW JERSEY RELIEF BEFORE THE SIEGE

New Jersey is like most other states. Some large cities with some important industries, some small towns, some farms, a fairly thickly populated state for its size. At the beginning of April 1936, there were about 270,000 on the relief rolls (116,000 of whom were children under the age of sixteen) and about 90,000 others working on the WPA. The standard of relief was no better and no worse, and the relief administration no more heartless, than in any other state in that part of the union. You could walk into the Trenton State House and look over the gentleman of the Senate and the Assembly, and you would find them pretty much the same bunch of shysters, tricksters, disgusting clowns, cheap demagogues, hypocritical careerists, small-town politicians, "socially minded" old maids, loud-mouthed windbags, pretentious ignoramuses interspersed with the few very puzzled, vacillating liberals that you would find in any state; the kind of men who never pass a law in the interests of the working class when they can slip out of it, who slip out of it whenever mass pressure isn't applied on them, and on whom mass pressure is never applied sufficiently. The unemployed of the state are no more shiftless and no more lazy than any other workers, and the vast majority of them, as in other states, have spent most of their lives working, piling up the millions for the rich, building, creating, making this country the wealthiest in the world, and would still be doing it, no doubt, if they could only find employment. . . .

The middle of March found the state without any more money appropriated for relief. The gentlemen of the legislature sat in their seats, played at the game of being very busy, and, as far as settling the question of relief funds went, did . . . nothing.

The Workers Alliance of New Jersey, knowing well that this could go on forever, applied the pressure. Led by Ray Cooke, at that time state chairman of the Alliance, a large number of unemployed, after protest demonstrations, filled the building and forced the gentlemen of the Assembly to grant Cooke the floor. Straight from the shoulder, he spoke, mincing no words, presenting the situation as it was in all its dire aspects, and demanding that they take immediate action on it. The Assembly came across, a couple of million dollars was diverted from the state highway funds, and there was now enough money to tide things over until the middle of April.

The money went fast enough, and the state was faced with the same situation on April 15. Again the gentlemen refused to act, again they dawdled around, again they began to pass laws affecting hunting and fishing regulations, making it illegal to shoot certain game in certain seasons or catch so many fish in certain streams, again, by ignoring the needs of the starving citizens who had elected them, they demonstrated that they were more interested in the welfare of fish than children. You see, this time they didn't want to do anything—either appropriate or refuse to appropriate money—because primary elections were little more than a month away, on May 19, and they wanted to let things slide until then so no one could accuse them of having given too much or having refused to give any relief to the unemployed. (That's one characteristic of the politician under this system, whether he sits in a small Council chamber or a State House hall or the White House: Offend no one, but if you must offend someone, make sure it's not the rich man, the boss, or the banker.) As a rule, a gentleman of the Assembly will almost slobber a reporter to death if he can get his name into the papers, and he'll give his right arm to a photographer who snaps his picture and spells his name correctly—but there was nothing the New Jersey Assembly would have liked better, as far as the relief situation went, than being completely disregarded by the entire state, than being totally buried in silence. They weren't seeking a method of providing funds to feed the starving; they were seeking a method of being reelected. And the best way to do that, they figured, was to lay low and keep on doing what they had been doing . . . nothing. So they brought up a luxury tax bill (that would provide about $6,000,000, that is, one-sixth as much as was needed) and they debated over it very loudly and made it look very important and they all frowned very seriously as they talked about it and then they let it go to the Senate and the Senate defeated it, and they adjourned for five days and went home to "rest up." Oh, they sat back and prayed, if only we can keep on doing this until after May 19!

It was a vain hope. Only a gentlemen of the Assembly could be stupid enough to imagine, while he and his colleagues wrangled playfully over trivial points such as the size of a fox trap, while men and women whose stomachs felt actual pangs of hunger were undergoing further torture having to listen to their babies' pitiful cries for milk, while the State Relief Council reported that it had left only $500,000, enough only to last until the following Monday, that the unemployed would just forget all about the question of relief until such a time as the legislature reminded them about it! Only a gentleman of the Assembly could be stupid enough to imagine that in such a situation not only the unorganized but the organized unemployed as well would be content to remain silent and meek while their landlords tried to evict them from the holes they called homes for nonpayment of rent by the government! But it is hard to realize that even a gentleman of the Assembly could have been stupid enough to hope that after the unemployed organizations had united they would not be twice and three times as militant as formerly![1]

THE WORKERS ALLIANCE
SEIZES THE STATE HOUSE

On April 20, a Monday, the legislature reconvened. By this time affairs were in a serious condition. In one community there were unemployed who had received no relief since the first of the month, and the overseer of the poor had nothing to feed them but apples. Municipal officers of Mercer County had met, declared relief was a state problem, and called on Governor Hoffman to appropriate funds to carry things along until the legislature acted. The honorable governor answered that all action was up to the legislature and did (what the legislature was doing) nothing.

The *New York Times* carried a report revealing that many of the communities intended to profit from the misery of the unemployed by forcing them to work for their crumbs, thus forcing the wages of labor down: "In North Plainfield, as in several other communities, plans were made to care for the needy on a 'no work no eat' basis. Funds for relief would be made available, but in return for it the recipients would be expected to work in parks, on the roads, and on other public projects." The mayor of South Hackensack, after being refused help by the American Red Cross, wired for federal aid to Roosevelt, announcing that in the town there were 113 on relief, $350 to care for them, and no credit to be obtained from the merchants.

What happened in the legislature this time? David Lasser, national chairman of the Workers Alliance, addressed the Assembly and warned them that they were sitting on a volcano. Governor Hoffman, too, addressed the legislature and explained that the people of the state were sick and tired of their actions. Members of the Workers Alliance picketed the State House, carrying signs calling for immediate appropriations. The gentlemen of the Senate showed what they thought of all this by defeating again—not merely once, but twice in the same evening—the luxury tax bill, once before the honorable governor spoke and once after.

The next day the gentlemen of the Assembly met late in the morning and during its three or four hours of session didn't discuss the relief problem for even a minute, although Ray Cooke did bring it to their attention in a short talk during which he reminded them that they had the power to force the honorable governor to divert another $2,000,000 for relief, pointed out that the Workers Alliance, a relief organization, was feeding 150 people a day while they sat there and did nothing, and promised them that if nothing was done, "we'll give you a real demonstration in a short time." And then—because even such horsing around makes the gentlemen of the legislature very, very weary—they decided they might just as well adjourn until the next Monday and spend the time until then thinking up new laws about the size of fish it would be legal to catch. That would be wasting almost a whole week, they exulted, and bring them just that much closer to May 19.

Again the Workers Alliance intervened.

For months now, members of the organization had attended every session of the Assembly, had come to know all the mannerisms of the individual gentlemen, had quietly and intently studied the bills having bearing on the relief problem before the legislature, and had become well acquainted with parliamentary procedure. For months now, as their bellies grew leaner and their faces more pale, they had had an unparalleled opportunity to observe the insulting, sneeringly indifferent, and openly unmoved attitudes of "their" legislators. And as the crisis deepened, with day after day going by and the gentlemen of the Assembly moving not a finger to meet and settle it, this indifference, this wanton disregard for suffering and want, were more than enough to convince the Workers Alliance members seated in the gallery that afternoon that they would have to act now, and act decisively.

When word spread through the building that the gentlemen on the floor were going to adjourn, the unemployed in the gallery (little more than twenty) held a hasty conference. Ray Cooke (now national secretary treasurer), John Spain (a ruddy-hued, genial-looking, but oh! how resolute WPA worker who was soon to be elected state chairman), and State Secretary Powell Johnson related a plan they had hit upon a few days before in a discussion with Lasser to meet just such an emergency as adjournment. It was discussed for a few minutes, accepted unanimously by all present, and voted upon almost immediately.

They split up into groups of two and three and followed Spain and Cooke down the stairs to wait behind the glass barricade opening up into the Assembly chamber. When the motion to adjourn until the following Monday was carried at 3:30 PM and the Speaker of the House banged his gavel to signify the House was adjourned, the members of the Workers Alliance walked into the room, circled around the back, and quietly occupied the seats of the gentlemen of the Assembly as the gentlemen left them.

The gentlemen ignored them, anxious to get out of the building and away, a few of them probably just a little ashamed of the brazenness of their behavior. Some of them probably thought these bums had a hell of a lot of nerve sitting in their seats. A few did march over to the State House policemen on guard and ask what was the meaning of this outrage. The poor cops didn't know what to make of it, didn't know whether they should start kicking them out, or whether as citizens they hadn't a perfect right to sit there in those seats as long as they wanted to; they weren't doing anything, after all, just sitting there at the desks, disturbing nothing, a few talking to each other in low tones; the cops decided to let them alone for the time being.

Very few of the people who witnessed all this realized its meaning. Practically none of them realized that there was now to be enacted in this building a play—burlesque mixed with tragedy—that would shock the nation, that would expose in all its rottenness and turn the eyes of the nation toward the politics that held ruthless sway over the relief problem of the state, that would graphically record the *peaceful protest* of the suffering against their conditions and torturers, and give warning that protests in the future might be less peaceful. . . . The Workers Alliance, without a shout, had seized the State House! The Army of Unoccupation, without a shot, had occupied the Assembly chamber! The Trenton siege was on!

THE MOCK ASSEMBLY LEGISLATES

The gentlemen of the Senate adjourned, too—after voting down for the second time in two days a resolution calling for the appropriation of $5,000,000 for temporary relief—and as they left the building, they looked into the Assembly and saw about twenty people sitting around, some dozing, some talking together, some playing rummy, Cooke, Spain, and Johnson talking to a few reporters, telling them they had decided they would not leave the building until the Assembly came back to legislate funds for relief, promising there would be no violence or disorder if no attempt were made to remove them.

And nothing else happened until night came and their number had grown to about fifty. After members of the Women's Auxiliary of the Workers Alliance brought in some food and tobacco, sandwiches were prepared on the clerk's desk, and their spirits had been raised a little by the food they ate, however, John Spain walked to the front of the room, climbed up into the Speaker's seat, banged the gavel, and declared the House in session.

At once two or three of the men put their feet up on the desks, leaned far back in their seats, puffed away on imaginary cigars, and began to read newspapers—as indifferent to what was going on in the House as true gentlemen of the Assembly. "I am glad to see that some of us know how real 'legislators' act," said Spain, "but this is, at present, an Assembly of the Workers Alliance, not the gathering of the bunch of miserable buffoons that you usually witness in this building. So let's show whoever's watching that we know how to conduct ourselves in a way the gentlemen of the Assembly don't know how to do, like decent people, like workers. . . ." The men sat up straight again.

"Now we've got some serious business to attend to, business that the working class, unemployed and employed, wants attended to this week, tonight. Something our predecessors have played around with for months, and something they have made no real effort to solve because it wasn't to their best interests to solve it. It's up to us, therefore, to settle it as rapidly and as efficiently as possible, to show the state that there are people who can sit in this building and legislate honestly and intelligently—even though it's never been done before. Let's make the workers of this state realize what kind of people they have elected here by showing them what kind of people they should have elected. This is a serious business, and I trust that all of us will remember that, will bear in mind that to us and the hundreds of thousands of unemployed in the state the question of passing legislation appropriating money for relief is a vital and paramount issue."

And then began a wonderful session! Then began legislation such as the walls of the chamber had never heard before. Then was witnessed a sight that will never be forgotten!

Bills and resolutions that affected the relief problem in any way and that had been put before the New Jersey Assembly during its 1936 sessions came up and were dealt with, were discussed carefully, intelligently, and at length, and were decided on one way or another. Bills and resolutions were debated, explained, and acted on—not used to waste time, to befuddle the public, to advance the careers of certain ambitious men, not tabled or buried in committee at the order of powerful reactionary interests. The sales tax was taken up, the "assemblymen" discussed it, made clear how monstrously unfair it was to tax an unemployed worker the same amount for his food as a banker would be taxed for his, how it was a method of taxing the unemployed and making those who had no money provide a part of the little they were supposed to be getting—and, in the interests of the working class, voted it down unanimously. An income tax bill was studied, debated, and, after a few amendments to make its meaning unambiguous and clear, was passed. A corporation tax bill (and everyone, in spite of the gravity of the situation, had to smile at the thought of this bill being passed in the real legislature) was given the same treatment. Resolutions calling for the reopening of idle factories, for unemployment insurance, for a thirty-hour week, and many others were adopted with no opposition. So it went with all of them. What was in the interests of the workers was passed. What was against the interests of the workers was defeated.

But even then they were far from done. The fun was just beginning, in fact.

A mock assembly was called to order by Spain. Now the Workers Alliance was to give a picture of the gentlemen of the legislature as they are, not as [they] might be. Now the unemployed were to begin a show that was to last over a week, to give an exhibition that was to be characterized by the gentlemen of the legislature themselves a few days later in the following words: "They have made a joke of the legislators," "It has made a laughingstock of the legislators," "I don't look upon it as a political move. Nor is it anti-American. These people had to express their ideas on the relief problem and they did." Ridicule was the weapon that the unemployed were to use for the time being against the indifference of the gentlemen of the legislature to their needs. And a powerful weapon it seemed to be: when people begin to laugh at a politician he's pretty near done for, in just the same way that a system—parliamentary, political, economic, or social—is pretty near its finish when people begin to laugh at it.

All the time the unemployed had spent watching the gentlemen of the Assembly at their "work" had not been wasted. These workers knew all the formalities, all the technicalities, all the stupid little trivialities of the parliamentary system. They used Harvard accents that sounded as phony as those of the real gentlemen of the Assembly did. They bowed when they addressed each other. They sneered and they bristled in anger. They addressed each other as "the gentleman from Essex," "the gentleman from Mercer," "the gentleman from Camden." They appointed a majority leader and a minority leader and they divided up into factions and factions within factions and factions within factions within factions. They paid very little attention to each other's talk. They turned every once in a while in their seats and looked insolently up into the gallery (at the unemployed who were not there). They used long, pompous, legal-sounding words, rolling them out as the gentlemen of the Assembly did, looking about to see if the other "assemblymen" noticed their vocabulary, striking poses, throwing their hands about eloquently, pounding the table, peeking over to the press box to see if the reporters were taking down everything they were saying. A clerk was appointed, a fellow with a loud, incoherent voice, a clerk who could read the roll call so rapidly that no one had time to answer. And Spain—Spain had not watched the Speaker of the Assembly in vain, either. For nine days Spain was to act as Speaker (except for the few times Powell Johnson took his place) and he was to do it excellently. Pounding his gavel, making the most arbitrary decisions possible, calling a question and declaring it passed before the "assemblymen" had time to even answer aye or declaring it defeated after a resounding aye vote and no nay vote, glaring up into the (empty) gallery every once in a while and growling, "Any more demonstrations, and the sergeant-at-arms will have to clear the gallery"—in short, by insisting on every formality from the "assemblymen" and ignoring all of them himself, Spain portrayed the typical Speaker of the typical House of Assembly.

For a few minutes everyone was busy writing bills and resolutions. The clerk read the first resolution:

> Whereas, the unemployed of this great and sovereign state of New Jersey have for the past few months been raising a great hue and cry about the miserable conditions they claim they had had to undergo, and
>
> Whereas, it is generally felt that something must be done to remedy this condition by us, the House of Assembly here convened, or blood will run in the streets and riots flare up everywhere, Therefore, be it resolved, that our pay be increased 100 percent at once.

At once ten hands were flung into the air and ten voices were yelling, "Mr. Speaker! Mr. Speaker!" all screeching for the floor. Mr. Speaker Spain recognized the Republican majority leader, the gentlemen from Bergen, and banged for and finally got order. "Mr. Speakah," said the gentleman from Bergen, and he said it in long, loudly drawn out, refined tones. He looked about him very impressively and he paused and began all over again. "Mr. Speakah. . . ." Everyone waited expectantly; it seemed he was going to say something very important, something of deep wisdom. "Mr. Speaker," and his words came out very slowly, very deliberately, "I think this is a very good resolution." And he looked around at the others smirkingly, to see if everyone had understood this very remarkable remark. "I think this is a ver-r-r-y good resolution, and I hope that everyone will vote for it. In fact, this is the best resolution concerning the relief situation I have ever heard of in all my life, and I want to say that I, for one, shall vote for this resolution every time it is brought up for debate. In fact, I should like to see this resolution brought up at every session, and I have no reason to doubt, Mr. Speakah, that if it is brought up at every session, that this is one resolution that will always be passed unanimously by this honorable House."

A long discussion followed, but there was really no disagreement on this resolution, every one of the "assemblymen" stated that he was glad to see such a resolution brought up and that he felt that if this good work was kept up that the relief problem would be solved in short order, and the resolution was adopted unanimously.

The next resolution and the discussion following its reading were more typical of those to follow:

> Be it hereby resolved, that we solve the relief problem by turning the Delaware and Raritan Canal over to the relief clients, letting them catch fish there for their meals.

This resolution provoked a furious fight on the floor. Accusations and recriminations flew back and forth. Names were called and threats were made. Voices were loud and angry and faces grew red and hot. The majority leader claimed that it was an effort on the part of certain elements to bankrupt the state. The minority leader maintained that the majority leader was trying to dodge the relief problem, to which the majority leader replied: "Aren't we all?" Another "assemblyman" admitted that there might be something to this question of people being in need, "but after all, gentlemen, let's not go to extremes, let's not be too extravagant, they won't appreciate it if you give them so much, it'll make them lazy and shiftless." "But elections are coming soon," said another, "and we need votes." "That's why we shouldn't be too hasty about solving this problem. If we do it rapidly, they won't appreciate it." . . . One red-faced "assemblyman" jumped up and accused the majority leader of working in behalf of certain corporations and having orders from them to see to it that the resolution was defeated: "And it is our sacred duty to our constituencies, it is our inviolable obligation to the high-minded American ideals of the sovereign people of this state, to see that this resolution is adopted!" The majority leader was very indignant, very hurt, aggrieved-looking: "Working for the corporations? Who, me? Why . . . I don't even know what a corporation is!" And he concluded his address by exclaiming: "And it is our sacred duty to our constituencies, it is our inviolable obligation to the high-minded American ideals of the sovereign people of this state, to see that this resolution is defeated!" . . . "Think of the taxpayers," said another; "consider what they will say when they learn that we are pampering the unemployed by giving them everything they want. No, gentlemen of the Assembly, this will not do. We must defeat this bill. And if we can't defeat this bill, then it might be wise for us to adjourn for a month or so. Huh? Whattaya say?" . . . "Mr. Speaker, I guess I am a funny sort of a guy to be in a place like this, but I, for one, believe that we ought to settle this problem as soon as possible. I think we ought to give them the canal. What the hell, they're unemployed and they won't have money to buy fishing rods anyhow, so it'll be no loss of ours. And it'll satisfy them by getting them to think that we're giving them something. And if they do get rods it'll keep them occupied all day long—and there aren't any fish there anyhow—and it'll keep them out of mischief for quite some time. We won't be losing a thing, and they'll be so busy that they won't have time to listen to this organization that's always telling them to organize to fight for better conditions, the Workers Alliance." "But, gentlemen of the Assembly, we must not forget that this is a question of *principle*. We'll be setting a dangerous precedent if we start giving the unemployed *anything*. Give them a fingernail and they'll want your arm up to your shoulder. We must teach them to rely on themselves, or they'll always be coming to us with complaints, whereas, if we just ignore them, they'll see we're not interested and they won't bother us any more. Besides, will the gentleman from Burlington submit to a question?" "Will the gentleman from Burlington submit to a question?" asked Spain. "I will, if it's not too technical." "He will," said Spain. "Isn't it true that you have a brother-in-law who is the third vice president of a fishing supply company?" "Mr. Speaker! I have never been so insulted in all any life! I never heard of such a thing! This is a slander and I hurl it back into the teeth of the gentleman from Hunterdon! He can't insinuate such things about me and get away with it! I'll sue him for defamation of character! He can't insinuate that I am personally interested in seeing this bill passed! He can't insinuate that I am interested in seeing this bill passed at all! He can't insinuate that I am interested in anything that goes on in this place! And now will the gentleman from Hunterdon submit to a question?" "Will the gentleman from Hunterdon submit to a question?" "I will." "Are you a citizen?" . . .

The bill was defeated, and, as Spain remarked parenthetically, "Good thing. If anything were accomplished in this place, we wouldn't be giving a lifelike picture of the 'legislators.' We'll just sit here and do nothing— like good 'assemblymen.'"

INSIDE THE STATE HOUSE ...AND OUTSIDE

When they got tired, they went to sleep—on the floor, on the desks, in their seats. When they became hungry, food (contributed by local merchants or paid for by sympathizers) was prepared on the clerk's table and eaten. When they grew discouraged and disheartened, there were telegrams and messages of solidarity and confidence sent by labor organizations from all over the East to be read, there were fellow members of the organization arriving from all over the state to take up the siege with them, there were every day bigger and bigger reports of the siege in the newspapers and louder and louder protests from the gentlemen of the legislature themselves, there was the remark made on the third day by a well-dressed, gray-haired man listening to the burlesque from the gallery: "I've watched the New Jersey Assembly for twenty years now and I'll be damned if these aren't the most intelligent people I've ever seen sitting in those seats. . . ."

On the second day they sent a delegation to Governor [Harold] Hoffman to demand that he call a special session of the legislature to meet at once to provide funds to care for the needy. The honorable governor did issue a statement to the press asking the legislature to please return and stay in session continuously until they arrived at some suitable decision, and he did advise the unemployed to keep putting pressure on the gentlemen of the Assembly (adding that what they were doing—the siege, picket lines around the homes of the more prominent gentlemen of the legislature, and so on—was not the proper way to do it), but he did absolutely nothing else. He fooled no one. Everyone knew that the reason he wanted the legislature to return was so that they would pass the sales tax he so favored and the unemployed so opposed and fought, everyone knew the "suitable decision" he referred to was the sales tax, and it was unmistakably clear to everyone that the honorable governor was no better than any other politician.

On the third day there was almost some trouble. A civil service examination was slated to take place late in the morning in the Assembly chamber. Spain and Johnson had agreed two days before that they would leave the chamber for the morning and afternoon and return after the exams were over. Then they had found out that the exams were to take place, not for one afternoon, as they had been promised originally, but for three afternoons. Considering the agreement broken by the other side, the Workers Alliance voted on Thursday morning that they would not leave the room.

The chief of the State House police entered and was given the privilege of the floor. He explained that he was only obeying orders, that it wasn't his fault that the misunderstanding had arisen, that he was prepared to give his word of honor that as soon as the exams were over they would be permitted to return, and that he would do everything in his power to help them out if they would help him out. One of the "assemblymen" asked if the gentleman would submit to a question. Spain asked the gentleman if he would submit to a question. He would. "Isn't it also true that in that original agreement it was understood that we were to get another hall in the building while the exams were going on?" That was up to the custodian of the building, said the chief, and he didn't know anything about it. Would the gentleman submit to another question? Would he? He would. "Will you go to the custodian and explain to him why we decided we would not leave, and ask him whether he would open the Senate so we can have it in exchange for this room, it being understood that we have the right to return here after each of the exams?" The chief went out.

The "assemblyman" explained that if they left the Assembly to hang around in the corridors they would be admitting a defeat, would be giving in when the other side had broken an agreement. But if they got the Senate, which was a much better decorated, a much more costly and imposing-looking chamber, they would be winning a victory. He moved that if the custodian agreed to this that they leave for the duration of the exams. "After all," he said, "we don't want to prevent anyone else from getting jobs, do we? Those people outside are workers just like ourselves, who want to take exams so they can get jobs. Let's give them the chance we haven't got for ourselves." The motion was carried unanimously, and when the chief returned to tell them they could have the Senate, they moved out and into the Senate.

Now they were "senators," no longer measly "assemblymen," and they strutted about more cockily than before, they were more dignified, more bombastical than before, and they were just as careful not to utter an honest or intelligent thought. Spain was now Mr. President, and he acted it, too. They introduced a resolution to raise the pay of the State House police 40 percent as a reward for their gentlemanly behavior. And then—this was a bombshell—they voted to cut their own salaries in half! "We can't afford to take too much in a time like this when people are supposed to be starving," said the speaker for the resolution; "it'll look as though we're trying to help out in this crisis, and that'll make us go over great with the relief clients. . . . Besides, even presidents have been known to use this stunt." "Mr. President, I want to protest most vehemently against a resolution such as this. I have never heard anything so outrageous in all my political life. This proves my contention that there are foreign agitators right here in our very midst, stirring up trouble and trying to undermine the American government! Why, good God, how will I ever be able to pay my chauffeur if you cut my salary in half?" The "senator" who had introduced the resolution got up, gave him a withering look (as though to say, anyone can see that you're a newcomer to the Senate), and answered with five short, contemptuous words, "Why with graft, you dope." Astonishment appeared on the face of the rookie "senator," then relief, happiness. "Oooooh!" he said, and sat down.

By this time the newspapers had riveted public attention on the siege and the public demanded more news, more information on the true state of affairs of New Jersey relief. And things were happening now, and the public got what it wanted.

In the town of Ewing all funds for relief were exhausted. The 296 families on the relief rolls continued to ask for relief. They were forced to fill out paupers' certificates, and then they were given begging permits! The mayor of the town promised that they wouldn't be arrested for begging—which was very nice of him. A member of the township committee

said, "There is nothing left for us to do,"—which was very helpful. . . .
The cities of Camden and Neptune planned to close down their schools
and use the school money for relief. . . . Trenton claimed it was $337,000
short of the $350,000 necessary to take care of the needy. . . . The State
League of Municipalities warned that it would be absolutely impossible
for them to carry the burden by themselves for any appreciable length of
time. . . . Some newspapers predicted hunger riots and bloodshed in the
streets unless the gentlemen of the legislature tackled the problems honestly and at once.

Maybe it was this ridicule that was being showered on them, maybe
it was public opinion and the realization that they would be held responsible for whatever unpleasantness might arise, maybe it was the picket
lines around their homes, maybe it was just fear for their own hides—but
anyhow, the Speaker of the Assembly, Marcus W. Newcomb, gave in, and
late on Thursday sent telegrams to the gentlemen of the Assembly
announcing that the Assembly was reconvening the next morning instead
of on the following Monday as had been originally intended. (And the
president of the Senate, although still calling the next meeting of the
Senate for Monday, advised the gentlemen of the Senate "to come prepared to stay until this relief problem is solved.")

It looked like a real victory! The members of the Workers Alliance
felt they had a right to feel proud and happy. It seemed that they had actually won what had at first seemed a hopeless battle. It seemed that they
had actually stampeded the gentlemen of the legislature into coming back
and doing something for the starving. It seemed that ridicule was as powerful a weapon as they would ever require. . . .

WAITING FOR THE GENTLEMEN

But their elation was short-lived. The Assembly did not meet the next
morning and the thing was postponed to the following Monday again. For
some reason that seemed good to them, or maybe because they got orders
from the higher-ups who were really paying them their salaries, they postponed the session. They probably figured that if they gave in on the date,
they would have to give in on the question of relief, too, and they weren't
at all willing to do that. Whatever their reason, they took what the mock

Assembly termed a "run-out powder," and showed the world again what they really were.

Leaders of the various factions of the Assembly and Senate met up in Newark to decide how they were going to get out of this mess without losing any votes (again showing that what goes on in the Assembly itself means nothing because everything is decided behind the scenes long before discussion takes place on the floor—a discussion that is carried on only to fool the people into believing that those whom they elected have minds of their own and are not dictated to by the heavy financial interests).

But if they had done all this in the hope that the unemployed would give up the siege in the disgust that it would be only natural for them to feel, they were soon disillusioned. In fact, when they called off that session, they succeeded only in making them more determined, more militant, more serious about the whole thing. It showed them that battles worth winning are not won easily, and that you've got to pack and use the harder punch if you want to win them. Indeed, the very fact that the gentlemen of the Assembly had almost given in convinced them still more that they would have to go on. And so, a little more haggard, a lot more grim, they settled down to wait for Monday night.

And during that wait a number of incidents took place that threw light on the character of the gentlemen of the Assembly and on the relief situation as it was while the gentlemen of the Assembly dilly-dallied.

A number of the gentlemen of the Assembly had not learned that the meeting was called off until they had arrived in Trenton, and they dropped into the State House to see what was what. One in particular, Hart Van Fleet of Union County, a typical specimen of an American statesman, even asked for the floor and delivered a talk to the unemployed. "I ask Almighty God for guidance in this hour," he said. "I voted for the sales tax, which means my defeat in this coming election, but I considered it my duty and I done it." One of the unemployed asked if the gentleman from Union would submit to a question. It seemed, after all the formalities had been gone through, that he would. The question was: "Will you vote for the Howe income tax bill?" And the reply of the gentlemen from Union: "I've got to study it first," made it very plain how much right he had to be in the Assembly when he didn't even know the nature of the bills before it and seemed to indicate that the gentleman had been spending so much of his time asking Almighty God for guidance that he had none to devote to legislation, and that even then he didn't have very good connections with Almighty God.

And there was another visitor who had a few words to say, an ex-gentleman from South Jersey, a Theron McCampbell. He got up and called them a lot of names. He said they were a bunch of loafers, bums, and paupers, that they didn't want to work, that they wouldn't work if they were given jobs, that by God he'd give them jobs, he'd give any one of them a job, and who would take it? No one would after one "assemblyman" from his part of the state got up and explained what kind of work it was and what the ex-gentleman paid for it. "You pick grapes and other fruit and vegetables, and he generously pays you every bit of from ten to fifteen cents an hour for it. But we're not scabs yet, and we're not taking him up on his kind offer, and I hope he'll be leaving here without any cheap labor, which is what he came up here to get." (Two cops escorted the ex-gentleman out of the room.)

A note of tragedy now appeared in the Assembly, after a report was made that, more conclusively than anything else could have, revealed the statement made by the gentlemen of the legislature after their conference in Newark (to the effect that the municipalities could carry on all right until such a time as they, the gentlemen, chose to quit playing around) as a lie. A member of the Alliance told them the story of George W. Elhoff, another member, who had just died of a bronchial affliction aggravated because he had been refused medicine by a local druggist on the ground that he had only a relief prescription and no money. Angrily, the members present drew up a resolution placing the responsibility for this wanton and unnecessary death on the New Jersey legislature for their failure to provide funds for relief. From this point on, the sessions of the unemployed grew less hilarious, their words more bitter, their determination to continue the fight more apparent.

Then there was the business of the honorable governor's telegram to one of the gentlemen of the Assembly. In answer to a request that he provide funds for immediate relief, he wrote: "Already there is grave danger that the constitutional prohibition against creating debt has been violated. Without the vote of the people, the state has no power to borrow money or to create debts of any kind except for war purposes, to repel invasion or to suppress insurrection. . . ." The patience of the unemployed with laws that permit the state to use money for the purpose of killing people and do not permit it to save people from starving to death was wearing thin. But if it was technicalities alone that prevented the honorable governor from producing money for relief, well, they (and he) could overcome that without much difficulty. And they did. They drew up and sent to him a resolution informing him that an insurrection against the state legislature was in progress. Now, they said, he had the power to come across. Well? . . . The honorable governor did nothing.

The conviction of the unemployed that they could expect nothing from these politicians except what they could force from them was further heightened by the slander they now began to resort to. The gentleman from Bergen, Horace R. Bogle, told the press that he had proof that the Army of Unoccupation was being paid $4.50 per day per individual to continue their demonstrations "for political purposes." Powell Johnson then sent him a telegram requesting him to bring his "proof" with him when he came to the Assembly Monday evening or to make another statement to the press admitting he had no such evidence and no right to make such a statement. The gentleman from Bergen did not bring his "proof" with him. And so he proved that he was a cheap, two-for-a-nickel liar, as shameless as Hearst.

But even worse than this gentleman from Bergen was another gentleman from Bergen, J. Parnell Thomas. This gentleman sent a telegram to the honorable governor in which he declared that he was disgusted by the performance staged by the unemployed in the State House (he called them professional agitators), and he called upon him to clear them out of the building. And if he wouldn't do that, the gentleman from Bergen said with intended irony, "I then suggest that you feed the crowd caviar and chocolate éclairs." The reply of the "insurgent assembly," it is true, showed in what contempt they held him: they invited him to a duel with cream puffs. But perhaps they didn't answer quite correctly, perhaps they should have pointed out to the gentlemen from Bergen that long ago, in the eighteenth century, there was a queen in France named Marie Antoinette, who, when she was told the masses of people were dissatisfied because they were hungry and had no bread, asked, "Why don't they eat cake?" or something to that effect, and they should have further pointed out that not many years after that these hungry people became so dissatisfied that they couldn't stand things as they were any longer, and they rose up in revolt, and before the dust settled down, the head of Marie

Antoinette, no longer on her neck, lay in a bloody basket. Perhaps the worthy gentleman from Bergen might not have opened his trap so easily after that. . . .

THE GENTLEMEN COME AND GO

It was Monday evening, April 27. The Speaker of the House, Marcus W. Newcomb, banged his gavel and called the Assembly to order. Thus began the climax of the Trenton siege.

The leaders of the Workers Alliance had conferred with Speaker Newcomb in the afternoon and had decided that the unemployed would retire to the gallery so that the Assembly could meet. ("We shall do nothing to prevent them from meeting to solve the problem," they said.) In return the unemployed were to have ten of their number on the floor of the Assembly, one to have the privilege of addressing the Assembly; the unemployed were to return to the floor immediately after the Assembly adjourned, if they so desired.

And so the unemployed were in the gallery. But not the mere 50, 100, or 200 that had at various times possession of the floor. The Workers Alliance had called a march on the State House of unemployed from all over the state. It had been expected that about 15,000 would respond, would choke the building with their presence and show the gentlemen of the legislature a force that would in short order convince them they'd better quit fooling around. However, they had had difficulty in getting transportation, and as a result only 5,000 showed up. But even these 5,000 packed the gallery, the halls, and corridors and filled the streets in front of and all around the building.

The gentlemen of the Senate, in spite of their president's message that they should come prepared to settle the problem no matter how long it might take, adjourned in fifteen minutes and rushed into the Assembly to witness what one paper called an "unparalleled session." Photographers were working like slaves in Ford's factories, the cops had a hard time clearing the aides, and the speakers often had to shout to make themselves heard.

This was the climax. To the newspapers it meant a good story; to the politicians it meant a ticklish position; to the unemployed it meant a last opportunity for the gentlemen of the Assembly to prove that they were really sincere in their "efforts" to solve the question of finances for relief, it meant an opportunity to judge the effectiveness of their weapon, ridicule, it meant—maybe—bread and butter. What would happen?

Permission to speak was given to three people, two clergymen who appealed for immediate action and the city solicitor of Burlington, who declared that unless the Assembly acted at once, untold suffering would result in Burlington County municipalities, most of whose funds were practically exhausted already. Then came a motion to grant Cooke the privilege of addressing the Assembly. On an overwhelming nay vote, the motion was declared carried.

Cooke spent no time beating about the bush. He read a letter from the Agricultural Workers Union of Cumberland County containing the information that the farmers there were taking advantage of the situation and were beating down the standards of labor by threatening to have the agricultural workers dropped from the relief rolls if they refused to work on their farms for ten and fifteen cents an hour. "And now I wish to become personal," he said. "Mr. J. Parnell Thomas sent a telegram to Governor Hoffman in which he called us a bunch of professional agitators. The governor answered him very well, but I am here to answer him, to tell him to his face that he is a liar."

Bedlam. Fifteen gentlemen of the Assembly demanded the floor. The first one to get it in all the noise and confusion didn't say much except that he didn't propose to be browbeaten into submission, and that as he understood the relief problem the state owed no one a living, and if anybody couldn't refrain from personalities, why, he said, put them out. It was a marvelous speech, but very stupid and disconnected; anyone could see that the gentleman was so excited and frightened that he didn't know what he was talking about. The next to get the floor declared that the Assembly, which didn't permit its own members to indulge in personalities, certainly wasn't going to permit outsiders to do so. "I move a resolution that this speaker who has indulged in disgraceful personalities be bodily ejected from this chamber."

Bedlam squared. The photographers earned another week's pay in the next five minutes. The gentlemen of the Assembly were standing up, screeching their lungs out in the most ungentlemanly manner. And in the gallery sat the unemployed, intent, silent, watching the proceedings, drinking it all in, uttering not a word.

And it was this tense waiting, this strained and pregnant silence, this significant calm that might so easily precede a storm that put fear into the hearts of the gentlemen of the Assembly. There's really no telling about these people, they thought: one of their leaders might suggest something to them and they're liable to jump down here and beat the hell out of us. So they got the maker of the resolution to amend it to merely deprive Cooke of the privilege of the floor, and it was passed, fifty to five.

LESSONS AND PERSPECTIVES

Well, the real story of the Trenton siege ends here. It is true that the gentlemen of the Assembly made and passed and tabled other resolutions that night (one to investigate the Workers Alliance to determine whether its members were really citizens and really unemployed!) and that the only bill they passed before adjourning (a bill to permit free trade zones in New Jersey, which would save big business the duty usually paid) showed clearly that while the legislature was too busy to even think of helping the unemployed, it was never too busy to help the corporations. And it is true that after the Assembly adjourned, the Army of Unoccupation returned to the floor and held a session where they discussed the need for independent political action and where they also endorsed the formation of a Farmer-Labor Party in New Jersey. And it is true that they voted to continue the siege and that they did continue the siege for two days more, and that they retired to the gallery again Wednesday evening and watched the scurvy knaves of the Assembly, now surer of themselves and more insolent, go through another whole session without discussing bills for financing relief, before they, too, adjourned ("Don't think this is goodbye; we're coming back," said Spain) and went home.

But they might just as well have adjourned Monday evening because at that time all the lessons of the siege were as plain as the fingers on your hand. And the point of the whole business was that there were lessons that had been learned, lessons even more important than the effects the siege left directly on the relief crisis, lessons which, if learned by all the unemployed in New Jersey and in every other state, constituted the force which would enable them to rise to even higher, more militant, and more successful struggles.

The interests of the ruling, the boss class, are opposite to those of the exploited, the working class; therefore, the workers can expect nothing but betrayal from the representatives of the ruling class, their politicians, and must be prepared to fight them for everything they want. This fight must be waged on the political field, and the weapon of the working class, independent political action, must be used to deliver political power (today used by the ruling class to oppress the working class) from the hands of the ruling class into the hands of the working class.

But meantime the fight on the economic field, the fight for bread, shoes, and a roof, must be carried on and raised to greater and greater heights. The weapon on which reliance must be laid must be mass action. (Ridicule is a good weapon, but as masterfully as it was used at Trenton it was not the ridicule itself which the ruling class feared, it was the mass action and mass resentment which such ridicule might sweep into play that had them sweating for a while.) But to have effective mass action, you must have the masses. The prime task of every advanced unemployed worker becomes recruiting into and building up the Workers Alliance. If we wish to reach a particular point, we always have to take a first step before we can take a second and third. Building the Workers Alliance is the first step of the unemployed on their way to a new and better society.

These lessons were learned well by those in Trenton. And that is why they left to return to their localities, knowing that the battle had just begun, knowing that their next task was to educate the masses around them, involve them in the struggle, and give them the leadership they were seeking. Conditions as they are in New Jersey, we must expect another outburst in the state in short time, a sharper and a deeper conflict. And the Workers Alliance, preparing for it now, will be in the vanguard.

NOTE

1. While it is true that the unity proceedings were not completed in New Jersey after the siege (May 30–31), still, in the face of a common problem of such importance, all the other organizations gave the Workers Alliance the fullest cooperation and support during the siege.

CHAPTER 9

WARTIME CRIMES
OF BIG BUSINESS
(1943)

George Breitman

Big business spouts patriotic speeches about "the boys in the fox-holes" every time the workers ask for a wage increase to meet the rising cost of living. But big business patriotism is only a hypocritical cloak for self-interest. Profits always come first with the capitalists—even during a war which they want to win. To get profits and more profits they do not even hesitate to endanger the lives of the men in the armed forces of this country and its allies. Here is the proof:

On January 17, 1943—more than a year after Pearl Harbor—the SS *Schenectady* snapped in half and sank off the West Coast, only a few hours after it had been delivered to the Maritime Commission. The American Bureau of Shipping reported the sinking was due to the steel plate on the ship which was "brittle" and "more like cast iron than steel."

The US Senate's Truman Investigating Committee took over the case and at a hearing before this body in Washington on March 23, 1943, the truth came out: the defective steel had been supplied by the Carnegie-Illinois Corporation, subsidiary of the giant United States Steel Corporation, whose officials had willfully and consciously delivered faulty material to the navy, Maritime Commission, and Lend-Lease administration and had falsified the steel test records to cover up their tracks.

Testimony before the Truman Committee showed that the faking of

Originally published as a pamphlet (New York: Pioneer Publishers, October 1, 1943).

tests had covered at least 28,000 tons of substandard plate; that minor officials and employees who had complained to their superiors about the faking of tests had had their "ears pinned back"; that high corporation officials "instead of cooperating (with the Truman Committee) . . . attempted to delay and obstruct the investigation." US Steel officials naturally "deplored" the situation, describing it as "so unnecessary," and tried to put the blame on "a few individuals" with good intentions who had grown "lax." This alibi, however, was decisively rejected by a federal grand jury in Pittsburgh in May, which refused to indict four individual employees offered as scapegoats and indicted the Carnegie-Illinois Corporation itself.

Equally indifferent to the murderous effects of its frauds was the Anaconda Wire and Cable Company, whose Marion, Indiana, plant (financed by the government) was indicted on December 21, 1942, for conspiring to sell the government defective communication and other combat wire, although its officials "well knew at all times" that use of such wire would "endanger the lives of men in the military service of the USA." The Pawtucket, Rhode Island, plant of the company was indicted a month later on similar charges.

The company was shown to have gone to great lengths to devise ingenious machinery for escaping government tests of its defective wire and thus getting the wire accepted for use by the armed forces of the United States, Soviet Union, and Britain. Senator Kilgore has pointed out:

> The batteries on all our warships, including the antiaircraft guns are fired, controlled, aimed and ranges set, over this self-same cable, and if the cable is defective, the ship is helpless against aircraft attack. Also, the safety and success of the entire land combat forces are frequently dependent on messages sent overland by these self-same cables.

The government charged that the conspiracy began about November 1, 1940, and continued up to October 1, 1942. Commenting on this, Senator Bone said:

> The fact that we were suddenly plunged into a deadly war did not in any wise induce the defendants to change the criminal practices outlined in the complaint. After Pearl Harbor, and while the boys were dying on the

battlefields, Anaconda and its officials continued their sordid work of defrauding the government by furnishing faulty cable.

Bone also declared the cable was "so defective that the persons deliberately creating the defects would be brought before a firing squad if they had done this in the war zones." Attorney General Biddle called it "one of the most reprehensible cases of defrauding the government and endangering the lives of American soldiers and sailors ever to come to the attention of the Department of Justice."

But it was no more reprehensible than the case of the Wright Aeronautical Corporation, subsidiary of the huge Curtiss-Wright Corporation, holder of the second-largest war contracts in the county. Wright's Lockland, Ohio, plant (financed by the government) was accused by the Truman Committee in July 1943 of falsifying tests on airplane engines, destroying records, forging inspection reports, changing tolerances allowed on parts, skipping inspection operations, etc. Inspectors who complained were intimidated or transferred. These activities were aided, abetted, and covered up by army inspectors and important army officials influenced by the corporation. The result, according to the committee's report, was:

> Engines were built and sold to the government which were leaking gasoline. . . . Unsafe material has been discovered in completed engines ready for delivery. The company's own reports from its field representatives indicate that these parts had failed in a substantial number of cases. A substantial number of airplanes using this engine have had crashes in which engine failures were involved. . . . More than 25 percent of the engines built at the plant have consistently failed in one or more major parts during a three-hour test run. Spare parts were shipped without proper inspection.

Accused of exaggerating the gravity of conditions at the Lockland plant, Truman retorted: "The facts are that they were turning out phony engines and I have no doubt a lot of kids in training planes have been killed as a result. The Committee was conservative in its report, in order to prevent too touch alarm over the situation."

A number of other and smaller companies were accused of the same crime during 1943: the Bohn Aluminum and Brass Corporation of Detroit, charged with fraud for willfully violating specifications for engine castings used in Rolls Royce airplanes; the Sandusky Foundry and Machinery Company of Sandusky, Ohio, whose officials pleaded guilty to faking tests on propeller sleeves used on navy vessels; the National Bronze and Aluminum Company of Cleveland, convicted for selling the government defective sand and aluminum mold castings which are used in combat planes; the Antonelli Fireworks Company of Spencerport, New York, indicted for deliberately selling the army faulty hand grenades and incendiary bombs; the Collyer Insulated Wire Company of Rhode Island, indicted for conspiring to avoid government inspection and deliver defective wire and cable.

Nor does this exhaust the list. In a speech in Chicago on August 23, 1943, Attorney General Biddle reported that big business frauds in this war are "much bigger than they were in 1917 or 1918"; he declared that 123 federal indictments had already been filed, with 1,279 investigations pending. Biddle did not indicate how many of these indictments and investigations involve fraud endangering the lives of servicemen, but there can be no doubt that a substantial number do.

In this same speech Biddle noted that so far seventy-one cases have been disposed of, with convictions or other penalties in about 90 percent of the cases. But, he complained, in many cases the offenders had gotten off with extremely light penalties. If anything, that was an understatement. While a few of the smaller companies have not gotten off scot-free and some of their officials have even been given prison sentences, the great majority of offenders—and particularly the powerful ones—have escaped thus far with at most a mere slap on the wrist. Typical was the trial in Fort Wayne, Indiana, June 1943, of the Anaconda Wire and Cable Marion plant.

"The most obnoxious fraud ever presented to a court of the United States!" That was how a prosecuting attorney described the Anaconda case. "Revolting" was the comment by Federal Judge Thomas W. Slick, who presided at the trial. Nevertheless, not a single one of the indicted Anaconda officials spent an hour in jail for their crimes. Some were fined and given prison sentences, but the judge ordered the suspension of the prison sentences upon payment of ridiculously light fines. Anaconda attorneys at the trial volunteered the information that the company had made $46,000 from the frauds, but the total fines imposed by Judge Slick came to $31,000. Thus, even after paying these fines, the company had a tidy margin of profit from its criminal activities!

The company got away so easily by pleading nolo contendere, that is, not contesting the charges and throwing itself on the mercy of the court. Its lawyers admitted "technical guilt" but not "moral guilt"; they explained their reluctance to go before a trial jury on the ground that such a course "would have impeded the war effort." The court, as has been shown, was exceedingly merciful. The judge explained the suspension of prison terms by saying he felt the guilty officials "could better serve the war effort by going back to work"; he did not say whether he meant the same kind of work for which they had been indicted. The judge also asserted that this disposition of the case would "stop anything of a similar nature elsewhere"—a view shared by almost no one else. Thus, the first important trial for wartime fraud endangering the armed forces indicated that big business can get away with murder.

"But," some people say, "these are the crimes of individual corporations, and big business as a whole should not be blamed for them." This is the position taken among others by AFL president William Green and CIO secretary James Carey. Contemptible as this argument is—especially from trade union leaders who are supposed to defend the interests of the workers against their big business enemies—it deserves an answer.

First, it must be remembered that US Steel and Curtiss-Wright are not two-bit businesses unrelated to the rest of industry. On the contrary, they are among the most powerful groups in American big business, being two of the twenty-five companies which hold 50 percent of the war contracts, and they are controlled by the same financial interests that dominate the national economy. Check the names of their chief stockholders and boards of directors and you will find listed the same respected bankers and industrialists who top the list of America's sixty families.

Second, let it be noted that the revelations of these wartime crimes have not evoked a single word of criticism or denunciation from a single important capitalist in this country. The employers' associations, the National Association of Manufacturers, the Chamber of Commerce—all have been as silent as the tomb, none has even implied that there is anything reprehensible in frauds that deliberately endanger servicemen's lives. This silence speaks volumes more than a million consciously deceptive statements by cowards like Green and Carey, for it indicates that the basic outlook of the corporations caught in the act is shared by big business as a whole.

Third, there is the behavior of the capitalist press, which reaps fortunes from the big patriotic advertisements inserted in their pages by the powerful corporations (and paid for out of the taxpayers' money). For every line they have devoted to incomplete and confusing accounts of the war frauds, they have printed ten lines whitewashing the corporations and trying to smear the Truman Committee. When used at all, the stories of the wartime frauds have been relegated for the most part to the inside pages where they will not attract the same attention as the huge headlines and editorials denouncing the miners and other workers forced to strike in order to secure a living wage. This is not because the capitalist press fails to recognize news when it sees it; rather, it is because the press recognizes that these crimes are a damning indictment of all capitalists.

Fourth, and most revealing, there is the following evidence about the steel and aircraft industries as a whole: A few days after the Truman Committee hearing on US Steel had been concluded, the steel barons began to talk about a threatening decline of 35 percent in national steel production. "Lower production prospects are due to the demoralizing fear the Senate inquiry has instilled into *every* steel plant," said the *Pittsburgh Post-Gazette* on April 16, 1943. These reports—inspired by the steel corporations in an attempt to get the Truman Committee to lay off—showed that the entire steel industry feared such investigations. The only logical explanation for this fear is that other steel corporations besides US Steel are engaged in illegal production practices.

Similarly, when the capitalist press was trying to blame the Truman Committee for an 85 percent decline in shipment of finished airplane engines at Wright's Lockland plant in the period between April and August 1943, it was shown that Curtiss-Wright was not the only company panic-stricken by the prospect of investigation: "Leading industrialists and production experts the country over are carefully watching the case," the *New York Times* reported on September 2. "The extent to which other companies and other plants of the Curtiss-Wright group have been affected by what happened at Lockland is difficult to estimate. Many other concerns are said to be worrying, however, lest they run into similar situations. . . ." But why should they be worrying if they are not guilty of the same crimes as Curtiss-Wright? Their apprehension is good reason for concluding that the Truman Committee investigations have scratched only the surface of big business crimes in this war and that further investigation would involve all the other big monopolies and corporations.

The sale of defective war material has shocked some people more than the other wartime activities of the corporations because it is so openly cynical and in such flagrant contrast to the high-minded sentiments spread over the newspaper advertisements. As a result, there is a tendency to look upon this practice as something exceptional and unrelated to the general policies of capitalism. But at bottom it is no different in kind from the other "scandals" perpetrated by big business every day in the year.

The explanation for the policies and activities of the monopolies and corporations is always to be found in the profit motive. No employer keeps his factory running unless there is profit to be made from it. This is as true in wartime as in peacetime, with only one difference: in wartime there is usually more profit to be made and the capitalists, maddened by greed, sweep aside all restraints and obstacles in the way of ever-greater profits. Rare indeed is the case of an employer who has said: "I have got enough." The tendency of the ruling class is always to go after more and more. Billions are being made on war contracts, but even the most powerful corporations do not disdain to pick up a few millions extra by manufacturing substandard products and then palming off the defective material as the article for which they are being paid such generous prices.

But in what sense does this differ from the normal practices of capitalism? In peacetime big business's concern for profits and profits alone often results in the shutting of the factories. The hardships this brings to the whole working class, the undernourishment it visits on millions of children, the diseases that follow in its wake, surely take as heavy a toll of human life and well-being as the war frauds. Who will say which is worse? Who will contend that the cause is different?

What about war profiteering? The people were solemnly assured that there would be no war millionaires this time. Yet profits were bigger in 1942, after the payment of taxes, than they were during the last war or in the boom year of 1929. And they were 14 percent higher during the first six months of 1943 than during the same period in 1942, according to a report by the Department of Commerce. Which scandal is more detestable—the war frauds or the war profiteering which will place heavy burdens on all the masses and act as a drag on their living standards for years to come? And who will deny the connection between the two?

No, the big business "scandals" of this war do not begin and end with their cynical disregard for the safety of the servicemen. They began long ago, they touch on every aspect of the war program, and they vitally affect the rights and conditions of every worker.

Ask the sailors at Pearl Harbor and they will tell you what they think about the manufacturers who sold the Japanese warlords the scrap metal used to make the bombs that were dropped upon them.

Ask the marines in the malaria-infested South Pacific jungles what they think about the capitalists who restricted the production of quinine and other drugs so that they could maintain high prices for these products.

Ask the aviators and the merchant marine men who survived the sinking of their ships what they think about rubber barons and oil magnates whose demand for monopoly control of rubber in the postwar period impeded the production of synthetic rubber necessary to build rafts and other lifesaving equipment.

There are shortages of aluminum, binoculars, critical chemicals, magnesium, tetracene, dyestuffs, tungsten carbide, etc., all important materials in wartime. The reason? Because Standard Oil, DuPont, General Electric, ALCOA, General Motors, and the other big corporations formed cartels with their fellow monopolists in Germany, Britain, France, Japan, etc., for the purpose of restricting production, maintaining monopoly, and raising prices. More lives have been lost in this war because of these cartel deals than because of the sale of defective material.

Other shortages affecting the war program can be traced directly to the fact that the big corporations have hogged the great majority of the government's war contracts. As Assistant Attorney General Tom C. Clark has reported:

> At the start of the war program in this country 175,000 companies provided 70 percent of the nation's manufacturing output, while today, two and a half years later, the ratio has been reversed to the point where 100 corporations hold 70 percent of the war and essential civilian contracts. This group, he declared, has obtained the bulk of the fourteen billion dollars' worth of new plants built at government expense." (*New York Times*, April 23, 1943.)

As a result many small plants have been driven to the wall; with them disappeared their productive capacity, while many of the new plants remain partly unused and unproductive. A typical example of how the monopolists impede production is the shipbuilding industry, where the revolutionary Higgins assembly-line production program was strangled because it was considered a competitive threat to the position of powerful companies like Bethlehem Steel.

Other wartime blessings for which the workers can thank big business are: the speedup, which resulted in 1942 in a greater number of casualties on the industrial front than on the military front; an artificially created manpower shortage—due to labor hoarding by the manufacturers and big agricultural interests, discrimination against Negro and women workers, managerial inefficiency—which is used to justify freezing the workers to low-paid jobs; an aggravation of the housing crisis in many war production centers, resulting in increased sickness, disease, child delinquency, and disruption of family life; food shortages designed to force price rises.[1]

Big business could not get away with all this if there were a government in Washington seriously interested in stopping it. But the government is itself the outstanding advocate of capitalism. The government is well aware of the attitude of big business, as was shown in Monograph No. 26, "Economic Power and Political Pressure," issued by the government's Temporary National Economic Committee in November 1940, and stating in part:

> Speaking bluntly, the government and the public are "over a barrel" when it comes to dealing with business in time of war or other crisis. Business refuses to work, except on terms which it dictates. It controls the natural resources, the liquid assets, the strategic position in the country's economic structure, and its technical equipment and knowledge of processes. The experience of the World War, now apparently being repeated, indicates that business will use this control only if it is "paid properly." In effect, this is blackmail, not too fully disguised.

Blackmail it may be, but the government has given in to it without complaint or rancor. It has given the employers the greatest profits in their history; and to pay for these profits, it has piled one scandalous tax bill after another on the masses, frozen wages and jobs, prohibited strikes, prevented effective price control, abolished all limits on big salaries. Big business has no reason to complain that it is not being "paid properly," according to its own lights. To make doubly sure that they don't muff any opportunities, the corporations have offered and the government has appointed a considerable number of dollar-a-year men to head the most important wartime agencies and posts. Even the New Deal Secretary of the Interior Harold Ickes admitted on July 21, 1943, that "it is the business men who are running the war." And while running it, they see to it that the interests of the corporations are well protected.

Even after Pearl Harbor the government was still trying to get industry to discontinue illegal practices hampering war production. Assistant Attorney General Thurman Arnold complained in his report to Congress on Jan. 3, 1942, about:

> the attitude of powerful private groups dominating basic industries who have feared to expand their production because expansion would endanger their future control of industry. . . . There is not an organized basic industry in the United States which has not been restricting production by some device or other in order to avoid what they call the "ruinous overproduction after the war."

The government pleaded with the corporations to cooperate, to discontinue their cartel deals and violations of the antitrust laws, and to let other companies use their patents for war production; the corporations flatly refused. Early in 1942 the government—in order to prevent the complete breakdown of the war program, that is, in order to protect the interests of the capitalist class as a whole—was finally compelled to institute a series of suits against a number of monopolies, making public the damning facts about which the government had been aware for many years.

The corporations had been caught red-handed. But the government, once having gotten their promise to permit the use of the patents during the war, dropped the charges and let these corporations escape virtually unpunished. Standard Oil, for example, whose restriction of synthetic rubber production had blocked the whole war production program, was permitted to plead nolo contendere and was given a $50,000 fine (which amounts to about the average profit this corporation makes every hour).

The other corporations got away even more easily. To make the government's attitude unmistakably clear, Arnold Biddle, Secretary of War Stimson, and Secretary of Navy Knox wrote Roosevelt on March 20, 1942, in the midst of the public revelations about the cartels, and said that "some of the pending court investigations, suits, and prosecutions under the antitrust statutes by the Department of Justice, if continued, will interfere with the production of war materials. . . . In those cases we believe that continuing such prosecutions at this time will be contrary to the national interest and security." This was some more "blackmail," a threat to hold up on production if the prosecutions were continued, with government officials covering up for the corporations. Roosevelt answered: "I approve the procedure outlined in your memorandum to me. . . ." Thus, punishment of the corporations for violating the laws has been postponed to some remote future in the postwar period, if then.

The same course has been followed in connection with the defective war material cases. Reluctantly the government has been compelled to prosecute in a few of the more flagrant cases, but each time high government representatives have stepped forward to make light of the corporation crimes.

The War Production Board held a closed meeting on the US Steel case, but its only outcome was a statement by WPB chairman Donald Nelson deploring a "more than usual" vigilance on the part of steel plant inspectors and a WPB telegram to several steel companies urging them not to lean over backward while seeking "unattainable perfection" in meeting production specifications. Other key government spokesmen issued statements implying that there was no need to worry about the practices of US Steel.

When a wave of protest arose after the Truman Investigation of Curtiss-Wright, Undersecretary of War Patterson, while not daring to deny the truth of Truman's charges, nevertheless issued a statement asserting that conditions at the Lockland plant were "much less sensational than some of the inferences drawn in recently published statements." An army investigation board under Lt. Gen. William S. Knudsen also had to admit the Truman Committee charges were accurate but sought to minimize their importance. Both these and other government officials seemed more concerned in quieting public indignation than in taking measures against the Curtiss-Wright criminals.

And during the period between Anaconda Wire and Cable's indictment and trial, the Offices of the Inspector of Navy Material in New York and Cincinnati went out of their way to commend Anaconda for its "good workmanship" and to announce that it was being considered for an "E" award. During this same period army and navy procurement officials showed how little concerned they were about the corporation's malpractices by awarding Anaconda's Marion plant almost $4,000,000 in additional business.

Whatever else one may conclude from these government actions, it is safe to say that they do not have the effect of strongly discouraging war frauds.

What is to be done about the criminal activities of big business? The administration and Congress have already conclusively shown that they either won't or can't take measures to make the punishment fit the crime. If anything is to be done, it will have to be done by the labor movement.

Some people have suggested the passage of legislation imposing the death penalty on manufacturers whose fraudulent practices endanger the lives of the men in the armed forces. A bill providing this penalty or a million-dollar fine has even been introduced into Congress. It is hard to imagine the present Congress—which is the servant, body and soul, of the big corporations—ever adopting legislation to punish them.

To get to the root of the problem, the Socialist Workers Party advocates that the ownership and control of industry be taken out of the hands of the capitalists. This course of action will be regarded by big business as far more drastic than any bill providing the death penalty and it will be fought by them with every weapon they have, but it is the only practical answer to capitalist mismanagement of industry.

At its June 1943 meeting in Toronto, the international executive board of the United Auto Workers, CIO, drew up a series of proposals designed to ensure full employment in the postwar period. One of these called for government ownership after the war of "monopolistic industries and of industries strategically essential to the national safety."

This is a sound idea, and offers the key to the solution not only of unemployment, as nationalized production has shown in the Soviet Union, but also of the criminal practices of the capitalist class. Let industry be owned by the government and operated under the control of committees democratically elected by the workers. The profit motive

would be removed, and with it would be removed the incentive to produce and sell dangerously defective products. The costs of production
would be lowered and the workers' committees, having no interest in
exacting profits from the blood of the soldiers, would guarantee production and honest testing in the interests of the masses of the people.

The UAW executive board proposes postwar government ownership
of industry. But why wait until the war is over? The contents of this pamphlet demonstrate that big business domination of industry menaces the
welfare and safety of the masses in wartime as much as if not more than
in peacetime. The war may last a long time, and so long as big business
is in control, the number of victims of capitalist greed will continue to
mount. Meanwhile the big corporations are using the war itself to smash
thousands of smaller businesses and to tighten their own grip on industry.
The longer the workers wait, the harder it may prove to expropriate the
capitalists. The time to act is now.

It will not be easy to put this program into effect. Union men and
women who have had to strike for a wage increase of even five cents an
hour know how vindictively the employers resist every challenge to their
profits; capitalist ferocity will be multiplied a hundred times when the
workers try to take the factories away from them. The daily press and
radio commentators will become frenzied in their denunciations and inci-
tations to violence against the workers; all the instruments of capitalist
propaganda will be turned on full blast to bolster the myth that production cannot continue without the capitalist coupon-clippers, that society
cannot function without parasitic exploiters. And, of course, the capitalists will be aided throughout in this campaign by their political parties and
their agents in the government.

The question of who is to own and operate industry is a political
problem. To make the change that is necessary, the workers will have to
conduct a political struggle against big business. The employers already
have their political organizations, the Republican and Democratic Parties,
and to fight them successfully the workers will have to create a political
organization of their own. The capitalist parties are last-ditch supporters
of the system of private property and private profit which enables the
employers to do what they wish with the means of production. The
workers need a party which will be just as firmly devoted to the program
of government ownership and workers' control of industry. That means an

independent labor party, based on the trade unions and running its own labor candidates in elections.

The present government has already shown where it stands on this question. The billions of dollars' worth of factories, properties, and equipment now owned by the government are going to be turned over at bargain prices after the war to the employers, who will use them to swell their profits and to further strengthen their monopoly control. That is why the workers and their party must fight for the creation of a new kind of government, one which will aid not oppose the struggle for government ownership and workers' control, a Workers' and Farmers' Government.

The wartime production crimes have torn away the mask from the rapaciously greedy countenance of big business. Now the working people must tear out of the capitalists' hands the power to continue their criminal activities.

NOTE

1. The full story of shortages deliberately created by the food corporations is told in *Your Standard of Living—What Is Happening to It*, by C. Charles (New York: Pioneer Publishers, 1942).

CHAPTER 10

SHOULD PROGRESSIVES WORK IN THE DEMOCRATIC PARTY?
A DEBATE BETWEEN
CARL HAESSLER AND GEORGE BREITMAN
(1959)

The following debate took place on May 8, 1959, at Eugene V. Debs Hall in Detroit, Michigan. It was the last year of conservative Republican Dwight D. Eisenhower's second term in the White House, when the Democrats controlled both houses of Congress and the state government in Michigan.

It was also the end of a decade that had brought about the decimation of the whole radical movement, thanks to the Korean War and the witch-hunts unleashed by McCarthy, Truman, and the union bureaucracy. Relative economic prosperity, although marred by intermittent recessions, contributed to the conservative climate. International events—the end of the Stalin cult in the Soviet Union; workers' rebellions in East Germany, Poland, and Hungary; and the spread of colonial revolution in Asia and the Caribbean—encouraged a regrouping of the badly battered American Left; in 1958 this situation had led several radical groups and individuals, including the Socialist Workers Party, to launch a United Independent–Socialist ticket in the New York gubernatorial and senatorial elections.

The debate was an exploration of the possibility of radical regroupment in Michigan, where the labor movement of the period was headed by Walter Reuther of the United Auto Workers, James Hoffa of the International Brotherhood of Teamsters, and August Scholle, president of the

---

This debate was originally published as a pamphlet by the Friday Night Socialist Forum, June 1959.

Michigan AFL-CIO. Carl Haessler was a longtime labor journalist and socialist who worked for the UAW Local 876 and for the Highland Park, Michigan, Dairy Workers Union, as their secretary-treasurer. He was an editor for the Michigan Federated Press.—ED.

PRESENTATIONS

Carl Haessler: I wonder why I was asked to participate in this debate. Knowing the gang that the first speaker, the affirmative speaker, would be up against, I suppose the manager of the forum decided it would take a brave man to come up here and present that point of view. I tried it about a year ago at the Central Methodist Church, where I was the unaffiliated speaker, and three other third-party speakers had the floor, and I got a pretty good drubbing, but it didn't bother me, especially as one middle-aged bourgeois member of the audience came up and said, "I thank you very much. You have the same persuasive character of presenting the subject as Dr. Henry Hitt Crane." And I don't know if he thought that was complimentary or not, but I have been compared to preachers before this, although that is not exactly my line.

However, I am serious in taking this side of the case, and not from inexperience. Almost fifty years ago, I debated on this general subject, except it was capitalist parties vs. Socialist Party, at the University of Wisconsin. One of my opponents, white-haired like myself, took one of the opposing views, and I imagine he'll take the floor in the general discussion tonight. I was a Socialist Party member, very active in Milwaukee after I was fired from the University of Illinois. I reached the glory of being a member of the City Central Committee of the Socialist Party there and also of the five-man State Executive Committee of the Socialist Party. Later on I was active in campaigning for Senator [Robert] La Follette when he ran for president in 1924, which was supposed to be the extension to the country as a whole of the third party—the Progressive Party—that had been founded in the state of Wisconsin. And when Henry Wallace, an ex-Republican, ran for president in 1948, also using the name of the Progressive Party, I was somewhat active in that campaign. In fact, I remember a debate here in which a lawyer for the Republican Party, a professor for the Democratic Party, and yours truly for the Progressive

Party discussed the platforms. Well, let's get down to the subject, "Should Progressives Work in the Democratic Party?"

I take that to mean, should progressives who are interested in organized political action work in the Democratic Party? If you are a progressive along general, vague social lines and don't spend much time on political parties, I would say, don't work in any political party. Why work in a party if you're not politically, organizationally interested? So I wonder if my adversary will accept that restriction of the subject. I hope he does, because he has plenty of ammunition besides that, because a year ago, the Democratic Party was much cleaner looking than it is today. Since the November victory, the sweeping November victory of the Democrats in the national election, great things were expected of that party by the labor people who supported it, supported them with money, with speeches, and most of all, with work in the precincts. So far, there has not been very much visible fruit on the national scale, for labor or for progressives, of this victory of the Democratic Party.

In the state of Michigan, of course, there has been some fruit. I should say, for instance, the victory of the Democratic Party in the last elections, not only in 1958, but in 1956, 1954, 1950, 1948—that those victories have paved the way, for instance, for the Democratic control of the state supreme court for the first time in the history of that body. Democrats were tied once before with the Republicans, but this is the first time that the Democrats have a 5–3 edge in the state supreme court. And it was due solely to the fact that Governor [G. Mennen] Williams, elected by original Democrats and by labor Democrats over and over again, had the opportunity to fill vacancies by appointment on the supreme court, and those appointees, in almost all cases, except for Justice Clark Adams, were elected when the time came for them to face the voters. And as you know, the greatest fruit of the state supreme court—Democratic control— was the decision in the Ford strike unemployment benefit case. They reversed the previous Republican decision that strikers in one plant of the Ford company would make all members thrown out of work—all employees thrown out of work at the Ford Motor Company—ineligible for unemployment benefits. The Republicans, representing General Motors and Ford, thought this was sound doctrine. The Democrats this year, representing labor and Democrats generally, thought the other interpretation was sound. Well, that's the most outstanding supreme court labor victory that has been achieved, I think, anywhere in the United States. And it has been achieved in a state where labor—organized labor—has for all practical purposes captured the Democratic Party.

The Democratic Party, without labor, in this state had been nothing except a governor once in a while who couldn't get anywhere with a Republican legislature. Now with the appointive power in Democratic hands for the courts for these many years—for the circuit courts, the probate courts, the common pleas courts—here and throughout the state, the judicial temper of a corporation-minded reactionary court in an industrial state has been decisively altered, and I ask you whether this could have been done by any other political means than the means that were actually employed. For instance, to make it personal, because that's what brings it down to cases, could the Socialist Workers Party, with its four thousand votes in the spring election in the state of Michigan, have done anything even approaching that? Could the Socialist Labor Party, with a few thousand more votes throughout the state, have done anything in that line? I don't have to ask you if the Republican Party could have done it. They could have, but they wouldn't have. The Democratic Party got in a position to do something on the supreme court and they did it.

Of course one of the justices on the supreme court is a socialist, a man who spent thirty days in jail in the good old militant days of 1937 for defying a Republican judge's antilabor injunction—Justice George Edwards of the supreme court; and of course the state chairman of the Democratic Party several times ran for office as a socialist, in and around Ann Arbor; and the man who controls the money bags of the Democratic Party, Walter Reuther, was a socialist within my own experience. In fact in 1938, when I was functioning to some degree as his brain truster—I founded his local union paper and edited it for a number of years—Reuther consulted me as to whether he should continue paying dues to the Socialist Party. I said no. And we discussed it, and I said if you want to rise in the UAW and reach an important position, and if you'll then want to spread your activities beyond that, don't get tangled up with a small group that's getting nowhere even faster than Norman Thomas is growing older, but get out from under. Don't have these entangling little alliances sticking to you. Free yourself. And he did. And he freed himself to such a great degree that a few weeks ago, when Jimmy Hoffa, who used to be his friend in West Side strikes, accused Reuther of being a socialist,

Reuther said he hadn't ever been in the Socialist Party except one year, during the depression. I know myself he had been a Socialist Party member for five years, and his father had been for thirty or forty years before that, but he's entitled to a change of opinion and he's entitled to change his memory of the facts, too. If there are other people with better memories than he has, well, that's their hard luck, because he'll deny it, and everybody will believe him and nobody will believe those who have counterevidence.

Well, you see, with three former socialists at the controls of the Democratic Party in this state, things are beginning to be done. But you still have a die-hard Republican senate, as a result of that overbalanced legislature created by an amendment to the constitution, but even that will crumble. Some senators are fearing for their seats, some Republican senators; some of them, while they're not exactly afraid for their seats, are ready to make deals with the majority party in the senate and even more so in the house, and so I think Michigan is a very good example of progressives working for organized political action in the majority party, the Democratic Party of this state.

Now, there are similar achievements, not quite so great, in other states. There is the state of West Virginia. I was sitting in the United Mine Workers office in Washington, talking to Denny Lewis, the brother of John L., and he was criticizing Reuther, saying he was wasting a lot of money on labor political action, "and we don't go in for that." And I said, "No, you don't, except in West Virginia." And he said, "Right, Carl." In West Virginia, the United Mine Workers controls the Democratic Party, and they've elected two US senators, ousting the Republicans in the last election, and they control the governor, most of the legislature. West Virginia has very good mining legislation, and considering that it's a hillbilly state, up in the mountains, not much doing industrially, West Virginia has a pretty fair record, legislatively, as far as states go. That legislative record was established by the Democratic Party, which is owned by the United Mine Workers of America.

Now let's take the state of Minnesota, where the Democratic Party is so thoroughly controlled by the old Farmers Nonpartisan League, the radical farmers in the state, and by the unions, that it really isn't even called the Democratic Party. It's called the Farmer-Labor Democratic Party. And in Minnesota, they've done pretty well, too. They elected a senator,

Eugene McCarthy, to supplant the old Republican diehard, Senator [Edward] Thye; they've elected a good number of liberal congressmen, they've got a Democratic governor, and things in that state are coming along, too. Of course, they've got judicial drags, and there are legislative drags; the press is not Democratic, to say nothing of being pro-labor, but there's a state on the move, too.

You take those three states—Michigan, Minnesota, and West Virginia—and you have a start for a pretty fair infiltration by progressive labor, meaning those people who are interested in organized political action, toward the beginning of a labor party under the Democratic name. Then if you consider that California went whole-hog against the Republicans in November, and the Democrats control not only all the state offices, except one, I believe, but both houses of the legislature, and that good legislation is going through, there's another state—a state, of course, of crackpots, especially around Los Angeles, but crackpots often make good organizers and good advance guards for the progressives in the party.

And then, north of California, the longshoremen, Bridges's union, the lumber men, and the building trades have had for many years a tight legislative conference which put the fear of labor, if not the fear of God, into the legislators; and lo and behold, in 1958, two of the remaining Republican congressmen—the state has four congressmen—were defeated; one Republican is left, three are now Democrats in Congress, and both Oregon senators are Democrats, where for years and years, no Democrat was ever sent east. The governor had been a Democrat. A liberal Republican defeated him this year, but the legislature keeps track of him, and Oregon is doing pretty well. The legislature, just a few weeks ago, adopted a resolution urging Eisenhower to relax the controls on trade with China. Of course, they did it for business reasons, but there you are, with one more state. North of Oregon is Washington, with a similar record, not quite so advanced, but getting there.

Then you take the state of New York in the East. Of course, the needle trades union sabotaged the promising third-party movement when they split the American Labor Party to form a liberal wing. The American Labor Party has since become defunct; the Liberal Party has not yet been buried, but maybe it will revive, or maybe something else will take its place. The defeat of the Democrats in New York City, New York State, because the party there listened to the Tammany gangsters instead of organized labor, is something that will be remembered, and there's a much better chance than for any of the splinter parties, the little parties, to work.

Now I'd like to make it plain again that I'm not opposed to small parties, to small parties as such; they keep the torch burning and are the vanguard of political thinking, and political feeling, which is even more important than thinking. But they don't accomplish anything in this country in an organized political way. It's the major parties, one or the other, that should be infiltrated, and then captured. And the Democratic Party, which is falling apart in two sections—has been for a number of generations—is the most promising, and the results I've cited should encourage us to go on with that. The other Democratic states of an industrial character, where the unions are strong, like Connecticut with its big sweep of Congress in the 1958 election; Massachusetts, where the Democrats finally got control of the state senate (they already had the lower house); New Jersey, where a Republican was retired for a Democratic US senator; and Ohio—I know Ohio is regarded by the *Militant* and other groups as a shining example of what happens when you use the Democratic Party instead of smaller parties for your work—but Ohio is just in the beginning of the Democratic capture, the Democratic infiltration by labor, and you'll see results there, too. Now what is the objection to this point of view? I've heard it before, and I'm not going to take away George's thunder by outlining it to you. All I want to say is that anything you can say against the Democratic Party you can say—and much more—against the Republican Party. I would like my opponent in this discussion to take up the points that I have presented, of considering the practicality of organized political action by taking over an already established party, instead of going through the agony of trying to set up one of your own.

The members of the Socialist Workers Party, who are very strong pluggers for third-party action, who work day and night, especially in campaign time, tirelessly, too, through the rest of the year, certainly excite my admiration. If their purpose is to keep alive a certain doctrine, presented to any who'll listen, I will say that's fine. But if their purpose is to capture political control of the community, of the state, or of the nation, then I think they are taking the road that is long, tortuous, full of detours, obstacles, costly, and in the end, barring a revolution, unsuccessful. And why?

Well, I think the Socialist Workers Party members know the difficulties, for instance, of merely getting on the ballot in industrial states. The fatigue, the disappointment, the cheating against petition circulators that those in control of political action exercise, if they fear they might lose some precinct or some ward or some district because a third party is in the picture. And then, also, the inability to attract followers, in that the American voter is swayed not by reason but by emotion, and the emotion of enjoying a defeat is not widespread enough to make a good third party feasible. There should be some prospect of winning once in a while, in order to attract the mass American voter. I don't see it in any of the third parties that have emerged so far.

I have one more point. The organization of a party, of a third party, is a terrific job, and a very disappointing job, and if you have a party shell already set up for you, why not take it over? It's a good Wall Street game, like the American Car and Foundry Company being taken over by lawyers and financiers, to become A. C. F. Wrigley's—Wrigley's Super Markets. The corporate setup is all there. And so with the Democrats, the political setup is all there. And if you think you can't sneak up and capture it, you have less imagination and power of adaptive action than I give you credit for. You've captured three key states—Minnesota, West Virginia, Michigan—then you capture another state, and then for a while there's a setback because the glowing prospects that were held out by the party speakers don't come true all at once. The takeover has to be postponed a little bit. There are obstacles, but at least you're on the right road. Now, George, you knock that down!

George Breitman: I shall begin defining what I have in mind by the terms "progressive," "work in," and "Democratic Party."

By "progressive" I mean two things: First, the great social forces that have the power to decide the future—the working class and its allies, the working farmers, the Negro people, and the youth. Second, I have in mind the smaller, radical groups and individuals who are repelled by the capitalist system, its anarchy, militarism, depressions, regimentation, inequality, and debasement of human and cultural values, and who favor the replacement of this system by one based on cooperation planning, brotherhood, and promotion of the interests of the majority. In short, I use the term "progressive" for those who are pro-labor or anticapitalist, who are antiwar, antifascist, and anti–Jim Crow, pro-socialist.

By "work in" I mean belong to, become a member of, vote for, support, or endorse.

Now, about the nature of the Democratic Party. Socialists say that political parties represent, express, reflect class interests. This doesn't mean that parties necessarily say they represent class interests; nor that all their members think they do; nor even that all their members came from the same class. (The truth of this proposition doesn't depend on what socialists say, or what antisocialists say. It can be tested by facts, the evidence of history, objective analysis.)

When socialists say the Democratic Party is a capitalist party, they don't mean that most of its members are capitalists. Obviously not. If the capitalists had to depend on their own numbers, they couldn't elect a justice of the peace, for they are a tiny part of the population. Actually, most supporters of the Democratic Party are workers, farmers, and members of the middle classes. But they aren't the ones who decide the real aims of the party.

Nationally, the Democratic Party is a coalition—of capitalists and union leaders, of southern white supremacists and northern Negroes, of corrupt machines in the cities and unorganized or loosely organized farmers on the land, of conservatives and liberals, et cetera.

This coalition explains why the Democratic Party says the things it says, why it writes the platforms it writes—for it appeals to conflicting interests and tries to hold them together. It also explains why the Democratic Party sometimes says different things than the other capitalist party, the Republican Party, for the Republican Party has a somewhat different composition and following, making its major appeal for support to the middle classes and nonunionized sections of the working class.

But it doesn't determine which interest controls, dominates, runs, and uses the Democratic Party. We say it is dominated, as the Republican Party is dominated, by a minority of its members—by a small group of monopoly capitalists who also control the economy, the government, the means of communication, and the educational system.

It doesn't matter what the Democratic platform says—the chief function of this party, as of the Republican Party, is to protect the interests of the monopoly capitalists at home and abroad. It doesn't matter what the candidates of this party say during election campaigns (they usually say what they think will win votes, not what they think)—what counts is what its officeholders do about the important issues of the day. Only a few examples are possible now.

The overwhelming majority of the people of this country, and of the members of both capitalist parties, want peace, the relaxation of international tensions, a ban on nuclear explosions, and so on. But what do they get? Wars, war crises, preparation for war, militarization, the draft, a permanent arms economy, and crushing taxes to maintain it; the continuation of the cold war and cold war propaganda. And the Democratic Party's chief complaint against the Republicans is that they don't appropriate and spend enough for these purposes! On this issue the Democratic Party surely serves the interests of the ruling class faithfully and consistently.

The Democrats differ from the Republicans occasionally on what to do about unemployment, because the Democrats usually have greater support among the unemployed and want to retain that support. But their differences are minor, sometimes insignificant. They agree on the basic things: that the present economic system must not be reorganized to abolish unemployment; that when workers are laid off through no fault of their own, *they* should suffer cuts in their living standards, rather than the employers; that jobless compensation should not be paid for the duration of unemployment; that the workweek should not be shortened. These are things the capitalist class thinks, too.

The Jim Crow system in the United States is the scandal of the world. Nevertheless, the American ruling class shows no intention of abolishing it within the lifetime of anyone now living. In the South the Democratic Party is a one-party dictatorship dedicated to maintaining white supremacy. In Congress, it provides the bulk of the votes against meaningful civil rights legislation. Northern Democrats have to make some gestures to keep the Negro vote, but their liberalism is rarely more than skin deep on this question. If you elect liberals like [Senators Philip] Hart and [Patrick] McNamara, who swear undying devotion to the civil rights cause, the first thing they do when they get to Washington is vote to elect the southern Democratic enemies of the Negro people to the key congressional posts, which are used to block civil rights and all other progressive legislation. Liberals like Governor Williams will make impassioned speeches about injustice to Negroes in the South, but no one has ever heard him utter a single word about the most Jim Crow city in the North—right on his own doorstep—Dearborn, whose mayor boasts that no Negro can live there. So it would be putting it mildly to say that the Democratic Party's policy on civil rights is in accord with that of the ruling class, which always benefits from hatred and discord among the workers.

My final example is civil liberties. We are still suffering from the effects of the witch-hunt launched to silence all opposition to the cold war. The record shows that the Democratic Party served the capitalist class just as zealously in this witch-hunt as the Republicans. The Democrats passed and enforced the Smith Act to gag political dissent. Democratic presidents transformed the FBI into a political police force. The Democrats started the misnamed government "loyalty" program. A Democratic president initiated the "subversive" blacklist. Democrats spearheaded the passage of the Internal Security Act of 1950. Liberal Democrats took the lead in passing the Humphrey-Butler "Communist Control" Act of 1954. We tend to think of this as the era of McCarthyism, but the Democrats, liberal as well as conservative, were in there doing their fair share of gnawing away at the Bill of Rights. And not only in Washington, but in Lansing, too. The Trucks Law of 1952 was the worst and most repressive law ever passed in Michigan. All the Democrats in the legislature voted for it. Williams, begged by the civil libertarians to veto this bill that would turn Michigan into a police state, said he could see no reason not to sign it, and sign it he did. For the next four years he ignored all appeals that he call for its repeal. It would still be on the books if it had been left up to him rather than the US Supreme Court, which finally struck it down.

Having given an analysis of the Democratic Party, for better or worse, I want to indicate now why it is wrong from just about every conceivable angle for progressives to work in it. I'll take up the labor movement first, the radical groups second.

Unions are created in the first place because there is a fundamental clash of interests between workers and capitalists. A necessary condition for the effective functioning of unions is that they be independent of the capitalists; as we all know, a company union, an organization dominated by the employers, does not and cannot defend the workers' interests. I believe it can be stated as a law: the more independent a union is of capitalists, of individual capitalists and of the capitalist class as a whole, the better able it is to defend the workers' interests. Or if you don't care for the word *law*, let me put it this way: Independence of the labor movement is a first principle, recognized and expounded by the best union leaders, like Debs and [William "Big Bill"] Haywood.

This has always been true, but it is especially true today, when the monopoly stage of capitalism expands the role of the state and gives all struggles, including labor struggles, an openly political character. What labor in our country needs above everything else is a party of its own, which can fight for the needs and aspirations of the workers on the political field as unions can on the economic field. (The present steel negotiations show how inseparable these two fields are becoming.)

But instead of having a party of its own, the labor movement is dependent, in the political sphere, on a party controlled by the capitalists and promoting the interests of the capitalists. It is a tail to the Democratic kite, as one union leader put it. This must be designated as a violation of the principle of independence on the basis of which the union movement was created. It is not only wrong in principle, however. It is also harmful in practice, and the cause of most of the ills besetting the labor movement today.

It was reported not long ago that the unions spent more money on the last congressional election than the Democratic campaign committees did. What have they gotten in return? UAW Secretary-Treasurer Emil Mazey said about a month ago: "We won an election last November, but until now we have not received a single thing from this victory." This is true after *every* election.

The present Congress, controlled by the Democrats the unions helped to elect, has refused to end the filibuster. It has refused to extend jobless compensation for a year. It is on the verge of passing the Kennedy-Ervin bill to further restrict the independence of the unions by subjecting them to government control, a bill which becomes worse and worse every time Congress takes it up. And at the recent conference on unemployment in Washington, all the AFL-CIO could get from the leaders of the Democratic Party was a promise to study the question.

No wonder Jack Crellin of the *Detroit Times* commented after the jobless conference that the AFL-CIO seems to be getting a "mighty poor return on its investment." And, he added ironically, "At least Jimmy Hoffa gets 6 percent on his."

Hoffa is not our idea of a model labor leader, any more than Reuther is. But sometimes they tell the truth, too. I think Hoffa did that in a recent interview with the *Detroit Free Press.* Asked to comment on the alliance between the UAW and the Michigan Democratic Party, he said: "The

UAW has less power that way. If I got you, I don't have to worry about you. The Democrats control the UAW in Michigan. Reuther has got himself into a trap and doesn't know how to get out." Reuther knows how to get out all right, but except for that, I think Hoffa's statement comes close to the truth, which I would put this way: Thanks to this alliance, the Democrats have much more influence in the labor movement than the labor movement has in the Democratic Party.

The Democrats can take the unions for granted because they feel they have them in their pocket; because the unions, having sworn not to create their own party, have nowhere else to go. Who can deny this? Dixiecrats get more concessions from the Democrats than the union leaders do because they threaten to bolt and form their own party. The union leaders not only have become dependent on the Democratic Party, they have become its captives. And this is one of the reasons why the Democratic Party has been moving steadily to the Right year after year. So labor's support of the Democrats is wrong in all respects—from the standpoint of principle, from the pragmatic standpoint of results.

What the labor movement and its allies need is to make a clean break with both capitalist parties and form an independent labor party dedicated to winning control of the government and putting into effect a program that will meet the needs of the majority of the people.

For radicals and socialists, the situation is even more clear-cut. Our goal—the creation of a new society through working-class political action—requires that we help the labor movement to break away from capitalist parties and capitalist politics; and that we expand the influence and organization of radical and revolutionary groups and parties fit to provide leadership to the workers in a fight for a better society.

Neither of these objectives can be served by working in the Democratic Party. Again, it is wrong in principle and wrong in every other way that can be measured. The highways are littered with the political corpses of radicals and socialists who entered the Democratic Party with the idea of making it radical, and who ended up by becoming mere liberals or even conservatives themselves.

The main function of the radical movement today is educational and propagandistic, pending the time—not as distant as some radicals think— when it once again can lead the people in great actions and struggles. To educate means first of all to say what is, to tell the people the truth. What good is a radical, what right has he to any hearing, if he doesn't meet this minimum condition?

But you can't be in the Democratic Party and tell the truth to the people. The first thing demanded of you in the Democratic Party is that you support its candidates, that is, help spread the propaganda that the election of Democrats is in the interests of the people. If you do this, you have to lie, you have to cover up the fact that the Democratic Party stands for the cold war, more armaments, little or no help to the unemployed, racial oppression, restrictions on the Bill of Rights, retention of the Taft-Hartley Act, maintenance of the status quo generally.

In short, the condition for working in the Democratic Party is that you must abdicate the primary function of the radical. If everyone did it, it would mean the death of all organized radical opposition to capitalism.

The final test of a policy is in its results. The policy we are debating tonight is not a new one, and it has been tested for a long time. The labor movement has been working in and supporting the Democratic Party for the last twenty-five years: Isn't it true, Brother Haessler, that the Democratic Party today stands to the Right of where it stood twenty-five years ago, and not to the Left? The main sections of the radical movement have been supporting the Democratic Party, directly or indirectly, with only a few lapses, for over twenty years: Can you claim, Brother Haessler, that radical influence in the Democratic Party is greater than it was twenty years ago? Can you claim that radical influence in the country is generally greater today than it was in the days when the radical parties considered it their duty to oppose the Democratic Party at the polls?

Supporting the Democratic Party is at best an exercise in futility for radicals, and one of the causes contributing to their decline. At worst, it is a betrayal of anticapitalist principles that are at the heart of radicalism, and without which it must decay and die.

It is also a repudiation of the whole past of American radicalism. If it's right to support the Democrats today, if it's wrong to oppose them at the polls and to work in every other way to expose their reactionary character, then everything the old socialist movement did in its best days was also wrong and should be renounced rather than pointed to as an inspiration for the future. If it's right to support the Democrats today, then Debs was wrong in helping to organize the Socialist Party, in running those magnificent election campaigns, in teaching that it is unprincipled for socialists to support capitalist candidates; then Debs was just a hopeless sectarian, whose example has little to offer us today. (Which, incidentally, is what William Z. Foster and the Communist Party now are saying.)

Speaking of Debs reminds me of the question that people sometimes ask: What happened to the old idealism of the socialist movement, the self-sacrificing spirit of solidarity and militancy that the American radical movement used to know? What happened to it was that the leaders of the movement, lacking or losing confidence in the capacity of the workers to change society and govern themselves, began to find all kinds of pretexts and rationalizations for deserting the policies of class struggle and embracing the policies of class collaboration. One of the manifestations of this change was the change from the old principle that it's the duty of socialists to oppose capitalist party candidates, to run independent candidates and use election campaigns to expose the nature of capitalism and present the truth about socialism—a change from this tradition to arguments that independent campaigns achieve nothing, that you must not let yourself get "isolated," that you must adjust yourself to the politics of the labor bureaucrats rather than fight them.

You can't create idealism, you can't maintain militancy and devotion to the great goals of the socialist future through such maneuvers. Take the workers into the Democratic swamp of opportunism, horse trades, and dirty machine politics, where any piece of filthy work is justified if it helps win the next election, and you can't expect anything but that it will sap the workers' militancy, devotion to principle, and class consciousness—if they remain there and don't drop out of politics altogether demoralized.

The future lies with the youth—the young people just beginning to recover from a decade of cold war conformism. They've heard enough lies to last them for a lifetime. What they need is the truth, simple and direct. Only if they get it will they respond with those reserves of militancy and bravery that are especially characteristic of the young, that seem to be the prerequisite of every genuine revolution, and that can revitalize American radicalism as an effective fighting force. You'll get nowhere feeding the youth white lies or half-truths about the Democratic Party. You'll be shirking your duty to them and to the future if you tell them to go work in the Democratic Party.

Therefore, the policy dictated to progressives is to oppose the Democratic Party, not to work in it or get others to support it. Those of us who are workers should strive in our unions to bring about a break with capitalist politics, and the formation of an independent labor party. Those of us who are radicals and socialists should do everything we can to fight the two-party system, utilize election campaigns to spread socialist ideas and influence, and run socialist slates for office, *if* possible along the general lines of the Independent-Socialist ticket in New York in 1958.

That ticket, bringing together independent radicals, former Progressive Party members, and Socialist Workers Party members in a united socialist campaign against both capitalist parties, was an encouraging progressive alternative to the compromising, demoralizing, self-defeating policy of working in the Democratic Party. The Socialist Workers Party advocated similar united left-wing tickets here in Michigan in the 1957 and 1958 election campaigns. The other radical groups in the state rejected its proposals in those years. We hope they will respond differently to proposals for a united ticket of radicals, socialists, and progressives in the 1960 campaign, nationally and locally. If they don't, we promise we will still try to act as socialists should, by placing a socialist ticket on the ballot in Michigan and running a campaign that will help promote independent working-class political action by openly telling the truth about capitalism and socialism.

REBUTTALS

Haessler: Let me say first that many of the things that Brother Breitman said about the Democratic Party as a whole are true enough. And I had no thought of denying that when I presented the case. What I was arguing was effective political action as against propaganda action, and I notice that one of the most significant things that Brother Breitman said was that for some time to come, radical third-party action would have to be of a propagandistic nature.

The Democratic Party is regarded by my opponent as one of the few things in the world that doesn't change. Everything else is changing, even the Republican Party; some of the Republicans are liberal, vote in the senate on the liberal side. But the Democratic Party does not change. It's a stinking mess of corruption and reaction. Just summarizing in three words what we've heard for the last thirty minutes. Now that is obviously an exaggeration. It's permissible in partisan debate, and I won't try to knock it down. I notice that nothing was said by Brother Breitman with regard to my opening point, which was the capture of the Michigan Supreme Court by the labor-backed and labor-financed Democratic Party.

Certainly Governor Williams signed the Trucks Act. The Republican state supreme court upheld the Trucks Act, and then it went to the US Supreme Court; and the US Supreme Court knocked it out. Did one person go to jail in the meantime under the Trucks Act? Was one person fined in the meantime? Very effective debating, Brother Breitman, but let's have all the facts. And so we can take up other things that were mentioned.

Certainly in the US government President Truman started the loyalty program for government employees. But why did he do it? I don't know if he should have done it even in view of all the facts, but the reason he did it was that McCarthy and his gang, both Democrat and Republican, in the Senate, were starting a witch-hunt, and Truman, mistakenly or not, thought that this loyalty program was one way to stop it. It wasn't that Truman's heart was in the red-baiting campaign, but you know McCarthy's heart was there, and Truman, as well as those who advised him, thought that this was one way to put a brake on the witch-hunt movement, Of course, people suffered; they would have suffered even more if this hadn't been put up. But it was not, as Brother Breitman says, one of the worst smells of the Democratic Party in Washington. It was an attempt to keep a bad thing in check.

So I think we would proceed more fruitfully in this matter if we came down to cases in our own state, where things are getting along pretty well. Of course you say that the Democrats rule labor in this state. Nobody thinks so except the speaker and a few of those who agreed with him beforehand. The whole complaint in this state, in the press, in private party councils of the Republicans and of the old-line Democrats themselves, is not that the Democrats have captured the UAW and its sister unions, but the other way around. Who is the national committeeman from Michigan? Is he a labor man, or a pro-labor man, or is he an old-line Democrat? Who got the biggest vote of all the candidates in the spring election for public office? Was it an old-line Democrat or was it Brother Woodcock, vice president and crown prince of the UAW, a man who used to be on the National Executive Committee of the Socialist Party? Those are the kind of Democrats that own the party in this state.

And my program to you is that there are other states emerging into a similar situation, where organized labor is strong enough, where it has the money to put up, which talks in political campaigns, as our splinter parties know only too well (they could talk a lot louder if they had a lot more money). Those are the things that are promising and those are the things that the youth of our country, if they are interested organizationally, politically, and not just as a pure sect of propagandists, if they're interested in getting things done politically, helping to guide their course, that's the kind of direction that the youth interested in political action should take.

Now I've heard, and I used to spout it myself, and I believed it for many, many years, that what Brother Breitman has proposed tonight is the true course. I no longer think so. We have to recognize conditions in this country, that it's the two-party system, very hard to overthrow, that you start working politically effectively by getting into that party, and you realize that the national party doesn't mean anything except once in four years. It's a coalition of state machines, and when you begin to get your hand in the state machine, you're getting to be one of the little levers, and then you and your friends reach out and get hold of bigger levers, and finally you control the whole thing. You get into that Democratic car, and when the time comes, you grab the wheel and then you run it. You run it the way you and your other labor members want it run, and then the Michigan car, the New Jersey car, and the Minnesota car, and the California car, and the Pennsylvania car, and the West Virginia car, and all the others, then you get together, you'll have a national fleet of cars. Not run by old-line Democrats.

In fact, enlightened northern Democrats have begun to realize that the party doesn't need the Dixiecrats in order to win nationally. They're telling them to go to hell. And the Dixiecrats aren't doing it. You watch 1960, the Dixiecrats know they can no longer run the Democratic Party but they know that by the seniority system, which Brother Breitman thinks is so terrible, the Dixiecrats can still hang on to certain committee chairmanships. They now have both the speaker of the House and the majority leader of the Senate. But what did those two men do just a few months ago? They formally severed their connection with the Dixiecrat caucus, the southern group, and affiliated with the western caucus. Both

Speaker [Sam] Rayburn and Senate majority leader [Lyndon B.] Johnson. Now Brother Breitman may think they did this with the full intent of running the western states. My opinion is that they climbed on a bandwagon. And in time, Rayburn, who is way up in his seventies, will retire on a fat pension, or he'll die. Other southerners will die, too, some will get defeated by younger men, the chairmanships will go around, and you take a freshman senator like [Phillip A.] Hart, coming up to Washington and asking for his committee appointments, and he's apt to be in the Senate for a long time. I know he married a millionairess—the daughter of a sweatshop manufacturer of the worst odor in Detroit, the late Mr. Briggs, who used to pay his women ten cents an hour and cheat them on overtime. Well, Briggs isn't in control, and I doubt whether Miss Briggs, now Mrs. Hart, controls Hart himself. I know that Hart has wrong things about him, I know that in the last campaign he bragged he was one of those who red-baited against the Communist Party. Of course, all sorts of people have red-baited against the Communist Party; Norman Thomas has done it as effectively as Walter Reuther has done it. But that's political opportunism and not conviction. Because one of the grievances that the Socialist Party in my opinion has against the reds, against the Communists, is that the Communists have made a going concern of a number of countries and the Socialists never have. But that's just family bickering, apart from the main course tonight. What should a progressive who is interested in organized political action do? Should he work in the Democratic Party? Yes, that's what I repeat for George's rebuttal.

Breitman: When Brother Haessler says that the Democratic Party can become a labor-dominated party, he puts me in the position of trying to prove a negative, which is a difficult thing to do. On the bus the other day I overheard two teenagers: One asked if the other believed in ghosts. The second said, "No, there are no such things." The first said, "How can you say that when you can't prove it? Go ahead, prove that there are no ghosts." All the second could do was mutter that you can't prove the moon isn't made of green cheese, either.

It's hard to prove a negative to the satisfaction of all. I've tried to show how the unions and many radicals have been working for a long time to move the Democratic Party to the Left, and all that's happened is that it's moved to the Right. I say it's your job to disprove that. Or to show why efforts to reform the Democratic Party will have any different results now than they had in the past. It's not enough to merely assert that the Democratic Party can be changed from an instrument of the capitalist class into an instrument of the working class—you have to demonstrate this possibility by current developments and trends, by logic, by the lessons of experience, which I've tried to use.

But Brother Haessler makes my job easier when he claims that the Democratic Party already has changed, and already has "for all practical purposes" been captured by labor in Michigan, among other states. This is a question of fact which all of you can test for yourselves. Let me cite a few of the many examples you will find showing that the labor movement, far from controlling the Democratic Party in this or any other state, is a captive of the Democratic Party; is a prisoner of the [L. Mennen] Williamses and the [Neil] Staeblers; is the tail, not the dog.

Just four months ago the Michigan AFL-CIO decided to conduct a fight for a state law to pay unemployment compensation for the duration of unemployment. This was a big step forward for the labor movement. They showed they were serious when they got the Democratic minority leader in Lansing and other Democrats in the House to agree to sponsor and introduce the bill. Then Williams stepped in. He didn't attack the bill directly, just said that it was different from what he favored, and he would have to study it. But that did it. The Democrats in Lansing backed away on the double. Not one of them would introduce the bill after that. The AFL-CIO helped to elect sixty-seven Democrats now in Lansing, but not one of them will even introduce this bill. However, that's not the worst part; the most miserable thing of all is that the AFL-CIO then dropped the proposal, too—its own proposal. They don't advocate in May what they said was necessary in January. Three days ago the AFL-CIO held a conference in Lansing on unemployment, and failed to even mention this bill that they said was necessary in January—even mention it as one of their long-range objectives. Labor supplies the money and the votes to elect the Democrats, but the Democrats have a greater voice in determining labor's program than labor has in determining the Democrats'.

Another example of who's captured whom: We in Michigan pay among the highest consumer taxes in the country. The Democratic platforms of 1948, 1950, 1952, 1954 pledged opposition to additional consumer taxes. In January 1955, the Republicans introduced a road construction program involving an increase of a gallon in the consumer tax paid on gasoline. The CIO denounced this plan. So did Williams. He called it a "political plunderbund," and said, "It almost made me gag." Almost—but not quite. Because less than a month later, he accepted a so-called compromise in which the added consumer tax was set at one and a half cents, rather than two cents. The CIO then dropped its opposition to added consumer taxes. And its members in the legislature voted for the increase. Of course if a Republican governor had violated his platform in such a fashion, the CIO would have denounced him from hell to breakfast as a man whose promises were worthless, whose platform wasn't worth the paper it was printed on. But that's not the point I'm trying to make now. The point is, this is another example of how the labor movement's own program becomes conservatized as a result of its alliance with the Democrats, another example showing who is the master in this alliance. You are urged to be practical, but I really can't think of anything more utopian than the idea of trying to capture the Democratic Party away from its bosses. It's not a democratic organization controlled by its members. It is a highly bureaucratic structure dominated from the top. You can't take it away from its bosses. If you did in this or that isolated case, you'd either be expelled or the antilabor elements would walk out and get the recognition of the national party. And you would end up having "captured" only yourselves.

The second thing to understand about this is that the union leaders don't want to capture the Democratic Party. They're as much against capturing the Democratic Party as they are against forming a labor party, because they don't want labor to have its own party, no matter how it originates. Until 1952, the CIO delegates at the Michigan State Democratic Convention used to meet in a caucus to discuss what they, the CIO delegates, were going to do. But at the spring convention in 1952, some of them talked incautiously about "taking over." Well, they were quickly squelched by Gus Scholle, who told them, "You won't capture anyone but yourselves." Since 1952, the labor delegates at the Democratic convention no longer even meet as a caucus, as a separate group. They have less intention of "taking over" than ever before. My point here is, you'll have just as big a fight on your hands trying to get the unions to capture the Democratic Party as you will in trying to get them to decide to form a labor party. The difference is, when you win the labor movement to a labor party, you'll have something, while if you finally succeed in getting the unions to try to take over the Democratic Party, you'll have accomplished little, because the Democratic Party won't let itself be captured. From a purely practical standpoint, which has been invoked here, it is far more realistic to keep fighting inside the unions for a labor party than to try to make the unions try to capture the Democratic Party.

Brother Haessler speaks about great accomplishments from labor infiltration of the Democratic Party in Michigan. He spoke on it at some length, but in the end he had only one concrete example of an accomplishment, and that was the decision of the Michigan Supreme Court on unemployment compensation. But this decision is not really as remarkable as he says. All it provides is that under certain conditions, workers laid off as a result of a strike in other states shall be eligible for unemployment compensation. But, according to Williams and the UAW, around thirty-five other states in the country already have provisions similar to that. And nobody would seriously claim that their having such provisions is the result of the Democratic Party or courts being controlled by the labor movement in those states.

Brother Haessler asks if this could have been done through any other force than the Democratic Party; if it could be done by the Socialist Workers Party or any of the other small radical groups at the present time. Obviously the answer is no. They are not in a position now to get a majority of the state supreme court. But it doesn't follow that labor therefore is forced to rely on the Democratic Party. It can get concessions of this modest caliber by exerting mass pressure on both capitalist parties, without supporting either. And it can get much bigger concessions by forming its own party to fight both old parties. The alternative should not be restricted to the small radical parties of today or the Democratic Party of today; the choice for progressives is also between the Democratic Party of today and the labor party that the union movement is now capable of building.

Brother Haessler points to the difficulties of building a labor party. I think he overstates them. The labor movement in the United States is big enough to build its own party; it is bigger than the labor movement in other countries that have labor parties. It can do it if it wants to. In its very first election, a labor party would sweep the big cities in the United States. Here in Detroit it could elect five or six labor congressmen to replace the Democrats. It could do this in all the other big cities, too. From the very beginning it could have in Congress a large bloc of congressmen who would fight for the things labor wants and which it doesn't have there now. From the start it would emerge as the second party, rather than a third party, because the Democratic Party minus the labor movement will amount to very little. What's lacking for this is not personnel, what's lacking is not the people with the experience to run such a party, or to be its candidates, or to get it on the ballot, or to do its precinct work. What's lacking is the will, which is paralyzed by the opposition of the top union leaders. The job of progressives in the labor movement is to fight to crystallize that will by opposing the political policies of the leadership, not to support and aid them.

I might say, if we're going to mention "all the facts," that Justice George Edwards, who is presented here as something of a hero because he spent thirty days in jail as a union organizer in 1937, also has another achievement in his record—namely, that in 1949, as president of the Detroit City Council, he was the one who introduced and pushed for the passage of the reactionary City Loyalty Investigating Committee. And it is Edwards, among others, who is pointed to as one of the bulwarks of liberalism on the supreme court. It is like the attempt here to defend the Democrats pushing through witch-hunt measures on the ground that they were trying to prevent the Republicans from pushing through worse witch-hunt measures, which seems to me to be carrying the argument of the "lesser evil" to the point of absurdity.

I was interested by Brother Haessler's advice to Reuther to abandon the Socialist Party and avoid those "entangling little alliances." Reuther was to some extent perhaps persuaded by him; at any rate, we know he left the Socialist Party for substantially such reasons. The trouble is that he got engaged instead in one big alliance, with the Democratic Party, and it's that in which the labor movement is badly entangled and hamstrung.

For progressives to spend their time and effort working in the Democratic Party is neither progressive nor practical. This policy does not result in teaching workers that they cannot trust capitalist politicians and parties. Instead, it results in strengthening illusions that the Democratic Party is a lesser evil and that they can solve their problems through that party rather than needing a new party. It does not educate the workers to act along the lines of class struggle in politics. On the contrary, it encourages and justifies the continuation of class collaboration in politics. You cannot serve the cause of socialism and progress by telling the workers that the Democrats are worthy of support despite their pro-capitalist, pro-war, pro-witch-hunt, pro–Jim Crow program. Therefore, we appeal to Carl Haessler and all other progressives who favor spending their considerable talents in the Democratic Party to reconsider.

The world tide is now against capitalism. Workers have ended it in many parts of the world. In the United States, too, incurable sicknesses are coming to the fore—growing discontent with foreign policy, a new permanent army of unemployed, a deepening demand for integration, an intense restlessness and instability. New opportunities are about to open up for radicals. Let us try to work together to meet them. We still have differences among ourselves. Without denying them or forgetting them, let us work together in those areas where we see eye to eye—in our political opposition to war, depression, racial oppression, infringements of civil liberties. Let us get together on these issues and do in 1960 what the progressives and socialists did in New York last year: let us put in the field a united Independent-Socialist ticket that will challenge both capitalist parties and educate all the people that it can reach to understand the necessity for a new party and a new society.

Haessler: I have a few minutes in what you might call rerebuttal. I haven't anything to say against Brother Breitman's peroration. I think the ideals expressed are noble, are ideals that I agree with. I further have nothing to say against his appeals for certain people to devote themselves to the organizing of an independent labor party. If they wish to, let them do it. And let me say further that I myself am not enough interested in political organization work to work in the Democratic Party. What I've been presenting is a practical program for those who are politically, organizationally interested. If you want to work and achieve practical political results in this state and a number of other states, do it through the Democratic Party. Don't waste your time trying to achieve practical results in these nonexistent or barely existent third parties of all sorts. That's all I was proposing.

To come down to a few trivial points, I didn't parade George Edwards as a hero; he's not one of my heroes. I was simply showing the course of evolution by labor control of the Democratic Party in this state. Here was a jailbird, in jail for the contempt of the courts in our state. He is now sitting on the topmost court in the state, and bawling out lower judges for not acting in a progressive manner. It was just an incident in political evolution, and not a parade of my heroes. In fact, I haven't mentioned any of my heroes tonight. Brother Breitman has—Eugene Debs was one of my longtime heroes, and the first picture ever taken of my first baby was when Debs held him in his arms. I sent that off to the relatives at Christmastime, and one of them replied, "We're so glad to see a picture of your baby, but please send us next time a picture that we can love."

Well, as for the future, I want to see a land of plenty, a land of peace, a land of happiness. I want to see the dreams come true of the couples with two incomes in the family, the wife working, too, and she saying, "When we get rich, I want to have a vacuum cleaner upstairs as well as downstairs," and the man says, "Yes, Sally, when we get rich, I want to use a blue blade, both edges on one shave." And the time will come when those dreams will be realized, and many bigger dreams than those. I'm for a practical third party. I don't want you to waste your time on any if it's not going to be practical. If you want to be practical in an organizationally political way in this state, and in a number of other states, the practical and effective way is, as I've said, through the transforming of the Democratic Party.

CHAPTER 11

IS IT WRONG FOR REVOLUTIONARIES TO FIGHT FOR REFORMS?
(1969)

George Breitman

Among young radicals, white and black, there is a certain amount of misunderstanding about problems connected with reform and revolution and their relation to each other.

Such misunderstandings are sometimes expressed in current notions:

- That it is incorrect for revolutionaries to advocate and fight for reforms;
- That revolutionaries should not bother trying to organize the masses to fight for anything that can be won under the present system;
- That the only kind of demands it is proper for revolutionaries to raise and organize around are those that cannot be used, misused, distorted, or "co-opted" by the ruling class or opportunists; etc.

Perhaps these questions can be clarified by reexamining the concepts "reform" and "revolution" from a Marxist standpoint.

For present purposes, a reform can be called a change in social, political, or economic institutions or arrangements that does not necessarily imply or require a fundamental change in those institutions or arrangements. In contrast, such a fundamental change, involving the overturn of

Originally published in the *Militant,* February 28, 1969.

the social-political-economic system itself and the replacement in state power of the former ruling class by a new ruling class, is what we usually mean when we talk about revolution.

Examples: When Congress passed laws in the 1930s recognizing the legal right of the workers to organize unions and bargain collectively, that was a reform. When the Supreme Court ruled in 1954 that school segregation is unconstitutional, that was another reform. The New Deal initiated by Franklin D. Roosevelt in the 1930s was not a revolution, just as the more recent Great Society was not a revolution, because the prevailing class and power relationships were not changed basically, as they were in the Russian, Yugoslav, Chinese, Cuban, and Vietnamese revolutions of this century.

Some reforms are initiated by the ruling class itself, because it thinks them beneficial to the interests of its system. Some are resisted by the ruling class for a long time and granted only after bitter struggle convinces them that it is a lesser evil. Some reforms are won peacefully, others only through the most violent conflict. Some ruling classes have been known to refuse to grant certain reforms right up to the point where they were overthrown. (Not every ruling class makes all decisions wisely or always acts truly in its own self-interest; this is especially true in revolutionary situations and crises.)

Revolutionary Marxists, starting with Marx, have never been opposed to the struggle for reforms; on the contrary, for revolutionaries to oppose such struggles or refuse to join and try to lead them would be to doom themselves to permanent isolation and futility. Except in revolutionary situations (and not always then) most of the exploited and oppressed masses do not see the necessity or possibility of winning anything but reforms (no matter how radical or numerous the reforms they want may be).

The essence of Marxist strategy, of any revolutionary strategy in our time, is to combine the struggle for reforms with the struggle for revolution. This is the only way in which to build a revolutionary party capable of providing reliable leadership to the masses and of enabling them in revolutionary situations to make the transition, in consciousness and in action, from the struggle for reforms to the struggle for power and revolution.

The United States is not now in a revolutionary situation. This is unfortunate, but true; and it is from this truth that revolutionaries must proceed in the development of strategy and tactics. On the other hand, it is also true that there is considerable social unrest, frustration, alienation, and the start of sizable radicalization in this country today, especially among young people, who provide the chief forces for revolution.

FAVORABLE SITUATION

That means there is a favorable situation developing for conscious and dedicated revolutionaries—a growing body of people who can be won to the cause of revolution even before a revolutionary situation actually arises. The development of significant revolutionary cadres is more possible now than at any time in the last third of a century.

But the gathering, education, and toughening of revolutionary cadres, while indispensable for a revolution, isn't enough to guarantee one. There are still all those people "out there"—the millions and millions who are not ready to make a revolution, although they are certainly in favor of reforms that can affect their living conditions and personal destinies. (This applies not only to the population generally, but also to the overwhelming majority of black people and young people, among whom the radicalization process is more advanced.)

Even though a revolution is not possible today, the development of a revolutionary strategy is. But you can't develop one unless you take into account the way to win those millions toward independent and revolutionary motion.

So revolutionary Marxists cannot be opposed to the struggle for reforms. What we oppose is reformism.

Reformism is the tendency which holds that the basic problems of society can be solved, or even that socialism can be achieved, by the gradual accumulation of reforms, one by one. That concept, not fighting for reforms, is what revolutionaries are and should be against.

Reforms can be sought in various ways. Reformists work for them in a class-collaborationist, conciliatory fashion, attempting to convince the exploited and oppressed masses that the system is "workable," that their interests and those of the exploiters and oppressed can and should be reconciled, that class and national struggles should not be fought out to their logical conclusion.

Revolutionaries fight for reforms, but they never stop teaching the masses the truth about the inadequacies of reforms so long as the ruling class is not displaced from power, about the ease with which reforms can be canceled or withdrawn or made meaningless by ineffective or discriminatory enforcement as long as the ruling class remains in power, about the need to go beyond reforms and reconstruct the foundations of society on a planned and rational basis.

In the struggle against fascism, for example, reformists seek to reinforce illusions about and reliance on capitalist democracy, and oppose antifascist methods that might go beyond the framework of capitalist democracy and thus incur the displeasure of the democratic capitalists. Revolutionaries, on the other hand, try to help the masses to understand the unreliability and treachery of the democratic capitalists and the need to combine antifascism with anticapitalism.

Another distinction is that reformists propose at best halfway measures aimed at avoiding showdown conflicts while revolutionaries encourage independent mass action and independent mass organization as the only way to win and keep reforms, to deepen consciousness and extend the conditions for continuing social change.

ONLY REFORM?

James Haughton and Timothy J. Cooney of Harlem's Equal Employment Council, which seeks construction work for blacks, think they have an airtight case when they argue that because the United States is not about to have a revolution, therefore the black man "has only one course of action: the hard, unromantic road of reform." That they actually mean the road of reformism is made clear when they add: "He [the black man] must have a legislative program and a political strategy for putting it across. He must grit his teeth and politely testify before hostile congressional committees. He must make alliances of convenience with people he doesn't like. He must learn that awful business of compromise," etc. (*Manhattan Tribune*, November 20, 1968).

The flaw in their logic is obvious. Black people have to fight for reforms, but that doesn't mean that they have to fight for them in a reformist way. They have the alternative of fighting for them in a revolutionary way—by militant mass action rather than polite testimony, and as part of a strategy consciously aimed at mobilizing the masses to change the system. You don't have to become a reformist just because revolution is not around the corner. In fact, that is the way to assure that revolution will never come—just as, conversely, a refusal to fight for reforms, in a revolutionary fashion, is also a way of postponing revolution.

In a similar way to Haughton and Cooney, Harold Cruse thinks he is making some kind of telling point when he asserts that Malcolm X cannot be considered a revolutionary because the program of his Organization of Afro-American Unity "was definitely written as a reformist document" (*The Crisis of the Negro Intellectual*, p. 442). He means, of course, that the OAAU programs of Malcolm's time urged black people to organize to fight for reforms.

But why does that disqualify Malcolm as a revolutionary, any more than it disqualifies Marx, Engels, Lenin, Trotsky, Mao Tse-tung, Castro, or Ho Chi Minh? The real question is whether Malcolm intended to fight for those reforms in a revolutionary way, and to utilize the organization, education, and experience acquired in the course of the fight for them to promote revolution. The answer is affirmative, although it will not be found in Cruse's writings. It is clearly apparent from Malcolm's teachings, summarized in his declaration: "By any means necessary."

To approach the problem another way: it is instructive to contrast SNCC [the Student Nonviolent Coordinating Committee] with the black student unions that have arisen in the last year or two. SNCC is an organization to whom all revolutionaries owe gratitude as a pioneer of the present radicalization; historically, it will surely be ranked with the IWW [Industrial Workers of the World] as a forerunner of the American revolution. But its present stagnation and isolation cannot be attributed solely to the savage persecution it has suffered at the hands of the government. In part, it has been hamstrung by its own antileadership fetish, by the unfortunate theory held by some of its leaders that "repression" will produce radicalization and revolution, and in the recent period by generalizations about revolution that somehow discouraged or minimized participation in the partial struggles that got the label of "nonrevolutionary."

On the other hand, the black student unions, which might have served as a major base for the revival and expansion of SNCC, have been healthily free of certain abstentionist inhibitions. Without excessive rhetoric, they have struck stunning blows at the status quo from one coast to the other. And what are their demands? Nothing but reforms, and reforms of only the schools at that!

But because they are fighting for reforms in a radical way, they have raised the campus struggles to a new level, strengthening the whole movement immensely, and making possible the widening of the youth radicalization, including whites as well as blacks. And because they are fighting in a radical way, they are winning more than if they had fought in a reformist way, even where they cannot win all of their demands. Dr. Nathan Hare is absolutely correct in his retort to Roy Wilkins when he says, "Our cries for more black professors and black students have padded white colleges with more blacks in two years than a decade of whimpering for integration ever did."

FALSE LIMIT

If we limit ourselves only to those demands that the ruling class and opportunists will not try (often unsuccessfully) to distort, manipulate, or co-opt, there will be very few demands we will ever be able to raise. In a revolutionary situation the ruling class will try to co-opt even revolutionary demands. For example, in the German revolution at the end of World War I, when the masses began to organize workers and soldiers councils (soviets), the ruling class and its social-democratic henchmen offered to "recognize" the councils and incorporate them into the government as an official institution (where, of course, they would have been subordinated, housebroken, and emasculated).

There are few if any demands so simon-pure that they can be guaranteed forever immune to manipulation by the enemy. The cure lies in education, alertness, flexibility, and in the creation of movements with a high level of revolutionary consciousness—not in the search for perfect but elusive formulas, and not in abandoning or abstaining from the struggle for reforms that have the potential of organizing and educating the masses.

(The Cuban Revolution developed as a struggle for reforms—end of the dictatorship, land for the peasant, lower rents, homes, schools, jobs for the workers—but because the Fidelistas mobilized masses in a revolutionary struggle for these reforms and educated them to the need to struggle for these things against any force that opposed them, they carried the struggle to a conclusion that brought the first socialist revolution in the Western Hemisphere.)

Nothing in the world can be done to prevent the government, the Ford Foundation, or various black opportunists from trying to give their content to the popular demand for black control of the black community, from interpreting it as "black capitalism" or "decentralization" or the election of black Democrats, etc., and from seeking to deflect the struggle for this demand into safer channels. (Attempts to dampen down movements with concession can boomerang, too. This, for example, was the intent in giving ghetto youth college scholarships and grants. Now they've got a panther by the tail.)

The way to combat efforts of the ruling class to co-opt demands is not to conclude that such demands are worthless but to give them a revolutionary content. To do otherwise can only guarantee the continued influence of the reformists among the masses.

For example, the school issue is a major one today for black people in New York and other cities. The reformists, supported by sections of the ruling class, try to keep that struggle within the limits of simple school decentralization. It is the obligation of revolutionaries to join the school struggle precisely to counterpose the revolutionary concept of black control of black schools to the reformist concept of an "improved," "less bureaucratic," "decentralized" education system.

The negative attitude of some black radicals to the struggle for black control of the black community has been paralleled by the disparaging attitude of some white radicals toward certain demands and aspects of the fight against the war in Vietnam, which has already radicalized millions of young Americans despite far-from-perfect leadership.

ANTIWAR MOVEMENT

The current antiwar movement had hardly got started in 1965 before some leaders of SDS [Students for a Democratic Society] and certain ultraleftist groups began to complain that they were "tired" of broad antiwar demonstrations and marches demanding the withdrawal of the GIs from Vietnam. Why? Because they weren't stopping the war, or because they were "too square," or because they weren't sufficiently anti-imperialist, or because they concentrated on trying to reach wider sections of the population instead of seeking "confrontations" with the cops, or (during the 1968 election campaign) because the liberal capitalist politicians were trying (with partial and temporary success) to exploit, deflect, and co-opt the antiwar sentiment and movement.

The Vietnamese liberation movement has a more realistic and a much more favorable estimate about the value of the antiwar demonstrations, and does not concur in the American ultraleftist judgment that they are now "passé."

But independently of the Vietnamese opinion, surely there should be more American radicals capable of appreciating the tremendous contributions the antiwar movement, with all its defects and limitations, has made up to this point, and is still capable of making—providing the American radicals don't turn their backs on it now.

Similar criticisms can be made about some of the current radical attitudes to antiwar referendums, and to electoral activity in general. (Barry Sheppard's refutation of the *Guardian*'s no-vote position on the 1968 election campaign, in the November 15, 1968, *Militant*, was perfectly correct, but probably will have to be repeated many times before electoral abstentionism is fully understood for the childish nonsense it is.)

VOTING AGE ISSUE

Lowering the voting age to eighteen is nothing but a reform, and one which has been granted even in reactionary states in this country. But a fight for this reform, led by revolutionaries and conducted with some imagination, could have a profoundly radicalizing-politicizing effect, especially among young people.

I lived in Michigan a few years ago when a referendum on this issue was held in that state, and I must report my disappointment at seeing the revolutionary socialists, adult and youth alike, confining themselves to routine endorsement of the lower-age reform instead of dramatizing and leading the campaign to enact it. Perhaps their underreaction was due to the fact that both capitalist parties, the labor movement, and just about everybody else also endorsed the proposition. (But it was badly defeated in the referendum vote.)

It is healthy for radicals, old and young, to beware of the dangers of reformism, but it is dangerous to mistake the baby for the bathwater or the bathwater for the baby. The American Communist and Socialist Parties did not become reformist because they participated in the struggle for reforms; the reasons have to be sought elsewhere. And the Socialist Labor Party did not remain revolutionary by deciding to oppose participation in struggles for immediate and partial demands; their hostility to every working-class revolution of this century testifies to that.

Capitalism always attempts to buy off every popular movement that it cannot pervert, misdirect, or crush. But there are limits on what it can accomplish along these lines, as the fact that one-third of the world has been torn out of its grip demonstrates. The dangers of co-optation must not be underestimated, but neither should they be overestimated. The reforms and concessions of recent years have not mollified, conciliated, or co-opted the masses of black Americans (even though they bought off some potential leaders). It really takes a lot of faith in the power of capitalism to believe that it is capable of satisfying the demands of the black masses—the only kind of "co-optation" that could end their struggle.

Struggle is the school of the masses. All demands that move the masses into struggle and raise the level of their consciousness are worth raising, fighting for, and incorporating into the overall revolutionary strategy.

None should be excluded because they are "only reforms," or because through sharp struggle they may be won partly or wholly under capitalism, or because the capitalists will try to utilize them for their own purposes, or because they don't conform to the dogmas of sectarians and abstentionists, who have so little self-confidence that whenever they get involved in anything outside of their own tight little warm circles they begin to ask, "What are we doing wrong?"

CHAPTER 12

THE LIBERATING INFLUENCE OF THE TRANSITIONAL PROGRAM
THREE TALKS
(1975)

George Breitman

1. THE LUDLOW AMENDMENT

Many of you know that in our movement there are no official versions of history, whether it's the history of our own movement or anything else. But for the benefit of those who don't know it, I want to mention it at the outset. The only thing you have to accept in order to join our party is its program and the obligation to promote it in accord with its rules and constitution, which of course includes the right to try to persuade the party to change this or that part of its program or constitution. You don't have to agree with every conclusion in Trotsky's *History of the Russian Revolution*, with every formulation in Cannon's books about party building and the development of the Socialist Workers Party (SWP) and its predecessors, with every opinion in the books by Farrell Dobbs and Art Preis on the Teamsters and the CIO, or the writings of George Novack on the philosophy of Marxism, of Mary-Alice Waters on the relations between feminism and the Marxist movement, of Evelyn Reed on anthropology and the matriarchy. We publish and circulate these works because of their value for our Marxist education, because of their general consonance with our revolutionary program, but it would be as silly to demand that all of us must agree with everything they write as it would

---

Originally published in the *Socialist Workers Party Discussion Bulletin*, May 1975.

be to demand that they should write only what we would all agree with 100 percent.

This is my way of saying that my remarks today about certain aspects of the early history of our party, centering around the year 1938, are neither "official" nor "approved." All they represent is my opinion, which is based partly on my memory of that period and partly on recent research, including the reading of documents that I had not seen at that time. I think that the facts I will cite are reliable, and I hope that you will be able to distinguish without difficulty between those facts and my interpretation of them.

In November of this year [1974] it will be forty-six years since James P. Cannon, Max Shachtman, and Martin Abern, expelled from the leadership of the Communist Party, began publishing the *Militant.* But it wasn't until New Year's 1938, in the tenth year of our movement, that the Socialist Workers Party was founded at a national convention in Chicago. Nineteen thirty-eight was also the year when the Fourth International was founded at an international conference in Paris in September, one year before the start of World War II. At this founding conference the delegates adopted as their major programmatic document a resolution written by Trotsky in Mexico, entitled "The Death Agony of Capitalism and the Tasks of the Fourth International," which later came to be referred to as the "Transitional Program."

I am going to talk about some of the problems that arose in the process by which the SWP endorsed the transitional program and changes resulting from this endorsement that continue to influence the SWP to this day. If I do not speak as much about the transitional program itself as the title of this talk might have led you to expect, it is because of (1) a lack of time, (2) the belief that most of you already know about the transitional program, and (3) the abundance of literature available on the subject in the book *The Transitional Program for Socialist Revolution.* Published last year, that book contains the transitional program resolution itself, a series of discussions by Trotsky with different SWP leaders and members about the program, and at least two useful introductions by Joseph Hansen and George Novack. A second edition of this book has just been published, and that contains a number of additional stenograms of Trotsky's discussions on the transitional program, taken down before the program itself was written, some of which are relevant to my talks.

However, I do want to say a couple of things about the transitional program and the transitional method. Of Trotsky's many valuable contributions to Marxist theory there are two, in my opinion, that stand out above the others. One is his theory of the permanent revolution, conceived when he was twenty-six years old, which challenged the conventional wisdom of the movement of his time about the possibilities and perspectives of revolution in most of the world and, after it was confirmed by the Russian Revolution of 1917, became a keystone in the reorientation of the international Marxist vanguard (although for a number of years after 1917 the term "permanent revolution" was not used by anyone).

The other contribution of which I speak was made by Trotsky in 1938, when he was fifty-eight years old and completing the fortieth year of his revolutionary career. Here, in his full maturity, a few weeks after Stalin's liquidation of Bukharin and Rykov in the third big Moscow trial and two and a half years before his own death, Lenin's collaborator and continuator drew on the experiences of the most eventful four decades in revolutionary history and put them together in a new synthesis that we call the transitional program.

That is usually what new great ideas consist of—a rearrangement of old ones, the sifting out of some, a new emphasis for others, a recasting of priorities and relationships. In and of itself, there was not much that was new in the transitional program; some of the parts dated back, as Trotsky noted, ninety years to the *Communist Manifesto*; other parts were so recent that they had not yet been assimilated or expressed in writing, deriving from the actions of the workers themselves, such as the sit-down strikes in the mid-1930s in France and the United States.

Trotsky's contribution was to take these parts and put them together, to unify them, in a way that even his closest collaborators were at first to find unique, maybe even disturbing. His aim was to write a program that would help the revolutionary vanguard to intervene successfully in the class struggle in a period when conditions were objectively prerevolutionary but the masses were still under the influence of the counterrevolutionary Second and Third Internationals or without any leadership at all. As he put it:

> The strategic task of the next period—a prerevolutionary period of agitation, propaganda, and organization—consists in overcoming the contra-

diction between the maturity of the objective revolutionary conditions and the immaturity of the proletariat and its vanguard (the confusion and disappointment of the older generation; the inexperience of the younger generation). It is necessary to help the masses in the process of the daily struggle to find the bridge between present demands and the socialist program of the revolution. This bridge should include a system of *transitional demands*, stemming from today's conditions and from today's consciousness of wide layers of the working class and unalterably leading to one final conclusion: the conquest of power by the proletariat.

The transitional program was written for specific purposes, in the midst of a world depression, on the eve of a world war, for the founding conference of the Fourth International. That has led some people to question or belittle its usefulness for today or tomorrow, when conditions are different. This seems to me the worst kind of formalist thinking, if thinking is the right word. In the first place, it overlooks the fact that the essential conditions are not different—that the contradiction between the maturity of the objective revolutionary conditions and the immaturity of the proletariat and its vanguard is even greater and more pregnant than it was in 1938. If not all the 1938 demands are applicable today (some weren't even applicable yet in 1938), the essential tasks are the same, and the *method* of the transitional program as it was written in 1938 is absolutely applicable today. In fact, the transitional method, in my opinion, is an even greater contribution than the transitional program itself.

In presenting the transitional program, Trotsky emphasized its continuity with the past, rather than what was innovative in it. He said that it "draws the balance of the already accumulated experience of our national sections and on the basis of this experience opens up broader international perspectives." But this was even truer of the transitional method than of the transitional program itself. The transitional method was being used by us before the transitional program was written—after all, the disparity between the maturity of objective conditions and the subjective immaturity of the proletariat and its vanguard did not begin in 1938, and the need for bridges between the vanguard and the masses had existed for a long time.

But before 1938 we weren't conscious of the transitional method that we used on occasion; we certainly were not fully conscious, and we used it haphazardly therefore, or incompletely, or empirically. Trotsky generalized it, concretized it, drew out its implications, showed its logic and necessity, named it, and indelibly imprinted it in our consciousness. For most of us the exposition of the transitional method was quite a revelation, bigger than the one the Moliere character had when he learned that he had been speaking prose all his life.

In 1938 the SWP was rather an exceptional organization. That also is an opinion, but there is plenty of objective evidence to back it up. It was the only organization in the United States that fought against the prevailing tidal waves of New Deal reformism and Stalinist opportunism from a revolutionary standpoint, and it was the only organization inside the Movement for the Fourth International that approached the norms of Bolshevism in the quality of its cadres, the solidity of its principles, and the level of its organizational practice. This is not to say that it was free of serious weaknesses, but it is to say that it had serious strengths as well. This was Trotsky's opinion, and it was for this reason in 1938 that he turned to the SWP leaders for discussion before writing the transitional program and that he asked the SWP to adopt and sponsor it at the founding conference of the Fourth International.

A history of our movement in this country from its inception in 1928 to the founding of the SWP in 1938 has been written by Comrade Cannon in the book called *The History of American Trotskyism*. It will have to suffice here to say that the first major turning point in this history came in 1933, after Hitler's victory in Germany, when our movement discontinued its efforts to reform the Communist International and its affiliated parties and set out here in the United States to gather the cadres of a new Marxist party as part of a new, Fourth International.

This meant that we now turned our primary attention away from the Communist Party, and that our main activity, the dissemination of propaganda, began to be combined with intervention and action, where possible, in the class struggle. At the end of 1934, after the Minneapolis strike had shown our competence in intervention and action, our movement merged with a left-centrist current led by A. J. Muste (this became the Workers Party) and then, in the spring of 1936, we entered the Socialist Party in order to merge with young revolutionary elements who had been attracted to that organization. Our forces, considerably augmented, were expelled from the Socialist Party and its youth organization, the Young People's Socialist League (YPSL), in the summer of 1937 (although they represented the majority of the YPSL). The expelled left-wingers then called a national convention to create a new revolutionary party affiliated with the Fourth Internationalist movement and, after an extensive internal discussion, that is how the SWP came to be founded in 1938.

The discussion preceding that convention was very rich, covering a broad number of current international and national problems as well as the fundamental principles to govern and guide the new revolutionary party. From Mexico, Trotsky, who had recently completed his historic work of exposing the Moscow trial frame-ups, participated in this discussion to some extent, but chiefly on the so-called international questions—the Spanish civil war, the Sino-Japanese war, the class character of the Soviet Union, and the nature of democratic centralism in general.

A declaration of principles and a constitution were adopted; a political resolution, resolutions on trade union and unemployed work, resolutions on the Soviet Union and Spain, a resolution on organizational principles and standards, reports on the international movement, the youth movement, the election of a national committee—these were only some of the important things taken up and acted on at the convention. As a young delegate to the convention, I left it not only tired but inspired and certain that we had taken a big step toward the American revolution, and I am sure that that attitude was shared by most of the rank-and-file delegates.

In 1937 Trotsky had been pressing for an international conference to found the Fourth International. He felt that the international conference of July 1936 had made a mistake in not taking that step then, and he kept urging after his arrival in Mexico in 1937 that it be done by the end of that year. But it didn't prove possible, for various reasons, one of them being that the US leadership felt that it had to concentrate first on the founding of the SWP. So after the new party was launched, it was agreed that a delegation of SWP leaders would go to Mexico for talks about the international conference and related matters. And this took place at the end of March 1938, less than three months after the SWP convention.

The SWP delegation consisted of Cannon, Shachtman, V. R. Dunne, and Rose Karsner, and they met with Trotsky and others at Trotsky's home for an entire week. After some initial, introductory discussions, more formal sessions were held on six consecutive days, four of which were devoted entirely or largely to the transitional program and the method it implied. Stenograms were made of these six discussions, which were not corrected or revised by the participants but gave the essence of the exchanges. For security reasons mainly—to protect Trotsky's right of asylum in Mexico—these six stenograms were shown only to the National Committee members of the SWP at a plenum the next month and then were retrieved.

None was ever published in any form, not even an internal bulletin, during Trotsky's life, and until just this year none was ever published anywhere, with one exception—a discussion about the labor party, which was printed in an SWP educational bulletin in 1948. Fortunately, copies of the six stenograms were kept by Trotsky and included by him in the archives sold to Harvard in 1940. Last year Pathfinder Press got access to the stenograms for the first time and permission to print them, and they have just been published as material added in the second edition of *The Transitional Program for Socialist Revolution*. There, in the back of the volume, you can read the material from the four stenograms that dealt with the transitional program (and next year you will be able to read the rest of these stenograms, dealing with other questions, in the second edition of the *Writings 1937–38*). The newly added material should not be confused with the other stenograms about the transitional program in that book, most of them from the period *after* Trotsky wrote the program, which were in the first edition.

No memoirs or reminiscences of the discussions have been published, but it is clear from the stenograms—not just by reading between the lines, but from some passages—that the SWPers must have been startled and even shaken up by some of Trotsky's proposals and arguments and his way of looking at certain things that struck them as new.

On the fourth day of the discussions transcribed, Trotsky began the session by saying, "In the preceding discussions some comrades had the impression that some of my propositions or demands were opportunistic, and others that they were too revolutionary, not corresponding to the objective situation. And this combination is very compromising, and that's why I'll briefly defend this apparent contradiction." Perhaps Trotsky was exaggerating a little here, but he apparently felt that he had not yet fully convinced the other participants in the discussion because they were not sure about the "orthodoxy" (a word I dislike) or the realism of his positions.

In a number of places the stenograms show them asking Trotsky the same questions, getting him to restate his arguments so that they can grasp them better; in other places, they voice doubts or reservations; in still others, disagreement (Shachtman in particular could not see how slogans on workers' control and workers' militia were applicable in the United States in 1938).

Such a thing is of course quite common, even inevitable, in any free political discussion where new proposals are introduced that require reconsideration of long-established patterns of thought. Besides, this was not an ordinary discussion or an abstract discussion. Some of the positions Trotsky was asking them to reconsider had been passionately reaffirmed less than three months before, in the declaration of principles and the political resolution adopted by the founding SWP convention. So they wanted to be damned sure that they understood what Trotsky was proposing because even if they were convinced, that wouldn't settle it—they would still have to go home and convince first the Political Committee, then the National Committee, and then the party as a whole. So nobody reading those stenograms today is entitled to cheap feelings of condescension toward those comrades, who bore heavy responsibilities in this situation and acquitted themselves well.

Trotsky himself was aware of the problem facing the SWPers, and his tone throughout was patient, friendly, and pedagogic, for he was talking to close comrades, not opponents. And by the time they left to return to the United States, they had become convinced, if perhaps not fully aware of all the implications, and had agreed that they would ask the SWP to sponsor the transitional program at the coming international conference and to modify certain important points in its national program.

Before continuing the narrative, I am going to turn to two of the questions on which Trotsky wanted the SWP to change its positions. These, I think, are at the heart of the transitional method, and discussing them in some detail will be my substitute for discussing the transitional program and the method as a whole, which I've said has already been done more than adequately by Comrades Hansen and Novack in their introductions to the transitional program book. I should add that I am inclined to do it this way because these two questions were the ones that I personally, as a young SWP activist, found the hardest to figure out. These two questions were the Ludlow amendment and the labor party.

In the 1930s, as the American people began to learn more about

World War I, partly through muckraking congressional investigations, and as the threat of World War II began to come closer, a considerable antiwar or pacifist sentiment developed in this country. One of the forms this took was that of so-called isolationism, an expression of a desire not to get involved in foreign wars. Beginning in 1935, the Stalinists attempted to exploit this antiwar sentiment by channeling it behind Roosevelt's foreign policy and the policy of "collective security," according to which war would be prevented through an alliance by the peace-loving countries (the United States, USSR, etc.) against the bad, aggressive, peace-hating countries (Germany, Italy, and Japan).

In 1935 a Democratic congressman from Indiana named Ludlow introduced a bill in the House to amend the US Constitution so that Congress would not have the authority to declare war until such a declaration had been approved by the people voting in a national referendum. Of course the bill had many loopholes, one of which was that this limitation on the war-making power of Congress would not apply if the United States were invaded or attacked; and this wasn't its only weakness. Support began to build for the amendment as fears of war were deepened in this country by the Italian invasion of Ethiopia in 1935, the Spanish civil war in 1936, and the Japanese invasion of China in 1937. The Ludlow amendment was reintroduced in the House in 1937 and in the Senate by La Follette of Wisconsin, and it finally came to a vote in the House in January 1938, nine days after our convention.

The Roosevelt administration was bitterly opposed to the amendment and used all its patronage pressures to bring about its defeat. The Communist Party also opposed it, charging that it was in the interests of the reactionaries and fascists because it would limit the ability of the US government to deter the fascist powers from starting a war. Just before the vote in the House, a Gallup poll showed that 72 percent of the population favored the Ludlow amendment. Most of the new industrial unions supported the bill, along with the National Farmers Union. The pro-Ludlow sentiment in the United Auto Workers (UAW) was so strong that the Stalinist members of its executive board were forced to vote in favor of it. In the House of Representatives the bill was defeated 209–188, a rather close vote, considering all the circumstances.

So far I haven't been able to find any references to the Ludlow amendment in our press before the vote in the House in January 1938, but without any specific articles in our press, I knew at that time what our position on the amendment was, and I approved of it wholeheartedly.

Before explaining what our position was, I shall have to make a correction of what Comrade Hansen said about it in 1971 in a speech included with the introductory matter in the transitional program book. After telling who Ludlow was and what his amendment called for, Comrade Hansen said, "Comrade Trotsky proposed that the Socialist Workers Party should offer critical support to the Indiana Democrat's proposed amendment to the bourgeois constitution of the United States. After a bit of hesitation by some comrades our party adopted this position. Trotsky considered the matter so important that he included a paragraph about it in the transitional program." I am afraid that Comrade Hansen must have relied on his memory here instead of checking the facts—perhaps because he didn't have access to the records when he was making the speech, but in any case, he doesn't have it right.

The fact is that we were opposed to the Ludlow amendment before Trotsky had any opinion about it. If we had had a member in the House on January 10, 1938, he would have voted against the amendment, after making or trying to make a revolutionary speech differentiating the SWP from the nonrevolutionary forces opposing it. And if you had been a sympathizer in 1938, asking me why we were opposed, I would have answered at length along the following lines: "Pacifism is one of the most pernicious elements obstructing the revolutionary struggle against imperialist war. It misleads and disarms the workers, delivering them defenseless at the crucial moment into the hands of the war makers. Lenin and the Bolsheviks taught us that implacable opposition to pacifism and the illusions it creates is obligatory for all revolutionaries. All the documents of the Left Opposition and Fourth International stress the principled character of the struggle against pacifism in all its forms. Our stand on this question demarcates us from all other tendencies. The Ludlow amendment is a pacifist measure, designed to create the illusion that it is possible to prevent war at the ballot box while leaving power in the hands of the capitalists. It misdirects the workers from the real struggle against war, and therefore we cannot support it or assume any responsibility for it. Not to oppose it would be a betrayal of our revolutionary principles."

On the same day that the House voted down the Ludlow amendment, the newly elected Political Committee (PC) of the SWP held its first meeting. The PC minutes of that date show that under one point on the agenda Burnham proposed launching an antiwar campaign, consisting of eight "concrete points." The eighth point read as follows: "For the Ludlow amendment on the general motivation of the opportunities which it, as an issue, provides." All the points were approved, except the eighth, which was defeated by a vote of six to one. A countermotion to that eighth point was made by Shachtman, as follows: "That in our press we criticize the Ludlow amendment and the pacifist agitation connected with it from a principled revolutionary standpoint." This was carried—six for, one against.

In accord with this motion, our paper, the *Socialist Appeal*, carried a front-page article by Albert Goldman, introduced with an editorial statement pronouncing it to be "the Marxian view on the amendment." Goldman's article begins by saying that the Ludlow amendment poses an old problem in a new form for Marxists and workers generally. But, he assures the readers, "It is only necessary to apply the accepted principles of revolutionary Marxism to solve the problem correctly." Applying them, he showed all the shortcomings of the Ludlow amendment and the pacifist illusions fostered by its advocates, demonstrated that it would not really prevent war, differentiated our position from that of the Stalinists, and pointed to the destruction of the capitalist system as the only solution to war. I might add that he also said that the Ludlow amendment carried even greater dangers than other pacifist schemes precisely because it added "an element of democratic procedure."

Also in accord with the PC motion were two editorials in the next issue of our magazine. The longer one, which could have been written by Burnham, denounced the pro-imperialist forces that voted down the Ludlow bill and explained why. The shorter editorial, which could have been written by Shachtman, sought to "represent the standpoint of revolutionary Marxism." Among other things, it said:

> Where pacifist nostrums are not outright frauds and deceptions, they are pernicious illusions which drug the masses into pleasant dreams and hallucinations and paralyze their fighting power. To teach the masses that they can "prevent war" by a popular referendum is to foster a disastrous illusion among them. . . . Like the panacea of "disarmament," or "international arbitration courts," the referendum illusion diverts attention from the need of an intransigent class struggle policy against war

every day in the year, because it cultivates the idea that when the "real" war danger faces us in the remote future the masses will be able to avert it by the mere casting of a ballot. . . . In sum, to support the Ludlow resolution is to inculcate in the minds of the workers the idea that war can be "prevented" or fought *by some means other than the class struggle*, that imperialist war can be averted otherwise than by the revolutionary socialist overturn of capitalist rule.

The PC minutes of February 18 have a point called "Ludlow Amendment," followed by this information: "Letter read supporting Burnham's position on the Ludlow Amendment." Not included with the minutes, and not identified as to author, this letter turns out to have been written by Trotsky, although it was signed "Hansen" for security reasons; its text can be found in the second edition of *Writings (1937–38)*, which should be out next year. The letter was addressed to Cannon, whom Trotsky gave permission to show it to Burnham if he wished. Cannon did, and he also turned it over to the Political Committee as a whole. The letter said that on the Ludlow question Trotsky was with Burnham, not with the majority of the Political Committee. He felt that after the congressional vote the question was settled practically, but he wanted to make some comments on the important question of methodology. The government position against the Ludlow amendment, Trotsky wrote, represented the position of the imperialists and big business, who want their hands free for international maneuvering, including the declaration of war. What is the Ludlow bill? Trotsky wrote:

It represents the apprehension of the man-in-the-street, of the average citizen, of the middle bourgeois, the petty bourgeois, and even the farmer and the worker . . . looking for a brake upon the bad will of big business. In this case they name the brake the referendum. We know that the brake is not sufficient and even not efficient and we openly proclaim this opinion, but at the same time we are ready to go through this experience against the dictatorial pretensions of big business. The referendum is an illusion? Not more or less an illusion than universal suffrage and other means of democracy. Why can we not use the referendum as we use the presidential elections? . . .

The referendum illusion of the American little man has also its progressive features. Our idea is not to turn away from it, but utilize these progressive features without taking the responsibility for the illusion. If the referendum motion should be adopted, it would give us in case of a war crisis tremendous opportunities for agitation. That is precisely why big business stifled the referendum illusion.

Today's average SWP member will not find Trotsky's thinking on the Ludlow amendment extraordinary or controversial; in fact, it may seem rather commonplace and hardly worth the time I am giving it. This testifies to the political development of our movement since 1938; in certain respects we have come a long way; we live on a higher political plateau now. But what seems simple now to a new member didn't seem at all simple to the politically most astute leaders of our party then, as we can see from what happened after Trotsky's letter was read by the Political Committee.

Trotsky thought that because the referendum had been rejected in the House nothing more could be done about it. The members of the Political Committee knew better, realizing that the amendment would continue to be an important American political question for some time. So they decided, after hearing Trotsky's letter, to formulate their position anew. Goldman introduced a series of four motions, some of which were amended by Shachtman. The first two motions stressed the need to use the interest aroused by the amendment to expose the war preparations and the bourgeois and Stalinist opponents of the bill and to expose all pacifist illusions by clearly stating at all times that whoever says any kind of referendum will stop war is seriously mistaken. The third motion declared that we cannot assume responsibility for the amendment under any circumstances, and it is impermissible for us or our members in mass movements to organize or participate in or endorse any campaign for the amendment.

Up to this point it's clear and consistent. Goldman's fourth motion, however, says that since the amendment has been adopted by the most progressive forces of the labor movement, since the working class learns through experience, and since we need to be closely connected with those forces, our comrades in the mass movement are instructed to vote in favor of the Ludlow amendment and to introduce pro-Ludlow clauses in antiwar resolutions, "at all times making clear our position on the amendment."

Shachtman disagreed with Goldman's point four and amended it to instruct our comrades to state our specific position on the Ludlow amendment, either orally or in writing, and to abstain when the vote is cast.

Instead of stopping there, however, he added an exception: in those exceptional circumstances where our comrades hold the balance of power between the Stalinists and patriots on one side and pro-Ludlow forces on the other, our comrades are instructed to defeat the Stalinists and patriots by casting their vote for the Ludlow amendment with the qualifications given above.

And this was the position adopted by the SWP on February 10, by five to two (Cannon was absent)—to abstain, except in special circumstances where we should vote in favor in order to defeat the Stalinists and patriots. And although the Political Committee held other discussions on antiwar work during February, this was and remained the SWP's position when its delegation went to talk with Trotsky the following month.

In the back of the second edition of the transitional program book you will find the stenogram of the discussion in Mexico about the Ludlow amendment. There we can see Shachtman especially—who was the chief formulator of the abstentionist position, although of course the Political Committee as a whole was responsible for it—still dragging his heels: "there is great danger that in jumping into a so-called mass movement against war—pacifist in nature—the revolutionary education of the vanguard will be neglected. At the same time, not to enter the movement leaves us mainly in a propaganda position." And at the end, returning to a point he had made in the February magazine article, he asks: "How do you distinguish between our support of the Ludlow amendment and our attitude toward disarmament programs, international arbitration, etc.?"

Trotsky's answer: "They have nothing to do with one another. The Ludlow amendment is only a way for the masses to control their government. If the Ludlow amendment is accepted and made part of the constitution, it will absolutely not be analogous to disarmament but to inclusion in the right to vote of those eighteen years old"—that is, a democratic right.

Trotsky's arguments in this discussion were so persuasive that the others were convinced. The Ludlow amendment was not the subject of much debate at the stormy plenum of the SWP National Committee held a month later. It was not taken up until the last hours of the plenum. Then two motions were presented.

Cannon's motion said: "That the Plenum finds that the Political Committee took a correct principled position on the Ludlow amendment but made a tactical error in failing to give critical support to this movement without making any concessions whatever to its pacifist and illusory character."

Motion by Carter: "That the Plenum reverses the position of the Political Committee on the Ludlow amendment and declares it incorrect; that the PC be instructed to issue a statement in support of a popular referendum on the question of war, with a critical declaration in reference to the pacifist and illusory tendencies in the pro-Ludlow movement."

Seven members spoke during the discussion, and then Cannon made a substitute motion for the whole: "The Plenum finds that the Political Committee was correct in principled opposition to the pacifist illusions contained in the Ludlow amendment—an opposition that was fully justified—the PC nevertheless took a purely negative position which prevented the party from utilizing the entirely progressive sentiment of the masses who supported the idea of submitting the warmongers to the control of a popular referendum before the declaration of war. The Plenum instructs the PC to correct its position accordingly." This substitute motion carried, and the Carter motion was defeated, the vote not given.

A month later, our paper printed a public National Committee (NC) statement reporting the change in the SWP's position on the Ludlow amendment and explaining why. At this point it could be said that the error was corrected and the differences liquidated—so completely that three months later, in August, nobody thought that it was out of order for the Political Committee to send the National Committee members the copy of a draft written by Goldman for an improved version of the Ludlow amendment, that is, one free of the defects in Ludlow's bill, which we were to try to get some member of Congress to introduce so that we could use it in our antiwar propaganda and agitation.

I have traced the course of this thing, perhaps in too much detail, because I think that a study of mistakes of this kind, frankly recognized and correctly analyzed, can be at least as useful educationally as a study of correct policies or actions. Everybody makes mistakes, even geniuses like Marx, Lenin, and Trotsky. The Russian Revolution of 1917 would have been impossible if the Bolsheviks had not learned many valuable lessons from the defeat of 1905. In politics, mistakes are unavoidable, said Trotsky; what is reprehensible is clinging to mistakes and refusing to correct them. This of course does not apply to the Ludlow dispute. But the

Ludlow thing was important methodologically, as Trotsky said in his letter to Cannon, so it deserves further comment.

Reading Trotsky's approach to the Ludlow question now, I am struck by how much more rounded and all-sided it was than the one we had at the time. This enabled him more effectively to select out the major elements of the problem—for example, he began with a concrete class analysis, taking off from the fact that the ruling class was opposed to the Ludlow amendment, whereas that fact was subordinated in our analysis, which tended to center on a secondary factor, the illusions that the Ludlow forces fostered. Of course, what the ruling class wants in a particular case need not always be conclusive (sometimes they make mistakes, too), and sometimes it is not even clear what the ruling class wants (that certainly was the case with the impeachment problem last year). But what the ruling class wanted on the Ludlow amendment was both relevant and clear, and it fructified Trotsky's thinking. For us, the position of the ruling class was something of an embarrassment that we didn't care to dwell on and didn't altogether explain, even poorly, concentrating instead on the question of illusions.

Illusions and the necessity to combat them were a prominent feature not only of the Ludlow discussion but also of other questions facing the SWP at that time. This stems from the abiding obligation we have to help the masses overcome bourgeois ideology in all its forms and variants, including illusions about the nature of bourgeois democracy. Recently, for example, our propaganda and action around Watergate had to take into account, and include material to counteract, the illusions widely generated about Congress, the courts, and the Constitution.

But here, as with everything else in politics, a sense of proportion is needed, and I am afraid that it was sometimes lacking. Sometimes, like today's TV housewife who is driven frantic by the absence of sparkle on a drinking glass or the presence of a ring around her husband's collar, we were a little obsessed by the illusion factor. Perhaps "obsessed" is too strong, perhaps a better word is "overpreoccupied."

But the struggle against illusions is not an end in itself. It is only a means toward an end, and not the central means. Its weight varies from one situation to another, sometimes considerably. And the way in which we struggle against illusions is not uniform and unvarying in all situations; in one case it is best done head-on, in another a more indirect approach proves more effective. And since effectiveness is or should be a paramount factor, a distinction has to be made between merely making the record against illusions, no matter how loudly and vehemently, and setting into motion forces that actually help people to raise their political consciousness.

We tended to throw all illusions into one bag marked "Dangerous, Expose at All Costs." Trotsky was more selective, more discriminating. In a different context, in a 1930 pamphlet that will be in English later this year, he had occasion to refer to the consciousness, mood, and expectations of the revolutionary workers in Russia at the time of the October revolution, and there he discussed what he called their "creative illusion in overestimating hopes for a rapid change in their fate." It was an underestimation of the effort, suffering, and sacrifice they would be required to make before they would attain the kind of just, humane, socialist society they were fighting for. It was an illusion in the sense that between that generation and that kind of society lay civil war, imperialist intervention, famine and cannibalism, the rise of a privileged bureaucracy, totalitarian regimentation and terror, decimation in the Second World War, and much more that they did not foresee; it was an illusion based on an underestimation of the difficulties that would face them after the workers took power in backward Russia, which would have been infinitely smaller if the revolution had succeeded in spreading to the rest of Europe.

And it was creative because the workers' expectations enabled them to deal the first powerful blow against the world capitalist system and open up the era of proletarian revolutions and colonial uprisings. The record shows that the Bolsheviks did not spend much time or energy combating such illusions; they were too busy trying to imbue the masses with the determination to make the revolution.

In any case, Trotsky was able to differentiate among illusions if he could designate some as creative. Even more important, he was able to distinguish different sides or aspects of an illusion, as in the Ludlow discussion. Instead of a single label on the illusion or illusions connected with the Ludlow amendment, he called attention to the fact that certain aspects were progressive at the same time that others were not.

The idea that war can be abolished or prevented without ending the capitalist system that spawns war does not have much to recommend it from a Marxist standpoint. But if the spread of that idea leads masses of people into action to try to prevent the government from going to war, or to set limits on its power to declare war, isn't that a good thing from the standpoint of Marxists? Even if the idea that sets them into motion against the capitalist government is not scientific, and is therefore wrong and illusory, isn't it good, that is, progressive for them to conduct such a struggle? Isn't that precisely the way that they can learn what is wrong and illusory about their ideas on how to end war?

When I read you the second position adopted by the Political Committee on the Ludlow amendment, in February 1938, after Trotsky's letter was read, you may recall that in one place Goldman's motion said, "the working class learns through experience." This was a commonplace in our movement; everyone subscribed to it. But the difference was that Trotsky held that the workers' experience with a struggle for something like the Ludlow amendment was exactly the thing that could help them learn about and go beyond their illusion. The Political Committee, even as it was saying "the working class learns through experience," took the view that we should try to discourage the workers from having such an experience with the amendment and that we should dissociate ourselves from the experience if they went ahead with it anyway.

The PC view was that this is an illusion, therefore we can only expose and denounce it. Trotsky's view was that this is an illusion, but it has a progressive potential. Therefore, without assuming any responsibility for the illusion, and without hiding our belief that it is an illusion—but without making our belief that it is an illusion the major feature of our approach to it—because it has a progressive potential, let us encourage and help the workers to fight against the government on the war question. Let us join this movement and become its best builders, because this is the most effective way of helping them overcome some of their illusions about war and democratic capitalism.

It seems to be the difference between the approach of narrow propagandism and the approach of revolutionary activism. In the first case, you write an article explaining "the Marxian principles on war" and hand it out to those who are interested in such matters; you won't affect many people that way, but you have done your duty and presumably can sleep well. In the second case, you intervene in the class struggle, helping to set masses into motion against the ruling class or to provide bridges for those in motion from the elementary, one-sided, and illusory conceptions they start out with toward better, more realistic, and more revolutionary concepts about capitalism and war and how to fight them.

I do think that the source of our error was in great part the remnants of the narrow propagandism that prevailed in the first years of the Left Opposition in this country, when we were restricted almost entirely to trying to reach the ranks of the Communist Party with our written and spoken ideas. Subsequently we consciously set out to transcend this phase, with increasing success. But occasionally, especially when new problems were posed, we had a tendency to slip back. The transitional method that Trotsky recommended to us was precisely the thing we needed to enable us to say good-bye forever to such lapses.

If it was not an error of propagandism, then it is hard to explain the thing Shachtman said in Mexico that I have already cited: "There is great danger that in jumping into a so-called mass movement against war— pacifist in nature—the revolutionary education of the vanguard will be neglected."

At first sight this seems like a non sequitur. Why should jumping into a mass movement, or only entering one with more dignity than jumping provides, present a danger, a great danger, that the revolutionary education of the vanguard will be neglected? How does it follow? What is the possible connection? It doesn't make sense unless the reasoning is being done from the standpoint of propagandism, where you feel that the most urgent task you have is to present your entire program without ambiguity or possibility of misrepresentation on all occasions—a necessity that occurs to you because you lack confidence about the revolutionary education, the ideological solidity of the vanguard, that is, of yourselves.

In such a case, if you are not sure of it, the main thing becomes the strengthening of the revolutionary education or ideological condition of the vanguard group, and doing something about that seems more important, much more important, than taking advantage of an opportunity to intervene in the class struggle.

By contrast, let us consider how we would pose the same problem today, after having absorbed the meaning of the transitional method. We would say, "Here is a mass movement that we can enter, where we can win over people to our revolutionary positions and help raise the consciousness of many more. It is a pacifist movement, which means that in order to work effectively there our own members must be well educated about the nature of pacifism, what's wrong with it, and how to counter its influence. Which means, therefore, that before we enter and after we enter we must make sure that our members are immunized politically against pacifism, if that is not already the case. That is, instead of neglecting, we must increase the revolutionary education of the vanguard on this point." Shachtman counterposed mass work and revolutionary education of the vanguard. We, on the other hand, combine them, because not only the masses learn that way, but we, the vanguard, do, too.

Methodologically we also seemed to be suffering from a confusion about the relation between principles and tactics. Principles are propositions embodying fundamental conclusions derived from theory and historical experience to govern and guide our struggle for socialism. Relating broadly to our goals, they set a framework within which we operate. Although they are not eternal, they have a long-range character and are not easily or often changed. In fact, we have essentially the same principles today that we had in 1938. The dictatorship of the proletariat, or the struggle for a workers' state, as the form of state transitional between capitalism and socialism—that is a principle with us. Insistence on class-struggle methods against class-collaborationist methods—that is another. Unremitting opposition to pacifism in all its guises because pacifism is an obstacle to revolutionary struggle—that is a third.

Tactics, on the other hand, are only means to an end. "Only" in this context is not meant to disparage them; without the appropriate tactics, principles cannot be brought to life, so there is clearly an interdependence between principles and tactics. But tactics are subordinate in the same way that means are subordinate to an end. They are good if they enhance and promote the principle, not good if they don't. In addition, tactics are flexible, adjustable, variable. They depend (or their applicability depends) on concrete circumstances. To advance a particular principle, tactic A may be best today; but it may have to be replaced by tactic B tomorrow morning, or tactic C tomorrow night. Meanwhile, the principle remains unchanged.

Principle tells us to oppose pacifism, but it does not tell us whether or not to participate in a certain mass movement; it only tells us that under all circumstances, whether participating or not, we should so function as to counterpose revolutionary ideas and influence to those of the pacifists. There is not a single tactic that follows from any principle; after understanding and grasping the principle, we still have to consider tactics; and tactics, although they are subordinate to principles, have laws, logic, and a domain of their own. Tactics must not, cannot, be in violation of principle (no tactical considerations could even get us to say that we think war can be abolished through a referendum vote), but tactics are not limited to formal reaffirmations of our principles—they are not worth much if that is all they are.

What was the nature of the Ludlow amendment problem? Was it for us a matter of principle or a matter of tactics? If the SWP in 1938 had had any doubts about pacifism, any ambiguity about it, then the matter of principle would properly have been foremost. But if ever there was any party whose members had been trained, indoctrinated, drilled, and virtually bred on a hostility to pacifism, surely it was the SWP. I can testify to that personally; long before I knew some of the most elementary ideas of Marxism, I had been taught about the dangers of pacifism.

Let me try to suggest an analogy: Comrade Smith takes the floor to propose that the branch should participate in a local election campaign by running our own candidates and explains not only the benefits that would accrue to us from such a campaign but also the facts demonstrating that we have the forces and the resources to run such a campaign effectively. But I take the floor to oppose Comrade Smith's proposal on the grounds that the workers have electoral illusions and that these illusions can only be reinforced and perpetuated if we, the revolutionary opponents of bourgeois electoralism, take part in these fraudulent elections. No, I say, our revolutionary principles forbid our participation in bourgeois elections and require that we call on the workers to boycott the elections; any other course would be in violation of our principled opposition to bourgeois parliamentarism.

Such a scene has never occurred at any SWP branch meeting, although it could occur and probably does in some of the Maoist and other sectarian groups in this country. Something not too different occurred in the Fourth International as recently as five years ago, when the French Communist League ran a presidential campaign dominated by the theme that its main task was to combat the electoralist illusions of the French workers.

Such a scene has not occurred at any SWP meetings, but if it did occur, there would not be any lack of comrades, new as well as old, who would point out that Comrade Smith had raised a tactical question and that instead of answering him on the level of tactics I had switched the discussion to the level of principles, leaving aside the question of whether the principles I had invoked were at all relevant to the point at issue.

Nobody in the SWP has ever done this—mix up principles and tactics—in relation to elections and our participation in them. But isn't that precisely what happened in connection with the Ludlow amendment?

From the very beginning of the discussion in January, when Burnham proposed support for the amendment, all that was needed was an answer on the level of tactics, assuming that there were no differences on the level of principle. But Shachtman, instead of giving a tactical answer, replied with a motion to criticize the amendment "from a principled revolutionary standpoint." And even at the end of the discussion, at the plenum in April, Cannon's initial motion, later withdrawn, wanted to affirm that the Political Committee had taken "a correct principled position" on the amendment "but made a tactical error" by not giving the movement critical support. But it was even worse than that, methodologically, in my opinion. When we are confronted with the need for a tactical decision, to be offered instead a "correct principled position" is to be offered at best an irrelevancy, and at worst an evasion, but in all cases not what the situation calls for politically. Pointing in such circumstances to the correctness of the principled position may provide us a measure of psychological consolation—"see, we were only 50 percent wrong"—but how much correctness can a principled position provide in real life if it is given as a substitute for a tactical position?

I think that I have been justified in devoting so much time to the Ludlow dispute for at least three reasons. First, I think that the details were needed, because without them, you would have only some generalizations and would lack the data through which to judge my conclusions.

Second is that the problems posed in that dispute related rather closely to other questions of importance. For example, there was the slogan of the workers' and farmers' government in the transitional program (which more recently we have shortened to the slogan of the workers' government in this country). The stenograms show that the SWPers kept putting questions about this to Trotsky—did he mean by the workers' and farmers' government the same thing that we meant by the dictatorship of the proletariat?—lurking behind which was the implied question: if the workers' and farmers' government means something different from dictatorship of the proletariat, don't we have the obligation to state this very forcibly, to emphasize it, in order to counteract the illusions that the workers may have in anything less than the dictatorship of the proletariat?

In tomorrow's talk I shall show additional evidence of the prominence in the thinking of the SWP leadership of the illusion factor, as well as more about the confusion over tactics and principles. But my point is that clarification of the issues involved in the Ludlow dispute helped the SWP to better understand the transitional program and its method as a whole. And without that clarification, if we had continued to cling to the SWP's first and second positions on the Ludlow amendment, what do you think would have happened decades later when a mass movement against the Vietnam War began to develop in this country? One thing you can be sure of is that we could never have played the role we did in that movement if we had not previously learned the lessons of the Ludlow question through the transitional program discussion. In that case, the SWP would be considerably different from what it is today, and I don't mean better.

The other reason I feel justified in giving so much time to the Ludlow dispute is because it helps us to view our party, its cadres, its program, and its method, the same way we try to view everything else—historically. Sometimes there is a tendency to think that they suddenly developed out of nowhere, fully formed and finished, with results and acquisitions that can be taken for granted. But it wasn't like that at all. We got where we are ideologically, politically, and organizationally as the result of a good deal of sweat, heart's blood, sleepless nights, trial and error—and struggle.

And that's how it will be as we continue to develop further. We have the advantage over our predecessors of not having to plow up the same ideological and methodological ground that they covered. If we really absorb the lessons they learned and the methods they pioneered, then we should be able to go beyond them and plow up new ground. And we certainly can do that better, the more realistically we understand how they did their work.

Two comrades whose opinions I respect made some suggestions after seeing the first draft of the notes for this talk a couple of weeks ago. I didn't succeed in incorporating most of their suggestions into the talk, mainly because it got so long without them, but I would like to take them up now.

One comrade thought that the emphasis of my talk might be misleading, especially for those who were not familiar with the early years of our movement. After all, he pointed out, we were not on the whole sectarians or abstentionists before 1938; even with our small forces and limited resources, we did some very good work when the opportunity came along. Furthermore, he added, although we didn't have the words "transitional method" or "transitional demands" in our vocabulary then, we did frequently and even effectively use that method and raise such demands in our work, especially after the big turn in 1933. Otherwise, he said, some of our most important work of that period—such as the Minneapolis experience—is inexplicable.

I must say that I agree with his concern, and if I did, or to the extent that I did, derogate or seem to derogate the party or its leadership in the pre–transitional program period of our existence, I certainly want to correct that now. There isn't any trace of muckraking or debunking in my motives for giving these talks. I don't know anyone who has a higher regard than I have for the pre-1938 party and its leadership. I said that it was a remarkable organization, and the more I think about the conditions of that period, the more strongly I hold this opinion. From my own extensive activity in the three years before 1938, I know that the party was not at all sectarian, and it was not abstentionist or dogmatic or doctrinaire.

If it had been, it could never have accepted the transitional program, it could never have absorbed the transitional method so fast. Certainly no other organization in this country ever understood them at all.

So please understand what I have been speaking about in that context. We were not abstentionists, but sometimes we made abstentionist errors, and the transitional method helped us to overcome them once we understood it and incorporated it into our arsenal. Does telling this story discredit the comrades of that time? Not at all. On the contrary, it seems to me greatly to their credit that they were able to correct their errors and lift the whole movement onto higher ground.

The other comrade's criticism was that in my discussion of principles and tactics, I entirely omitted the question of strategy, which he feels is the area where the transitional program makes its central contribution. I think that he is completely correct on this latter point: the transitional program did provide us with a coherent and viable strategy or set of strategic concepts, perhaps for the first time in this country, and certainly on a scale we had never known before.

(Strategy, I should say parenthetically, was explained by Trotsky as follows in 1928: "Prior to the war [World War I] we spoke only of the tactics of the proletarian party; this conception conformed adequately enough to the then prevailing trade union, parliamentary methods which did not transcend the limits of day-to-day demands and tasks. By the conception of tactics is understood the system of measures that serves a single current task or a single branch of the class struggle. Revolutionary strategy on the contrary embraces a combined system of actions which by their association, consistency, and growth must lead the proletariat to the conquest of power." Tactics are subordinate to strategy, and strategy serves a mediating role between principle and tactics.)

But I did not go into the question of strategy in my talk deliberately because it was virtually omitted from the 1938 discussion in the SWP; the focus was almost entirely on the principle–tactic relationship. The stimulus given to strategical thinking instead also marked an important step forward, thanks again to the transitional program. My not going into that aspect was not intended to deny that or minimize it. Anyhow, I hope that the comrade who made this criticism will, as I suggested, some day himself speak about the danger of what he calls "tactical thinking that is not rooted in strategical thinking," and how the transitional program relates to this.

Tomorrow I shall resume the narrative, concluding my account of the chaotic plenum of the National Committee held in April 1938 after the return of the SWP delegation from Mexico, with major attention on the dispute over the labor party question. The following day, I shall make some comparisons between the SWP of then and the SWP of today, based upon a recent reading for the first time of the 1938 minutes of the Political Committee.

2. THE LABOR PARTY QUESTION

I can't repeat the ground covered yesterday, but I'll give a brief chronology.

1928—Our movement begins when Cannon, Shachtman, and Abern are expelled for "Trotskyism" from the American Communist Party (CP).

1929—The Communist League of America (CLA) holds its founding convention and adopts its platform.

1931—The CLA holds its second convention.

1933—The International Left Opposition, to which the CLA is affiliated, makes the most important shift in its history, giving up its efforts to reform the Comintern and calling for a new International. In this country, the CLA ceases to consider itself a faction of the CP and sets out to build a revolutionary Marxist party. This means the beginning of a turn away from almost pure propagandism directed at the CP toward intervention in the class struggle, with the aim of linking up with leftward-moving tendencies to construct the cadres of the revolutionary party.

1934—The CLA merges with the American Workers Party (AWP) headed by A. J. Muste to form the Workers Party of the United States (WPUS).

Spring of 1936—We dissolve the WPUS and join the Socialist Party (SP) and the YPSL in order to win over to the Fourth International young revolutionaries recently attracted by those organizations.

Summer of 1937—We are expelled from the SP and YPSL, with our forces considerably increased, and begin a discussion in preparation for the founding convention of a new party.

New Year's 1938—The SWP is founded at a convention in Chicago that adopts a declaration of principles and other basic documents to guide the new organization.

End of March 1938—Cannon, Shachtman, Dunne, and Karsner go to Mexico to meet with Trotsky to discuss plans for the founding conference of the Fourth International (FI) to be held later that year.

Trotsky introduces to them the idea of the transitional program, to be written as the basic program of the FI founding conference. They discuss this and related problems for an entire week, and then agree that they will go back to the United States to ask the SWP to approve it and act as its sponsor at the international conference, even though it will require changing certain positions previously adopted by the SWP. One of these is the SWP's position on the Ludlow amendment to the US Constitution for a referendum on war, which I discussed yesterday.

The other is the SWP's position on the labor party, which I shall discuss today. Before doing that, however, I would like to carry the narrative further as regards the disposition of the transitional program as a whole, aside from the labor party question.

Cannon and Shachtman got back to New York in time for a Political Committee meeting in mid-April, nine days before a plenum of the National Committee. The Political Committee adopted an agenda for recommendation to the plenum, which was to be changed a week later on the eve of the plenum; they changed the rules for attendance—previously it was to be open to all members, now it was to be closed except for NC members and a few invited guests—and they received reports from the delegates, the minutes reporting only, "Comrades Cannon and Shachtman give full reports on their journey."

There is no record of the Political Committee deciding to recommend anything regarding these reports; it only designated Cannon, Shachtman, and Dunne reporters to the plenum but did not take a position on anything, which is not how it is usually done. We can assume that the Political Committee wanted time to think over the transitional program and related proposals.

In referring to this plenum yesterday, I called it stormy and chaotic, and I don't think that is an exaggeration, although the minutes contain only motions and a few statements made specifically for the record. In the first place, the plenum was extended from three days to four, an unusual thing; and even so, a considerable part of the agenda was not acted on, and at the end had to be referred to the Political Committee.

The first point on the agenda was a report by Cannon on the matters discussed in Mexico, supplemented by brief remarks on factory committees by Shachtman. The second point was questions from the National Committee members, answered by Cannon, Shachtman, and Dunne. The third point was a five-hour recess to study documents (the first draft of the transitional program had arrived shortly before the plenum), including stenograms of the talks with Trotsky (those that dealt with the transitional program have just been published for the first time in the second edition of the transitional program book).

Then the political discussion began on transitional demands and related questions. But when the political discussion ran out, instead of a vote being taken, voting was deferred to the third day of the plenum; in fact, before the vote was taken, time was consumed with local reports on the branches, labor party sentiment, the antiwar movement, the CP, etc. The members of the plenum were plainly not in a hurry to vote on the key proposals. But the clearest sign of uncertainty or confusion was the nature of the motions presented and finally voted on.

A motion was made by Maurice Spector, supported by Cannon and Abern, that the SWP approve the transitional program, and a motion was made by Shachtman, supported by Burnham, that the SWP approve the transitional program, and the debate over these motions became one of the two focal points of the plenum, leading to roll-call votes duly recorded in the minutes and a division that was sixty to forty. Of course the motions were not exactly the same. But I had to reread them several times before I detected a possible nuance, and three of the twenty-eight who voted—Goldman, Clarke, and Cochran—voted for both motions, with a statement that they considered them essentially the same.

The possible nuance was this. Spector's motion "endorses and adopts" the thesis written by Trotsky, whereas Shachtman's "endorses the general line of the thesis . . . and adopts it as a draft of an analysis." But this thin line is made thinner yet by the fact that a second part of Spector's motion "subscribes in principle to the conception of the program of transitional demands proposed" in the thesis. So one endorses and accepts while subscribing in principle, and the other endorses the general line and adopts it as a draft of an analysis. The vote was seventeen for Spector's motion, eleven for Shachtman's.

The same thing happened with the second part of these motions, directing the Political Committee to prepare a program of actions based on the transitional program and the conditions and needs of the American working-class struggle. To me, the two motions seem the same, but they led to a thirteen to twelve vote in favor of Spector's. There was agreement only on the third part of the motion, that the program to be prepared by the Political Committee be submitted to the membership for discussion and referendum.

When such a thing happens, when a National Committee is divided thirteen to twelve over motions it is hard to distinguish between, then it is safe to conclude that the situation is not normal, or, to put it another way, that it contains the potential of a crisis. In my interpretation, there were two elements involved. One was what may be called personal. Cannon had been convinced by Trotsky, and he wanted the SWP leadership to endorse the transitional program without equivocation or pussyfooting. Others, including Shachtman, probably still had some reservations, hence wanted to affirm only "the general line." They resented being pushed or pressured; they wanted more time to try to square the new line with what they had said in the past, and they reacted against the motions supported by Cannon as a way of expressing their dislike of him as a "hand-raiser" for Trotsky, as someone who unthinkingly went along with whatever Trotsky proposed, in contrast to themselves as independent thinkers.

This was closely connected with something that had happened the previous year, 1937, when we were still in the SP. Trotsky was the first, in a confidential letter to the leadership, to conclude that the SP experience was coming to an end and that we should prepare to be expelled and set up our own party. Cannon, agreeing, quickly sent a letter from California, endorsing Trotsky's perspective. Shachtman and Burnham, who were in the New York leadership, almost flipped out when they got this letter, because they had settled themselves in for an extended, an indefinitely extended, stay in the SP, and they were bitter about Cannon "the hand-raiser," even after they were compelled to agree with his proposal.

The difference between them was that Cannon was a more astute politician, saw things faster, and did not feel that there was anything shameful about endorsing a good idea just because Trotsky had made it; whereas they, being perhaps less self-confident, had greater psychological difficulty in reaching a decision.

But the other element, a purely political one, played the main role in producing the strange situation of a fight over two similar motions. That was the one I referred to in some detail yesterday—namely, that the SWP leadership was being asked to sharply change positions on important questions like the labor party, which they had held for several years and which they had reaffirmed just a few months before at the founding convention of the SWP; and that the reasoning Trotsky used in the transitional program seemed in some ways new to them, so new that at first they were jolted by it.

Supporting this part of my interpretation are the facts about what happened after the plenum. A Political Committee subcommittee was set up to draft a national program of action based on the transitional program, which was to consist of two parts, one on transitional demands, the other on the labor party question. In June, Spector and Burnham brought in separate drafts on the transitional program, but as they worked on them, the realization grew that really there were not any significant differences, and what emerged was a joint document. There were differences over various passages, but these were settled by majority vote (except workers' gov-

ernment or workers' and farmers' government), and in the end the comrades who had voted against each other at the plenum all accepted the
final draft, which was submitted to the membership for the referendum.

So the leadership should be credited with the good sense to reach
agreement, once they had a little more time to assimilate the transitional
program. They should also be credited with avoiding a factional situation,
which was unwarranted and would have done great damage, since there
was no political basis for it. Their united presentation of the document did
a lot to win the support of the party ranks for both Trotsky's transitional
program draft and the American adaptation of it. A full-scale discussion
took place in the ranks, and in the referendum that followed, over 90 percent of those voting endorsed the international resolution, and about 95
percent endorsed the American program of action (I'll report on the labor
party vote later).

I do not mean to imply that everybody in the party, leadership or
ranks, absorbed the full meaning of the transitional method all at once or
quickly. Late in the fall, two members of the Political Committee were
still trying to get us to replace the slogan of the sliding scale of wages
with a "rising scale of wages." There were also some strange things said
during the discussion.

One that I remember now with some amusement is a debate that was
never settled, echoes of which I still encountered in the 1950s among certain kinds of comrades. That was over the question of whether transitional
demands can be realized under capitalism, the implication often being
that transitional demands were good or acceptable only if or when they
could not be realized under capitalism and could not be supported if they
could be realized under capitalism, the further implication being that supporting demands that could be realized under capitalism would lead us
into some kind of horrendous trap and make rank opportunists of us all.
It sounds more amusing now than it did then.

Anyhow, my point is that we did not grasp the meaning or master the
use of the transitional method all at once—it took time, in my own case
it was a matter of years, not months. But we did grasp it in part relatively
quickly, which testifies to the maturity of both the leadership and the
membership, and to the fact that our past had prepared us for this leap forward, for in practice we had been learning basic elements of the transitional approach before 1938, but without ever having generalized it or

concretized it or theorized it or worked out the relations between the different parts as Trotsky did for us in 1938.

Now let me get back to the labor party question. Lenin waged a fight in the early years of the Comintern against those sectarian elements who refused to work in or give critical support to the candidates of existing labor parties, and this fight was so successful that hardly any communist thereafter held such a position. The question that concerned our movement in the 1930s was not whether to work in a labor party created by other forces, but whether it was permissible for revolutionaries to advocate the formation of a labor party. In a few moments I will trace the history of our movement on this question, but I will start by referring to my own experience, which began in 1935, when I first joined.

In 1935 the CIO and the new industrial unions were just being born; soon they were to turn their attention to politics—openly capitalist politics, as in their support of Roosevelt in 1936, but also hybrid politics, as in the formation of Labor's Non-Partisan League (LNPL) nationally and the American Labor Party in New York, which had the potential of taking an independent labor party direction. Nineteen thirty-five was also the year when the Stalinists dropped their third-period policies, including opposition to labor parties as social-fascist formations, and began to call for the formation of a national labor party. Labor party resolutions began to be discussed in various unions and other mass movements and often were adopted at union conventions, although that was about as far as it went.

What I learned as a new member was that it was impermissible for us to advocate the formation of a labor party. We could advocate independent labor political action in general because that encompassed the idea of revolutionary workers' politics, but we could not advocate formation of an independent labor party because a labor party, necessarily reformist, would inevitably betray the workers. I remember that in 1936, when I was writing a pamphlet to be published by the unemployed movement in New Jersey, I felt it necessary, in reporting action taken by this movement, to try to distinguish between its endorsement of independent political action (which we favored) and its endorsement of a farmer-labor party (which we didn't).

In 1936 we joined the SP and YPSL, and our labor party position immediately became, and remained, the clearest point of distinction between our faction, called the Appeal Association or Caucus, and the centrist faction, called the Clarity Caucus. They advocated a labor party, for reasons that sometimes sounded radical and other times sounded opportunist, and we opposed advocacy. In the year and a half we spent in the SP and YPSL, there must have been thousands of individual discussions and debates around the labor party, no one ever joining our faction without coming to accept our antiadvocacy position. In fact, it was often the crucial point for the revolutionary-minded youth of the SP and YPSL dominating their decision on whether to join the Appeal or Clarity Caucus.

At our founding convention there was no debate on the labor party question. Instead there was agreement, you could say unanimity, with the statement in the Declaration of Principles that the revolutionary party cannot "properly take the initiative in advocating the formation of Labor or Farmer-Labor Parties," and with the statement in the main political resolution, "Faced with the prospect of the formation of a national Labor party of one kind or another, the [SWP] has no need of altering the fundamental revolutionary Marxian position on the Labor Party question. The revolutionary party cannot take the responsibility for forming or advocating the formation of a reformist, class-collaborationist party, that is, of a petty-bourgeois workers' party."

But having settled accounts with the SP and having turned our eyes to the union movement, it began to be clear to the leaders of the new party that considerable pro-labor party sentiment was developing in this country and that the party had better pay attention to it. Burnham took the lead in this respect in the Political Committee, but Cannon also was starting to concern himself with it. Burnham then wrote an article called "The Labor Party: 1938," reviewing the recent developments and urging an active orientation toward them. Even he, however, felt it incumbent to tip his hat to the convention formula: "The revolutionists are not the originators or initiators of any labor or any other kind of reformist party; they not merely give no guarantees or false hopes for such a party but, on the contrary, warn against the illusion that such a party can solve any major problem of the working class. The central task of the period ahead remains the building of the revolutionary party itself."

In the Political Committee, Burnham explained the strategy behind his article: he said that "there is now a labor party movement, and that we have to find ways and means of working in it." With this approach, the question of advocating a labor party could be skipped over; a movement already existed, so we didn't have to advocate it, all we had to do was get in. He asked the Political Committee to endorse his article and recommend its approach to the plenum coming in April. The Political Committee decided merely to refer the whole matter to the plenum, and that is how things stood at the time of the talks in Mexico.

Trotsky also wanted us to work in the labor party movement, but he didn't see any need to be devious about it. Instead, as you can tell from the transitional program book, he argued that we should change our position and begin to advocate the formation of a labor party, and he sought to convince the SWPers that they should do the same.

In the discussion at the beginning, Cannon said that he thought the prevailing sentiment of the party was to join the LNPL and become aggressive fighters for the constitution of a labor party, as against the policy of endorsing capitalist candidates. If we can do that without compromising our principles, that would be best in the sense of gaining influence. Shachtman, too, was concerned about the possible compromising of our principles. More than once he reminded Trotsky that we cannot advocate a reformist party and yet he (Trotsky) was advocating something that seemed just that.

Trotsky replied that he was not advocating a reformist labor party. He was trying to find a pedagogical approach to the workers. "We say [to the workers], you cannot impose your [political] will through a reformist party but only through a revolutionary party. The Stalinists and liberals wish to make of this movement a reformist party, but we have our program, we make of this a revolutionary—"

Here Cannon interrupted: "How can you explain a revolutionary labor party? We say: The SWP is the only revolutionary party, has the only revolutionary program. How then can you explain to the workers that also the labor party is a revolutionary party?"

Trotsky: "I will not say that the labor party is a revolutionary party, but that we will do everything to make it possible. At every meeting I will say: I am a representative of the SWP. I consider it the only revolutionary party. But I am not a sectarian. You are trying now to build a big workers' party. I will help you but I propose that you consider a program for this party. I make such and such propositions. I begin with this. Under these conditions it would be a big step forward. Why not say openly what is? Without any camouflage, without any diplomacy."

Cannon: "Up till now the question has always been put abstractly. The question of the program has never been outlined as you outlined it. The Lovestoneites have always been for a labor party; but they have no program, it's combinations from the top. It seems to me that if we have a program and always point to it."

Shachtman was still not convinced: "Now with the imminence of the outbreak of the war, the labor party can become a trap." He was very much on guard against traps and illusions. "And I still can't understand how the labor party can be different from a reformist, purely parliamentarian party."

Trotsky: "You put the question too abstractly; naturally it can crystallize into a reformist party, and one that will exclude us. But we must be part of the movement. . . . [W]e always point to our program. And we propose our program of transitional demands."

It is obvious from reading the stenograms that the SWP leaders were hung up by some of their previous formulas on the labor party question. Trotsky tried to bring new light on the matter, and the way in which he did this, in line with the transitional program as a whole, appeared to them to represent something new. "The question of the program has never been outlined as you outlined it," Cannon said. The problem seemed solved: the only thing that remained was how to explain the change. If the new position was correct, how about the old position? Had the old position been correct in the past but became invalid as the result of new and different conditions? Or had it always been wrong? If so, what was the source of the error?

The voting on the labor party at the April plenum was very much like the voting on the transitional program, except that this time there was a third position presented by Glen Trimble of California, whose motion would simply reaffirm the position taken at the founding convention, that is, would continue to oppose advocacy. Trimble's motion was defeated seventeen to four. The two major positions were expressed in motions by Cannon and Burnham.

Cannon's was very short: "That we adopt the draft statement distributed to members as the position of the Plenum and instruct the Political Committee to take this as a basis, concretize it and elaborate it, and submit it to the Party for discussion culminating in a referendum vote." The draft statement he referred to was one written by Trotsky, which appears in the transitional program book under the title "The Problem of the Labor Party."

The motion by Burnham was longer and more detailed, generally along the lines of his recent magazine article, but at no point in real contradiction with the line of Cannon's motion. The vote was closer this time: twelve for Cannon's, ten for Burnham's, two abstentions (weeks later one of the abstentions was changed to a vote for Cannon).

When the time came to draw up the document authorized in the Cannon motion, almost the same thing happened as with the transitional program. That is, virtually everyone who had voted for either the Cannon or the Burnham motion realized that there were no real differences between them on the labor party, and they all voted for a common NC majority resolution and jointly defended it in the referendum discussion against an NC minority resolution introduced by Hal Draper.

But the results in the discussion and the voting were not the same as with the transitional program. Despite the virtual unanimity of the leadership, a large part of the SWP membership (and of the youth) was and remained against the change of position. The new position received only 60 percent in the referendum, as against 90 percent for the transitional program and 95 percent for the American adaptation.

Here I must differ with a statement George Novack made in his introduction to the transitional program book. He notes that the labor party question is not included in the transitional program and says, "This is for good reason. The problem is peculiar to our country, which is the most politically backward of all the advanced capitalist countries," the only one where the workers don't have a party of their own. But obviously this was not true of all countries in 1938 and it is not true today. There are many countries in the world, especially colonial, semicolonial, and neocolonialist countries, where the workers don't have a party of their own class, and where the general labor party approach could be appropriate. And although the Soviet Union was the only workers' state in the world, that didn't stop Trotsky from writing a lot in the transitional program about the problems that were "peculiar" to that country.

But comrade Novack was correct in saying that there was good reason for the labor party not being included in the transitional program. And the reason was that the leaders were aware of the opposition of many members to the new labor party position and were afraid that if the questions weren't separated, so that they could be voted on separately, this might endanger adoption of the transitional program first of all in this country, and second, indirectly in the rest of the international. This was good and sound reasoning in my opinion. In my own case, I could not have voted for the transitional program at that time if it had included a provision in favor of labor party advocacy. At least 40 percent of the party would have been in a dilemma if they had had to vote on the two matters in a single package.

Today, when there isn't anybody in our movement who disagrees on the pro-advocacy position, it may be difficult to appreciate the heat that accompanied that discussion in 1938. The source of the difficulty was that, for several years before 1938, we, the members, had been taught that it was unprincipled to advocate the formation of any party but the revolutionary party. And the difficulty was compounded because the leadership, instead of forthrightly stating that this was a mistake that now must be corrected, denied that it had been considered a principled question or tried to sweep it aside as irrelevant. This way of handling the change, which is not typical of Bolshevism or of our movement before or since, complicated the whole situation, distracting the discussion away from the essence of the problem into side issues, and made it more difficult for the members to resolve the question correctly.

"The question of the labor party has never been a question of 'principle' for revolutionary Marxists." That is the opening sentence of Trotsky's draft statement, printed in the back of the transitional program book, which was incorporated with a few changes into the National Committee majority resolution in the referendum. In my opinion, that sentence was wrong. It *had* been a question of principle, and when I say that, I am not concerned with whether it had been formally labeled a principle, but with how the party membership had been educated to view the question.

In the National Committee draft, that sentence was changed from "The question of the labor party has never been a question of 'principle' for revolutionary Marxists" to "The question of the attitude toward an existing labor parry has never been a question of principle for revolutionary Marxists." In my opinion, the changed sentence was correct, as it stands, but in the context, it was an evasion of the problem that was troubling and confusing many party members.

I have decided not to try to prove what I have said here—that before 1938 we treated labor party advocacy as a principled question, even if we didn't label it that way. I'll merely repeat what Cannon said in Mexico, that our party would become aggressive fighters for a labor party "if we can do that without compromising our principled position." I'll assume that is sufficient until somebody challenges my statement.

At that time I thought that our principled position had always been against advocating a labor party, and in the course of that discussion, both written and oral, nobody, absolutely nobody, ever said that we had previously had any other position. If they had done so, it would surely have shaken me and the other 40 percent of the membership that voted against the new position and might have persuaded us that we were wrong. But nobody ever mentioned our having had any other position or even said when we had adopted the one we had up to 1938. You may think that odd, but in those days—before offset printing made possible relatively inexpensive production of the old bound volumes of the *Militant*, and at a time when the resources of our party did not make available the old internal bulletins and documents of our movement—the general membership was not as well informed about the history of our own movement, in the form of accessible documents, as it is today. Anyhow, in the course of that discussion, which I followed closely and anxiously because, for the first time, my confidence in the leadership was shaken, *nobody* ever asked or said when we had adopted our pre-1938 position or if we had had a different position before that.

And so it wasn't until a few weeks ago, in preparing this talk, that I learned that our pre-1938 position had first been adopted in 1931, and that we had indeed had a different position before then—a contradictory one, in fact.

A few months after our expulsion from the CP in 1928, the *Militant* printed a long document by Cannon, Shachtman, and Abern, "The Platform of the Opposition," filling most of the paper's eight tabloid pages. One section was called "The Perspective of a Labor Party." I will read a few passages from it:

> The perspective of coming mass struggles involves the question of developing these struggles in a political direction and unifying them in a centralized form. The movement for a Labor Party is today at low ebb as a result primarily of the passivity of the workers and the decline in movements of struggle in the past period. The coming period of developing economic struggles will very probably be reflected in tendencies toward the revival of the Labor Party movement.

It is not reasonable to expect that the masses of the American workers, who are still tied ideologically and politically to the bourgeois parties, will come over to the Communist Party politically in one step in a period not immediately revolutionary. All past experience, and particularly the recent experiences in the mining, textile, and needle trades industries, where the workers who supported Communist leadership in strikes did not vote for the Communist ticket, do not sustain such expectations. The perspective of a Labor Party, as a primary step in the political development of the American workers, adopted by the Party in 1922 after a sharp struggle in the Party and at the Fourth Congress of the Communist International, holds good today, although the forms and methods of its realization will be somewhat different than those indicated at that time.

It is therefore necessary to keep the perspective of a Labor Party before the eyes of the Party and the working class. We speak here not for the immediate formation of such a party and surely not for the adventurism and opportunism that has characterized this work in the past, particularly in the organization of fake Labor Parties that had no genuine mass basis. The Labor Party must have a mass basis and must arise out of struggle and be formed in the process of struggle. To this end, the propaganda slogan must be really revived, and as soon as it has found roots in the masses and their experience in the struggle, it must become an agitational, and finally an action, slogan.

The rest of this part of the 1929 platform discusses what a labor party of the kind we would propagandize for cannot be—it cannot be a two-class party, or an enlarged shadow of the CP, and so on, so I won't read those parts.

That was February 1929. We then decided to hold the founding convention of the CLA in May, and the platform containing this position on the labor party was introduced as the leadership's main document for the convention, serving as the basis for discussion first in the branches and then at the convention. There, according to a report on the convention by Cannon in the *Militant*, the labor party question was one of the two sharply debated on the convention floor. After describing minority viewpoints, including some who wanted nothing to do with any labor party even after it was formed, and some who were against advocacy but would work inside a labor party, Cannon wrote:

It was the opinion of the majority that, although it certainly is not a pressing question of the moment, the labor party question has a great importance for the future when the radicalization of the workers will begin to seek political expression. Therefore it is imperative to have a clear and definite stand on it. A misjudgment of the probable line of development of the American workers or a sectarian doctrine which would prevent us from approaching and influencing new upward movements, might have the most serious consequences later on. The formulation of the Platform on the Perspective of a Labor Party was adopted by a majority after a thorough discussion.

I wish that I had known in 1938 about this stage of our thinking on the labor party nine years earlier. I think it might have helped me avoid a serious error because, in my opinion, our 1929 position was substantially correct. It did not make a principle out of what was actually a tactical question. It did not reject taking a clear and definite stand merely because there was no labor party movement of significance in existence. It distinguished between the labor party as a subject for propaganda and the labor party as a subject for agitation or action. And it had what proved to be a realistic perspective on the relative future growth of the revolutionary party and the mass movement.

That was the position at our first convention, in mid-1929, before the start of the big depression and at a time when all factions of the Communist Party, right, center, and left, were in favor of advocating a labor party, although their motivations and reasoning varied greatly. This position was changed, and even criticized, at our second convention in mid-1931, when the depression was over a year old and when the CP, now deep into its third-period madness, also was opposed to any pro-labor party development.

I don't mean to suggest that the CP's opposition to labor party advocacy was the same as ours. To the CP, anybody who advocated a labor party was a social fascist. We condemned their position, first of all because the whole theory of social fascism was false and suicidal from start to end, and second, because if that was all their opposition to a labor party rested on, it was insufficient, because it meant that when they ultimately gave up social fascism they might or would return to advocacy of a labor party. (Which, incidentally, they did, in 1935.)

The political resolution adopted at our second convention, in 1931, was a long document, and the section called "Social Reformism and the Perspectives of the Revolutionary Movement" was also long. Contrary to the CP, we warned that the basis for social reformism, far from being "narrowed down," was being extended in the form of a growth of a leftist bureaucracy in the unions and a revival of the social democracy. Most of the section is devoted to a discussion of how to fight the reformists—how the CP should fight them, through the united front correctly understood and applied and so on, in a period when it must not be assumed that the United States was fated to be the last capitalist country to enter the revolutionary crisis.

The labor party question was presented in this context. The resolution saw the AFL bureaucracy, "their socialist assistants and the 'Left wing' progressive toadies of the Muste school" working consciously to erect barriers to the growth of the revolutionary movement in every area. "On the political field most of these elements seek to erect a barrier in the form of a 'Labor' or 'Farmer-Labor' party, that is, a bourgeois workers' party in the image of the British Labor Party."

The 1931 resolution then criticizes the many false formulations of the labor party question held in the American CP from 1923 to 1928, saying that none was based on a Marxian conception of the role of the labor party or of the nature of our epoch. Of course many of these formulations and policies had been adventurist or opportunist, or a combination of both. Now, said the resolution:

> [A]ll these conceptions and practices must be thrown overboard because they were originally wrong. . . . The American Communists cannot undertake to organize a petty bourgeois workers' party "standing between" the bourgeoisie and the proletariat.
>
> Abstractly considered, to be sure, were there a mass movement which would organize a labor party, the Communists would have to take up the question of working within it as a revolutionary nucleus. But this is a different matter entirely. Moreover, it is a matter which has less of a timely significance today—even abstractly—than in past years, since there is no substantial movement at all for a labor party in the 1932 elections.
>
> It is the reformists of all shades, the Thomases and the Mustes, who seek to set up this petty bourgeois party as a wall against the workers' progress towards Communism; in this work, they are only fulfilling their mission and role of prolonging as much as possible the "reformist period" in the development of the American working class. It is no accident that the right-wing liquidators of the Lovestone group have as the

central point in their program the idea that the Labor Party's formation is an essential and imperative step for the American workers, which the right wing is ready to initiate, to form and build up. It is this perspective which it recommends to the Communist movement as a whole to adopt. The Left Opposition, at its formative stage, leaned in the direction of this reformist perspective which constituted to a certain extent an uncritical carryover of the preceding group struggles in the party, prior to the time when the left wing took shape and was established as a political grouping distinct from all the others in the movement. The firmer establishment of its Marxian position dictates a break with this early standpoint and the adoption of the one outlined here. The adoption of this revised point of view, the result of clarification in its own ranks, marks a step forward that will enable the Opposition to bring greater clarity on this vital problem into the revolutionary and labor movements as a whole.

That was 1931. A year later, Trotsky had talks in Turkey with Albert Weisbord, the leader of a small group that was making an approach to the Left Opposition, although it shared many of the ideas of the Right Opposition, including its labor party position. After their discussion, Trotsky wrote a letter to Weisbord and a statement on the labor party, both printed in *Writings (1932)*. In the letter he praised the position taken by the CLA at our second convention "because in the theses not only was a correct position taken on the essence of the question but also an open and courageous criticism of its own past was made. Only in this way can a revolutionary tendency seriously assure itself against backsliding."

In the labor party article, he said that he found the CLA convention position on the labor party "excellent in every part, and I subscribe to it with both hands." It is an article very worthwhile, especially for those who may think that we should have been or should be in favor of the formation of a labor party under all circumstances. But I leave all that out to quote two passages:

A long period of confusion in the Comintern led many people to forget a very simple but absolutely irrevocable principle: that a Marxist, a proletarian revolutionist, cannot present himself before the working class with two banners. He cannot say at a workers' meeting: "I have a ticket for a first-class party and another, cheaper ticket for the backward worker." If I am a Communist, I must fight for the Communist Party.

And a little later, after mentioning how the Comintern's policy toward the Kuomintang and the British Labor Party in the 1920s produced an opportunistic adaptation to the will of the Comintern's allies and, through them, to that of the class enemy, he said:

> We must educate our cadres to believe in the invincibility of the Communist idea and the future of the Communist Party. The parallel struggle for another party inevitably produces in their minds a duality and turns them onto the road of opportunism.

It should be noted that there had been no explicit reference to a principle about the labor party in the 1931 convention's resolution, but Trotsky's use of such a term was not inconsistent with that resolution; it merely spelled out what was implicit in the whole approach of the resolution.

By now it must be plain that there was a principle involved in the thinking behind the position we held between 1931 and 1938. And it was a most fundamental principle—the principle of the need and primacy of the revolutionary party, whose construction is indispensable for everything else. Those who depart from this principle, or subordinate it, or compromise it, like the social democrats or the Lovestoneites, cannot possibly have the right position on the labor party.

But it does not follow that everybody who advocates a labor party is necessarily subordinating or compromising the principle that the building of the revolutionary party comes foremost for Marxists. It does not follow that advocating a labor party is contradictory to building the revolutionary party; in fact, advocating a labor party is not only consistent with building the revolutionary party in certain conditions but also a means toward building the revolutionary party, if the revolutionaries know what they are doing and how to do it right.

So on the labor party there was a confusion between principle and the tactics that were presumed to flow from the principle, which, as I showed yesterday, is the same thing as happened with the Ludlow amendment. The difference is that the Ludlow amendment mistake was of relatively short duration, a few months, whereas the labor party mistake lasted for seven years and therefore was harder for many of us to correct. The transitional program, or, more exactly, the transitional method that it taught us, enabled us not only to understand this mistake, some of us sooner than others, but also to better grasp the dynamics of unfolding class struggles and how to relate to them in a way that was positive and creative rather than purely propagandist, abstentionist, or dogmatic.

It showed us that advocating a labor party does not necessarily make us responsible for everything that happens in connection with a labor party that is formed under the leadership of other forces any more than advocating a strike makes us responsible for everything that happens during a strike under the leadership of other forces. The nature of our responsibility depends on the nature of our program and the way we present it. We are responsible only for what we advocate, not for the victory of opponents over what we advocate.

It showed us that advocating a labor party does not necessarily mean that you are advocating the formation of a reformist party. It depends on how you advocate it, on what content you give your advocacy, on what program you advance for the labor party. The posing of the question—can a labor party be revolutionary?—which seemed unreasonable to us before 1938, was very useful educationally. Trotsky did not give the question an absolute or direct yes answer. We will try to make it as revolutionary as we can, he said, and he might have added, just as we do with the unions.

It showed us that advocating a labor party does not inevitably produce in the minds of the revolutionary cadre a duality regarding the primacy of the revolutionary party or turn the cadre onto the road of opportunism. It can do these things, but it need not, if the cadre is firm in principle in the first place and if the leadership is always alert to maintain the cadre's educational-political level and consciousness. Advocating a labor party can result in these retrogressive things, but it does not follow that it must, therefore it does not follow that the mere possibility must compel us to abstain from what can be a fruitful tactic for the building of the revolutionary party.

Of course it is true that a party that is weak on the principle of the revolutionary party will get into trouble with a labor party tactic. But the SWP was not weak on that principle, so that general truth was irrelevant in this case.

In 1931, when we replaced the 1929 position, we said that it had been wrong, for which Trotsky praised us. In 1938, when we replaced the 1931 position, we did not make any such explicit judgment. We said only that the 1931 position was abstract and that conditions had changed sufficiently to make the abstract formulas of the past obsolete. These were valid criticisms, and it is to the credit of the party and its leadership that, with help from Trotsky and the transitional program, we were able to arrive at a correct position, in a relatively short time, without the loss of cadres and without serious damage to morale. Perhaps this was the most that could have been achieved under those conditions.

I did not think so at that time. I resented what I took to be the leadership's refusal to make a judgment about the 1931 position, so much that my resentment prevented me from understanding what was correct and progressive in its 1938 position. In addition, I was basically wrong because I thought that the 1931 position was correct. Later I saw and now I see that the 1931 position was not just abstract but wrong, not just rendered obsolete by new conditions but wrong before the coming of new conditions—not in every word, but on the whole. I think that the public opinion of the party will reach this conclusion, too, actually though not officially, when in the not too distant future we will make these old documents more available for study by the membership.

The personal lesson that I learned, rather painfully, was the need to be more objective in the analysis of political problems. It was hard for me to admit to myself that we had been mistaken, that I had been mistaken, so hard that I wanted to cling to the error. And I justified clinging to it by the less than perfect arguments used by the leadership to motivate the correction. That's not a good way to reach a decision. A position may be correct even though its proponents do not defend it in the best way possible. We have the obligation to recognize a correct position independently, so to speak, of the arguments of others who find it correct. It took me almost three years after the end of the 1938 discussion before I was able to do that with the labor party question. Fortunately, the party was not so slow.

Although the subject of these talks played a decisive part in my political life, that is not the main reason that I have gone to the trouble of telling you about them.

Building the revolutionary party is a difficult and arduous process. Recently I read the translation of a 1933 article by Trotsky about how hard it is to achieve a healthy society even after the workers have come to power, written for an American bourgeois periodical but not published at that time.

"To achieve harmony in the state," he wrote, "—even on the basis of collective ownership and planned management encompassing all facets of the economy—is only possible as the result of an indefinitely prolonged period of efforts, experiments, errors, crises, reforms, and reorganization." That description struck me as appropriate also for the task of building a party capable of leading the revolutionary workers to power—"a prolonged period of efforts, experiments, errors, crises, reforms, and reorganization."

We have reason to be proud of the achievements of the SWP. It is qualitatively superior to any of its opponents in this country, and, thanks to the continuity of its leadership, which enabled it to avoid repeating the same errors over and over, it enjoys several advantages over other sympathizing groups or sections of the Fourth International. This did not come about by accident or sheer good luck; it is the result of struggle and consciousness. A correct appraisal of the SWP and its achievements, which is necessary for further progress, is furthered by an awareness of the difficulties it has encountered and the way it overcame them, rather than by an ignoring of those difficulties or a depreciation of their magnitude.

The other reason that I think discussions such as this are justified is that they contribute to party consciousness-raising about the abundance of weapons in our political and theoretical arsenal. The metaphor most commonly used to call our attention to the debt we owe our predecessors is that we are "standing on their shoulders," which explains why we can see some things that they couldn't. I think I prefer a less athletic figure of speech, that of the arsenal. It was built by the pioneers of the Marxist movement and expanded by their successors. It is bigger, and its contents are more varied and useful than anything they had at their disposal. Available to us now are not only the actual weapons—the ideas, theories, programs, principles, strategies, tactics, and so on—but the history of their development, refinement, and improvement, which includes trial and error and experiments that failed as well as those that succeeded. We don't have to start from scratch, with the bow and arrow, and we are not doomed to repeat errors merely because we don't know their history. We can learn from the past, both what to continue and perfect and what to avoid.

No other movement has such a rich arsenal; the others would like to forget the past. The Stalinists, for example, would never dream of reprinting the books they published in the early 1930s, during the period of social fascism; we, on the other hand, are using precious resources to print material from the 1930s by Trotsky and others that we were too poor to print in permanent book form then and that we are determined to add to our arsenal for the benefit of the youth of today and tomorrow.

This arsenal is big, but it's going to have to be bigger before humanity turns it into a museum. You are going to have to build new weapons to hasten that day, but before you can do that you have to master the ones in our present stockpile. These talks are intended as a contribution to that process.

3. THE SWP, THEN AND NOW

A by-product of the preparation of these talks, which required that I read the minutes of the Political Committee, the National Committee, and the founding convention of 1938, most of them for the first time this year, was an almost involuntary comparison between the state of the party in 1938 and the state of the party now. I should warn you that these comparisons are drawn from data that is fragmentary at both ends, and that they inevitably reflect the special or subjective concerns I have about certain aspects of party life. And since they have little to do with the overall title of these talks and some of you may feel that you were brought here through false advertising, I hope you will feel free to leave now or whenever you realize you are not interested.

First of all, I should say that I am working comparisons between organizations that are roughly the same size, although I think that the SWP and the Young Socialist Alliance (YSA) together are a little bigger than the SWP and YPSL were between the founding convention in 1938 and the split with the Shachtmanites in 1940.

I have noticed a tendency among some of the younger members, when they look at the older members who have survived from the 1930s, to forget that the older members were once as young, energetic, and inexperienced as they are or were. So I will compare the age levels, since a normal revolutionary party will be a young party. At the 1938 convention, age data about the delegates was not reported, probably not collected. But it was reported the following year, at the 1939 convention, when it could not have been much different from 1938. The average age of the regular delegates was twenty-eight and a half, of the alternates thirty. Comparable figures at our convention last year were not given, but an estimate based on those that were given is between twenty-six and twenty-seven years for the regulars, and between twenty-five and twenty-six for the alternates. So the age levels of the membership are not much different.

The age levels of the central leadership were wider apart, but not as much as you might expect. Cannon was forty-eight in 1938, but he was exceptional. Shachtman was thirty-five, Abern forty, and most of the other PC members were in their thirties, I would guess. Their average age might be between thirty-five and forty, whereas the average age of their successors today might be between thirty and thirty-five. Not a big difference. The central leaders of 1938 had had a longer experience in the movement, which of course is important, but qualitatively this is hard to measure or compare.

There are no statistics about the class composition of the party in 1938. But I think that I should caution you against a tendency to imagine that the differences were greater than they actually were. In those days, when the depression was eight or nine years old, the occupation a person was going to end up with was harder to foresee and more dependent on accident. A college graduate might be working as a busboy and might have jumped at the chance to work on an assembly line; it was only when the war liquidated unemployment that things got sorted out and it turned out that he was going to be a school administrator or a sales executive. This distorts the picture a little so far as comparisons go.

Anyhow, class composition varied considerably from branch to branch. In Newark, where I was city organizer, we had four branches; one of these was made up entirely of workers, most of them unemployed or working on Works Progress Administration (WPA) jobs, and most of them black; in the other branches, perhaps one-fourth belonged to unions; the great majority were college-age youth who couldn't afford to go to college and were either unemployed or holding low-paid jobs because, at the moment, there was nothing else. This was probably a more proletarian local than some others, including the New York local.

Trotsky, as you may know, was very dissatisfied with the class composition of the SWP, and he felt vindicated two years later when the split of the petit bourgeois opposition headed by Shachtman and Burnham cost us around 40 percent of our membership. He kept pestering the SWP leadership with his solution, which was to reduce to the status of sympathizers all members who failed to recruit a worker in six months. The leaders thought that this was too drastic and preferred to concentrate instead on colonization of members into industry. And in fact, in the next few years, especially when the war began and jobs became available, a considerable proportion of the nonproletarian members who did not leave with the Shachtmanites was successfully colonized.

An artist became a steelworker; a young woman who had studied to be a musician became an electrical worker; a student became a seaman; and so on. But this transformation was the result of politics, of decisions by the party and by the members involved, and it transcended class based on birth or accident. And even if we had useful figures, there's not much to be gleaned from a comparison of the relative class compositions that does not begin with a firm understanding of the primacy of politics and concreteness.

An area in which I regret to report no progress is our almost total lack of interest in cultural problems and questions. Reading through the many long resolutions of our 1938 and 1939 national conventions, I noted sadly but without surprise that although the word "cultural" appears three or four times; neither in our resolutions, nor in our press, nor in our political or theoretical work did we display the slightest interest in cultural change or struggle, or any except the most superficial interest. Despite our urban location, we have always had more to say about agriculture than about culture.

This was one of the weaknesses of our movement at that time—its one-sidedness, its bias or blindness to everything except the most obviously political or economic aspects of life in the United States. This one-sidedness can be explained and, for the beginnings of our movement, to some extent it can even be justified. But I hoped that this defect would be corrected someday, and at the first Socialist Activists and Educational Conference four years ago, when Mary-Alice Waters made some remarks about the so-called cultural and sexual revolutions, I welcomed them and said:

> The sickness of a society that has outlived its usefulness takes many forms, and millions enter the radicalization process at personal and cultural rather than social and political levels. The beginning of the breakup of the authority of American capitalism can be seen in changing attitudes to morals, in revaluations of sexual norms, in the many varieties of escapism we can see around us. To better understand this breakup and its political significance, we ought to pay more attention to the cultural superstructure, beginning with our press. Perhaps the next time we have a conference like this we can have a full session on this question.

This is the fourth conference we've had since then, but there's never been a single talk or class on any aspect of culture. Our press confines itself for the most part to reviews of books and movies, and it often gives the impression that these are printed only when there is a hole to fill.

It took us one-third of a century after his death before we printed one of Trotsky's books on culture, but it is underread and underpromoted in our party, and it would never occur to our educational department to prepare a study guide for it or to recommend its use in party classes.

I had hoped that the present generation of the party, itself very much shaped by the rapid cultural changes since World War II, and sensitive to the problem of workerism, would fill this gap that my generation left in our outlook and analysis. But it hasn't happened yet, and it's difficult to discern any signs of progress.

One of the indisputable disadvantages of our party now as compared to then is that we do not have the benefit of Trotsky's advice and help. The only word to describe their value is enormous. Of course, since he was not in this country, his suggestions were not always practicable, but on the other hand, his physical distance from the problems and pressures sometimes gave him a broader and better view, as in the Ludlow and labor party questions. In addition, he sometimes tended to think that things could be done faster than actually proved possible, which must have been upsetting or exasperating to the comrades involved. But on the whole he was the wisest of teachers and the most loyal of collaborators, and this collaboration was fruitful for both our party and the international.

We haven't had the advantage of direct guidance by Trotsky for a long time. But as partial compensation we have the benefit of a much greater volume of his writings in English, available to all of us, than anybody had in any language in the 1930s. We can still learn much from Trotsky through these writings, if we take the trouble to study them and their method—from Trotsky's writings and from the writings, activities, and example of those who have continued his work during the last third of a century, starting with Comrade Cannon.

Another counterbalancing factor, which constitutes a big plus for us today, is the fact that the SWP leadership is now more homogeneous, more united, than it was in the 1930s. Reading the 1938 minutes convinced me, reconvinced me, that our central leadership at that time included several exceptionally talented and even brilliant people—but people who give the impression of sometimes pulling in different directions. Not all the time, not most of the time, some of the time. The Cannon leadership set out to correct this after Trotsky's death, not in an arbitrary or mechanical way, and the long-range effects have been very positive and noticeable. Our leadership now not only knows how to work as a unit, as a team, but it does it almost automatically, without having to think or strain about it. The consequences can be detected in all areas of party life if you know how to look for them, and they are good in virtually all respects.

Another area of big contrast between then and now is our electoral work, as I've already said in *The Party Builder.* The differences are bigger than between night and day, and they are qualitative as well as quantitative. If I dwell on this too much, it is because I was one of the few ardent advocates of electioneering at that time, long before the central leadership awoke to its opportunities. And since I was usually wrong when I differed with the National Office, I take satisfaction in calling attention to the few times I was right.

Most of the comrades looked down their noses at election work in the 1930s; they weren't opposed in principle, but they didn't see how revolutionaries could take it seriously or devote precious time to it. Most of our few so-called election campaigns consisted of announcing a candidate two or three weeks before election day and printing an article in our paper urging a write-in campaign for Comrade So-and-So (usually Cannon). They never bothered to tell readers how to cast a write-in vote, and even our own members didn't know how. It was the closest you could come to complete abstentionism in electoral activity without renunciation of our principled position.

I had learned better during our sojourn in the Socialist Party, and the other comrades there had the same opportunity to learn better, but most of them shut their eyes to this side of the SP experience, or never opened them. In all of 1938 we had only two places where we even tried to run candidates of the new party—in the mayoral primary in St. Paul at the start of the year and in congressional and state legislative races in Newark. In the first case, we had to settle for a write-in vote, I think, and in the second, we actually went out and got petitions, got on the ballot, and got a respectable vote.

(Minnesota, one of the few places where we were interested in elections, was of course the model center of our party for trade union work; and at the founding SWP convention, the New Jersey party's work in the unions and the unemployed movement was cited as being the next best—a circumstance I find worth mentioning because I think that a branch's attitude to election work is a good index to its political health and sagacity and its real attitude to reaching outward and talking to people other than ourselves.)

Our record was so bad that when the National Committee had a plenum at the end of 1938, it adopted a resolution that was printed in the *Socialist Appeal* under the title "Political Committee Rapped on Election." This resolution criticized our failure to try to get on the ballot where it was possible, put the responsibility on the Political Committee, and directed it to correct the faults shown in the 1938 elections. But there was little improvement until around the end of World War II.

In 1948 we ran our first presidential campaign, and the change really began to sink in. But it was interrupted by the cold war and deepening isolation in the 1950s, and we did not really get back into stride until our 1968 campaign. Since then the progress has been monumental, in every respect. And all this will be seen as only a tune-up for 1976.

Finances, or rather financial woes and worries, are frequently reflected in the 1938 minutes. Comrade Cannon's *History* told of the poverty under which the movement tried to operate in its earliest years. We were bigger in 1938, and the financial situation was probably better then, but not much better, considering the fact that we were trying to organize a party rather than a faction.

Several times the minutes report that a competent member of the staff has had to be laid off—the national labor secretary, an editor, etc.—because we could not find the fifteen dollars a week they and their families needed to live on. A report is made that the party car can be sold for sixty dollars, with the money to be allocated for fieldwork in Michigan and Indiana. Sixty dollars was a lot of money then. A report is made in January that we are going to send thirty dollars to the International Secretariat (IS). When Cannon tells Trotsky in March that the sum sent to the IS had by then risen from thirty dollars to fifty dollars, Trotsky is overjoyed: "Oh, that's very, very, good."

When it is decided to send two delegates to the founding conference, a big campaign is launched in May to collect one thousand dollars for their expenses. The money comes in slowly. When half is raised, Cannon sails off, but Shachtman has to wait. In July he is still waiting, and in the end some members have to take out a loan to get him onto a ship. Of course, one thousand dollars then was a vastly different magnitude.

Trying to make allowances for the inflation and the very different economic situations of the two periods, I have asked myself if it was possible to make a comparison of the levels of financial responsibility to the party between the membership of then and the membership of today. That is, taking the different circumstances into account, was the party membership as ready in those days to make financial sacrifices as it is today? I finally decided, reluctantly, that I could not answer this question with any assurance, but I will tell you my impression, based on memory rather than the minutes: today's membership, which I think performs very well in this area, compares favorably with that earlier generation.

Related to finances and what it says about the membership's morale is the size of the party's staff, or the number of full-time workers. I don't call them professional revolutionaries, for as I understand that term, it applies to a larger part of the membership, including those who are not on the party staff but who make themselves available to the party where and when they are needed, whether on the staff, in a factory, on a campus, or wherever. So I am referring now only to the number on the staff. And I do that because it is a most significant index of the fighting capacity of the party, the best quantitative measure of the party's ability to turn word into deed, to carry out our decisions electively, to intervene in a serious way in the class and national struggles that will take us beyond radicalization to revolution.

As I've already said, the size of our movement at the end of the 1930s, party and youth combined, was approximately the same as our present size, perhaps a little less then, but approximately the same. Not in the minutes but in an internal bulletin of that period, in a speech by Comrade Cannon after a trip to France in which he compared the SWP with the French party in 1939, I was able to find a figure about the size of our national staff of that time, including full-time workers in the various branches. And the figure was—approximately—one-sixth or one-seventh the size of our full-time staff now.

The membership size is approximately the same; the size of the staff is between six and seven times as large as it was then. Thinking about this ratio may make you more conscious, as it did me, of what a powerhouse, relatively, our still small movement is today and of what a powerhouse it is, relatively, compared both to our opponents in the radical movement in this country and to the revolutionary movements in other parts of the world.

I think you know that I am not emphasizing this ratio in order to encourage complacency or smugness. I do it in order to heighten consciousness about the uniqueness of certain of our accomplishments, the moral being not only that more is possible now, but also that more is expected of us than of our predecessors.

I did not expect to find much in the 1938 documents about the black struggle, nor did I find much. There is a short section in the declaration of principles adopted by our founding convention, entitled "Negroes and Other Oppressed Racial Groups." Everything said in this section—about the origins of racial antagonisms, the need to combat chauvinism among white workers, the need for common struggle, and so on—is correct and necessary. But it's not complete. Not complete merely by our present standards, but by the standards our party was to adopt a year later, at our next convention, when we first really began to think about the black struggle and try to intervene in it. This turn in 1939, one of the crucial ones in our history, was, as is known by readers of the pamphlet *Leon Trotsky on Black Nationalism and Self-Determination*, stimulated and encouraged by the results of another visit to Mexico by a delegation from the United States, this time including C. L. R. James, which went to talk with Trotsky in April 1939 about the black struggle, among other things.

I didn't know it in 1939 because the records about our history weren't as accessible to the members then as they are now, but that was the second time Trotsky had held discussions with US visitors on the Marxist approach to the black struggle. The first time was in 1933 when Trotsky, then in Turkey, had told Arne Swabeck that he thought that the Stalinist position on self-determination at that time was more correct than the Communist League of America's position. That was certainly unusual—that the Stalinists were more correct on anything than we!—but I never heard a word about that in the 1939 discussion, or for many years after, until I inherited an old internal discussion bulletin.

I mention this, although it is a little off the track, because I discovered something else that everybody had forgotten only a few weeks ago, when I was delving into the old *Militant*s about the evolution of our position on the labor party. That is that the 1939 convention, which I thought was our first to discuss the black struggle thoroughly, including its aspect as a national struggle, was actually the second where this question was discussed and debated.

The story, briefly, is this: In February 1929, a few months after the CP's expulsion of Cannon, Shachtman, and Abern, they published in the *Militant* a long document entitled "The Platform of the Opposition." This included a section entitled "Work among Negroes," which said in one place:

> The Negro question is also a national question, and the Party must raise the slogan of the right of self-determination for the Negroes. The effectiveness of this slogan is enhanced by the fact that there are scores of contiguous counties in the South where the Negro population is in the majority, and it is there that they suffer the most violent persecution and discrimination. . . . The Party must at the same time decisively reject the false slogan of a "Negro Soviet Republic in the South" at this time. This theory is still being propagated in the Party press and in official Party literature despite its rejection even at the Sixth Congress of the Comintern.

The Platform of the Opposition, including this section, served as our program until the founding convention of the CLA in Chicago in May 1929, and the platform served as the major document both in the preconvention discussion and at the May convention. Two parts of the platform were the subject of considerable dispute at the convention—the one on the labor party, the other on the slogan of the right of self-determination. Cannon's report on the convention in the *Militant* says:

> Following a discussion of the disputed section of the Platform on the Slogan of the Right of Self-Determination for the Negroes it was decided to defer final action until more exhaustive material on the subject can be assembled and made available for discussion. . . . In view of the profound importance of this question and the manifest insufficiency of informative material and discussion pertaining to it, this decision to defer final action was undoubtedly correct.

Final action was to be deferred ten years, until the 1939 convention, and a deep grasp of the question was not to be reached until the black radicalization in the early 1960s helped us understand it more concretely and better. Our progress in this field, theoretically and practically, has been tremendous. Its full extent can be measured only by closer acquaintance with where we stood in 1938 and 1939 and, as it now turns out, ten years before then.

A few remarks about the role of women in the party: At the 1938 convention, the credentials committee was occupied mainly with contests in some branches by competing candidates for delegate seats, and it gave little data about the delegates as a whole. But one roll-call vote was taken, over the resolutions on the Soviet Union, and the minutes give the names of all the delegates and how they voted. Out of seventy-seven voting, three were women. The number of alternates and their sex are unknown. It was a little better at the next convention, in July 1939. Out of seventy-eight delegates, six were women; out of thirty-eight alternates, nine. So, at the 1938 convention, around 4 percent of the delegates were women; at the 1939 convention, around 8 percent. The percentage of women in the membership was of course higher than that.

Anybody who has attended recent party conventions and conferences, national or local, knows that the change in this area has been as big as it is progressive. At our convention last year [1973], 39 percent of the delegates and 35 percent of the alternates were women. I don't think that there has been any change in our party in these three and a half decades bigger or more important than this one. And I don't thing that the younger members can fully appreciate its magnitude.

There has been as a result literally an explosion of revolutionary energy and talent previously untapped or underutilized throughout the party, from the highest committee to the lowest. Organizers, public representatives, candidates, campaign managers, department heads, teachers of classes, writers, editors, translators, coordinators, fraction heads, delegates abroad, and Janie Higginses—wherever you look, you find the women of the party well represented, making serious contributions to its work. In fact, if they weren't there, it simply wouldn't be recognizable to anybody as the SWP. No section of the radical movement in this country even comes close to us in this respect, and I don't think most of the sections of the Fourth International do, either.

This release of revolutionary energy, this liberation of revolutionary energy, has transformed our party and made it a better instrument for its great historic tasks. I am not interested in allocating credit for this change. In great part, of course, it was brought about by the radicalization of the last decade and a half, especially of women, with results that penetrate every nook and cranny of this society. But in part it was also made possible by our responsiveness to this radicalization, our capacity to see what was happening and to meet it constructively, in both our public work and our internal relations and practices. How much credit we deserve for the change is not what interests me here. What I am after is to try, if possible, to make you more conscious of its magnitude.

In this connection I want to say a couple of things about Mary-Alice Waters's pamphlet *Feminism and the Marxist Movement*, based on a talk here two years ago. I consider it an excellent piece of work, a real contribution to the literature of our movement. I fully approved of what I took to be its main aims, which were to refute slanderous and ignorant misrepresentations by anti-Marxists about the record of Marxism in the women's struggles and to prod backward and sluggish elements in the Fourth International who were dragging their feet instead of meeting their revolutionary responsibilities toward the new women's liberation movement.

I happen to disagree with her conclusion that the two traditions of the women's struggle in the Marxist movement coincided generally with the main division in the movement between revolutionaries on one side and reformists on the other. I think that it was more complex than this, and that the evidence shows that there were two traditions among the revolutionaries, too, some understanding and championing the women's struggle, and others rejecting it or paying it only lip service. Our line of continuity is with the former, and we have no reason whatever to minimize or ignore the shortcomings of the latter, merely because on other questions they were on the right side.

Comrade Waters's pamphlet has a section called "The Fourth International," but it doesn't have much to say about the Fourth International's theory and practice on the women's movement, and the reason for that is that it didn't do much in this area until recently. Comrade Waters warns us against ahistorical thinking—against "project[ing] backward in time our current level of consciousness or stage of development instead of judging the past by what was known and what was possible then." I endorse that warning wholeheartedly. To it I would add a corollary: avoiding ahistorical thinking does not mean and does not require shutting our eyes to the shortcomings or mistakes of the past, whether by our predecessors or ourselves.

The truth is that in recent years a big leap has been made in the SWP and parts of the Fourth International in both the theory and practice of the women's struggle. The SWP has added something important to our arsenal here. How much and how important this addition is can be measured accurately only by those who have a clear-eyed, historical view of what the situation was before the addition.

So, in summary: There has been much change and considerable progress since the founding of the SWP. Much of this we owe to the pioneers, without whom we couldn't have done half of what we did. But we would have perished if we hadn't gone beyond the pioneers, and we have gone beyond them, learning how to sharpen the ideas and improve the practice that they initiated or developed. And this is good because the time is coming closer when we shall have to storm revolutionary heights that the conditions of their time prevented them from reaching.

The last thing I want to take up is not a comparison, but an estimate of the party in the late 1930s. In a discussion I had with two comrades a couple of weeks ago, after I had related some of the things that happened in the Political Committee and the National Committee in 1938, one asked me about the composition of the Political Committee at that time. It consisted of seven people, I said, making a pedagogic point that in those days a Political Committee of seven was not considered inadequate, and I named the seven, noting that within two years six of the seven had left the SWP.

There were Cannon, Shachtman, Abern, Burnham, McKinney, [B. J.] Widick, and [Nathan] Gould, representing the youth. All but Cannon left the SWP in the 1940 split by the petit bourgeois faction that set up the Workers Party. Burnham quit the Workers Party at its birth and became a reactionary Republican in the course of time. Abern died in the Workers Party. McKinney left it before its members went into the SP, and today he is with the Shankerite A. Philip Randolph Institute. Widick became a professor and commentator on the labor movement, and Gould quit early for refuge in some Jewish organization. "Only one out of seven remained, and that was Cannon himself," said the comrade. "That confirms my feeling that we didn't have a real Trotskyist leadership until the 1940 split."

I've thought about it since this conversation, and I don't agree with his conclusion. To say that we didn't have a real Trotskyist leadership until the 1940 split would be like saying that we didn't have a real Trotskyist organization until then. And that's just not a tenable conclusion.

The SWP was superior to all other groups in the International at that time; if it wasn't really Trotskyist, then they weren't, either, and neither was the International. Trotskyism then must have been some kind of ideal that did not come into real existence until 1940, or later.

Exactly when, I cannot say. Because if you apply this criterion—of how long the central leadership lasted in the movement—to determine whether it was a real Trotskyist leadership, you would get some baffling results. Take, for example, the Political Committee that was elected October 1, 1939, the first elected Political Committee after the seven-member Political Committee of 1938–39. The war had begun, and so had the faction fight, and the PC was being reorganized to reflect the fact that the National Committee had decisively voted for the majority view on the Soviet Union. The Political Committee was enlarged to eleven, the minority being given three posts (Shachtman, Abern, Burnham), the majority taking eight and, of course, choosing them itself. The eight were Cannon, Morrow, Weber, Clarke, Cochran, Gordon, M. Stein, and Murry Weiss.

This was the Political Committee at the time of the split in 1940, its main additions at that time being Dobbs and Goldman. Well, what happened to these eight? Morrow and Weber succumbed to Stalinophobia during the war and were out soon after. Clarke and Cochran lasted longer, until the Korean War. That is, four of the eight defected in a dozen years. Three of the remainder dropped out individually for various reasons: Gordon, Stein, and Weiss. So out of the PC majority of eight, only one survived to old age in the movement, again Cannon.

The same thing occurs when you examine the International Executive Committee (IEC) elected by the 1938 founding conference of the Fourth International. Out of fifteen, three were murdered: Trotsky and Ta Thu Thau by the Stalinists, Leon Lesoil by the Nazis. Of the remaining twelve, ten defected by the end of the war, leaving only a possible two who still stood with the Fourth International seven years after its foundation. The certain one of this possible two was, again, Cannon.

So it's better to see the SWP and its leadership as development in process, starting in 1928 and continuing through today into the future. When Cannon, Shachtman, and Abern began in 1928, they had less knowledge of some aspects of what is called "Trotskyism" than many people in this room today. But they all made big contributions, including Shachtman and Abern, despite the fact that they defected after a dozen years, and the party was a product of their collective work. The weak and negative sides of Shachtman and Abern came to the fore later, but that shouldn't blind us to their contributions in their best days any more than [Georgi] Plekhanov's ultimate betrayal of the revolution can detract from the progressive role he played in his earlier years in preparing the way for Lenin's party.

Under their collective leadership, or, if you wish, under a bloc of Cannon with Shachtman and Abern, the SWP *never* made the kind of serious mistakes that the Bolsheviks made in March 1917 before Lenin's return to Russia. Under their leadership, the SWP went through some serious tests in the 1930s.

One of these was the French turn, that is, our entry into the SP. That was not an easy thing to carry out without losses or demoralization; it required an organization solidly based in principle and led by people who were tactically very flexible. The French turn was carried out in this country much more electively than in France, where the Molinier–Pierre Frank split occurred right after the expulsion from the SP and paralyzed the party until World War II; the fact that such crises were averted here says something for the quality of our leadership and movement, and what it says is highly favorable.

Then there was the test of the transitional program, and I've told how that was met. And, soon after, there was the test of World War II, which we also met with success. So it was, on the whole, a pretty good party before 1940, a party developing in the right direction. In my own way, that is what I have been trying to show in these talks, among other things.

CHAPTER 13

THE ROCKY ROAD TO THE
FOURTH INTERNATIONAL,
1933–38
(1979)

George Breitman

One of the good things about Trotsky's *History of the Russian Revolution* is that, along with the clash of hostile class forces in that revolution, it presents the disputes and struggles that took place inside the monarchy, the bourgeoisie, the petty bourgeoisie, and the proletariat, and the parties that spoke or tried to speak for them. Most valuable of all is the story it tells about what went on inside the Bolshevik Party—not only its decisions and actions, its strengths and victories, but also its hesitations and uncertainties, its mistakes and weaknesses, and how it resolved them through debate and conflict.

Believing that to be the best method for studying revolutionary history and hoping that that aspect of Trotsky's *History* will serve as a model when the history of the Fourth International is written, I offer the following as a contribution to the study of an important segment of that history, the five-year period that ended in the foundation of the Fourth International in September 1938. This was the period that Trotsky called the second and final phase of the "prehistory" of the Fourth International.

Originally published as an *Education for Socialists Bulletin* in 1979. An abridged version of this talk was given at a socialist educational conference in Oberlin, Ohio, on August 5, 1978. Subheads have been added.

REVOLUTIONARY INTERNATIONALISM

Internationalism was at the heart of the Marxist movement from its inception. When their *Communist Manifesto* called on the workers of the world to unite, Marx and Engels did not mean this in a merely rhetorical or symbolic sense—they meant that revolutionary workers must build an international organization as well as national parties—and when the opportunity arose they helped to organize and lead the First International. Nobody who claimed to be a Marxist in the 1930s disputed the necessity of a Marxist International, although there were differences about the kind that was needed. This was before Stalin dissolved the Communist International during World War II, that is, before Stalin decreed that an international party had become outmoded, a view that is still championed by all the branches and offshoots of Stalinism today.

So in 1933 the critical problem facing revolutionaries was not whether to have or build an international Marxist party but a related though separate question: What do revolutionaries do when an international party becomes corrupt or degenerates and departs from its originally revolutionary principles and practices? Do they remain members of such an international trying to correct its course or do they, at a certain point, decide that such efforts are hopeless, break with the old International, and try to build a new one?

A certain body of experience had already accumulated around this question. In the 1870s Marx and Engels agreed to the dissolution of the First International they had founded rather than let it fall into the hands of the anarchists. This cleared the path after Marx's death for the formation of the new Second International, which united the Marxists of the world and played a generally progressive role during the next quarter of a century. In 1914 Lenin called for a new International because the Second had betrayed Marxism by supporting the imperialists in World War I. This orientation guided the Bolsheviks and other internationalists through the war and the Russian Revolution and led, more than four years after Lenin's first call, to the foundation of the Third, or Communist, International.

These developments supplied what might be called precedents for the decision that presented itself in 1933, but of course precedents alone could not determine a decision of such gravity: the chief criterion was objective necessity. And that was the criterion that prevailed at the meeting of the International Left Opposition's executive committee in France in August 1933, which voted to start work toward the formation of a new revolutionary International. It was undoubtedly the single most important decision in the fifty-five-year history of our movement.[1]

For ten years, since 1923, the Left Opposition had been working to reform the Communist International and return it to the path of Leninism and the revolutionary internationalist principles developed under Lenin's leadership at the first four congresses of the Comintern. Although expelled from the Comintern and its affiliates, the Left Oppositionists regarded themselves as a faction of the Comintern, demanding reinstatement and disdaining any intention of becoming an independent movement in competition with the Comintern.

But Hitler came to power early in 1933, not only because of the cowardice of the Social Democratic and union leaders but also because of the policies of the Stalinized Comintern, which fought bitterly and successfully to prevent any united front struggle against the Nazis. And in the months that followed, the executive committee of the Comintern, refusing to acknowledge any responsibility for the fascist annihilation of the powerful German workers' movement, unanimously reaffirmed the policies that had produced the German catastrophe. This reaffirmation convinced Trotsky and other leaders of the Left Opposition that the Comintern's degeneration had passed the point where its reform was any longer possible, that it was finished as a revolutionary force, and that a new International to replace it was the most urgent need of the international working class.

It was a striking example of simultaneous continuity and change. The principles of Leninism remained the same, but in order to promote and realize those principles it now became necessary to radically change the movement's orientation, organizational character, and tactics. Previously, the major, the virtually exclusive, work of our movement had been the preparation and dissemination of propaganda directed at the Communist parties [CPs], their ranks and their periphery, seeking to persuade them to change their policies so that the Communist parties could become capable of leading proletarian revolutions. Now the axis of our work was fundamentally changed. We ourselves were going to undertake the responsibility of building the Leninist International and parties—not alone of course, but together with other revolutionary forces, including those that could still be won from the CPs. Propaganda would continue to be essential, but its form would have to be altered and widened because it would be aimed at non-CP as well as CP audiences, and it would have to be combined with work in the labor and mass movements and with other independent activities to build the cadres of the new Leninist parties.

ASSETS AND DIFFICULTIES

To appreciate the magnitude, the audacity, and the difficulties of the undertaking requires an effort of historical imagination and some knowledge of the state of the Left Opposition at that time. For ten years its members had been recruited around the idea that a Leninist faction in the CPs was needed, not a new party; they had been educated around this idea after being recruited, and most of their activity had been devoted to spreading this idea among their contacts. *Faction—not party* thus had the status almost of a tradition. So it might be expected that there would be a strong psychological resistance to the new orientation. But in fact it was surprisingly small and brief. A dissident group split away in France but it probably would have split over another issue if this one hadn't come along, and here and there individual members could not adjust to the turn and dropped out. Opposition was so minimal that the leaders felt it was possible to make this momentous change without holding an international conference.

The near unanimity testifies to a relatively high level of political consciousness among the members of the Left Opposition, who had tried to influence the outcome of the fight against fascism in Germany before it triumphed and who grasped the main implications of the worst defeat the workers' movement had ever suffered. And it testifies to the exceptional authority held by Trotsky, whose arguments in favor of the new orientation seemed irrefutable to the members. But it may also have reflected an inadequate awareness of the towering obstacles that lay ahead, which nobody could have foreseen in all their concreteness.

One of the principal assets of the Left Opposition has already been mentioned—the fact that its members were better educated ideologically and politically than any other tendency of the period. But on the other side, it was a small, weak, and poor movement.

An international conference in February 1933 had been attended by representatives of the Opposition from eleven countries: ten in Europe[2] and the United States. The Soviet and Italian sections were organizations in exile, and most of the German leaders had to go into exile after Hitler's victory. By that time the Opposition in the Soviet Union no longer existed as a functioning organization, its remaining supporters having been isolated, exiled, or imprisoned by the Stalinist repression, cut off from each other as well as from Trotsky and the Opposition center abroad. The Greek and Spanish sections were the largest, each having over a thousand members. The other main sections had memberships averaging a few hundred, and many of the sections were smaller. Most of the sections were unable to publish regularly even a four-page weekly paper. One reason why an international conference was not held late in 1933 was the material poverty of the movement, which had held a conference in February and couldn't afford the expense of another so soon. In fact, the next international conference was not held until 1936.

Both the Second International and the Third International at this time had millions of members. There were two other international groupings on the Left—the International Communist Opposition or Right Opposition, which was led by Heinrich Brandler, and the loose centrist coalition of left Social Democrats and dissident Communist tendencies expelled from the Comintern for opposing the ultraleftism of the Stalinist "third period," which later came to be known as the London Bureau. Both of these two groups in 1933 had affiliates with memberships many times larger than the maximum of four or five thousand then adhering to the Left Opposition. The mightiest movements always begin small, so smallness is not a sin, provided it is not persisted in. But smallness is also never a virtue or an advantage for those whose aim is to win a majority to change the world.

Besides its small numbers, the Left Opposition had the handicap of an unfavorable class composition, most of its sections having a large percentage of petty-bourgeois elements, intellectuals, and students. This, too, is not uncommon in the early stages of workers' movements but invariably creates critical problems for them. In addition, many of the members were immigrants who were not well acquainted with the country where they lived or its labor movement. Most of the members were young and had little previous political or organizational experience. Some had prior experience only in the Communist parties in the years when they were being Stalinized, where they were seriously miseducated on many questions.

The leaders of the sections tended to be a little older and more experienced. Some had roots in the workers movement extending back before the Russian Revolution or World War I, and a few of the national leadership, such as the Belgian and the American, had the important advantage of having worked together in the CPs instead of having met, so to speak, for the first time in the Left Opposition. But none of them had yet completely freed themselves of the concept that prevailed in the Comintern after Lenin and before it was completely subjugated by the Stalinist faction—namely, the concept that the revolutionary party is a federation of factions rather than a combat organization striving for political homogeneity and a collective leadership. Unprincipled factionalism and even cliquism frequently undermined efforts to achieve political and organizational stability in the national sections of the Opposition and their leading bodies.

EARLY STEPS

Until 1933, the only international coordinating committee the Left Opposition had was the International Secretariat [IS]; in that year, it was supplemented by an executive committee, which was really only an enlarged IS. The composition of the IS was partly accidental because the national sections lacked money to send representative and authoritative members to serve at the center in Paris. Most of the IS members were young and its composition changed frequently, often as a result of factional changes in the national leaderships, especially in the French section. It had only one full-time staff member, the administrative secretary, the other members devoting most of their time to the work of their own sections. All in all, the independent authority of the IS in this period was never very high.

Our greatest asset in the thirties was the leadership provided by Trotsky. In his person was represented direct continuity with the experiences of the Russian Revolution, the long uphill struggles that preceded it, and the lessons of the Comintern in both Lenin's and Stalin's times. This continuity enabled the Left Opposition to escape most of the ruinous mistakes and false starts that plague movements starting out from scratch. His authority—moral, political, and theoretical—towered over that of all the other Opposition leaders. He knew, better than anyone else, about the shortcomings of the IS, but he also knew, as any good branch organizer does, that you have to work with the forces available and not reject them because they are less than ideal or perfect. Trotsky had an unshakable belief in the capacity of the workers to free themselves from class exploitation and oppression, given adequate leadership, and the conviction, which never left him, that the working-class vanguard was capable of forging such a leadership. These were the sources of both his patience with others and his own unceasing activism even when he was hemmed in like a prisoner in a cell. And so he worked with the members of the IS and the national leaderships, trying to educate them in the methods of Marxism and principled politics, in collective leadership for the whole movement. It was often frustrating work because all of them were operating under murderous pressures—the pressures of isolation and an unending series of defeats and setbacks, the pressures of imperialism and of Stalinism, repression of every kind, the spread of fascism, the poverty and demoralization resulting from mass unemployment, and much more—and most of the leading peoples in the thirties were gone from the movement by the end of World War II. Trotsky by himself could not compensate for unfavorable objective conditions or IS leadership weaknesses, but he could and did limit their impact on the work of the movement, sometimes decisively.

The first results of the August 1933 decision to work for a new International were quite encouraging. A week later there was an international conference in Paris of the centrist groups in and around the London Bureau, and the Left Oppositionists participated in order to raise the call for a new International and win allies around this call, which came to be known as the Declaration of Four. Trotsky had pointed to the inevitability of ferment in the radical movement as the lessons of the German catastrophe sank in, and to the likelihood that this would result in the emergence or strengthening of left-wing tendencies inside the centrist and social democratic organizations. This was confirmed at the Paris conference where three national groups joined with the Left Opposition in signing the Declaration of Four.[3] Two of these groups soon changed their minds about a new International but the third, a Dutch organization led by the veteran communist Henricus Sneevliet, joined the Left Opposition as its Dutch section and he himself became a member of its executive committee, playing an important role in it during the following five years.

Shortly after the Sneevliet group's adherence, the International Left Opposition changed its name to the International Communist League (ICL), the name by which we were known internationally until 1936.

The new orientation had healthy effects in several of the sections. In France it motivated the Opposition's youth group to initiate serious faction work inside the Socialist Party's youth group, which led to valuable results a year later. In the United States it provided a favorable climate for the resolution of an internal crisis between the supporters of James P. Cannon on one side and of Max Shachtman and Martin Abern on the other that had crippled the American section for three years. Thanks to the help of Trotsky and the IS, the old differences were put aside and there ensued a period of fruitful collaboration between Cannon and Shachtman that lasted through the founding conference of the International, in 1938, making the American section the strongest in the movement and the one that went farthest along the road of transforming itself from a propagandist group to a workers party of mass action.

But not all the results were positive. I have mentioned that a small group split from the French section when the new line was adopted, but its members had been on their way out for two years, and their departure was a blessing. More serious was the fact that behind the scenes they had the encouragement of an IS member in Paris, Witte [party name of Mitsos Giotopoulos] of the Greek section.[4] When the IS and Trotsky called Witte to order, he quit, and under his influence, the Greek section, the largest in the Opposition, also broke away from the ICL.

The political reasons for the split were not too clear at the time; the Greek leadership contended that only organizational principles were in contention. But soon after splitting from the ICL in 1934, they affiliated to the London Bureau, which was adamantly opposed to a new International. Objectively, it would appear, the split involved divergent views on the need for a Fourth International even though the Greek leaders never posed the issue that way before the split.

One of the London Bureau groups that attended the Paris conference was the centrist Independent Labour Party [ILP]. The ILP delegates voted against the Declaration of Four, but some of its leaders were interested enough to visit Trotsky in France to discuss perspectives. Because of these talks and his reading of the ILP press, Trotsky concluded that an important part of the ILP was in motion toward the Left, and he proposed that the members of the year-old British section of the Left Opposition should enter the ILP in order to win support for the Fourth International perspective. The IS agreed with this proposal and formally recommended it to the British section.

In what resembled a dress rehearsal for a much bigger debate over "entrism" a year later, the leaders of the British section, which had only forty members and not much independent experience, responded with shock and indignation. What! Right on the heels of calling for a new International and new revolutionary parties, we should go into a miserable outfit like the ILP? Wasn't this in contradiction to the principle that the independence of the revolutionary party must be maintained at all times! Trotsky tried patiently to explain that forty members were not yet a revolutionary party but only a nucleus for such a party, that the nucleus could expand only through organizational flexibility and tactical suppleness, that the nucleus could preserve its political independence by functioning as a disciplined fraction inside the ILP, and soon. But the sectarian formalists in the British leadership would not listen, and even though the entry proposal was only a recommendation and not a command, they expelled a minority that favored entry and split away from the International Left Opposition. Later, most of them were to join the ILP but not as a revolutionary fraction of the Fourth Internationalist movement.

As these and other examples in 1933 and later show, merely adopting the new orientation, although necessary, was not sufficient. Cadres in the revolutionary movement cannot be measured only by the good resolutions they vote for or adopt. What counts even more is how they implement those resolutions. Almost everybody in 1933 voted for a new International. But many did not really understand what they were voting for or how to carry it out in practice, and others changed their minds along the way when they saw or felt the immensity of the task.

At the end of 1933 the four organizations that had signed the Declaration of Four held a conference to consider their next steps in elaborating a program for the future International and the areas of collaboration that could take place among the four organizations. It was held in Paris, and Trotsky was part of the ICL delegation. It was agreed to hold another conference six weeks later and to prepare programmatic documents for that, but the exchanges between the ICL representatives and those of the German and Dutch centrists were so sharp that the prospects did not look promising; in fact, this was the last joint meeting of the Four, and the proposed February conference never took place.

I mention the conference mainly to call attention to the composition of the ICL delegation, whom I shall designate as the Eight, because they personify and illustrate some of the central problems and developments of the period. One, there was Trotsky. Two, Sneevliet, the leader of the new Dutch section. Three, Erwin Bauer, the leader of the German section, who was then administrative secretary of the IS. Four, Alfonso Leonetti, a founder of the Italian section. Five and six, Pierre Naville and Pierre Frank, founders of the French section. Seven, Leon Sedov, Trotsky's son, a leader of the movement in his own right. And eight, Rudolf Klement, Trotsky's German-language secretary and later administrative secretary of the IS.

These eight Europeans were not the entire leadership of the ICL at the end of 1933, but they included most of the central core. Sedov and Klement were both to be murdered by the GPU [Russian Civil Political Service] in 1938, in the months before the International's founding conference. As our narrative continues, we will take note of what happened to the other six.

Pulling together the forces of the Fourth International was not only and it was not mainly an organizational problem. It was a political problem primarily. When we were a faction of the Comintern, it sufficed to criticize the errors of the Comintern. But an independent International, if its existence is to be justified and if it is to attract people who will dedicate their lives to it, must have its own positive program, distinct from all others. Reaffirming the basic principles of the first four congresses of the Comintern was not enough; the new International needed a program that would draw the necessary lessons from the cataclysmic events since those congresses and answer the burning strategic and tactical problems facing the revolutionary movement in the 1930s. In fact, the organizational sides of the struggle for the Fourth International in the five-year period under examination were directly connected to, interlaced with, and dependent on the programmatic sides, the development of which fell mainly on Trotsky.

THEORETICAL UNDERPINNINGS

If I dwell on the organizational history rather than the programmatic contributions, which were undoubtedly the main achievement of our movement in this period, it is only because the organizational side is less well known. A crucial advance in our analysis of the Soviet Union was made only a few weeks after the decision to work for a new International. Then, like now, we characterized the USSR as a degenerated workers' state, which revolutionaries must defend against imperialist attack. Until then, however, we had advocated not only reform of the Russian CP but also reform of the Soviet state. This, we decided late in 1933, was no longer realistic. The CP, we concluded, could not be reformed but would have to be opposed and replaced by a Soviet section of the Fourth International; and forcible action to oust the bureaucratic Stalinist caste from power (not just reform) was needed to restore workers' democracy in the Soviet state and society. Subsequently refined as the concept of the political revolution, this has been our bedrock position on the Soviet Union and degenerated and deformed workers' states ever since. Hardly anyone in the ICL disagreed with it when Trotsky formulated it in October 1933[5] but differences about the class character of the USSR and what to do about it did begin to grow as the years went by and the crimes of Stalinism mounted. Our position was rejected by a third of the delegates to a national conference of the French section in 1937, and it was a major source of the important SWP split in 1940, where almost half the members were against defending the USSR when it came under imperialist attack in World War II.

Making a correct analysis of Stalinism as it evolved was only one of the important programmatic achievements that put their stamp on the Fourth International and conditioned its internal crises and conflicts in the thirties. Others related to our basic positions on fascism and the united front against it (Germany), People's Frontism (France and Spain), civil war (Spain), national liberation struggles against imperialism (China), and revolutionary policy in the fight against imperialist war. It would be hard to recognize the Fourth International without these programmatic positions. But they did not come easily or automatically. Reaching them required bitter struggle inside the movement as well as outside.

FRENCH DEVELOPMENTS

We now have come to the year 1934. In February, right-wingers and fascists tried to overthrow the French bourgeois-democratic government; also in February, the Bonapartist government of Austria crushed an armed uprising by the social democratic workers; and in October, the Spanish right-wing government crushed an armed uprising led by the Socialist Party. Trotsky considered the French developments to be the most crucial.

France is now the key to the international situation, he wrote in a manifesto published in March; he had used the same terms to apply to Germany in the 1930–33 period. By this he meant that the center of revolutionary gravity in Europe had shifted to France; that a struggle decisive for the whole world had opened in that country, that a correct policy there could create the conditions for a revolutionary victory, with all the international repercussions that that would bring, and for a qualitative change in the growth of the movement for the Fourth International.

In keeping with his analysis of the potential situation in France, Trotsky threw himself and everything he had into trying to influence its development. He was hampered when the French press launched a big witch-hunt against him in April and the government ordered him deported, because this meant he had to leave the metropolitan area where he had been able to attend IS meetings. Thereafter his direct participation was limited to what he could write or tell an occasional visitor to his home in a remote Alpine village. But his concern with the French section and its work never flagged.

The attempted French coup d'état in February 1934 brought a militant response from the French workers, first a general strike and then overwhelming sentiment for a workers' united front against fascism. This was so strong that first the Socialist Party and then, more slowly, the Communist Party had to consent to a united front. Along with this grew talk and pressure for a merger of these two parties. At this point, in June 1934, Trotsky, who was on the run from one place to another and had not yet been granted permission to live in the French Alps, made an audacious proposal to the French section of the ICL: that it should formally dissolve and join the SP, which permitted tendencies inside the organization to exist and publish their own newspapers. This, he felt, would enable it to avoid isolation outside of the new united front and put it in a position to make recruits to its ideas among the large number of left-wing SP members who had joined or become radicalized since Hitler's victory.

THE ENTRY TACTIC

Trotsky was the initiator of this entry tactic or maneuver, which came to be known as the "French turn." And he had to explain and defend this proposal with all the vigor and eloquence at his command[6] because it met much bigger resistance in the French section (and elsewhere) than the call for the new International had received. After a heated discussion and a near split averted only by IS intervention, the entry proposal was adopted by a majority of the French section at a national conference held at the end of August. It was supported by one of the two principal French leaders, Raymond Molinier, and opposed by the other, Pierre Naville. Shortly after the conference, the Naville group split from the section, and although it later decided to enter the SP, too, it refused for a long time to join the Bolshevik-Leninist Group in the SP, which was the name now taken by the members of the French section.

The entry tactic was an affront and a blow to everyone in the ICL who was tainted by formalism, schematism, sectarianism, routinism, and passivity, and hid these traits behind radical rhetoric about revolutionary principles and Bolshevik firmness. These traits all came gushing out now. Some were opposed to the entry proposal on the ground that it was impermissible in principle under any circumstances; others were against it on tactical grounds, like Naville; and still others were opposed on any and all grounds.

It can be argued that entrism was only a tactic, and one which applied only in very specific circumstances. This is true enough, but in my opinion Trotsky's proposal was one of his finest contributions in the 1933–38 period. Aside from other benefits it produced, the discussion it provoked shook up a lot of people and led to the first major liberation of our movement from the diseases of dogmatism that had been carried over from the Comintern or had been reinforced by different waves of recruits from third-period Stalinism. It also helped to rid us of people who were hopelessly unassimilable and could only hamper the healthy growth of our movement.

The repercussions in the IS and the ICL executive committee were bigger than those in the French section. Several members were opposed to the turn on various grounds, and most of them were incensed against Trotsky because he had taken the entry proposal to the French section before taking it up with the IS. Bauer, the IS secretary, denounced the proposal as a violation of Bolshevik principles and accused Trotsky of capitulating to the Second International. He could not even wait for the meeting of the ICL executive committee that was called for October to assess the French turn, but quit on the spot, and joined the German affiliate of the London Bureau. Sneevliet, the leader of the Dutch section, and Vereecken, the secretary of the Belgian section, were also opposed to the French turn, largely on tactical grounds, but Trotsky diplomatically persuaded them that even if they voted against the turn, they should agree to let the French section, then already inside the SP, complete its experiment. The leadership of the Spanish section, long estranged from the ICL although still part of it, was vehemently against the French turn. The vote at the October meeting, which Trotsky could not attend, would have been even closer if Bauer had not quit so quickly and if the Spanish had not boycotted the meeting. As it was, Sneevliet, Vereecken, and Pietro Tresso, a supporter of the Naville group, voted against the resolution written by Trotsky, which was adopted by a vote of six to three.[7] One of the supporters of the resolution was Cannon of the American section, who had come at Trotsky's urging and was given the assignment of meeting with Bauer, Naville, and others and trying to persuade them they should not split the movement over a tactical question. Another of the supporters of the resolution was Molinier, who favored its main parts but objected so strongly to a provision in it inviting the Naville group to return to the French section that he threatened to resign from the executive committee. And it was at this time, Cannon later reported, that Sneevliet tried to convince him the whole ICL should join the London Bureau in order to take it over and into the Fourth International.[8]

Thus this 1934 dispute accounts for the departure of two more members of the 1933 group of eight leaders: Bauer and Naville (although Naville was to return before leaving for good in 1939). Bauer's defection to the London Bureau and Sneevliet's illusions about the London Bureau in 1934 also tell us something significant about the quality of their commitment to the Fourth International only a year after they became two of the four signers of the Declaration of Four.

BRIGHT SPOTS

Things began to pick up after the October meeting. The brightest spots were in France and in the United States.

The American section had decided early in 1934 that the way to apply the new 1933 orientation in the United States was to propose a fusion with the left-centrist American Workers Party [AWP], headed by A. J. Muste. (Contrary to the legends, this proposal originated with the American leaders, not with Trotsky, who approved it; and it was made before the Musteites wrote a glorious page of labor history in the Toledo Auto-Lite strike and before the American section showed its revolutionary caliber in the Minneapolis Teamster strikes.) There had been attempts in 1933 to fuse the German and Dutch sections with centrist groups in the London Bureau, but they had fallen through. So the fusion of the American section with the AWP around a month after the October ICL meeting was the first time that this particular merger experiment was carried through. And it was a successful experiment, uniting the American cadre with an important group of effective mass workers and integrating most of them into the movement for the Fourth International.

One notable feature of the fusion was that the new Workers Party of the United States did not have any international affiliation at its birth. This was because the AWP had not had such affiliations and was not ready to adhere to the ICL. But this was only a temporary arrangement; seven months later, virtually the whole leadership of the Workers Party voted to join with the ICL in working for the Fourth International. The success of the American fusion was contagious, at least in Holland, where the Dutch section and a centrist group headed by Peter Schmidt finally merged a few months later, early in 1935. This new Dutch party decided to belong to both the ICL and the London Bureau for the time being.

But the major advance took place in France, the key to the international situation. Within a few months, the Bolshevik-Leninist Group had tripled its membership and begun to influence thousands of left-wing Socialists; in the SP's youth organization, they effected a bloc with the left-centrist leaders that soon had the reformist leaders worried. Even the die-hard sectarian Vereecken had to admit grudgingly that the Bolshevik-Leninists were doing good revolutionary work inside the French SP.

The Moscow bureaucracy finally began to junk its ultraleft third-period policies in the middle of 1934, when it gave permission to the French CP to form a united front with the SP. But neither Stalin, nor the French CP leaders, nor the French SP leaders, as it soon became clear, were interested in forming a united front of the workers against the capitalists. What they all wanted, for various reasons, was a front of the workers *with* some capitalists (bourgeois democratic capitalists) against other capitalists (reactionary or fascist capitalists); that is, an alliance based on class collaboration instead of class struggle, which bore the name of People's Front when it came into existence. Stalin dropped the other shoe in May 1935 when he signed a nonaggression treaty with French imperialism and gave his blessings to French rearmament. What he was after was an alliance, in the name of "collective security," with peace-loving democratic imperialists (like France) against war-loving fascist imperialists (like Nazi Germany), and to get this alliance he was ready and eager to handcuff the French workers and deliver them into the custody of the French imperialists. That was the meaning of the People's Front that was organized by the bourgeois Radical Socialists, the Social Democrats, and the Stalinists later in 1935.

All this put the French Bolshevik-Leninists in an extremely favorable position, precisely because they were inside the SP, to expose the real nature and aims of the People's Front and to rally the left-wing workers to a revolutionary mobilization against the coming war. And this was also precisely why the SP leaders, egged on by the Stalinists, realized that they would have to expel the Fourth Internationalists from the SP and isolate them as much as possible as fast as possible.

CRISIS IN THE FRENCH SECTION

Trotsky left France for Norway in June 1935, just as the SP leadership was preparing to move against the Bolshevik-Leninist Group. Sizing up the situation realistically, he advised his French comrades that their days in the SP were numbered and that they should orient quickly toward the construction of a new revolutionary party; for tactical reasons, they should take advantage of the democratic clauses in the SP's constitution to resist expulsions, expose the motives of the SP bureaucrats, and solicit the sympathy of left-wing workers, but all of this had to be subordinated to the political mobilization of an independent revolutionary party.

Trotsky also felt that the new social-patriotic policies of the Stalinists, which were universalized at the Seventh (and last) World Congress of the Comintern in 1935, and the worsening of the war danger, illustrated by fascist Italy's open preparations for the invasion of Ethiopia later in 1935, required an intensification of public work for the Fourth International, which had temporarily been subordinated to the exigencies of the French turn in France, Belgium, Poland, and elsewhere. So he wrote the text of a new document, the Open Letter for the Fourth International, which reaffirmed the 1933 Declaration of Four and brought it up to date in the light of the new developments since then. This was published in the summer of 1935.[9]

Unfortunately, an important part of the French leadership, headed by Molinier, did not agree with Trotsky's views on what to do in France, and the rest of the leadership, following Jean Rous and Naville, proved incapable of providing decisive action toward the construction of a new French party. Molinier thought the SP experience was not concluded and that additional gains could still be won in the SP. He felt this so strongly that he violated discipline and began publishing his own paper. The French section was plunged into the worst crisis in its history. Molinier's group was expelled at the end of 1935 and set up its own party. Precious time was lost. Many of the new recruits and sympathizers gained inside the SP were demoralized by the factionalism and drifted away. The two groups were reunited in June 1936 and then split again a few weeks later. It was a real mess and accounted in part for the insignificant role the French section played during the big 1936 strike wave that followed the electoral victory of the People's Front and the reduced role it played inside the Fourth International from then until World War II.[10]

In the heat of the dispute, which consumed much energy, Trotsky charged that the conduct of the Molinier group represented a capitulation to the social-patriotic pressures generated by the bourgeoisie in preparation for World War II and promoted by the Stalinists and social democrats. Then and later the Molinierists indignantly denied this charge, contending that the differences arose only over conflicting estimates as to how best to build a Fourth Internationalist party in France, and it is true that their subsequent evolution as an independent group did not have a social-patriotic character. But it seems equally true that if only tactical differences were involved, then splitting the French section at such a critical juncture was an irresponsible act that inflicted grave damage to the Fourth International in their own country and elsewhere, raising questions about the depth of their understanding about the need for the Fourth International as a united and disciplined movement. In any case, the splits resulted in the departure from the movement's leadership not only of Molinier but also of Pierre Frank, another of the group of eight in the 1933 international leadership. Frank did not return to the leadership until after World War II, during which the two French groups were finally reunited.

DISSENSION AND CONFUSION

The French, Spanish, and Belgian workers were radicalized in 1935 and 1936, but the radicalization was channeled into the People's Fronts, which came to power in France and Spain in 1936. People's Frontism became the central political issue, and the major obstacle to the growth of the Fourth International. Our movement produced a large body of propaganda and educational material on People's Frontism, but only a small vanguard was receptive to it at the time, although it represents political capital off which we are still living today. At the beginning nobody in the movement directly disputed the positions taken by Trotsky on People's Frontism, but again, as we shall see, it was a case for some members and leaders of abstract agreement at first, later followed by concrete serious divergences.

Before discussing the differences of People's Frontism, however, mention should be made of our international conference in July 1936. Although it was the only international conference we held between 1933 and the founding conference in 1938, and although it casts light on the state of the movement around the halfway point in our story, it is rarely discussed in our literature.

The Open Letter for the Fourth International in 1935 had proclaimed the need for its supporters to correlate and unify their work on a world scale under the banner of the Fourth International and held out the perspective of an international conference when conditions permitted. In 1936 the ICL decided the time had come for such a conference, and set it for April. But the conference was poorly prepared. Sneevliet and Peter Schmidt of the Dutch section were put in charge, but instead of organizing the conference, they ignored or obstructed it, and it had to be postponed from April to July. In the final weeks the Dutch leaders even let it be known that because of organizational grievances against the IS and Trotsky, they did not intend to attend the conference. The main resolutions had to be written at the last minute, chiefly by Trotsky in Norway, so that there was no real preconference discussion. Trotsky also organized pressure on the Dutch section, so that Sneevliet finally had to attend. Altogether, only eight sections were represented.[11] Others were invited but could not attend or did not receive invitations.

The July 1936 gathering was held a couple of months after the big French strike wave, two months after the American section publicly announced its members were entering the Socialist Party, around a week after the start of the Spanish civil war, and a few days after the second split in the French section.

Designating itself as the First International Conference for the Fourth International, this conference dissolved the ICL, established the Movement for the Fourth International (MFI), and expressed hope that a first constituent congress of the Fourth International could be held in seven or so months, after further discussion and the preparation of programmatic documents. The minutes of this conference were lost. For the last nine years we have been trying to get a complete picture of its proceedings, but most of the delegates are dead and most of the others either do not remember what happened or won't discuss it with us. The excellent political resolution on the new revolutionary upsurge in France and Spain and the other resolutions adopted—on the need for political revolution in the Soviet Union, on the London Bureau, etc.—are all available and in print.[12] We also know about the structure chosen for the organization and its personnel: a General Council, equivalent to an international executive committee; an International Bureau of eleven; and an International Secretariat of five. But at least one aspect of the conference can now be clarified.[13]

The time has come to put to rest the principal legend about this conference, which I must admit with regret I have been helping to circulate for the last decade. I refer to the legend according to which Trotsky proposed that this conference should found or proclaim the Fourth International and according to which the delegates to this conference rejected or refused to accept his proposal. How did this legend arise? There isn't the slightest basis for it in any of the surviving documents of the conference, or in the presently available correspondence about the conference in 1936 by Trotsky or anyone else.[14] None of the conference delegates interviewed in the last decade could recall any "proclamation" proposal by Trotsky at the conference or any action by the delegates to reject such a proposal. And some correspondence by delegates in 1936, which has become available to us only in the last year, thoroughly contradicts the legend.

So what is its source? Probably the statement Trotsky made two years later, in 1938, when he was arguing in favor of dropping the name "Movement for the Fourth International" and in favor of establishing the International at the international conference later that year. "This name [Movement for the Fourth International] seemed pedantic, unfitting, and slightly ridiculous to me even two years ago, when it was first adopted." But all that says is that Trotsky didn't like the name adopted; it doesn't at all follow from this statement that he made any proposal or that the delegates rejected it. Stretch that statement however you like, it cannot offer the slightest scrap of evidence for the alleged proposal and the alleged rejection.[15]

Discarding the legend and its implications about the delegates should not lead us to the opposite error of imagining that the conference was marked by nothing but harmony and agreement on perspectives. Sneevliet, who already was steering the Dutch section away from the Fourth International and toward the London Bureau, was the main adversary of the ICL leadership at the conference. He did not discuss his views on the International at the conference; in fact, he walked out of it because he did not like the order of the agenda. It is not likely that he would have gotten any significant support at this conference for his views on the International, and I think it is likely that most of the other delegates would have voted for a "proclamation" proposal if Trotsky had made one. But Sneevliet was not the only delegate in 1936 who left the movement before the founding conference in 1938; the Fourth Internationalist convictions of several other 1936 delegates crumbled or expired in the next two years. We will get fuller details in 1980, when Harvard will open the last of the Trotsky archives, but we already know that there were different concepts in the movement about the nature of the Fourth International, and different degrees of commitment to it, three years after it was first proposed.

PEOPLE'S FRONT AND CIVIL WAR IN SPAIN

Returning now to the problem of People's Frontism: Trotsky called attention to a dangerous tendency in the French section as early as October 1935, a few weeks after the People's Front was organized. Some members, he noted, were against raising a slogan calling for the Radical Socialists to be ousted from the People's Front; they thought that the workers "had to go through the experience" of having the People's Front in power, and therefore we had to support the People's Front as a whole. These comrades were not for People's Frontism themselves, of course not, but they held that we had to go along with the workers who were

going along with the People's Front, and, therefore, . . . the people holding such and similar views were a minority of the movement but are
worth remembering as evidence that even on questions as elementary as
People's Frontism, our present positions did not come to us automatically
but as the result of struggle against rather strong pressures. Sad to say, this
position was not limited to new members recently won from the Socialist
Party; it was also advanced by Ruth Fischer, the former German CP
leader who was then a member of the IS and the ICL executive committee, who wanted our movement to call for power to the People's Front
(including the bourgeois Radicals).

But the principal and most disruptive division over People's Frontism
came around the Spanish POUM (Workers' Party of Marxist Unification),
its adaptation to the People's Front, and the defense of the POUM by
important MFI sections and leaders. The POUM was formed in September
1935 as a merger between the centrist Workers' and Peasants' Bloc led by
Joaquín Maurín and the Spanish section of the ICL, led by Andrés Nin. The
Spanish section had supported the call for a new International in 1933, but
its disaffection with the IS and Trotsky soon led it to withdraw from all
activities in the ICL while not formally disaffiliating from it. In 1934 it
denounced the French turn and refused to join the Spanish SP even when
the SP's youth group passed resolutions calling for a new International.

After the merger the POUM voted to affiliate to the London Bureau.
But the ICL did not terminate relations with the POUM until January
1936, when the POUM, using the pretext that this was the only way it
could get on the ballot in coming national elections, publicly endorsed the
electoral program of the Spanish People's Front. Trotsky called this a
betrayal of the workers, and after the Spanish civil war began in July, this
characterization became the focus of a bitter debate in the MFI.

The POUM played a prominent role in driving back the fascists at the
start of the civil war, and for a short time the ICL leaders hoped that in
the crucible of war the POUM would correct its mistakes and that a reconciliation would take place. Trotsky also supported such an approach,
volunteering to help by moving from Norway to Barcelona if possible.
But in September Nin accepted the post of minister of justice in the
Catalan People's Front government, and Trotsky resumed implacable
criticism of the POUM, calling for the establishment of a Fourth Internationalist party in Spain after the POUM prohibited a pro–Fourth Interna-

tionalist tendency in its ranks. It took longer before other leaders and the principal sections of the MFI gave up their hopes that the POUM could be reformed, as a reading of their press late in 1936 shows. And some of the leaders never gave up their hopes and sympathy for the POUM.

The most outspoken defenders of the POUM in the MFI were Sneevliet, Vereecken, and Victor Serge, an Oppositionist who was allowed to leave the Soviet Union in 1936 and was elected to the MFI's General Council at the 1936 conference. They did not advocate People's Frontism and on occasion they even criticized the POUM's "mistakes" in this respect, but they denied that these mistakes were decisive and demanded that the MFI give complete political support to the POUM as the only revolutionary force in Spain. Their adaptation to People's Frontism took the form of pro-POUMism. This was the issue on which Serge broke from the MFI in 1937 after a meeting of the International Bureau rejected adaptation to the POUM. This was one of the issues on which the Dutch section separated itself from the MFI, although the actual formal break did not come until 1938. And it was the issue on which Vereecken fought a rearguard action against the IS throughout 1937, although he, too, did not resign until 1938.

IMPACT OF THE MOSCOW TRIALS

Two weeks after the MFI conference, and even before its documents could be published anywhere, Stalin shocked the whole world by announcing the opening of the first big Moscow "confession" trial. [Gregory] Zinoviev and [Lev] Kamenev were the chief defendants in the dock, but Trotsky and the Fourth International were the chief targets of this frame-up: its aim was to drive them out of the workers movement throughout the world, to isolate them permanently as political pariahs whom no decent worker would talk to. Trotsky and the MFI had to, in effect, put everything else aside for almost a whole year in order to defend themselves in this life-or-death struggle. On the whole, they acquitted themselves well in exposing the frame-ups and their meaning. But little energy was left for other party-building and International-building activities in this period, and as a result the projected founding congress of the International had to be postponed.

The price of the Moscow trials went beyond that, however. The trials were a serious blow to the morale of revolutionary workers everywhere. Anti-Bolshevik tendencies appeared or were revived among workers previously sympathetic to the Russian Revolution. Many activists, influenced by the joint bourgeois and Stalinist propaganda that Stalinism is the logical continuation of Leninism, became disillusioned with politics and withdrew to the sidelines; and the MFI was not immune to such defections and backsliding—neither its sympathizers, nor its members, nor its leaders.

It must seem strange to some that leading people who had been calling and working for the Fourth International should renounce and desert that work because of the crimes of Stalinism; after all, those crimes had been part of the reason they decided a new International was necessary. Yet that is precisely what happened with people like Muste and Schmidt, who had both been elected to the General Council at the 1936 conference. Barely a month after the conference and a few days after the first Moscow trial, they both resigned, Muste returning to pacifism and the church from which he had come originally, Schmidt returning soon after to the social democracy. Bourgeois pressures work in different ways on different people to destroy their belief in the capacity of the workers to liberate themselves from the oppressions of class society, and Stalinophobia, the fear and hatred of Stalinism to the exclusion of every other consideration, has been one of the most effective mechanisms for undermining and obliterating revolutionary consciousness during the last four decades.

CONTRADICTIONS

We must remember that at the same time the Stalinists were murdering and imprisoning millions in the Soviet Union, they were winning millions of supporters in other countries by being the most active and ardent architects of alliances that they said would stop fascism and war. In 1939, of course, Stalin signed his pact with Hitler and that pact signaled the start of World War II, but in the preceding years many people were attracted to the Stalinists because they were the chief force calling for resistance to fascism and the coming war. Among these were not only newly politicized elements but political veterans like Alfonso Leonetti, a founder of the Italian CP, a founder of the Italian Left Opposition, and a member of the IS from 1930 to 1936 who was elected to the International Bureau at the 1936 conference. Leonetti had come to our movement during the Stalinist third-period and sectarian madness, and when the Stalinist line was switched he was as critical of People's Frontism as any other ICL leader.[16] But seeing no other mass alternative to war and fascism, he began gradually to see possible positive features in People's Frontism, and soon after the 1936 conference he became inactive and then dropped away. The pressures operating on him became more evident during the war, when he collaborated with the Stalinists in France; and after the war he applied for readmission into the Italian CP, where he was accepted and is now a "Eurocommunist."

Leonetti was the last of the eight leaders we singled out for 1933. To repeat: three were murdered by the GPU (Trotsky, Sedov, and Klement) and one capitulated to the Stalinists (Leonetti). Two split away from the movement temporarily because of tactical differences (Frank and Naville, Naville later leaving permanently because of deeper differences). And two split away to join the centrist London Bureau (Bauer of the German section and Sneevliet of the Dutch section). Bauer was a sectarian formalist while Sneevliet adapted himself to POUMist opportunism, but they both ended up in the same centrist pit, and Naville would have joined them if the London Bureau had not gone out of business before he got there. Leonetti's adaptation to People's Frontism led him to Stalinism while Sneevliet's adaptation to the POUM's participation in the People's Front led him to the London Bureau, but in both cases it led away from the Fourth International. Anyone who thinks the ICL and the MFI were immune to People's Front pressures has to overlook such evidence about what was impeding the Fourth International internally. Our list of defectors could be extended, but the losses among the eight are sufficient to show what a variety of pressures beat down on these people, with a force that drove some of them far from the goal of the Fourth International that they had set themselves only a couple of years before.

In Mexico Trotsky completed the major part of his historic exposure of the Moscow trials in mid-1937. Then he turned again to the internal problems of the movement, and he reached agreement with the IS on the need for another and better-prepared international conference, tentatively slated for October 1937. But it had to be postponed, partly because the American section had been expelled from the SP and needed time for adequate preparation of the convention that established the SWP at the end of the year.

PREPARATIONS FOR THE FOUNDING CONFERENCE

In March 1938 an SWP delegation, consisting of Cannon, Shachtman, V. R. Dunne, and Rose Karsner, visited Trotsky in Mexico to discuss the proposed international conference. Transcripts of the major discussions, which also involved several important American problems, will be found in the books *The Transitional Program for Socialist Revolution* and *Trotsky's Writings (1937–38)*. They are worth reading, or rereading, on the occasion of this fortieth anniversary because they provide an excellent example of Trotsky's method of collaborating with other leaders of the movement. First of all, he did not just talk to them or at them—he also listened very carefully, and he learned as well as taught. Benefits of this approach are to be seen in the main programmatic document he wrote for the founding conference, but they extended far beyond the most important document because the method Trotsky used promoted the spirit of teamwork, which is indispensable for the creation of a collective leadership.

In the first of the discussions in Mexico agreement was reached on the nature and timing of the international conference, on the documents that had to be prepared, especially a programmatic series of transitional demands, and so on. Then Cannon said:

> On the organizational side of the question—shall we consider this conference as a provisional gathering or as the actual founding of the Fourth International? The prevailing opinion among us is that we would actually form the Fourth International at this conference. We think that the main elements of the Fourth International are now crystallized. We should put an end to our negotiations and maneuvers with the centrists and henceforth deal with them as separate and alien groupings.

Trotsky replied that he agreed "absolutely" with what Cannon said. And for the benefit of the SWP leaders who would be attending the international conference, he listed the forces in the MFI that would or might be opposed to such a conception of the Dutch. "Naturally we are a weak International," he said, "but we are an International." He urged the Americans to push their position energetically.

Cannon then continued:

Some comrades have taken the tactic of maneuvering and making concessions to centrists as a permanent policy, whereas we think that all our maneuvers with the centrists have been exhausted by now. We were justified two, three, or four years ago in delaying organizational action, in order to complete the maneuvers and experiments with those people, but not now. We noticed in our discussions that there are some comrades who want to carry over the tactic indefinitely—some kinds of maneuvers which are doomed in advance to defeat. And for this reason I believe we have to explain this matter to the comrades.

Trotsky said he subscribed to every word of Cannon's along these lines. The exchange is significant only because it would not have taken place, and would not have been necessary, if the views it expressed were shared by everyone in the MFI. And remember, this was only five months before the founding conference.

In May Trotsky submitted a very emphatic letter to a Czech comrade as a contribution to the international preconference discussion. It was entitled, "'For' the Fourth International? No! The Fourth International!" On reading this letter, Vereecken resigned from the movement. Sneevliet and the Dutch section had already departed. There was some French opposition to founding the new International but it was a minority view. At the conference itself nineteen of the delegates voted in favor of a statute proclaiming the founding of the International, while three voted against: the two delegates from the Polish section and Yvan Craipeau of the French section.[17]

The Polish delegates in 1938 were not opposed to founding the International, they said, but they were opposed to doing it at this time, because it would be a meaningless gesture, because we were too small, and because the first three Internationals had all been founded in periods of revolutionary upsurge.[18] The three opponents of the founding did not specify how deep a revolutionary upsurge would have to be before they would agree to a new International, but in any case they did not wait around too long. One of the Poles became a Zionist, the other dropped out of politics, and Craipeau quit after the war to join a series of centrist outfits who were all opponents of the Fourth International. The supporters of the founding generally agreed with Trotsky's view that the existing national sections needed a clearly defined international organization and leadership, whatever its size might be.

It is tempting to speculate how the vote would have gone if Trotsky and the SWP had not taken such a strong stand. By the end of the war and the political holocaust it visited on the revolutionary movement, five of the fifteen International Executive Committee members elected at the founding conference had been killed, and of the remaining ten only two were still active in our movement: Cannon and Carl Skoglund of Minneapolis.

The other great achievement of 1938 was the transitional program, which Trotsky wrote and asked the SWP to sponsor in the international discussion. It is unquestionably the most valuable programmatic document produced by the revolutionary movement since Lenin's time. It draws upon the actual experiences of the workers internationally in the epoch of imperialism, summarizes and synthesizes the lessons of their struggles, and projects a program and a method for leading the workers and their allies at their current levels of consciousness across the bridge to the struggle for workers' power. Despite different conditions, the transitional method is as relevant and usable today as it was forty years ago. The transitional program put an indelible stamp on our movement—the Fourth International and the SWP would be quite different and much weaker without it. I am not sure that they would have survived the crippling adversities of the forties and fifties without such a program and method.

THE INDIVIDUAL IN HISTORY

That completes our narrative, but leaves us with a couple of questions to consider. One of these, almost poking us in the eye, is whether the Fourth International would have been founded at all in 1938 without Trotsky. His role was so overwhelming that our critics at that time derided it as a one-man International, certain to disintegrate and fall apart as soon as Trotsky was gone. This prediction was soon put to the test when Trotsky was murdered in 1940, and it was refuted in the maelstrom of World War II, when the International was badly maimed and mauled but succeeded nevertheless in holding fast to its principles and remaining the authentic continuator of revolutionary internationalism. As Cannon said at a 1940 memorial meeting, Trotsky had built this movement around his ideas, not personalities, and the ideas survived after his death.

The question we are raising is very much like the one that is asked about Lenin: if, early in 1917, a brick had fallen off a roof in Zurich where Lenin was in exile and had fallen on Lenin and killed him, would the October revolution have taken place in Russia later that year? Most of the people who pose that question think it is very cute: if you say yes, the revolution would have taken place without Lenin, that proves you are blind to the facts and dogmatically denying the importance of the role of the individual in history. If you say no, the revolution would not have taken place without Lenin, then you are convicted, in their eyes, of violating the doctrines of historical materialism, underestimating class forces and the role of the masses, and giving an exaggerated, unwarranted, and idealistic significance to the role of great individuals or heroes in history.

But leaving games aside, Marxists don't have to make concessions to anybody when they examine the concrete developments in 1917 and conclude that without Lenin the October revolution in all probability would not have taken place when it did or would not have been successful if attempted. Genuine Marxism finds no contradiction between the role of the revolutionary masses and the role of exceptional, even indispensable revolutionary leaders; both are needed for success. It is true that in the early years of this century, when much of the movement was still in its theoretical adolescence, some of its leaders propounded a version of Marxism that was steeped in fatalism, in a vision of socialism arriving through the inevitable advance of impersonal economic forces and ignoring or underestimating the crucial role of leadership. But since 1917 and the assimilation of Bolshevism as the revolutionary essence of Marxism in the epoch of imperialism, these errors have been corrected among authentic Marxists, who reject fatalism, understand the limits and pitfalls of spontaneism, and accord a more correct weight to the indispensability of leadership in theory and in practice, especially collective leadership.

In a 1935 discussion about underground activity in Nazi Germany, Trotsky warned the German comrades against what he thought was a tendency to take a supercilious or contemptuous attitude toward those members of our underground movement who were not well educated in Marxist literature and theory. I can't describe the whole discussion here, but I want to cite one passage from Trotsky that I think is pertinent:

> Moreover, one makes the revolution with relatively few Marxists, even with the party. Here the collective substitutes for what the individual

cannot achieve. The individual can hardly master each separate area—
it is necessary to have specialists who supplement one another. Such
specialists are often quite passable "Marxists" without being complete
Marxists. The whole Bolshevik Party is a marvelous example of this.
Under Lenin's and Trotsky's supervision, [Nikolai] Bukharin, [Vyash-
eslav] Molotov, [Mikhail] Tomsky, and a hundred others were good
Marxists, capable of great accomplishments. As soon as this supervision
was gone, even they collapsed disgracefully. This was not because
Marxism is a secret science; it is just very difficult to escape the colossal
pressures of the bourgeois environment with all of its influences.[19]

It would be totally misleading to read this passage as meaning that
Trotsky was indifferent to the education and training of Marxist cadres;
his whole life was dedicated to developing them. What he is actually
saying, in my opinion, is that while we are engaged in training Marxist
cadres, we must not set ourselves impossible or ideal standards but must
recognize that as long as the bourgeois environment continues to press
down upon all of us, not everyone is going to turn out to be a "complete"
or perfect Marxist. We must use the forces available, even with their
defects, attempting to strengthen, guide, and supervise them so that they
make the most effective contributions to our common revolutionary
work. In addition, it seems to me, Trotsky is making the bigger point that
while there are few "complete Marxists" *their* role is of decisive importance because on what they do or do not do depends the success or failure
of all the others, the less-than-complete Marxists, and therefore of the
movement as a whole. Far from belittling the role of Marxist leadership,
Trotsky here was attributing to it, in a very concrete way, a centrality and
decisiveness such as I have not found expressed elsewhere in his or
Lenin's writings. It is not an elitist conception at all, but an understanding
of the unprecedented leadership responsibilities that the most competent
Marxists bear. And this understanding permeated everything he thought
and did about the Fourth International.

When Trotsky wrote in his diary in 1935 that he thought the building
of the Fourth International was the most important work he had ever
done, commentators like Isaac Deutscher found it impossible to believe
that a person of Trotsky's intelligence meant or could mean this literally.
But Trotsky did mean it literally, and he acted accordingly, with every
resource at his disposal.

We all knew that Trotsky was the theoretical leader of the movement; every one of our many conquests in this area in the thirties originated with him or bore his imprint. But we did not all know, until the recent publication of the *Writings* series, how much Trotsky was also the practical-political leader of the International. The circumstances of his exile did not permit him to attend our international conferences, and he was able to participate in meetings of the IS for only a few months while he lived in France. But despite all the legal restrictions and the obstacles of time and space, he succeeded in various ways in placing himself politically at the center of the leadership and of participating in all the major decisions, not only the strategic ones but very often the tactical ones, too. His role in the active leadership of the Fourth International and its predecessors was bigger and lasted longer than that of Marx and Engels in the First International, Engels in the Second, and Lenin in the Third.

I also suspect that few of us have adequately appreciated how much the fate of the Fourth International in those years depended on the will of a single person. (I use the words *will*, *will power*, or *determination* to reach your goal where Trotsky's critics would say "fanaticism" or "dogmatic stubbornness" or "doctrinal blindness to reality" or something like that.) Fortunately for the movement, Trotsky possessed this element in great abundance—enough to keep him going against great odds, with enough left over to provide the stimulus for others whom he drew along, perhaps dragged along, beyond their normal capacities while he was alive, after which some of them wilted and dropped away.

URGENCY OF THE FOUNDING CONFERENCE

I didn't think I had to persuade this audience that revolutionary workers need to be organized internationally as well as nationally or that the founding of the Fourth International was necessary and progressive. But there is a corollary question that may need clarification here: Granted that the International had to be founded, why was its founding in 1938 so urgent, what difference would it have made if it had not been founded until later?

The main answer is World War II. It almost broke out in the Munich crisis the same month the conference was held, and it did actually begin just one year later. Next to revolution, war is the supreme test for revolutionary organizations. It submits them to overwhelming pressures, it often isolates them or isolates them further from their base, it strips them of illusions, it crushes the weak and wavering elements, and it poses life-or-death challenges to the strong. Within weeks or months, World War II swept away the London Bureau and the remnants of the Brandlerite international like gnats in a hurricane.

The small and weak Fourth International was not immune to these destructive and disintegrative influences. On the European continent, the national sections were driven underground and reduced to a handful by ruthless repression. Some members of the 1938 International Executive Committee were murdered at their posts: Trotsky by a GPU agent in Mexico, Leon Lesoil by the Nazis in a concentration camp, Pietro Tresso by the Stalinists in France, Ta Tu Thau by the Stalinists in Vietnam. Others withdrew to the sidelines or defected. Pioneers like Shachtman, even before the United States entered the war, buckled under the weight of bourgeois-democratic opinion, rebelled against the perspectives of the Fourth International they had voted for at the founding conference, and led a damaging split of the movement. Slowly, our heroic comrades were able to reknit some of the European sections and resume activity against their formidable enemies, but they took over four years of the war before they succeeded in reestablishing connections among themselves in the form of the European secretariat of the Fourth International.

So it is safe to say that if the International had not been founded in 1938, it would not have been founded during the war. Eventually, sooner or later, it would have been founded, but it would have been a different and politically weaker body than the one that was established in 1938 and managed to survive the war with its banner and tradition unstained.

During the war itself, the existence of the International—cribbed, cabined, and confined as it was when the center was moved to the United States—was an enormous factor in maintaining revolutionary morale and ideological continuity in the midst of adversity. I can report personally how much it strengthened me as a youthful activist to know that the International and its partisans, even though cut off from each other, were continuing the struggle for our common ideas and goals. Later in the war, after I had been drafted into the army and sent to France, where political conditions were much more difficult than here, I had a chance to talk with many European comrades and to hear over and over again testimony about the unifying and inspirational effects that news (or even just rumors) about the existence and survival of the Fourth International had on the persecuted fighters in the concentration camps, prisons, armies, and underground cells. They fought better because of this, and it would have been harder for them to keep on fighting without it. And without it, it would have been more difficult to establish the political and ideological homogeneity that was established soon after the war.

Hard as it was to found the International in 1938, with Trotsky's help, it would have been harder to found it after the war, when the authority of the would-be founders would have been smaller and the precious continuity of the movement would have been sundered for several years. Not only would it have been harder to found it after the war, but it also would have been harder to maintain its unity after it was founded. Keeping the International together in the face of external pressures and internal disputes has never been easy, and sometimes it has not been possible, but it would have been much more difficult if the efforts to found it in 1938 had ended in failure.

The Fourth International, like the parties affiliated or sympathetic to it, is not yet strong or influential enough anywhere to complete the mission it undertook in 1938. But it is many times larger than it was then, larger than it has ever been, and still growing. It does not have a Trotsky to guide it, but it has a collective leadership, which it lacked in Trotsky's time. It still has to cope with many serious problems, but none are the fatal sort that wrecked the First, Second, and Third Internationals. It has lived longer than any of these predecessors, but it is still young, vigorous, able to learn and correct mistakes, and revolutionary in its outlook and practice. It embodies the revolutionary lessons, traditions, methods, and program of the past century and a third, and the destiny of humanity depends on its future. In large part this is due to the way it was conceived and nurtured in the five years we have examined.

APPENDIX A
THE INTERNATIONAL OPPOSITION AND
THE COMMUNIST INTERNATIONAL

The events that have unfolded in Germany and have resulted in the establishment of fascism and the bankruptcy of the German Communist Party have posed the question before the International Left Opposition of a new party in Germany, a question that has been broadly discussed in our ranks and has been definitively settled.[20]

On the basis of the German events, the May plenum unanimously adopted the orientation toward the construction of a genuinely communist party in Germany. Before this plenum, since the betrayal in Germany committed by the Stalinist Party, voices were raised in our ranks calling for a new international orientation. "How can we condemn the German party without at the same time condemning the Communist International, which led the party and bears the real responsibility for this betrayal?" was the usual way the comrades argued. The events in Austria and Bulgaria,[21] proving that neither the International nor the parties were capable of learning the slightest lesson from the German catastrophe, but instead, actively sought to justify the ill-fated policy followed in Germany, and even characterized the present situation as a victory—these events have broadened our criticism toward those who are really responsible for the German betrayal, and have forced us to pose the question of our attitude toward the International, and to settle it in a clear and definitive manner.

Should we continue to consider ourselves as a faction of the Comintern, or break definitively from it and disassociate ourselves from responsibility for the policies of the faction that leads the International? Should we persevere in our orientation toward reform, or put an end to it, and orient toward a new, independent regrouping of revolutionary forces on a world scale?

The International Secretariat has already explained to the sections in

---

This was a resolution adopted by the executive committee of the International Left Opposition at a meeting ("plenum") in Paris on August 19, 1933. It was the first official document of the ILO calling for a new International. Although it is in accord with Trotsky's position at the time, it is not written in his style and appears to have been drafted by a non-French member of the IS after a discussion with Trotsky. It is translated here by Jeff White from the French text reprinted in *Naissance de la IVe Internationale (1933–40)* (Paris: La Brèche, 1978).

its circular how the question has been posed. Even though the discussion is only just beginning in the sections, it seems that the proposal for the new orientation has been favorably received. It is necessary that this historically important turn be preceded by a full discussion in order to clarify as fully as possible all the questions related to it and to sift out the tasks that flow from it.

It is now time to draw the balance sheet on what our position as a faction in the Comintern has given us, and to establish our position in the light of the experience gained from the German catastrophe up to the present day. The Comintern's abandonment of the line of its first congresses has come about in stages—most notable, the policy of the Anglo-Russian Committee, the defeat of the Chinese Revolution, the gradual degeneration of the Russian Communist Party, and the treacherous capitulation before German fascism.[22]

This process of degeneration finds its expression in the international communist movement in the form of an ideological and organizational weakening of the parties. Although this whole degeneration has been determined principally by the establishment of the reactionary theory of "socialism in one country," it has nevertheless come about in stages, between which can be seen degrees of decomposition.

Our position as a faction has been determined by the reality out of which we came and in which we have been obliged to work. The proletarian character of the Soviet state and the existence of a party having the greatest traditions and of an international organization encompassing important revolutionary forces constituted the forces on which we had to rely for an entire period for the possibility of the reform that we advocated. We had to exhaust all the possibilities that flowed from that reality before we could pose the question of a new orientation. It was an indispensable stage in those concrete conditions, an inevitable experience we had to undergo, and on the basis of which we had to work out our position at a certain decisive stage.

Is reform possible after the German experience and particularly after the lessons of these last months? And if it is no longer possible, what purpose is being served by being a faction? Should we wait, fatalistically, for the same experience to repeat itself in every country, or for a catastrophe in Soviet Russia before abandoning our position as a faction? Or should we instead, as vanguard of the revolutionary movement, henceforth reject all responsibilities [for the Comintern], face up to reality, and enter on the road to the independent regroupment of the revolutionary forces on an international scale to wage the most bitter and effective struggle against world capitalism, and thereby give real support to the proletarian state?

Those are the questions we must answer. The force of the facts imposes a new orientation on us. This means that from now on we must look for every opportunity for unity and collaboration with the revolutionary forces who, since the German catastrophe, are beginning to break away from the influence of the Communist International led by the Stalinists, and from the Second International, and to orient themselves toward a communist movement founded on the principles formulated by the first congresses of the Comintern and on the experience acquired in the communist movement since the death of Lenin. This means that while rejecting responsibility for the Stalinists we must collaborate with the Stalinist organizations on the international, national, and local levels on the basis of the tactic of the united front, through which we must link up with and win over the best elements that still remain in the Stalinist parties. Even at the present stage of decay of the Comintern, the winning of these elements will constitute an important objective of our activity.

The lessons of the latest events after the German catastrophe have made our change of viewpoint on the international scale appear altogether logical. These lessons have also untied us from our attitude toward the Stalinist Party in the Soviet Union.

The question of our attitude toward the CP of the USSR must be considered in conjunction with that of our attitude to the Communist International. On the one hand, our independent activity in the capitalist countries by the regroupment of revolutionary forces on the basis of authentic communist principles will forge the most effective weapon for the defense of the proletarian state; on the other hand, our bold attitude inside the Soviet Union will throw into greater relief the state of decay of the Stalinist Party, arouse the attention of all the elements dedicated to the communist cause, show them the grievous danger that threatens the proletarian state, and give them a flag for struggling against reaction and sweeping aside the power of the centrist bureaucracy.

While adopting this new orientation in its general lines, the plenum underscores the heavy tasks that fall on our international organization in the coming period. More than ever the necessity is being brought home with particular force for strict cohesion in our ranks, for absolute clarity in our positions and principles, and for spreading our activity into all areas of action among the workers and oppressed layers.

These premises will allow us to apply a flexible tactic toward the currents that are oriented to communism and, on the basis of firm principles, to facilitate their assimilation of these principles and their definitive passage into the common camp of intransigent and merciless struggle for the overthrow of capitalism.

How Are We to Set Up This New International?

1. Consider ourselves as the embryo of the genuine communist party; establish in every section our program of very broad action; turn our backs resolutely on the work of reform and its particular characteristics; maintain fractions in all the labor organizations and handle our tactics in accordance with the relationship of forces.

Direct our fire mainly against the influence of the social democracy; be the propagandists and popularizers of communism and internationalism; strive to tear away the workers attached to the party by real action against the bourgeoisie and its lackeys. To that end, push the united front in action with the official CP at all levels. If the bureaucracy refuses, support the actions of the Stalinist parties if they are appropriate; oppose them if they are wrong.

2. With regard to the auxiliary organizations, International Red Aid,[23] etc., draw the conclusions from our new orientation. Wherever the International Red Aid shows it is only a tool of bureaucratic conservatism and of a tendency, create real organizations of revolutionary solidarity, according to our forces. What has been said on this subject is true for all the other auxiliary organizations of the party.

3. Declare that our previous analysis of the Soviet state as a workers' state with a pronounced bureaucratic degeneration is still our analysis, that the accentuation of the bureaucratic degeneration in the CPSU [Communist Party of the Soviet Union] and the Comintern involves a decisive danger for the workers' state, and that the reconstitution of a party in the USSR and the strengthening of the revolutionary proletariat in the world around a revolutionary International are decisive factors in the defense of the workers' state.

Rally the revolutionary forces in the world by denouncing the inability of the Stalinist parties to defend the USSR. Struggle in the USSR for the reform of the state, the complete reestablishment of the prerogatives of the proletariat, and the defeat of the bureaucracy. Support at all times the proletarian forces against the Thermidorean forces—this will be the role of our section in the USSR, whose indispensable creation as the incarnation of communist and revolutionary principles will be the greatest assurance of the existence of the October revolution. In no way does it follow from this demand that we are disposed to accept the creation of other parties in the USSR. On this point the Left Opposition has changed nothing in its demands for workers' democracy as the pivot of the dictatorship of the proletariat.[24]

4. Our present forces, acting as the embryo of a communist party can, by their political cohesion, their testing in action among the working-class organizations, and their resulting experience, exert an important attraction on other currents in the labor movement who have been repelled by the Third and Second Internationals, and who are moving toward communist positions. Our attractive power will be all the more pronounced when our position as a faction no longer exists as an obstacle between these currents and ourselves.

These are diverse formations; some are close to our position, others are still heterogeneous and require a great deal of work to assimilate to our positions. We must fight forcefully against the conception of an unprincipled grouping. On the contrary, the International Left Opposition must orient its forces to rally these scattered currents on the basis of communist principles.

It would not be a question of a regroupment between the Third and Second Internationals, but rather one based on the foundations of the Third International, which have been abandoned by the Comintern (the first four congresses in their main lines, enriched by the experience of the last ten years), and on the eleven points of the ILO preconference.[25]

5. Having defined the basis of political relations with the existing groups, the Left Opposition must understand the historical interest represented by the international regroupment of these scattered groups, who, without a foundation of well-defined principles and without organic ties, can degenerate in the present chaos or fall prey to the exterminative maneuvers of the Stalinists.

On the other hand, the ILO must also understand that the disintegration of the Second and Third Internationals will again give birth to further divisions and splits, and that in our relations with the groups that are moving toward communism we must demonstrate educational flexibility as well as political intransigence.

APPENDIX B
A REPORT ON THE 1936 CONFERENCE

Max Shachtman

Bronx, New York
August 13, [1936]

Dear Comrade Trotsky:

My last days in Paris were so occupied with the details of finishing off rag-ends of the postconference work and with the difficult business of obtaining passage back to New York during the tourist season that it is only now that I am able to write you some of my impressions.

On the whole, I would say that the conference accomplished everything that was to be expected of it and everything that we originally planned in Weksal. With one or two minor exceptions, we were able to deal with every point on the order of the day and to adopt motions or resolutions covering the most important problems, both political and organi-

Reprinted by permission of the Library of Social History, New York. Max Shachtman was one of Trotsky's principal collaborators in planning and carrying through the 1936 international conference. He knew better than anyone else exactly what Trotsky expected and hoped for from the conference. Shachtman and A. J. Muste were the delegates of the American section, which had recently joined the Socialist Party. Shachtman went to Europe early; he collaborated with the IS in Paris; he spent time in Amsterdam, putting pressure on the Dutch section to attend the conference; and he visited Trotsky in Weksal, Norway, to explain what the IS intended to do at the conference and to get last-minute suggestions on tactics from Trotsky. This letter was written two weeks after the conference, when Shachtman had just got back to the United States. It is a report about "internal" questions which Shachtman and Trotsky had discussed in considerable detail before the conference. Some of these problems were grave ones; others were minor and transitory. It is psychologically and politically impossible that Shachtman would have troubled to report their outcome while at the same time failing even to mention Trotsky's alleged proposal for the conference to proclaim the Fourth International and the conference's alleged refusal to accept this proposal.

zational, which were posed before the conference. When you consider that we had only three days at our disposal, that we have no large technical apparatus at our command, and that we had a large agenda, I think that our modest accomplishments were something of an achievement. To the difficulties should of course be added the attitude of the Dutch delegate,[26] which didn't improve the general efficiency of the conference.

We did not adopt a *special* resolution on France and Spain because the comrades assigned (Fero and Rous) [Alfonso Leonetti and Jean Rous] did not have the opportunity to finish it. Their draft was to be left to the incoming IS to edit and make public; in any case, the general resolution on the revolutionary upsurge covers the ground pretty well, and the lack of a special resolution is not fatal. Nor did we adopt the trade union thesis which came before the conference at the very last minute and only in a German translation; we were therefore compelled to refrain from considering it and decided instead to use it as the opening of an international discussion on the trade union question. Finally, I was unable to find the time for the communiqué to the bourgeois press, and the draft is to be turned over to Naville to elaborate, in view of his connections with various journalists who are in a better position to get us some "publicity." As I remember it, these are the principal shortcomings of the conference, and all things considered, we did not do so badly. After the conference, we met in two or three long sessions of the new IS during which the adopted resolutions and amendments were finally edited so that nothing stands in the way of their publication immediately (at least in French, to begin with) except the purely technical work of typing the stencils and running them off on the machine.

The most important "internal" question before the conference was of course that of the Dutch party. Sneevliet's conduct was something unprecedented. The same [Dutch] party leadership which conducts itself so gracefully and unultimatistically in the London Bureau conferences—presumably conferences of our enemies and theirs—could find no other way of conducting itself at *our* conference than by manifesting supreme contempt for it and by facing it with ultimatums at every turn. Adolph [Rudolf Klement] has told me that he has already written to you the details and I shall not therefore dwell upon them here. Sneevliet insouciantly came late to the conference; he stayed for an hour or two; he came that evening to the organization commission with a new ultimatum on the

338 MALCOLM X AND THE THIRD AMERICAN REVOLUTION

IS to be elected, in which he proposed to exclude all those who have had the misfortune to be defeated by Stalinism or fascism (i.e., the "émigré" sections, or as he calls them: the "abnormal" or "dead" sections); the next morning we receive a new ultimatum, threatening withdrawal, to which we reply in the most restrained and polite manner, despite our mounting indignation; the [Dutch] party bureau in Amsterdam, *by telephone*, directs Sneevliet to break with the conference, without troubling to hear our point of view—and Sneevliet, without another word, departs. (I recall, at this point, the outraged feelings of the Dutchmen when you sent us a telegram expressing your personal opinion about the "American turn," after having read both sides—a telegram which did not commit the American section; the Dutch, by telephone, on the basis of a one-sided report, *decide in two minutes* to break with the conference of the Fourth International, and in such a way that it can only be followed by further steps away from our whole movement and its political line. Apparently, these are the "organizational methods" that we are asked to substitute for "ours"!!!) As you know, we decided to write a letter to the CC [central committee] of the RSAP (Dutch section) concerning the whole affair; I drafted the text and sent it to the IS for approval and mailing. I hope that you find it a fitting reply both in tone and in content. As I see the aim of this letter, it is to set down, in a friendly and nonpolemical manner, the *facts*, first of all, relating to the convening and carrying through of the conference; second, the impermissible conduct of Sneevliet at the conference (*en passant* he did not even leave us the colonial thesis which he said he had brought along!); third, the *enumeration*, without yet taking explicit position, of the undoubted *political* differences that exist between us; fourth, an attempt at a popular explanation, so simple that even political philistines and amateurs should be able to understand it, of the dialectical relationship between politics and organization, between political line and organizational methods; fifth, a polite invitation to the Dutch leadership to express itself on these questions and to signify its future intentions with regard to participation in our movement. We decided (I believe correctly) not to go "over the heads" of the CC at the present time and to address ourselves to the membership. We merely say in the letter that we take it for granted that the CC will explain to its own membership the reasons for its fateful steps at our conference; and that if it does make this explanation, then it will surely have no objections to submitting to its membership also the other side of the story, such as is contained, for example, in your letter to the conference and in our [the IS's] letter to the CC of the RSAP. If the CC *refuses* to accept this elementary proposal for an intelligent discussion in the ranks, then we have the right to consider which ways and means are best adapted to reaching the membership of the RSAP without receiving the kind permission of their CC, and thus breaking down the blockade that has been established between the international movement and the Dutch party membership. We have a big advantage, it seems to me, in the fact that the CC will find it politically impossible to consummate a break with us at the present time, although Sneevliet's line leads, objectively, straight in that direction (objectively and perhaps even subjectively; I must confess that he made a highly unfavorable impression on me especially at the conference, not of a revolutionary politician but of a disdainful bureaucrat with a revolutionary past). The time left for us in Holland must be utilized to strengthen all possible points of support, so that if and when a break comes with the CC, we shall not be in the tragic position in which we found ourselves under similar circumstances in Spain.[27]

[Georges] Vereecken: He was completely isolated at the conference, although he tried to find some basis of a rapprochement with both Sneevliet and Molinier, as well as with Muste. But when he took his scandalous position with regard to the Molinier case,[28] I was forced to make a sharp attack on him. Muste had insisted on putting V. on the General Council or the [International] Bureau, and to avoid an additional struggle, we agreed; but after my attack on V.'s disgraceful unprincipledness, it was Muste himself who proposed that V.'s name be withdrawn from the list of candidates; so that V. was not elected on any of the three international bodies. So far as the record is concerned, by the way, Vereecken left his vote unqualifiedly (!) in favor of the list proposed by me in the name of the Org Com [organization commission].

Molinier: Here, too, except for Vereecken, we had no difficulty and the vote was therefore quasi-unanimous. I had another talk with Molinier and told him that so far as I was concerned, his readmission into the International was an open question provided that he showed in the next period (six months–one year) that he would not engage in or encourage any activities against our French section. Otherwise, we would have to crush any movement he sought to set afoot. I believe it made an impression on him, for he wants above all to do his work in *our* ranks. Whether he will conduct himself properly or not remains to be seen, of course; but it is not vitally important. His movement is dead and the events will only reduce it further. Your letter about his possible displacement to the United States came too late for me to act upon it (day before my departure from Paris), but I do not exclude it as a possibility. I originally proposed it in Paris to the IS, even before the conference and the visit to Weksal; on second thought I found the idea a bit far-fetched, but I still do not believe it is entirely out of the question. If the French comrades agree, I can take it up with our comrades here, and then we can put the question to Molinier. I am inclined to believe he would accept such a proposition, because he hinted at it the last time we had a private talk together.

Muste: Your fears were groundless. He did try to play the conciliator with Sneevliet, but the conduct of the latter and our own conciliatory position left no room for an "independent" position. But while Muste gave us needless admonitions about the need of "understanding" the Dutch situation and of "proceeding intelligently," he did not take a position against that adopted by the conference. He confined his differences on the Dutch question to remarks about "shortcomings on both sides" which, I regret, did not illuminate the situation very greatly. As to the question of Abern[29] I am very sorry that you agreed to Muste's written proposal. Fortunately, Muste did not propose Abern for the IS at any point during the conference or any of its commissions or in any personal conversation. I say "fortunately" because I would have been compelled to fight openly against it. Our CC has no *personal confidence* in Abern, who is so utterly factional in his dealings that he cannot even be trusted with confidential material which has nothing whatever to do with a factional fight. However that may be, the question did not arise at the conference and consequently no difficulties were connected with it. The list for the General Council, the Bureau, and IS was unanimously prepared and unanimously adopted (Muste and I finally "merged" our two proposals in the Org Com; I agreed to this because the differences in the two proposals were, after all, not decisive and certainly any concession made was a trifle in comparison with the value of averting "minority report"). Nor did we have any difficulties with the American resolution endorsing the entry. With one absolutely insignificant editorial change, the resolution was *unanimously* adopted; Muste also voting in favor of it.

As for my return to Brussels to work in the IS: Since my arrival in New York yesterday, I have only had the chance of speaking a few brief words with [Arne] Swabeck. He is entirely in favor of my going back. What the others will say I do not yet know but I think the prospects are fairly good that in a month or two I shall be able to leave New York again for a prolonged stay in Europe.

As soon as I have found my bearings here, I shall write about how matters stand with us in the SP.

Meanwhile, warmest regards to you and Natalia Ivanovna [Sedova] from my wife and me, and best greetings to the remarkable Knudsens.

Cordially,
Max Shachtman

APPENDIX C
TROTSKY'S POSITION IN 1936

Copies of the currently available correspondence in 1936 by Trotsky and the people who worked most closely with him in organizing and carrying through the international conference in July leave no room for doubt: he did not propose to the delegates that they should found the Fourth International at the July conference and they did not reject this proposal that was not made. What remains is to indicate what Trotsky did have to say on the subject in the period before the conference.

The Open Letter for the Fourth International, which Trotsky wrote in the spring of 1935 and which was published in the summer of 1935, briefly recalled "the struggle for its principles and ideas" since 1933 and said, "All this labor will indubitably proceed much better if correlated and unified on a world scale under the banner of the Fourth International." And it added,

---

The first generally correct discussion of this question that I have seen anywhere was by Pierre Broué, editorial director of the Trotsky Peuvres being published by the Leon Trotsky Institute in Paris. See the interview with him in the French magazine *Critique Communiste* 25 (November 1978). But a letter by Broué ("Trotsky and the Proletarian Revolution of the Twentieth Century," *La Verité* 588 [September 1979]) unfortunately recycles the Frankian legend.

The tempo and the time of the new revolutionary construction and its consummation depend, obviously, upon the general course of the class struggle, the future victories and defeats of the proletariat. Marxists, however, are not fatalists. They do not unload upon the "historical process" those very tasks which the historical process has posed before them. The initiative of a conscious minority, a scientific program, bold and ceaseless agitation in the name of clearly formulated aims, merciless criticism of all ambiguity—those are some of the most important factors for the victory of the proletariat.

This open letter was the link that led to the July 1936 conference. It shows that in 1935 Trotsky had an open and flexible attitude on the whole question. He saw the tempo and timing of the new International as dependent on the evolution of the class struggle, but noted that this in no way relieved the Marxists of their responsibilities in the construction of the new International. He did not even mention a "proclamation" or "founding" of the Fourth International.

In February 1936 Trotsky was visited by two members of the American section, Maurice Spector and Lyman Paine. Most of their discussion concerned a proposal that the members of the Workers Party should join the American Socialist Party, which was approved later that month by a Workers Party convention. Toward the end of the transcript, Spector asked, "How do you conceive the main stages in the development of the Fourth International?"

After citing recent developments in Belgium and France, Trotsky said,

Nothing has changed. As I wrote to Muste and Cannon at the time of the Open Letter, I looked on it [the collaboration with Muste] as a lifelong alliance. I do not know at what stage the Fourth will arrive. Nobody knows. It is possible that we will have to enter again into a unified International with the Second and Third. It is impossible to consider the fate of the Fourth International apart from the fate of the national sections and vice versa. . . . If we consider the Fourth International only as an international "firm" which compels us to remain independent propagandistic societies under any conditions, we are lost. No, the Fourth International is a program, a strategy, an international leadership nucleus.[30]

There is still no reference of any kind to "proclaiming" or "founding." The statement that the Fourth International is "a program, a strategy, an international leadership nucleus" might perhaps be interpreted to mean that the Fourth International already existed, since the program, strategy, and international nucleus also existed. But it should be noted that this statement comes a little after the one where Trotsky said he didn't know, and "nobody knows," when the Fourth International would "arrive."

Trotsky and the IS agreed in April 1936 that the international conference should be held in the summer. In April he also began corresponding with Victor Serge in Belgium. Serge was one of the early Left Oppositionists in the USSR, for which he was brutally victimized. The Stalin regime finally permitted him to leave the USSR with his family in the spring of 1936, after protest campaigns by French intellectuals and the ICL. Years of banishment, harassment, and isolation had caused Serge to lose touch with the thinking of the Left Opposition and the ICL, and to revive some of the syndicalist and anarchist sympathies of his youth. Despite this, Trotsky wrote him frequently in the spring and summer of 1936 in an effort to win him over politically to the ICL and to find a place in it for the literary contributions Serge was capable of making. One of the Serge letters, dated May 23 or May 27, 1936, which unfortunately was not available when the correspondence was printed in France,[31] must have asked Trotsky about perspectives or plans for the Fourth International. Trotsky's answer on this point, dated June 3, 1936, said:

> The Fourth International: I confess I do not understand what "founding" the Fourth International means. There exist in different countries organizations and groups that struggle under this banner. They try to determine together their position on all the world events. They are preparing a common program based on practical and theoretical concepts rooted in history. Some Ryazanov[32] of the future may at his leisure try to resolve in retrospect the question of when exactly the Fourth International was founded. But as for us, we have simply to develop our work.

When the Serge letter that Trotsky was answering is located, perhaps the significance of the reply will be clearer. Meanwhile here, for the first time in 1936 to our knowledge, Trotsky does refer to the "founding" of the

Fourth International. But not in a favorable way. On the contrary, he takes a critical attitude to the idea, or at least dismisses its practical significance for the groups in different countries already struggling under the banner of the Fourth International. Future historians might have the leisure to figure out "when exactly" the Fourth International was founded, but the partisans of the Fourth International had more urgent things to do now.

The letter to Serge was sent only a month before Trotsky wrote the major resolutions presented to the international conference. He touched on the "foundation" question in one of these resolutions, "The New Revolutionary Upsurge and the Tasks of the Fourth International," which dealt with the massive strike wave in France and the opening of the civil war in Spain. Point 15 of this resolution said:

> Thus, all the tasks of the revolutionary struggle unfailingly lead to one task—the creation of a new, really revolutionary, leadership, capable of dealing with the tasks and possibilities of our epoch. Direct participation in the movement of the masses, bold class slogans taken to their conclusion, an independent banner, irreconcilability toward compromisers, mercilessness toward traitors—here lies the road of the Fourth International. It is both amusing and absurd to discuss whether it is yet time to "found" it. An International is not "founded" like a cooperative, but created in struggle. The June days [in France] provide an answer to the pedants who discuss its "timeliness." There is no room for further discussion.

Here Trotsky is concerned primarily with the "timeliness" factor. He calls it absurd to even discuss that factor after the recent upsurge of the French workers has demonstrated the need for new revolutionary leadership. But he has something to add about the "founding" question: an International is not "founded" like a cooperative, but is created in struggle. (Whatever interpretation may be made of that, it is not the sort of statement that would have harmonized with a proposal for the conference to proclaim the founding of the new International.)

Another relevant point to be made about this and the other conference resolutions written by Trotsky is that in all of them he said, the Fourth International calls for this, the Fourth International stands for that, etc. In no place did his resolutions use the term "Movement for the Fourth International," which the delegates decided to adopt during the conference. This tends to support the probability that he never heard of the new name until after it had been adopted by the conference.

What do the various statements cited above suggest? The following, in my opinion:

We know of course that Trotsky wrote in 1935 and continued to believe until his death that the Fourth International was the most important work of his life. Hundreds of letters and articles in 1935–36 express his conviction, publicly and privately, that the solution of the most crucial problems facing humanity in that period depended on the creation of a strong and effective Fourth International as soon as possible. Nobody disputes the fact that everything he did and said in 1936 was intended to hasten the creation of the Fourth International, and no interpretation of what he said about "founding" makes sense if it contradicts that fact.

But Trotsky did not equate the creation or bringing into existence of the Fourth International with its "proclamation" or "foundation." In fact, he distinguished between them rather strongly. Since he usually put quotation marks around "proclamation" and "founding," and then spoke about them with sarcasm or hostility, it seems to me that he attached some special meaning to those words. For him, those who spoke about "proclaiming" and "founding" had a concept of how to create a revolutionary International which he believed to be misleading and unhealthy, and he was trying to alert his comrades to beware of that concept and its consequences. *It can't be done*, he was saying, *by issuing a proclamation notifying the world that a new International exists; it can't be done through some formal act like taking a new name or passing a motion pledging to fulfill the functions of an International; no, it can only be done by continuing and intensifying the struggle for the International we began in 1933 and not letting ourselves be distracted by irrelevant or trifling pseudo-problems; the new International is timely now, but its arrival and success depend on hard work; not on useless or harmful "proclamation" and "foundation" formalities.*

This interpretation of Trotsky's position up to the 1936 conference is based, I must admit, on examination of only a part of the 1936 correspondence and documents. When the papers containing the letters to and from Trotsky are opened at Harvard in 1980, perhaps more light will be cast on the nature of the concepts that Trotsky was trying to counteract and how widespread they were in the ICL. Perhaps they will also disclose elements of a semantic problem. But I am certain that they will not do anything to support the legend of Trotsky proposing the founding or proclamation of the Fourth International in 1936. He simply did not see any point in such a thing in 1936, when he thought that without the formalities the movement should call itself the Fourth International, as he did in the resolutions he wrote for the conference.

I repeat "in 1936" because Trotsky changed his mind on this question in 1938.

For reasons stated in his letter of May 31, 1938, Trotsky disliked the name chosen by the July 1936 conference (MFI). But he was in complete agreement with the conference decision to set up a commission that would write a draft program; its final version (the "foundation document") was to be adopted early in 1937, after a four-month discussion, by the "first congress" of the Fourth International. Because the July conference was quickly followed by the first of the big Moscow trials, which compelled the MFI to concentrate all its energies on exposing the trials, this schedule was completely upset and the next conference was postponed a number of times before it was finally held in September 1938.

Did Trotsky see any contradiction between his remarks before the 1936 conference and the MFI's plans to prepare a "foundation document" for what we now call the founding conference or founding congress in 1938? We cannot say, but others in the MFI who worked most closely with him did not sense any inconsistency. Rudolf Klement is a good example. He was secretary of the July 1936 conference and was administrative secretary of the IS until his murder two years later. In the latter post, it fell to him to write the IS circular-letter containing the formal call for the international conference in 1938. This first letter informing the national leaderships about the coming conference was dated April 1, 1938, less than two weeks after Trotsky's discussions with an SWP delegation about the conference. It was undoubtedly written in accord with Trotsky's views as Klement understood them, and he was better placed at the time to understand them than the other IS members. It is worth noting that Klement's letter referred to the coming gathering as the "Second International Conference for the Fourth International" (the official title of the July 1936 conference was the "First International Conference for the Fourth International"). Under this title he wrote:

[I]t is certainly not necessary to explain here the urgent necessity of this conference, in view both of the experiences lived through since the July 1936 conference and of the grandiose events to come. This will probably, in fact, be our last international conference before the outbreak of the world war and the revolutionary movements which it will inevitably engender. We must draw a balance sheet of our experience, verify, conform, and specify our program and our policies, consolidate the ideological and organizational bases of the Fourth International in order that it may effectively play the role that history has entrusted to it. Will it be a question of the "foundation" of the Fourth International? This certainly is a poor way of posing the question. The process of the formation of the Fourth International commenced a long time ago and will not cease in the immediate future. It is necessary, in any case, that those who throughout the world are fighting for the Bolshevik program of the Fourth International should build, consolidate, enlarge their international organization, adopt, on the basis of their common program, common rules of conduct, apply on a national and international scale democratic centralism. May the Second International Conference be an important new step in this direction![33]

It is plain from this that at least echoes of Trotsky's 1936 views on "founding" were still reverberating at the time that the plans for the founding conference were being communicated to the leaders of the national sections in April 1938. There are even traces to be found in the last chapter of the transitional program, which Trotsky completed in the same month of April 1938. Polemicizing against skeptics asking if the time had yet arrived to proclaim the foundation of the Fourth International, Trotsky replied that it

has no need of being "proclaimed." It exists and it fights. Is it weak? Yes, its ranks are not numerous because it is still young. They are as yet chiefly cadres. But these cadres are pledges for the future. Outside of these cadres there does not exist a single revolutionary current on this planet meriting the name. If our International is still weak in numbers, it is strong in doctrine, program, tradition, in the incomparable tempering of its cadres.

But the name used in the conference call (the "Second International Conference for the Fourth International") was abandoned soon after it was introduced, along with the implication that the 1938 conference would not do anything essentially different from the 1936 conference. And despite Trotsky's April 1936 denial that the Fourth International needed to be "proclaimed," it was proclaimed at the 1938 conference, and its formal founding was incorporated into the statutes of the new World Party of Socialist Revolution.

Trotsky did not oppose these steps; in fact, he contributed to them heavily by his letter of May 31, 1938. There he explained that the name chosen in 1936 (Movement "for" the Fourth International) was being seized on by elements inside the movement to oppose or delay the creation of a disciplined revolutionary International. The resulting "indecision and lack of self-confidence" could do great damage to the movement; it was necessary to check the vacillators and backsliders in the most unambiguous way. While his letter only reiterated the thought he had in 1936—that we are the Fourth International and that is what we should call ourselves—it had the effect of separating the real Fourth Internationalists from the phonies and of reinforcing the trend toward "proclamation" and "founding" formalities at the 1938 conference.

To fully understand what Trotsky meant—in 1936, 1938, or any other time after 1933—it is not always sufficient to read what he wrote or said. Sometimes it is also necessary to learn what the other leaders of the movement were thinking, saying, worrying about, or trying to do. Almost everything he wrote, including most of his public articles and books, was aimed at educating and consolidating an international cadre capable of the teamwork and discipline needed to build the Fourth International. Maybe Trotsky didn't always get the most accurate reports on what his fellow leaders were thinking, but he always took this question seriously, and it affected both what he wrote and how he wrote it. Since Trotsky was in general one of the clearest of writers, an examination of what his comrades were thinking is recommended whenever there is any uncertainty or ambiguity about what he was saying and trying to say.

G. B.
August 1979

NOTES

1. The ILO's August 1933 resolution is translated into English for the first time as Appendix A.

2. Germany, France, Britain, Belgium, Greece, Spain, Bulgaria, Switzerland, Italy, and the USSR. Other Oppositionist groups existed—in China, South Africa, Latin America, central Europe, etc.—but were not represented at this conference.

3. The three were the Socialist Workers Party of Germany (SAP), the Independent Socialist Party of Holland (OSP), and the Revolutionary Socialist Party of Holland (RSP). The SAP was organized in 1931 after a left-wing tendency was expelled from the German Social Democracy; although outlawed by the Nazis, it claimed over 10,000 members in 1933. The OSP originated in 1932 out of a left-wing split from the Dutch Social Democracy and had an estimated 4,000 members. The RSP was organized in 1929 after its leaders were expelled from the Dutch CP for opposing Stalinism; it had almost a thousand members.

4. The Archeo-Marxists were a tendency in the Greek CP that was expelled in 1924. After functioning as a propagandist group for some years, they became a serious competitor of the CP. They began to sympathize with the Left Opposition in 1930 and joined as its Greek section in 1932. Witte became a member of the IS the same year.

5. See "The Class Nature of the Soviet State," in *Writings of Leon Trotsky (1933–34)* (New York: Pathfinder Press, 1972).

6. Several articles on this subject are in *Writings of Leon Trotsky (1934–35)* (New York: Pathfinder Press, 1971).

7. See "The Present Situation in the Labor Movement and the Tasks of the Bolshevik-Leninists," in *Documents of the Fourth International: The Formative Years (1933–40)* (New York: Pathfinder Press, 1973).

8. See Cannon's 1945 speech "The Workers Party and the Minority in the SWP," in *The Struggle for Socialism in the "American Century"* (New York: Pathfinder Press, 1977).

9. See *Writings of Leon Trotsky (1935–36)* (New York: Pathfinder Press, 1977).

10. See *The Crisis of the French Section (1935–36)* (New York: Pathfinder Press, 1977).

11. France, Belgium, Holland, Britain, Germany, Italy, the USSR, and the United States.

12. See *Documents of the Fourth International.*

13. The following three paragraphs were rewritten in 1979 to correct erroneous statements made in the August 1978 talk.

14. A useful example of such correspondence is Max Shachtman's report to Trotsky two weeks after the conference, printed here as Appendix B.

15. The legend's earliest appearance in print that I have found was in Pierre Frank's short book, *La quatrième internationale* (Paris: François Maspero, 1969); the 1972 English translation in *Intercontinental Press* was recently republished under the title *The Fourth International: The Long March of the Trotskyists* (London: Ink Links, 1979). It had only two sentences about the 1936 conference, one of which said: "Trotsky wanted the birth of the Fourth International announced then and there, but his proposal was not accepted by the conference, which called itself merely 'Movement for the Fourth International.'" Frank himself was not a delegate to the conference, nor did he attend it, so his statement was not based on eyewitness experience. Although he did not cite any documentary or other evidence, I accepted it as a factual statement, and repeated it in many books and other places, assuming that when he wrote on the subject with more room at his disposal he would fill in the information gaps. That occasion arrived at the end of 1978 when the first volume in a series called *Les congrès de la quatrième internationale* was published (Paris: Editions La Brèche, 1978) with a substantial introduction by Frank that includes almost two pages about the 1936 conference. Alas, there are no more facts in these two pages than there were in his two 1969 sentences. The extra space is used by the author of the introduction for rhetoric and embroidery: "Why did he present this proposal? Why did the conference reject it? Why did the conference decide only to take the name of Movement for the Fourth International?" etc. But his answers, whether relevant or irrelevant, are locked so tightly between speculation and abstraction that mere facts cannot possibly wiggle their way in. Trotsky's May 31, 1938, letter, "'For' the Fourth International? No! The Fourth International!" is in *The Transitional Program for Socialist Revolution* (New York: Pathfinder Press, 1977). His 1936 views on when and how to found the new International are in *Writings of Leon Trotsky (1935–36)* and *Writings of Leon Trotsky (1934–40), Supplement* (New York: Pathfinder Press, 1979) and are discussed in Appendix C.

16. Leonetti's articles on this subject in the ICL press used the pseudonyms J. P. Martin and A. Feroci.

17. See "Minutes of the Founding Conference of the Fourth International" in *Documents of the Fourth International.* Eleven sections were represented by regular delegates at this conference: the United States, France, Britain, Germany, the USSR, Italy, Brazil, Poland, Belgium, Holland, and Greece. Several other sections expressed their adherence to the new International even though they were unable to send delegates. There is no evidence that the Fourth International as a whole had any more members at the time of its founding conference than the International Left Opposition had in 1933.

18. In the United States around this time, Walter Reuther was starting to explain that he was not opposed to the founding of a labor party, "but now is not the time."

19. See "Underground Work in Nazi Germany," a transcript of a discussion held around June 1935, in *Writings of Leon Trotsky, Supplement.*

20. The proposal that the German section of the ILO should stop working for the reform of the German CP and start working for the creation of a new revolutionary party in Germany was debated in the ILO from March 1933, when Trotsky first made this proposal, until May 1933, when the ILO leadership approved it at a plenum in Paris. The leadership of the German section was opposed to the proposal at first, but by May they had changed their minds and supported the new orientation for Germany. Trotsky's letters and articles on this question are in *Writings (1932–33)* and *Writings (1929–33), Supplement.* The May plenum resolution, entitled "On the Need for a New German Party" is in *Documents of the Fourth International.*

21. In the months following Hitler's victory in 1933, the Stalinists in Austria, Bulgaria, and elsewhere continued to oppose united front action against the fascists, as they had done in Germany. This led in Austria to the total suppression of the CP and in Bulgaria to the virtual suppression of the CP, in both cases with little or no protest from the workers.

22. The Anglo-Russian Trade Unity Committee existed from 1925 to 1927 as a bloc of "Left" bureaucrats in the British Trades Union Congress with the Stalinist leadership of the Soviet unions. The Left Opposition demanded that the Soviet representatives break up the bloc after the British representatives betrayed the 1926 general strike in Britain. The Stalinists clung to the bloc, claiming all kinds of revolutionary virtues for it until the British dissolved the committee by withdrawing in 1927. Trotsky's writings on the subject are in *Leon Trotsky on Britain* (New York: Pathfinder Press, 1973). The Chinese Revolution of 1925–27 was crushed because the Chinese CP, following the orders of Stalin and Bukharin, subordinated the interests of the revolution to their alliance with the bourgeois nationalist forces headed by Chiang Kai-shek. For Trotsky's position, see *Leon Trotsky on China* (New York: Pathfinder Press, 1976). The gradual degeneration of the Russian CP began while Lenin was still alive. See *Lenin's Fight against Stalinism* (New York: Pathfinder Press, 1975) for articles sounding the alarm against Stalinism written by Lenin and Trotsky in 1922 and 1923, when they planned a joint attack on bureaucratism in the CPSU and the Soviet state.

23. The International Red Aid was organized in 1922 as a Comintern auxiliary organization to defend class struggle victims; under Stalinist control in the 1930s it discriminated against and refused to support the cases of Left Oppositionists arrested by the capitalists. In the United States its affiliate was called the International Labor Defense (ILD), which was organized in 1925.

24. As this passage indicates, the Left Opposition, while fighting for the restoration of workers' democracy and the reconstitution of a revolutionary party in the USSR, was still unwilling at this time in 1933 to advocate a multiparty system of pro-soviet parties in that country. It was not until 1938 that the Fourth International, in the transitional program, adopted the demand for the legalization of soviet parties in the USSR.

25. This refers to the platform adopted by the ILO preconference in February 1933. One of the eleven points, still calling for the policy of reform in the USSR, was later changed to recognize the need for a new International and new national parties.

26. Henricus Sneevliet was the Dutch delegate. See the *Writings of Leon Trotsky (1933–36)* and the *Supplement* for several letters about the role of the Dutch leadership up to the conference.

27. This refers to the fact that when the Spanish section broke with the ICL to found the POUM and take it into the People's Front in 1936, virtually the entire membership of the section was lost for the ICL, and the movement for the Fourth International in Spain had to be started over again from scratch.

28. Georges Vereecken voted against the conference decision to endorse the recent expulsion of Raymond Molinier from the French section and to prohibit political or organizational collaboration with Molinier by any member of the movement.

29. Muste had suggested Abern for election to the new IS at the conference, and Trotsky accepted the suggestion and recommended it to Shachtman in a letter on the eve of the conference.

30. See *Writings of Leon Trotsky, Supplement.*

31. See *La lutte contre le stalinisme*, ed. Michel Dreyfus (Paris: François Maspero, 1977). All of the Trotsky letters to Serge are translated in *Writings of Leon Trotsky, Supplement.*

32. David Ryazanov, head of the Marx-Engels-Lenin Institute in Moscow in the 1920s, was in charge of research about the history of the revolutionary movement. Stalin purged him in the 1930s because he was an obstacle to the rewriting of history in the Stalinist mode.

33. See excerpts from this circular-letter in *Cahiers Leon Trotsky* 1 (January 1979).

III

THE LIFE AND LEGACY
OF GEORGE BREITMAN

CHAPTER 14

WRITER, ORGANIZER, REVOLUTIONARY

THE LIFE AND LEGACY OF GEORGE BREITMAN

Paul Le Blanc

George Breitman was, according to the *New York Times* (April 24, 1986), "a leader of the American Trotskyist movement." Trotskyists may have had an honorable history on the American Left, but they never had a membership of more than two thousand. The fact that Breitman's influence went far beyond this small group is hinted at by the *Times* obituary's comment that he "was considered an authority on the life of Malcolm X, about whom he wrote a book"—a remark that was certainly true, as far as it went. He was also the pioneering editor of the most extensive collections of the black revolutionary's speeches, and he was responsible for the English-language edition of writings by another twentieth-century revolutionary, Leon Trotsky. His considerable literary and editorial labors influenced the thinking of many people throughout the world. Indeed, his approach to such work flowed organically from his years as a political organizer. "He demanded serious, concentrated work and was impatient with routinism and inattention," recalled Naomi Allen, one of his editorial coworkers. "He took every assignment seriously, no matter how small. . . . And when he had a major project on his hands, such as the Trotsky series, he planned it in such detail that it often seemed inconceivable that our slim forces could carry it out."[1]

Paul Le Blanc is associate professor of history and dean of the school of arts and sciences at La Roche College. He is the author or editor of many books, including *A Short History of the U.S. Working Class* and *Black Liberation and the American Dream*, and the series editor for Humanity Books' Revolutionary Studies series.

Breitman's best-known works are the anthology *Malcolm X Speaks* (1965) and his influential study *The Last Year of Malcolm X: The Evolution of a Revolutionary* (1967). "Without his early, consistent, and persistent commitment to preserving and disseminating Malcolm X's legacy to the emancipatory struggle, much of that legacy might have been lost," was the judgment of political scientist Eugene Victor Wolfenstein. Malcolm X scholar Paul Lee (a consultant for Spike Lee's film *X*) has spoken of "Breitmanesque scholarship" as involving "a very conscientious, thorough, methodical, serious, direct type of writing." The noted journalist Earl Ofari Hutchinson has commented: "George Breitman did a major service in showing through Malcolm's words how he grew from narrow nationalist to international statesman. By doing this, Breitman combated the distorted media image of Malcolm as a race-hating demagogue." According to Henry Lewis, "Malcolm X was a witness for the oppressed peoples of the world and particularly black Americans. . . . Malcolm bore witness to our condition. George bore witness to Malcolm's condition, growth, needs, and evolution—he witnessed the witness." Wolfenstein concludes that Breitman "established an important and controversial interpretation of Malcolm's position, and in this way, too, contributed to our understanding of his significance. Even those of us who disagreed, in part, with that interpretation have learned from it." The ideas in Breitman's essay "How a Minority Can Change Society" were inseparable from his interpretation of Malcolm X. "No longer did I see blacks as a powerless, helpless 'minority' forever dependent on the whims of white America," Ofari Hutchinson tells us. "Blacks as a 'minority' could also move masses and transform society."[2]

Breitman's greatest contribution to Trotsky scholarship was in overseeing the editing of the fourteen-volume *Writings of Leon Trotsky (1929–1940)* and other works by Trotsky, including the three-volume *Challenge of the Left Opposition*, for Pathfinder Press—collaborating with and coordinating an extensive team of translators and coeditors over a period of more than fifteen years. The seasoned British working-class militant Harry Wicks referred to Breitman's effort to "so devotedly communicate Leon Trotsky's writings and thoughts to a new generation" as something that might "continue to inspire others with his example and meticulous concern for detail." Naomi Allen has described how "Breitman took primary responsibility for the task of locating manuscripts

from all over the world, selecting them, translating them from many languages, editing and annotating them, and shaping them into cohesive
form." Pierre Broué, the noted biographer of Trotsky and editor of his
works in France, commented that "the Writings [as edited by Breitman]
had been the 'foundation' of our work," adding: "It will likewise be true
of all the editions to come in all languages, and the work accomplished
by George and his team will not cease to be useful to anyone who in the
future will want to know the thoughts and deeds of Trotsky." Louis Sin-
clair, the Scottish scholar whose *Leon Trotsky: A Bibliography* (Stanford:
Hoover Institution Press, 1972) Breitman termed "monumental," once
described "the cumulative effect" of George's many businesslike letters
to him (and to the editorial project on which the letters focused):

> They show him patiently enquiring, methodically checking and
> rechecking. He would query a translation from a language he could not
> read, praise work done in the field. He spared no effort to do proper jus-
> tice to the work assigned to him and his team. And the outcome is so
> easy to read. The absence of contorted expressions, vague formulations,
> ambiguity, has the result that his notes and prefaces say what he wanted
> to say. . . . Today scholars throughout the world turn to the Pathfinder
> *Trotsky* as the standard version of Trotsky's writings in English. That is
> their tribute to George Breitman, to George Breitman and his team.
> . . .The same respect is shown to George Breitman for his work on black
> nationalism and on Malcolm X. And for the same reasons: for the com-
> prehensiveness of his outlook, for the precision of his arguments, and
> for the clarity of his expression.[3]

GUIDING IDEAS

But such accomplishments cannot be understood apart from Breitman's
intellectual and practical commitment, from his teenage years onward, to
the revolutionary socialist perspectives of Marx, Lenin, and Trotsky. It is
worth identifying elements in their orientation that became essential elements of Breitman's approach.

"To be radical is to grasp things by the root," wrote Karl Marx. "But
for man the root is man himself. . . . Man is the highest being for man,
hence the categorical imperative to overthrow all conditions in which

man is a degraded, enslaved, neglected, contemptible being." It was the hope of Breitman and the belief of others who followed Marx that the working class must create a "self-conscious, independent movement of the great majority, in the interests of the great majority" to "win the battle of democracy" to create a society in which—as Marx and Engels put it in the *Communist Manifesto*—"the free development of each is the condition for the free development of all."[4]

No less was he committed to the notion emphasized by Vladimir Ilyich Lenin that a revolutionary socialist's ideal should be "the tribune of the people, who is able to react to every manifestation of tyranny and oppression, no matter where it appears, no matter what stratum or class of people it affects." Lenin insisted on the need for a disciplined organization of revolutionaries that would rise above sloppiness and amateurishness, that would "train people to devote the whole of their lives, not only their spare evenings, to the revolution." The socialism that Lenin and Trotsky were struggling for as they led the Russian Revolution of 1917 was described in this way by Trotsky: "Socialism signifies a pure and clear social system which is accommodated to the self-government of the toilers. . . . Socialism would have no value apart from the unselfish, honest, and humane relations between human beings."[5] There is a striking harmony between this vision of socialism and the qualities that Trotsky insisted must animate revolutionary activists. "Revolutionary discipline has nothing to do with blind obedience," he explained. "A Bolshevik is not merely a disciplined person; he is a person who in each case and on each question forges a firm opinion of his own and defends it courageously and independently, not only against his enemies, but inside his own party."[6]

The absorption of this approach into his very being comes through in a tribute to Breitman by the well-known Marxist economist Ernest Mandel:

> He was . . . at home in the library as well as on the picket line, a gifted writer and an excellent organizer, great at organizing election campaigns and at helping others to develop theory, an outstanding editor and a real workers' leader. His qualities as educator and popularizer, which stemmed from a rare gift of perceiving the essential and expressing it in a clear and simple way so that many can understand it, did not prevent him from being at the same time a deep and independent thinker.[7]

Indeed, Breitman not only sought to live up to the Bolshevik injunction to be critical, courageous, and independent, but in doing so he was able (as one comrade later reflected) "to develop insights which changed the way the entire Trotskyist movement thought about certain kinds of problems."[8]

EARLY COMMITMENTS

Breitman was born in a working-class neighborhood of Newark, New Jersey, in 1916. His mother was a houseworker for better-off families, and his father was an iceman carrying fifty-pound blocks of ice up tenement stairs in the days before refrigeration. The father's premature death meant that George's older sister Celia had to quit school to support the family. Like many others throughout the world, she was inspired by the 1917 workers' revolution in Russia led by Lenin and Trotsky, and her involvement in the Young Communist League in the 1920s influenced Breitman's own political development. Among his childhood memories was attending, with his sister and hundreds of other Newark residents, a mass protest against the execution of anarchists Nicola Sacco and Bartolomeo Vanzetti in 1927. The Great Depression deepened his radical convictions. Unemployed after graduating from high school, he eventually found work in the Civilian Conservation Corps in 1934 (which temporarily shipped him off to Alabama), and later with the Works Progress Administration.[9]

A split in the early US Communist movement would profoundly affect Breitman's political evolution. In 1928, one of the central leaders of the American Communist Party, James P. Cannon, was expelled—along with two young co-thinkers, Max Shachtman and Martin Abern, and about a hundred others—on charges of "Trotskyism." They had agreed with Trotsky's criticisms of the Soviet bureaucracy that after Lenin's death had been consolidating, under Joseph Stalin, an authoritarian regime both inside the Soviet Union and within the Communist International.

It was important for Breitman to stress as well many positive elements in the US radical tradition, and the struggles to remain true to those positive elements, that were essential to American Trotskyism. "Before the Communist Party (CP) could expel Cannon for holding a minority viewpoint, the Communist International initiated by Lenin and Trotsky in

1919 had to be bureaucratized and the minority represented by Trotsky and the Left Opposition had to come into existence," he once insisted. "Before the CP could expel Cannon, one of its founders, it first had to be founded in 1919 as a revolutionary party. But before the CP could be founded, there had to be a prewar radicalization that is sometimes called 'Debsian,' the treachery of the Second International in World War I, the development of a revolutionary wing in the American Socialist Party and the Industrial Workers of the World (IWW), the Russian Revolution of 1917, and so on."[10]

These early heroic years of American socialism and communism were crucially important for Breitman. One of the greatest strengths of US Trotskyism, he affirmed, was "its continuity with the struggles from the start of the century—the IWW and revolutionary syndicalism, Debs's fighting election campaigns, opposition to US entry into World War I, efforts to absorb the meaning of the Russian Revolution and Leninism, the development of a left wing in the SP, the birth of the new CP and its early attempts to adapt to American realities." He emphasized that "Cannon and his comrades, especially the older ones like Carl Skoglund, V. R. Dunne, and Arne Swabeck, had not merely read or heard about these events; they grew up in them and were shaped by them." This fact "provided the basic political capital" of the American Trotskyist movement to which the young Breitman was attracted in the economic hard times of the Great Depression. By this time, the Trotskyists' organization, the Communist League of America (which played a key role in the 1934 Minneapolis general strike), had merged with the American Workers Party, an independent socialist formation led by A. J. Muste (which in 1934 played a key role in the Toledo Auto-Lite strike), to form an outward-reaching group called the Workers Party of the United States.[11]

By 1935, at the age of nineteen, Breitman had joined the Trotskyist movement as a member of the Spartacus Youth League, and not long after as a member of the Workers Party of the United States. His future wife, Dorothea Katz, visited him at his family's apartment: "His room was filled with papers and books everywhere," she recalled. "The written word—in pamphlets, books, current newspapers, piled up all over the place in his own manner of order." At the same time, at citywide meetings of the Workers Alliance he "was developing into an effective, respected, and well-liked leader of the unemployed. . . . He won his posts over political opponents with clear presentations and a program which appealed to those who listened."[12]

For Breitman, the influence of Jim Cannon was especially inspiring. "When I use the word 'inspired' I am referring not to the effects of his oratorical powers, although they were great," Breitman later wrote, "but to his ability to draw for our benefit on the vast fund of political and organizational knowledge he had accumulated in his early days, which he had reflected on very carefully, and which he polished and adapted so that we could use it and be certain that we were doing the right thing at the right time." Breitman believed that "an important responsibility of the older and more experienced members of the revolutionary movement is to help educate the newer and younger members. The main way is to set a good example, but when mistakes are made, direct criticism is necessary." Noting that "all the mentors and teachers in my eight-year apprenticeship [roughly 1935 to 1943] were considerate and restrained," he added that "no one was more tactful than Jim in making criticisms of the younger members."[13]

Breitman himself later reminisced that politically he "was relatively uneducated and inexperienced," but he knew more than many older colleagues. When he and about five hundred other Trotskyists joined the Socialist Party of America in 1936, he became friends with a member of the Newark Socialists, James Kutcher, who later recalled:

George Breitman helped me understand politics after he joined the Socialist Party in Newark in 1936 where I had been a member for a year or two without learning much. Although still young, . . . George taught us socialists the meaning of the Moscow trials which were just beginning, and he explained what Stalinism was. He also taught us about fascism and how Hitler had gained power in Germany. Other events closer to home interested him as well, and he tried to teach us to understand them and relate them to what was happening in the world.

George was one of the organizers of the Workers Alliance, the organization of the unemployed in New Jersey. He got me interested in the work of this organization. And through it we began helping some of the CIO [Congress of Industrial Organizations] organizers who were trying in those days to set up unions where there had been none before. One of my early memories of George is marching on a picket line with him. In actions of this kind I began to learn more about the class struggle in this country.[14]

This recollection gives a sense of the radicalization process, and the extremely energetic intervention in the Socialist Party of America, that enabled the Trotskyists in many areas to outstrip the influence of more moderate members around party leader Norman Thomas. This had not been what Thomas and the others had bargained for when they had allowed the Trotskyists into their organization. "Unable to contain our growing influence by other means," Breitman recalled, "the SP leaders tried to gag us and expelled us wholesale when we refused to accept the gag."[15]

While this conflict devastated the Socialist Party, it propelled the Trotskyists and their newfound converts—about fifteen hundred in all—to establish a dynamic new organization.

SOCIALIST WORKERS PARTY

Breitman attended the founding convention of the Socialist Workers Party in 1938, "feeling that the convention represented a milestone in the history of the American revolutionary movement. I am sure most of the delegates shared my conviction that we had participated in something truly significant: the launching—at last!—of the party that would lead the American workers in the coming socialist revolution." The theoretical and intellectual level of the gathering was significantly more advanced than that of previous defining moments in the history of US radicalism. No less important in Breitman's view was the impressive base the new organization had acquired in the new industrial unions:

> Our chief union stronghold was Minneapolis, where our comrades in the teamsters union led by Dunne, Skoglund, and Farrell Dobbs were showing the whole country what a union led by revolutionaries could do. It was our aspiration in Newark, and I am sure elsewhere, to meet the high standards they were setting. . . .
>
> Another gain of that time was the organization of our fraction in the maritime industry, starting on the West Coast. Although he was not at the founding convention, Tom Kerry was elected to the National Committee at this convention, partly in recognition of his work in this fraction, which also served as a model for the party.
>
> Most of our other activity was centered in the new CIO unions that

were being born at the time—steel, auto, electrical, and so on. We helped to sign up workers to join the unions, both in the plants and in their homes; we participated in strikes to win recognition and bargaining rights; we joined forces with others to gain, extend, or preserve democracy inside the unions.

The main difference was that the unions then were less bureaucratized and the workers had a greater interest in their unions than they do today [1982]. That made it easier for militants to get a hearing from the members in those days.[16]

The high hopes of the new SWP about the likelihood of dramatic organizational advances were not to be realized, in part because the early beginnings of World War II (including the Hitler-Stalin nonaggression pact; the Soviet invasion of Latvia, Lithuania, Estonia, and eastern Poland; and the Russo-Finnish war) initiated a sharp factional conflict. Max Shachtman and Martin Abern—joined by the SWP's most prominent intellectuals such as James Burnham, Dwight MacDonald, and C. L. R. James—broke with Trotsky over the issue of whether the Soviet Union continued to have any progressive features. Cannon and the bulk of the party's trade unionists sided with Trotsky. By 1940 Shachtman's faction, with almost half the membership, split away to form its own Workers Party (increasingly moving away from Trotskyist politics), while the SWP quickly elevated some of its younger cadres to help write for and edit the party's publications—the weekly *Militant*, the theoretical magazine *Fourth International*, and the books and pamphlets of Pioneer Publishers. In 1941 the US government initiated Smith Act prosecutions of the party's leadership, as the United States prepared to enter World War II.[17] This action drew Breitman into a more central role in the organization.

Shakespearean scholar and literary critic Paul Siegel, an SWP member, got to know Breitman in this period and remembered him vividly. "The special qualities I found in him were those which everyone who knew him were aware of: his luminous intelligence combined with modesty and unpretentiousness and his utter devotion to the revolutionary party, a devotion that put the cause of the proletarian revolution before all his personal feelings and relationships." Siegel was especially impressed with the "remarkable lucidity" of Breitman's writing. He remarked: "George Orwell once held forward as an ideal prose style one that is like a sparklingly clear window through which one can see reality without the writer's personality getting in the way. This was George's style." Charles Curtiss made a similar point: "He revered the simple declarative sentence as the glory of the language, and used the simplest terms to express the ideas, the logic, and the ideals of socialism so that the most untutored worker could grasp them." Yet Siegel was not satisfied to leave it at that. "A writer has to be able to understand the complexities of reality in order to convey them to the reader," he noted. "George's style may have been self-effacing, but the clarity of vision it gave to the reader was derived from his own clarity of thought."[18]

Breitman himself thought most highly of the writing style of James P. Cannon. "The articles that Jim submitted were the stuff that editors dream of—clean, carefully constructed, and complete. He worked and reworked them, rearranging and polishing them with the conscientiousness and devotion that both craftsmen and artists give to their work." Looking back on Cannon's *Militant* column titled "Notebook of an Agitator," Breitman was struck that many of the columns "consist of what today might be called 'cultural criticism,'" something to which much of his own writing was inclined.[19]

Breitman later recalled that in the years when he worked on the *Militant*, his relations with Cannon were friendly—but added that "by 'friendly' I mean that they were cordial, that we worked together easily, but not that we were friends. Our age differential and the teacher-pupil relationship militated against that." At the same time, Breitman insisted, "Jim felt as great an affinity for young revolutionaries and rebels as anyone could possibly feel." In turn, he and others especially savored the rich humor that Cannon brought to his revolutionary efforts:

> Jim's sense of humor had a wide range—sharp or savage when aimed at the class enemy; sarcastic toward opponents in the labor and radical movements; more on the wry or ironical side when it was about ourselves. At lunch he used to enjoy relating or hearing accounts taken from the day's newspapers that emphasized the ludicrousness of bourgeois politics or morality. Sipping his beer and fastidiously munching his ham or corned beef sandwich, he would lift his eyebrows and shrug his shoulders slightly as though to say, "What a crazy world—you'll go crazy if you don't learn to laugh."[20]

Breitman's veneration of Cannon was rooted in his own revolutionary convictions. "Because I believe the United States' future is socialist and that socialism will be attained through the kind of revolutionary party Jim was building," he commented after the old revolutionary's death, "I have no doubt that future generations will cherish his memory as one of the chief architects of the socialist society and will want to know as much as possible about him."[21]

Frank Lovell, a leader of the SWP's maritime fraction, recalled that "Breitman was a great favorite of Cannon's—I think because Cannon found in him a young man who was anxious to learn the method of scientific socialism, the logic of Marxism, and was capable of teaching it." Lovell also remembered: "In November 1943, shortly before Cannon and the others were sent to jail under the Smith Act, Cannon referred to George as a 'mere boy'—which George, who was then twenty-seven and about to be grabbed up by the US Army, deeply resented and never forgot—but it was intended as an affectionate reference because Cannon went on to explain that Breitman had taken charge of the weekly newspaper, the *Militant*, and was the kind of leader the working-class party needed." Charles Curtiss worked with Breitman on the editing and production of the paper at this time. "I remember the nights we put the *Militant* 'to bed.' Each word had to be carefully weighed so as not to give the government further pretext to indict others, while at the same time to affirm our stand for socialism and internationalism." He added: "And I remember the relaxed talk and camaraderie after the tension of the night's work. How precious are those memories."[22]

Drafted into the US Army late in 1943 despite physical disabilities that kept him out of combat, Breitman was later shipped to France. While absolutely opposed to all that Hitler's Nazism and Mussolini's fascism represented, he was nonetheless critical of what he and other Trotskyists perceived as essential elements at the heart of US foreign policy: the goal of the global predominance of powerful US business interests at the expense of the democratic and humanistic aspirations of the world's peoples. While not seeking to obstruct the US war effort militarily, the SWP refused to give it political support, criticizing it as part of a conflict between rival imperialisms for world domination. "It is absolutely true that Hitler wants to dominate the world," commented Cannon, "but we think it is equally true that the ruling group of American capitalists has the same idea, and we are not in favor of them, either."[23] The fact remained, however, as Breitman's wife, Dorothea, recalled, "George's only real vacation was his stint in the army in World War II." She elaborated:

> In training camp he and the other 4-Fers defied orders to be clean-shaven by growing beards. He was classified as an office worker and in the typing test he beat champion typists using only his two fingers where they used ten. By the time he got to Paris he was a master sergeant in charge of his quartermaster office. He and the guys who worked with him had a ball. They completed their eight hours of work in many less, chewed the fat, discussing politics and other things, and had much time off. It was the only time in his life that he weighed over 140 pounds. Before his discharge [in 1946] he participated in the "We want to go home" movement and attended meetings of the Fourth International.[24]

The "Bring the Boys Home" movement that Breitman participated in was initiated by young radical US servicemen stationed in Europe and Asia. They organized rallies and protests at the end of World War II to prevent their being utilized militarily to establish "the American Century" at the expense of the left-wing Resistance movements that had helped defeat the Axis Powers and now might want to push for far-reaching social change. But no less important for Breitman was helping to reorganize and rebuild the war-battered movement of the European Trotskyists. When French police raided a meeting of Fourth Internationalists, one of the people they arrested was Breitman, dressed in his US Army uniform. "I first met George when he was in Europe in the aftermath of World War II and assisted . . . in rebuilding a functioning center for our world movement," Belgian Trotskyist Ernest Mandel later recounted. "As the youngest participant in that effort, I learned a lot from him." Mandel added: "If I wanted to single out the persons from whom I learned most during the years following the war, I would name two SWP leaders: Morris Stein* and George Breitman."[25]

---

*Morris Stein was the "party name" of Morris Lewit (1903–1998), who as a teenager had participated in the Russian Revolution, after his 1920 immigration to the United States becoming involved in the early US Communist movement. After joining the Trotskyists, he and his companion Sylvia Bleecker edited the Yiddish-language paper *Unser Kampf*. When SWP leader James P. Cannon was jailed under the Smith Act in 1943, Lewit served temporarily as the party's national secretary. After World War II he came to Europe as a member of the top leadership body of the Fourth International, the International Secretariat. Illness removed him from political activity by the early 1960s.

Upon his return to the United States, Breitman again served as editor of the *Militant* in the late 1940s and early 1950s. It was in this period that he developed a deep friendship and extended working relationship with one of the SWP's most capable intellectuals, George Weissman, who for a number of years functioned as director of Pioneer Publishers (later to be renamed Merit Publishers and finally Pathfinder Press). Weissman sought creative ways to expand Trotskyist influence, later producing the widely read anthology *Che Guevara Speaks*, as well as encouraging the production of Breitman's *Malcolm X Speaks* and Jean Tussey's *Eugene V. Debs Speaks*. In later years Breitman also became centrally involved in the work of Pathfinder Press.[26]

Another important relationship of this period was that with Joseph Hansen, who had served as Trotsky's personal secretary during the last years of the revolutionary's life and—like Breitman—would play an extremely influential role in the SWP from the late 1940s through the 1970s. "The consensus, at least among those I knew, was that Breitman and Hansen were the outstanding creative political personalities of the old guard," recalled Les Evans of the layer of 1960s radicals who became part of the SWP. Hansen oversaw the work of a tiny staff that produced a sophisticated weekly news magazine, *World Outlook*, later renamed *Intercontinental Press*, that was one of the most effective publications of the US Trotskyists. Evans later wrote:

> Joe himself was a tireless worker and a fine journalist who worked long into the night week after week. But when he wanted to scold the staff, it was always Breitman he held up as the impossibly perfect role model. When Breitman was editor of the *Militant*, he never spent working time reading the comic strips and ads of the papers he was assigned to follow the way we did. No, Breitman always, legend had it, read the whole *New York Times* on the commuter train from Newark before he even got to work. And when we left to drag ourselves home at midnight on a typical Friday night, Joe would often remind us that Breitman not only worked the same schedule as we for years on end, but that he would come in at eight the next morning with an extra article that he wrote at home sometime or other during the night.[27]

Far from being obsessively narrow, however, Breitman's attention and energies embraced the larger world. His mind and heart engaged with a variety of intellectual and cultural currents—whether Hannah Arendt's writings on totalitarianism, or the literature of existentialism represented by Jean-Paul Sartre, Albert Camus, and Simone de Beauvoir, or the avante garde theater of Brecht and Beckett and Ionesco, or the surrealism of Andre Breton and others. When the Johnson-Forest tendency, led by C. L. R. James and Raya Dunayevskaya, abandoned the Shachtmanites to return (for a few years) to the SWP, Breitman certainly appreciated their vibrant involvement with cultural questions, feminism, and the dynamics of black liberation. In later years he made a point of highlighting and further developing the pathbreaking insights on black nationalism that had emerged from James's earlier discussions with Trotsky. In 1949 and 1950 a militant mineworkers' strike erupted in Pennsylvania and West Virginia. Dunayevskaya recalled: "I [began] sending a very new type of article on the miners' strike and interviews with miners' wives to the *Militant*, whose editor, George Breitman, greeted them as 'a breath of fresh air.'"[28]

But the promising expansiveness of the post–World War II radicalization (which also found reflection in the fact that SWP membership rose once again, in 1946–47, to almost fifteen hundred) was blocked by a combination of factors, including the lethal interplay of Stalinism's negative predominance on the US Left with the even more powerfully orchestrated cold war anticommunism that soon came to dominate American culture and politics (a destructive dynamic fueled by the Korean War). The unprecedented prosperity of American capitalism made it increasingly possible for more and more US workers to realize "the American dream," dramatically narrowing the social base for revolutionary socialism. More important still, the worldwide revolutionary upsurge that Trotsky had predicted, and that his followers had anticipated, for the post–World War II period did not take place. The anticolonial and anti-imperialist uprisings in Asia, Africa, and Latin America were not accompanied by the expected antibureaucratic uprisings in the Soviet Union and anticapitalist uprisings in western Europe. Nor did revolutionary socialism (as represented by the Fourth International) replace reformist moderation and Stalinism within the mass labor movements of any country.

The result for the Trotskyists was a devastating process of fragmentation and implosion. Anticipating the impending failure of revolutionary "inevitabilities," a small group around Felix Morrow and Albert Goldman had broken away from the SWP in the mid-1940s. The Johnson-Forest tendency left the SWP in 1951, also feeling that Trotskyism was no longer relevant to world realities, but optimistically (and wrongly, as it turned out) believing that greater class-struggle gains could be made if they formed their own group. Far more devastating was the crystallization of an opposition initiated by Bert Cochran, George Clarke, Harry Braverman (a close friend of Breitman's) and others, including a substantial section of the SWP's trade union cadres.

The Cochranites were aligned, temporarily, with the European majority leadership of the Fourth International, which included Michel Pablo (Raptis) and Ernest Mandel, among others. Pablo projected a global conflict between Stalinism and capitalism, predicting an economic downturn in the capitalist world and the coming of a Third World War between the USSR and the United States. In this context, he argued at the Third World Congress of the Fourth International in 1951 that Trotskyists should seek to enter and be part of the Stalinist organizations that would—because of "objective" pressures—be forced to play an increasingly revolutionary role. Several years later, leaders of the Fourth International concluded that "the theses of the Third Congress were in error on the prospects for war and on the economic situation."[29] But the error contributed, at that time, to a serious breach.

The "Cochranites" viewed the approach of James P. Cannon as far more problematical than any possible shortcoming of Michel Pablo. In a 1946 document nicknamed "The American Theses," James P. Cannon and others in the SWP had advanced their view that "the task of the Socialist Workers Party consists simply in this: to remain true to its program and banner; to render it more precise with each new development and apply it correctly in the class struggle; and to expand and grow with the growth of the revolutionary mass movement, always aspiring to lead it to victory in the struggle for political power." By remaining true to the perspectives traditionally associated with the Trotskyist movement, the party would be in a position to lead the US workers to victory. Writing seven years later, Cochran and his US co-thinkers charged that this approach had resulted in a devastating crisis in the SWP. Thanks to the overly optimistic "American Theses," the party suffered from "a six-year disorientation in the face of unexpected changes in the world and at home," culminating in "disappointment over the collapse of exaggerated hopes," as well as "an inability to cope soberly and analytically with the new reality created by the deepening reaction and the coming war."

Defending the traditional orientation—in the United States and in the Fourth International—was SWP leader Cannon, with whom Breitman, Hansen, and a majority of SWPers were aligned. The dispute culminated in a 1953 split in which the Fourth International was torn into two weakened fragments and many valuable members of the Cochran faction were lost forever. "As for the SWP minority," commented Fourth International historian Pierre Frank some years later, "no sooner did it break away from the party than it publicly expressed liquidationist positions and openly fought the Fourth International."[30]

Breitman concluded that Cannon's defense of the Leninist-Trotskyist tradition had been absolutely necessary, but he also went out of his way (unsuccessfully) to head off the split. In later years, as the political differences between the two major fragments of the world Trotskyist movement narrowed, he played an important role in bringing about the reunification of the Fourth International. Although it was not possible to bridge all of the political and personal barriers between the SWP and most of those identified with the Cochranites, Breitman made a point of reestablishing relationships with such old comrades as Harry Braverman, Jules Geller, and David Herreshoff. Herreshoff remarked on Breitman's "capacity to renew friendships which were casualties of the factional convulsions of our movement. He could renew friendships without belittling the importance of all the issues we have fought over among ourselves."[31]

The 1950s were a difficult time for revolutionaries, but Breitman remained committed to the SWP. With a membership barely exceeding four hundred, however, it was no longer the organization that Breitman and others had founded with such hope and enthusiasm two decades before. Tim Wohlforth, who shifted from Shachtman's Independent Socialist League to the SWP in the late 1950s, offers this comparison:

> Dues were paid and the *Militant* was always sold. The party was run in a modest, but smooth and professional manner. The problem was that the party was comprised of a generation of workers and intellectuals— those recruited in the 1930s and during World War II—which was getting old and tired. Cannon did a better job than Shachtman in holding on to his aging cadres and, on the whole, he and his followers kept the revolutionary faith. But as will and energy departed, faith was about all they had left. Cannon could not defy the general trends affecting the working class in the 1950s.[32]

In fact, by this time Cannon had gone into semiretirement, with a newer leader pushed into the position of SWP national secretary. This was Farrell Dobbs, a seasoned trade unionist who, in the opinion of revolutionary veteran Morris Lewit, on questions of revolutionary politics was "very green . . . not prepared for political leadership."[33] Playing a more aggressive role in the party leadership was another trade union veteran, Tom Kerry, who was more astute but had a reputation for being theoretically rigid and often intolerant of political differences. Murry Weiss and Myra Tanner Weiss, who had been close to Cannon, at times played a more creative and outward-reaching role, but they proved unable to coexist with the Dobbs-Kerry team. Breitman, Hansen, and prominent party intellectual George Novack were able to do so, however, and also became central to the SWP leadership in the late 1950s and early 1960s. Yet the meetings of the Political Committee on which they served could later be described by Wohlforth (at that time a leader of the newly created Young Socialist Alliance) in this way:

> The Political Committee functioned reasonably well in those days; its regular, brief meetings reflected the overall organizational efficiency of the Dobbs-Kerry regime. . . . It concerned itself with organizational matters and dealt with these matters largely in a routine fashion. World events were rarely discussed; one wonders if they were even thought about. Unlike the YSA, the Socialist Workers Party in general in the late 1950s was a rather dull place and Dobbs's PC was no different. A typical PC meeting was a two-hour battle to keep awake.[34]

Wohlforth's implication that party leaders never thought about world events inaccurately caricatures those being described, particularly Breitman. As a revolutionary in this period, Breitman was not satisfied to remain in a politically frustrating context like that which Wohlforth describes and jumped at the chance to help reorganize and build up the SWP's Detroit branch. From 1954 to 1967 this effort was a primary focus of his political attention and energies.

DETROIT ORGANIZER

George and Dorothea Breitman moved to Detroit in the wake of the dispute and split with the Cochran faction, joining Frank and Sarah Lovell, who had transferred in during the last stages of the fight. The Breitmans and the Lovells became close friends and comrades in this period, a political and personal collaboration that became lifelong.[35] Their collective political understanding and experience were certainly challenged by the situation they found themselves in. Detroit had been a stronghold of the Cochranites, and young activist Evelyn Sell later recalled that the split "left us with only eight members, no headquarters, [and] no mailing list or mimeo machine or basic resources." All of them had to get jobs to support themselves. Breitman worked as a proofreader and was a member of the International Typographical Union. For him the real job, however, was organizing the Detroit branch of the SWP—recruiting new (mostly younger) members, helping to educate them politically and train them to be effective activists, while at the same time helping the growing organization reach out to the larger population and influence the political life of the city. In a 1958 letter to a comrade, he described his view of this work:

> Those who sent me to Detroit didn't intend that I should stay there; they
> thought in terms of a year or two, an improvement in the internal situa-
> tion, etc. I told them I was going for good. . . . I had set my heart on . . .
> helping younger comrades, so far as I could, to develop all their powers,
> to realize their potential. I think I made a beginning at it. I know some
> a little, some substantially, some not at all. I know that I helped to create
> a healthier climate in the branch, in which development could be
> encouraged in the right direction.[36]

Over the next dozen years, the Detroit branch of the SWP attracted a growing number of people, especially with the youth radicalization of the 1960s. According to one observer, Breitman was "adored by the younger party members." Melissa Singler was a teenage activist involved in the 1960 picketing of Woolworths during the early days of the civil rights movement, and the first socialist class series she attended was taught by Breitman. "I was terribly excited by the classes," she remembers. "George was able to take a roomful of young people, most of whom had gone from six to sixteen in the silent 1950s, and have us hanging on his words." Impressed by "his straightforwardness and his creativity," Singler notes that "there was tremendous admiration on the part of those teenagers for this man who could so easily and humorously tell us about a history we had not been told about before."[37]

Evelyn Sell recalled, "he devoted special time, energy, and thought to helping younger comrades realize their potential," and he "paid extra-special attention to the development of women comrades." Breitman's deeply felt feminist commitment comes through in his discussion of Simone de Beauvoir (the existentialist he "admired the most"):

> In all of her novels there is much that is good, and some that's very good.... But her best book, and I think the best of that school is her [pioneering feminist] study, *The Second Sex.*... Its dissociation from Marxism is feeble and quibbling, I think. The spirit and tone of the whole work is Marxist to me. It is the work of a truly talented and cultured writer. (Maybe I felt a special impact; it had long been one of my conceits that I understood the woman question better than anyone else, including most women; and I was shaken up to find that after all I didn't know so much about how hard it is to be a woman.)[38]

Breitman's comprehension of working-class realities necessarily intersected not only with those of gender but also with those of race. As Michael Smith puts it, "He learned about black nationalism in Detroit. It was all-pervasive in that extremely nationalist and political city, and he was thus able to educate others, many others, about black nationalism, and about its shining prince and chief spokesman, Malcolm X, whom George never met but who more than anyone else is responsible for transmitting Malcolm's legacy."[39] Though some SWPers did not accept Breitman's perspective, it became the dominant perspective in the organization regarding black liberation.* Evelyn Sell captures an essential aspect of Breitman's achievement:

---

*In this, Breitman found himself involved in an extended polemic in the SWP with Richard Fraser, a thoughtful and energetic leader of the Seattle branch. (With his wife, Clara Fraser, in 1967 he and others in the Seattle SWP broke away to form the Freedom Socialist Party.) Fraser opposed to Breitman's embrace of black nationalism the quite different approach of "revolutionary integrationism." See *In Memorium: Richard S. Fraser, An Appreciation and Selection of His Work* (New York: Prometheus Research Library, 1990).

His empathy enabled him to have unique insights into the feelings and aspirations of blacks—and this gave the Detroit branch a special advantage in responding to the exciting developments in the black community: the emergence of a generation of black youths seeking militant and revolutionary solutions to racism; the outpouring of almost the entire black population for the 1963 civil rights march through downtown Detroit; the nationalist character of the Michigan Freedom Now Party. George's ability to be in tune with these developments didn't come solely from his brain but from the very core of his being.[40]

"I thought he was black like me," commented one reader of Breitman's works who was surprised, upon meeting him, to find that he was white. "I felt as if he was in my skin." Another young black student commented that initially "I looked upon the world struggle and the world situation as that of black vs. white—as oppressive whites who were responsible for oppressing nonwhites." Contact with Breitman contributed to a shift in perspective: "The struggle is really against avaricious capitalists who use racism and sexism as weapons in order for them to continue their exploitation and oppression of the working class of the world."

Paul Lee, in a perceptive discussion of Breitman's writings on Malcolm X, has added another important point:

It has been rare in my experience to meet white people who define themselves as *people* before they define themselves as *white*. That is, most whites that I've known see themselves and their culture as *the* norm, which implicitly or explicitly expresses itself in an attitude of superiority.

In George's case, I'm not sure if he had *any* attachment to his so-called whiteness or to his ethnicity. I am sure that I never felt judged or "different" in his regard because of my so-called blackness. I've been told the same thing by other African Americans who knew him, including the late Wilfred Shabazz [brother of Malcolm X], who was an exceptionally perceptive person.

I can't account for *why* this was so, but I do know that it gave him an advantage in dealing with people defined as black, who, after all, just wanted to be treated as people. He related to black people with an ease and unselfconsciousness that won him their respect and trust. Another revolutionary who happened to be white, John Brown, is said to have had a similar relationship with black people.[41]

With his pathbreaking work on Malcolm X, it became possible for Breitman to break out of two ghettoes. One ghetto was the rarefied circle of allegedly "sectarian" politics to which small left-wing groups (especially Trotskyists) were often restricted, certainly in the conservative political and cultural atmosphere that had been predominant in the United States during the 1950s and early 1960s. The other ghetto was much larger—that of so-called white America, which was traditionally sealed off from people of color in general and especially from African Americans. Of course, the person he had been all of his life had never accepted remaining restricted to such boundaries. But in the early 1960s, with the rise and acceleration of the black liberation struggle, Breitman's insights found resonance in the larger culture (as capitalist publishers and distributors of his Malcolm X books—ever drawn to new and expanding markets—quickly discovered).

And just as the color line was being challenged by the civil rights movement, so did the books, pamphlets, forum talks, and articles that Breitman produced cross the color line and connect with the thinking and activity of a significant number of African American activists. Some responded critically, some with suspicion and hostility, but many considered what he had to offer thoughtfully, reflectively, and with appreciation for his integrity, insights, and genuine contributions.

Over the years there have been many members of left-wing groups who, having genuine intellectual contributions to make, have become prominent in the larger culture while moving away from the seeming restrictiveness of organizational discipline and ideological "dogma," joining what Trotsky once termed, with characteristic annoyance, as "the herd of independent minds." One of Breitman's distinctive qualities, however, involved the persistent integration of his creativity with a deep and ongoing commitment to consistent revolutionary organizational work.

From semiretirement in the mid-1950s, Cannon, the grand old man of US Trotskyism, hailed the Detroit SWP branch for its "combination of all-sided activity." In what Frank Lovell later termed "a tribute to George Breitman," Cannon said: "I was overjoyed when I heard the report that our comrades in Detroit, despite their preoccupation with the Square D strike* and the [SWP] election campaign, got a nucleus established at Wayne University."[42]

---

*The Square D strike involved a militant 108-day struggle between the United Electrical, Radio, and Machine Workers of America (UE) and the Square D Company. The company was trying

One of the most important institutions that Breitman initiated in Detroit was the weekly Friday Night Socialist Forum. It was, Evelyn Sell points out, "a primary means of party-building, of educating members and nonmembers, of developing young comrades as speakers, and of creating a center for political and radical activities in the Detroit area." In time, SWP branches throughout the country duplicated this Detroit example—which became a national institution of the SWP, generally labeled the "Militant Forum" or "Militant Labor Forum" in other cities. But some Detroit SWPers felt there was something special about the forums organized under Breitman's leadership. Sell writes:

> From its inception, the Friday Night Socialist Forum invited speakers from a range of organizations. Although most of the topics were political, there were many dealing with art, music, and literature. A humanities professor from Wayne State University not only gave talks about music but brought his portable keyboard and played excerpts to illustrate his points. A comrade who was a relatively well-known sculptor gave a series of talks on art, including taking the whole forum audience to the Detroit Art Institute for a guided lecture tour. The forum devoted a weekend to an exhibit of Daumier prints along with showing of a film on the revolutions of 1848. The Friday Night Socialist Forum had theater nights when we presented portions of the writings and plays of Bertolt Brecht. As George wrote in a letter to me, Brecht was "the creative writer with whom I identify the most closely." He made Brecht fans out of many of us, and this was reflected in the Friday Night Socialist Forum.[43]

The forums would be held at the new SWP headquarters, which combined offices and a modest bookstore with a large meeting room and was dubbed Debs Hall to honor the great labor socialist Eugene V. Debs. Independent radical Dan Georgakas, coauthor of *Detroit: I Do Mind Dying*, frequently attended the Friday Night Socialist Forum, "the only regularly scheduled Left event in the city at that time" (from the late 1950s to the

---

to utilize the fact that the UE had been attacked (and expelled from the CIO in 1949) for being "Communist-dominated" in order to break both the strike and the union. Thousands of workers and local officials from the United Auto Workers—independently of the UAW national leadership—mobilized to support the embattled UE workers with a solidarity and militancy that propelled them to victory. An account of this incident can be found in the classic history by Art Preis, *Labor's Giant Step: Twenty Years of the CIO* (New York: Pathfinder Press, 1972), pp. 502–503.

mid-1960s). The initial presentations "were always followed by often spir-
ited question/answer/statements/debate periods," an intellectually stimulating format that added to its appeal. "Looking over the list of those who
attended various forums, one will find a virtual who's who of the Detroit
Left in the period which immediately followed [from the late 1960s through
the 1970s]," as well as "individuals who became part of the liberal establishment: at least one congressman and several judges, college administrators, union leaders, and city officials." Once the weekly forums became an
SWP institution, Georgakas notes, "over a period of time, in any given location, hundreds of people might attend one or more such forums," and
though most of those attending never joined the Socialist Workers Party,
"the cumulative impact of such forums was considerable."[44]

During this period, Breitman played several important roles.
According to Mandel, he was "one of the few in our movement who have
made a genuine contribution to the development of theory, in his case in
the field of black nationalism, and more generally the nationalism of the
downtrodden and the oppressed everywhere in the world." Beginning in
1956, Breitman also pushed forward the discussion that brought about a
reconciliation among many Fourth Internationalists, culminating in
formal reunification in 1963. Breitman's important role in the reunification of the Fourth International, recalled Frank Lovell, was "little known
to most members of his branch in Detroit at the time."[45]

To most members of the Detroit SWP, however, Breitman did provide
a model of what Sell called "a well-rounded, professional revolutionary,"
who "set an example simply by the way he did things"—specifically, as
someone who was prepared to assume responsibility in all phases of
political life of the branch, including the most "mundane." Sell empha-
sizes: "He took a serious attitude toward every task and assignment,
whether it was functioning as a branch organizer, or bringing a wealth of
ideas to executive committee meetings, or mopping the hall floors as a
member of the headquarters committee."[46]

THE NEW RADICALIZATION

Breitman developed a complex and multifaceted analysis of the radicalization of the 1960s to which it is worth devoting significant attention. He

advanced this in an impressive talk at a Socialist Activists and Educational Conference organized by the Socialist Workers Party in Oberlin, Ohio, in 1970. This presentation—combining profound insights with what turned out to be overly optimistic assumptions and predictions—influenced many young radicals of that turbulent time and helped set the trajectory for the SWP over the rest of the new decade.

"A period of radicalization is one in which large numbers of people, responding to material conditions and alterations in those conditions, change their attitudes about important questions, beliefs, values, customs, relations, arrangements and institutions—social, personal philosophical, political, economic, cultural," Breitman explained. "Things that were previously accepted or taken for granted begin to be questioned or rejected." Far from taking place "all at once," such a radicalization "is the result of a process that has multiple and complex roots and that develops very unevenly." He emphasized that a study of the 1960s radicalization would reveal the striking "unevenness of its development, the ways in which it spread and influenced new sections of the population, the ways in which it leaped ahead in one sphere when it was blocked or stagnated in another."[47]

Breitman also made a distinction between the concept of radicalization and the concept of revolutionization. "When masses of people become revolutionized, you have the major element in a revolutionary or prerevolutionary situation," he noted. "But that is not necessarily the case in a period of radicalization." To say that the United States is experiencing a deep-going radicalization is not the same as saying it has entered a revolutionary situation. Such a situation may develop out of a radicalization. "Radicalization can also be contained, deflected, or dispersed. Much depends on the quality or capacity of the leadership on both sides of the struggle." More than this, a revolutionary moment is of relatively brief duration, whereas a radicalization can unfold over a period of one or two decades. He concluded that the longer duration of a radicalization period allows the revolutionary movement to orient itself, prepare itself, and engage in and learn from struggles, while in a revolutionary situation the opportunity can be seized or lost much more quickly.[48]

Breitman identified three period of mass radicalization in the United States during the twentieth century:

The first came in what can be called the Debsian period, beginning around the time the Socialist Party was organized [1901] and extending at least until the First World War; the second came in the 1930s, and although much of it was overcome by the Second World War, there were still some powerful remnants visible in the big strike wave that followed the war, just before the cold war and its attendant [anti-Communist] witch-hunt took center stage. The third, in which we have the good fortune to be living now, began some time ago . . . and clearly has a considerable lifespan before it.[49]

"Each radicalization is unique, although they all flow from the contradictions of capitalism," he argued. Between one radicalization and the next, society had undergone "modifications that affect the relations between classes and between layers inside the same classes, that affect how people think and what they expect and how they act." Such assertions could be expected from many thoughtful people. Breitman's assertion regarding the third radicalization, however, was provocative: "The present radicalization . . . is the biggest, the deepest, the broadest—and therefore the most threatening to the ruling class and the most promising for revolutionaries."[50]

One striking feature of the new radicalization was that it was taking place in a period of relative prosperity, in the face of a US capitalist power structure that was far from weak. In the mid-1950s such prosperity and power of the dominant institutions were part of a situation in which the Left was in shambles, radical protest marginalized. The situation was now incredibly altered:

What produced the great change between then and now? It is an oversimplification . . . but I don't know any other short statement for it than alienation. This capitalist system, which long ago outlived its historic mission, which is overripe and rotten to the core, has managed to hang on at a frightful price to humanity, but it has not managed to convince growing numbers of people that this is the way life should be. It has alienated, repelled, and angered increasing millions of Americans, who do not yet agree on what should be done but who feel that things cannot, should not, need not continue the way they are.

The capitalist system is still very powerful, but large numbers of people now doubt that it is right. They cannot give you a scientific analysis of its structure, but many of its contradictions are now apparent even to junior high school students. The atom bomb was once the symbol of American imperialism triumphant, but the generation that has been born since the first atom bomb does not believe that it should live under the constant threat of annihilation; its consciousness, its alienation from a system that cannot eradicate that threat, is vastly different, perhaps qualitatively different, from that of preceding generations. More and more people reject the notion that a system which boasts of its affluence and unrivaled productivity cannot solve problems of poverty at home, cannot teach its children how to read, cannot provide decent health care for the sick, cannot let the old survive with a measure of dignity, cannot even keep the air breathable. They are affronted by a system which prates about freedom and justice but denies them to a majority of the population because of race or class or sex.[51]

The new radicalization was rooted, Breitman suggested, in "the technological and social forces that were unleashed" by World War II, as well as by "the world policeman role that Washington assumed, the resurgence of revolutionary nationalism in the colonial world, the promises that were made, and the betrayals that were committed." Central to this development was the rise of the civil rights struggles that began in the 1950s— "resistance and then revolt against the oppression of black people in this country." This was a reality that he underscored: "I don't think anyone will dispute the conclusion that the present black radicalization is bigger, in absolute numbers and proportionally, than anything that occurred in the Debsian or depression period, or that its revolutionary potential is more explosive now than ever before, despite the problems of organization, leadership, and program that have not yet been solved." While many had once felt that this racial minority could never be expected, through its own efforts, to play a decisive, vanguard role in changing society, "the catalytic effect of the black struggle on other oppressed minorities in this country (and in some cases outside this country) is now conceded." Indeed, the struggle had helped to generate and continued to influence deeply the broader radicalization process in society.[52]

"It need hardly be argued in 1970 that the current youth radicalization is the biggest in American history," Breitman observed. "There has never been anything remotely resembling it." Sharpened and propelled by opposition to the Vietnam War, the youth upsurge had culminated in a massive student strike that closed down hundreds of campuses throughout the United States in May 1970. Never in wartime had a mass antiwar movement taken to the streets in growing numbers, sustaining itself year after year, reaching growing numbers in the armed forces. "Another sure sign of how deep the radicalization is going is the development of women's liberation as an independent movement." While this was still a very new development in the summer of 1970, Breitman pointed out that while there had been feminist components of previous radicalizations, now "the women's radicalization begins again in an independent form, which, as we've seen with the black movement, can offer certain advantages and safeguards against being sidetracked." He predicted: "Eventually the women will work out their own forms of organization and operation, as blacks have been doing. When they do, the current radicalization will be at least twice as strong as now."[53]

Breitman pointed to "the nationwide character of this phenomenon. It has reached out of just the big metropolitan centers into the medium-sized cities and even small ones; there's hardly a part of the country now where you can't find radical quarters or clusters or groups." More than this, the radicalization was spreading throughout a variety of social layers—among artists and professionals and intellectuals, among people in prison, among those seeking new forms of cultural and sexual expression. More radical books, Marxist literature, and alternative newspapers and magazines were being produced and read than in the "red decade" of the 1930s.[54]

Of course, both the "red decade" and the "Debsian" radicalization had been marked dramatically by powerful labor upsurges. This seemed to be absent now, but Breitman gave particular stress to a point missed by many at the time—that a significant working-class component was integral to the mass protest movements opposing racism, the Vietnam War, and so on. He argued: "It is idiotic and insulting to think that the worker responds only to economic issues. He can be radicalized in various ways, over various issues, and he is." Breitman developed this point:

> The radicalization of the worker can begin off the job as well as on. It can begin from the fact that the worker is a woman as well as a man; that the worker is black or Chicano or a member of some other oppressed minority as well as white; that the worker is a father or mother whose son can be drafted; that the worker is young as well as

middle-aged or about to retire. If we grasp the fact that the working class is stratified and divided in many ways—the capitalists prefer it that way—then we will be better able to understand how the radicalization will develop among workers and how to intervene more effectively. Those who haven't already learned important lessons from the radicalization of oppressed minorities, youth, and women had better hurry up and learn them, because most of the people involved in these radicalizations are workers or come from working-class families.[55]

Nor was Breitman willing to acknowledge that the level of Marxist political thought was higher in the 1930s than in 1970—"the theoretical level of the radicalization of the 1930s was lower, not higher, than that of the current radicalization. I say that as one who does not think it is very high now." Although he was correct in asserting that "more people have demonstrated in the streets over the war in Vietnam than joined the CIO in the first five years of its existence," he also recognized that the United States still had far to go in regard to a self-conscious and organized radicalization that would embrace the working-class majority in a manner that would open up revolutionary socialist possibilities.[56]

Generalizing that "the political and theoretical level of a period of radicalization will not be any higher than the level of the party or tendency leading the radicalization," Breitman believed that the hegemony of a politically diffuse Socialist Party in the first radicalization, and of a Stalinized Communist Party in the second, had limited what could be accomplished in the earlier periods. Now there was a possibility that the revolutionary socialists of the Socialist Workers Party might have an opportunity to provide leadership. He emphasized: "Ours is the most optimistic tendency in the radical movement, and the most self-confident. This derives from our political analysis, not our personal traits. . . . The development of significant revolutionary cadres, the building of the Marxist party so that it can play the central role in the current radicalization and its aftermath, is more possible now than at any time in American history."[57]

With the benefit of hindsight, we can see that the impressive sweep and insightful qualities of Breitman's analysis were not matched by the accuracy of his forecast. The Socialist Workers Party proved incapable of playing the role that he had hoped it might. One could argue that this is related to the lack of working-class consciousness among the masses of radicalized activists he was talking about, some of whom did become part of the Trotskyist movement. Despite the objectively working-class social origins of many of them, their consciousness had been shaped by the "middle-class" culture of 1950s and early 1960s America. In fact, the reality of working-class life, experience, and organization in 1970 was not the same as it had been in the 1930s and 1940s, and although young activists might absorb the ideas of Marx, Lenin, Trotsky, and Cannon, there was not a simple way to apply them to the new realities. This would create a debilitating crisis within the SWP that Breitman did not antici-pate. The same problem, in one form or another, affected all other left-wing organizations, so that the revolutionary leadership Breitman saw as essential was forthcoming from no quarter. According to Breitman's own analysis, such a situation would mean that the radicalization would finally be "contained, deflected, or dispersed." And so it was.[58]

THE SOCIAL CONTEXT
OF DISAPPOINTED HOPES

Breitman had been one of the foremost representatives, among SWP old-timers, of someone who was open to new developments. In 1974, he had made this statement:

> There has been much change and considerable progress since the founding of the SWP. Much of this we owe to the pioneers [of American Trotskyism], without whom we couldn't have done half of what we did. But we would have perished if we hadn't gone beyond the pioneers, and we have gone beyond them, learning how to sharpen the ideas and improve the practice that they initiated or developed. And this is good because the time is coming when we shall have to storm revolutionary heights that the conditions of their time prevented them from reaching.

One could argue that this was overly optimistic in more than one way. The possibility of "storming the revolutionary heights" seemed closer to many in 1974 than it does in 2005. Worse than that, certain of Breitman's younger comrades ended up "going beyond the pioneers" in ways that appalled him, in fact falling far short of the revolutionary insights, achievements, and integrity represented by earlier generations (including Breitman's own). Despite the superficial continuity of American Trotskyism from the late 1920s through the late 1970s, the new layers of radicalized youth representing the SWP's future were qualitatively different—in historical context, life experience, and consciousness—from the layers shaped by the period of Debs and the IWW and the1930s labor struggles. A fundamental rupture in continuity had occurred in the 1950s. In part thanks to this (often unacknowledged) break in continuity, also in part because of the dramatic economic and cultural changes, the Trotskyism of the younger generation inevitably lacked the qualities that it had in Breitman.[59]

Even so keen a mind as Breitman's seems to have missed some crucial aspects of what was happening, at least initially. A profound sociological and cultural development fatally undermined the labor-radical subculture that had evolved from the post–Civil War period to the 1940s. By the early 1950s there had been a double erosion of the radical working-class base that had provided the decisive context out of which, or in relation to which, the Left in all its varied components had emerged. One aspect of the erosion was the fading out of immigrant radicalism and of the vibrant working-class subcultures that had been so important to labor's left wing since the mid-nineteenth century. The second aspect of this erosion was the fact that working-class struggles led by radicals had helped to make capitalist society a better place to live for many workers and their families, so they came to have much more to lose than the "chains" of capitalist oppression. The dividing line was World War II. As Frank Lovell commented:

> The war changed the world. It changed almost everything about the world that we had known. It changed class relations among people around the world. And of course it left vast destruction and devastation in its wake. But this was the very condition needed for the recovery and expansion of the capitalist system. Capitalism as a world system gained renewed strength from the process of rebuilding.[60]

"A new middle class arose which included a number of young people of working-class background," sociologist John C. Leggett has written, noting that many prospering working people had moved out of traditional working-class communities to become home owners in the suburbs. "The class struggle abated with the end of the post–World War II strikes, although repeated flare-ups between management and workers occurred during and after the Korean War." An important aspect of the new labor-management harmony involved "governmental boards and labor union unions [that] often helped minimize class conflict as unions grew more friendly toward companies which were willing to bargain with, and make major concessions to, labor organizations." He added that "even working-class minority groups [for example, some African Americans] improved their standard of living and sent sons and daughters into the middle class." A radical black autoworker named James Boggs asserted in 1963 that "today the working class is so dispersed and transformed by the very nature of the changes in production that it is almost impossible to select out any single bloc of workers as a working class in the old sense." By "the old sense" he meant the kind of class-consciousness that had made possible the "red decade" of the 1930s. "The working class is growing, as Marx predicted, but it is not the old working class which the radicals persist in believing will create the revolution and establish control over production. That old working class is the vanishing herd"[61]

From the 1950s through the 1970s there was, as Stanley Aronowitz has put it, a tendency "toward the replacement of all the traditional forms of proletarian culture and everyday life—which gave working-class communities their coherence and provided the underpinnings for the traditional forms of proletarian consciousness—with a new, manipulated consumer culture which for conveniences' sake we can call mass culture." Despite the flattening and fragmentation of much that had sustained the old radical working-class consciousness, it is hardly the case that workers' minds simply turned to mush or that they simply believed whatever their bosses or televisions told them. The distinctive philosophy of many disaffected workers, one participant-observer commented, was not any of the traditional left-wing ideologies, however, but cynicism: "Cynicism is a variant of anarchism—anarchism without ideals or ultimate illusions, apathetic, easygoing instead of strenuous, nonsectarian, hence more broadly appealing and far more suitable to the conditions and mentality of contemporary workers than the older tradition of militant idealism and self-sacrifice."[62]

The young activists of the 1960s and early 1970s emerged from an experience qualitatively different from that of earlier generations in the

Trotskyist movement. While they may have been attracted to and inspired by what Trotsky and Cannon and Breitman had to say, the young activists' understanding of these things was necessarily shaped by their own quite different context and experience. "I sometimes wonder," Cannon mused in his last year (1974), "whether our movement today, which is predominantly young, fully realizes where the power lies in this country. The power is in the working class." Cannon was aware, obviously, that the new cadres understood this on a theoretical level, but a "full realization"—one that is part of the very fiber of your being—comes from life, and the life experience of the young Trotskyists had been profoundly different from that of the Trotskyist veterans.[63]

While coming from working-class backgrounds, the young radicals of the 1960s were influenced by a consumer culture and a sense of "upward mobility" unknown to previous generations. A majority of those in the working class as a whole identified themselves as "middle class" rather than "working class." Many of the young activists were, for all practical purposes, déclassé—going through an extended period supported by their parents or by scholarships and financial loans as they went to college. Those who dropped out of college to do political work may have supported themselves through various jobs, but in many cases these jobs were peripheral to their "real" lives. Their "real" lives were immersed in a particular political subculture of the Young Socialist Alliance and Socialist Workers Party that—being composed of "students, petty-bourgeois radicals, a few older workers facing retirement, and [YSA and SWP] functionaries," as Frank Lovell later put it—had little in common with the actual daily lives of US working people.[64]

Within the consciousness of this upwardly mobile "middle class" layer of 1960s radicals—along with considerable idealism, creativity, and commitment—there were powerful strains of elitism, arrogance, and superficiality. Such strains combined with the activists' own lack of connection with working-class life, so important to the earlier movement, and distorted both theory and practice even as the SWP and YSA seemed to be moving on from one success to another. The organization for which Breitman helped provide leadership in the 1960s would make significant contributions in opposing the Vietnam War, combating racism, struggling for women's liberation, and spreading socialist ideas, but it would ultimately prove incapable of playing the role that he had envisioned for it.

Moreover, the revolutionary theory and principles to which Breitman and others of his generation had committed their lives would prove to be in contradiction to the quite different experience and consciousness of so many younger comrades. This set the stage for the crisis and fragmentation of the party to which he had devoted himself for so many years.

QUALITIES OF CHARACTER AND FINAL CONFLICTS

Breitman suffered from rheumatoid arthritis, which became increasingly severe as time went on. "One of the effects of George's arthritis was that his bones were softened by the medications he had to take," Paul Siegel recalled about the later development of the affliction. "He had to be careful every moment not to bump against anything lest he break a bone." Pierre Broué commented on "the ebbs and flows of his sickness," adding: "He only spoke to me when he had something to say, told me not to shake his hand roughly, no jovial backslapping, either; I might have broken his bones." He added that Breitman "never complained; he only mentioned that sometimes he could not do all that he wanted to." David Herreshoff remarked: "I am not personally acquainted with a comparable example of prolonged devotion to duty in the face of persistent, crippling disease." Siegel noted that "there was not an ounce of self-pity in his makeup—but . . . a kind of wry awareness of the trick fate had played upon him." He continued to work unremittingly despite the pain that was a daily part of his life.[65]

And there were ulcers. And then there was cancer—and finally the heart attack that brought his life to an end in 1986. But his struggles with illness lasted for decades, and he refused to allow them to deflect him from the efforts to which he had devoted his life.

In 1967 Breitman agreed to return to the SWP national headquarters in New York. There had been some additional splits, resulting in the formation of three rival groups, beginning with the semi-Maoist Workers World Party in the late 1950s. By the mid-1960s there was the crystallization of the Workers League and Spartacist League, both opposing the reunification of the Fourth International, the SWP's support of the Cuban Revolution, its embrace of black nationalism, and other perceived sins— many of them connected with Breitman's influence. Whether in spite of these splits or because of them, the SWP was expanding significantly in size and influence, becoming a central force in the movement to end the US war in Vietnam, and impacting significantly among other currents within the general radicalization of the 1960s as well.[66] Michael Smith offers a portrait of Breitman in the early 1970s:

> George was then an editor of Pathfinder Press, where I worked for the next five years. There were three editors, the three Georges: George Novack, George Weissman, and George Breitman. What a magnificent publishing project they led the party on in those years. What a splendid contribution to international socialist culture they made. It was the golden age of Pathfinder. We were the most prolific publisher of pamphlets outside the government, but ours were of topical political concern, and ours were read. Dozens of our pamphlet titles got distributed throughout the movement, tens of thousands were put into the hands of activists in the '60s and '70s. Some years we published up to thirty books, that is, over two a month. . . .
>
> I remember George at Pathfinder meetings. He sat in his own chair, a straightback chair to which someone had welded a headrest. He was always, always in pain. Terrible arthritic pain. He shielded us from the agony, though sometimes he would wince, and we would know the resolve and courage and continual willpower it takes to fight pain and still think clearly. Think clearly, be reliable, and be fastidious in your work. That's what we learned from George about our standards. His own personal standards became the yardstick for Pathfinder.[67]

Les Evans, at that time the capable editor of the SWP political magazine *International Socialist Review*, reports a caution and complaint that Breitman offered regarding a growing tendency among SWPers who edited the writing of others—that [in Breitman's words] "most of our editors in recent years (perhaps more than recent years) confuse their responsibilities and tend to overedit—to edit copy so that it says what *they* would say if they had written it, and even to say it in the way *they* would say it." The result was to make "so much of our writing . . . so flat, so uniform, and so interchangeable that if you shifted bylines around nobody could tell the difference."[68] The problem was not simply one of aesthetics but of politics—a growing tendency toward homogeneity, diluting individuality, discouraging creativity, blunting critical-mindedness.

Although Breitman had initially felt considerable optimism and confidence in regard to the SWP's rising new leadership layer, he was concerned about what he perceived as a tendency toward overcentralization in the development of national leadership. He sought to encourage a development away from this tendency in an essay written after the 1974 death of James P. Cannon. Toward the end of the essay he focused on Cannon's approach toward the selection of national leadership at SWP national conventions:

> Its essence was that the National Committee slate recommended to the convention should be the product of the delegates from the branches themselves rather than the choices of the outgoing national or Political Committees or of any of the central leaders, no matter how prestigious. Being delegates, too, regular or fraternal, the leaders of the outgoing committees had the formal right to try to influence the selection of the new committee, but the implication of Jim's proposal was that the interests of the party would be best served, and the most representative and authoritative committee would be elected, if they refrained from exercising this formal right.[69]

Overcentralization was disturbing enough while the SWP held aloft the Trotskyist banner and played an increasingly important role in the youth radicalization and mass protest of movements of the 1960s and early 1970s, but a leadership transition replaced the authority of Farrell Dobbs with that of an ambitious and aggressive younger leader named Jack Barnes. Barnes developed a new leadership team that increasingly became dominant, and new tensions soon developed within the party. With the end of the Vietnam War and rising challenges and expectations related to a slow radicalization of the working class, the new leaders made unrealistic projections, made mistakes, and increasingly fostered the notion that to be critical of the new leadership was to be "antiparty." And increasingly, after 1979, the new leadership began to doubt the old Trotskyism. It soon became convinced that the Cuban Revolution under Fidel Castro represented—through the spread of revolution through Central America and the Caribbean—the wave of the future.

Breitman was certainly not in tune with the new trend being fostered by the Barnes leadership. "He was somewhat dour and taciturn, speaking infrequently at Political Committee meetings," remembered Tim Wohlforth of the mid- to late-1970s.

> He had a cot in the room where the meetings were held and had to lie down from time to time because of his physical condition. This made George's intervention on Cuba all the more dramatic. In a quiet voice he simply asked that the question be placed on the agenda. When nothing happened over a period of weeks, he repeated his request. Finally he simply stated his political position on the matter. . . . Breitman stated that he believed Cuba had changed since the party had last pronounced upon it in the 1960s and that our position needed to be discussed again. He tended toward the view that it was now a deformed workers' state.[70]

This view was increasingly unacceptable to the now-dominant group led by Barnes. "It is a strong human tendency to go along with the authorities of whatever group one is loyal to," Les Evans reflects. "There is a deep and powerful tendency to conformity and to rationalizing even the most ridiculous pronouncements of leaders in order to avoid conflict and criticism." But while "the great majority of the members of the Socialist Workers Party went along with the turn toward authoritarianism of the Barnes leadership," Breitman was "too stiff-necked for that." Or as Alan Wald put it, "He had never made the mistake of confusing loyalty to ideas with loyalty to charismatic personalities and cozy institutions." Another participant recalled that in 1979 "George offered critical-minded written contributions which challenged some of the enthusiasms [of the Barnes leadership], and the word among the fashion-minded was that although Breitman used to be a good revolutionary, he was 'slipping.'"[71]

Far worse than insulting gossip were cynical deceptions and maneuvers by the Barnes leadership to cover up what would soon be an open and explicit junking of Trotskyism for Castroism, while at the same time tightening so-called Leninist norms of organization to choke off democratic discussion. And there was a conscious preparation to initiate mass expulsions of real and potential dissidents. In the face of this tyranny, and given the reluctance of a majority of SWP members to question the new leadership, the oppositional currents led by Breitman and others were doomed. There were several waves of expulsions (Breitman himself was expelled in 1984), accompanied by the falling away of many others who—while not prepared to challenge the ensconced SWP leadership—could not overcome a growing demoralization generated by the destructive turn of events.[72]

In the wake of the expulsions, Breitman was central in establishing the Fourth Internationalist Tendency.* This modest group sought to unify US supporters of the Fourth International while at the same time creatively applying the revolutionary Marxist perspectives of American Trotskyism to contemporary realities and struggles. "Although our expulsion from the Socialist Workers Party was a terrible negation of everything we had tried to build," his wife, Dorothea, wrote after his death in 1986, "it gave him an opportunity to again, as he had at the beginning of his political career, become an organizer." Unlike some of those who went through this experience, he was not inclined to turn away from his fundamental political commitments. "My idea is not that we're going to go back to the beginning of the Marxist movement and try to find out what is wrong with Marxism in order to discover what Barnes did," he argued. "And it's not my idea that we should go back to Lenin and to Leninism in order to find out what's wrong with Barnesism. I am very satisfied with Marxism and Leninism and with the American version of that, which came to get the name of 'Cannonism' in our movement. . . . We have to say that Barnesism is a negation of 'Cannonism,' not its continuation."[73]

All the while, he sought to transcend the effects of his illnesses. The tracks of this struggle can be found in his voluminous correspondence. "I should have written right away but I was very tired," he apologized at the beginning of one letter. Another began: "I have been sick most of the time since my last letter. Now I am having trouble with my right artificial hip and right artificial knee, which make it painful to stand on, or to sit down." One letter, a month before his death, begins: "I've had a lot of pain in the last month, making it difficult to sit or walk for long, so I'm largely confined to bed, where I can't read or type for long. Your last two

---

*This group, with a membership ranging from approximately thirty to seventy members, functioned from 1984 until 1991. Its members produced a rather impressive monthly magazine (*Bulletin in Defense of Marxism*, later renamed *Labor Standard*), a number of pamphlets, and a few books, and they also engaged—considering their numbers—in an impressive amount of political activity. Once it became painfully clear that the goal of unifying the fragments of the SWP would not be achieved, the group formally dissolved, its members going in somewhat different directions, although remaining active on the Left.

letters raise many points and I may not be able to answer or comment on all of them, but I'll feel better if I can reduce the number of unanswered points, while taking up a few of my own." Two days before his death, he dictated three letters from his hospital bed.[74]

A younger veteran and scholar of American Trotskyism who some-times disagreed sharply with Breitman's political judgments was Alan Wald, who nonetheless was moved to write that "in his historical research, I think, George lived closer to the world of fact than anyone else I had ever met," pointing to his "uncompromising interrogation of all empirical data" and to the fact that "no one was exempt from this interro-gation, including Trotsky and James P. Cannon. George possessed one of the most critical intelligences I think I have ever known." There was an essential integrity in Breitman's approach to exploring the history of US and global Trotskyism, going "far beyond immediate functional pur-poses; his laborious research was not undertaken in the service of proving a political line, smashing a factional opponent, or establishing certain cre-dentials for himself." In fact, Wald suggested, "George's passion for his-tory had a sort of aesthetic dimension to it. Like a novelist in the realist and naturalist tradition, who is driven to reconstruct the authentic life experience of his or her times, George was engaged in a struggle to recon-struct the political world of Trotskyism over the past five decades."[75]

Of course Breitman was concerned with more than reconstructing the history of Trotskyism. "George was obviously a very sick person," remarked Charlie van Gelderen (an octogenarian veteran of South African and British Trotskyism), recalling a 1983 visit, "but his mind was as active and creative as ever and his energies were entirely devoted to the movement which he had served with such dedication for half a century." Among the younger working-class activists Breitman inspired was Dave Riehle, who wrote that "George was an unforgettable example to all of us of how to wring every positive drop of productivity and meaning out of life," someone who "will be seen as one of those rare people who were indispensable to maintaining the thread of continuity of authentic Marxism." Another labor activist, Bill Onasch, added that "he made sure there was a cadre in place to continue the fight for revolutionary Marxism that he devoted his life to." Bob Fink, a Canadian writer and artist who had known Breitman in Detroit, recalled: "George was a socialist with a heart and soul . . . and not just a slogan socialist or a 'theoretical' socialist. . . . The word 'comrade' had all its meaning in the way I saw George relate to me and to many others. He had an instinct for social and personal justice that went beyond any theory or rationalizations for theory as we see in the SWP today. That heart and soul was based on a wide life's experience, and that's the source of all theory anyway."[76]

Steve Bloom, a younger comrade who worked closely with Breitman from 1981 to 1986, commented: "One quality that particularly impressed me was simply his willingness to respond 'I don't know' when someone asked a question on a subject about which he was ignorant." Breitman had little patience for the notion that because someone is a leader "he was somehow obliged to know everything." Bloom added that "George was capable of great anger. That, too, is a useful trait for revolutionaries when directed at the proper target." Exploitation, oppression, racism, sexism—such things as these made him deeply angry. "But he was capable of expressing anger at his comrades or coworkers as well, when he perceived some slackness, some weakness, some stupidity on their part." And he got "supremely angry" over the policies of the Barnes leadership of the SWP, for the betrayal of a trust and "for the way it has chosen to treat an entire generation of comrades who spent decades working to build the movement."[77]

What Bloom called Breitman's "broad and sweeping historic vision" was blended with remarkably fine personal characteristics that drew people to him. "In spite of the tremendous authority he had in our eyes, he treated us as equals in every way," Naomi Allen commented. "He could be withering in his sarcasm and reproof when he faced bureaucratic obstacles, incompetence, or indifference; but given goodwill and an honest effort, he treated the humblest correspondent and the youngest, most inexperienced member with genuine respect."[78] Melissa Singler put it this way:

In our lives we meet a number of special people, but George Breitman was indeed rare. Once I hiked down into Bryce Canyon and stood surrounded by cliffs, trees, sun, and sky, and at that precise moment three deer bounded by and I thought "how lucky can you get." Well, that's how I've always thought about George, "How lucky can you get to have known such a comrade." His inexhaustible energy and spirit in the face of pain, his richness of thought offered without ego, his humor made George an extraordinary person.[79]

There is much of this extraordinary person in the essays in this volume, and we are indeed lucky now to have them more generally available. They are part of his legacy to us, and they will challenge and contribute to the thinking of a broad range of readers—scholars and activists and others. They will especially resonate among those who are concerned with the same issues, opposed to the same injustices, and inspired by the same ideas and values that animated George Breitman.

NOTES

1. *New York Times*, April 24, 1986. Placing Trotskyism in the larger context of the US Left is facilitated by reference to *Encyclopedia of the American Left*, ed. Mari Jo Buhle, Paul Buhle, and Dan Georgakas (Urbana: University of Illinois Press, 1992). Actually, Breitman preferred such terms as "socialist" or "revolutionary socialist" as a self-description, explaining: "On the whole, the label 'Trotskyist' is a handicap, not an asset. To new people it gives the impression that we are some kind of cult, creating unnecessary obstacles to reaching them with our program, especially rebellious youth who are suspicious of cults." He added: "This was not a term we chose or sought. Trotsky never used it, except within quotation marks to indicate it was not his designation for our movement. Moreover, we ourselves generally did not use it during his lifetime" (Breitman, "Two Proposals," 1965 statement in author's possession). Allen's comment is from *A Tribute to George Breitman: Writer, Organizer, Revolutionary*, ed. Naomi Allen and Sarah Lovell (New York: Fourth Internationalist Tendency, 1987), p. 32.

2. Allen and Lovell, *A Tribute to George Breitman*, pp. 30–31, 125, 145.

3. Ibid., pp. 33, 89, 90, 92.

4. Karl Marx, "Toward the Critique of Hegel's Philosophy of Law: Introduction," in *Writings of the Young Marx on Philosophy and Society*, ed. Loyd D. Easton and Kurt H. Guddat (Garden City, NY: Anchor Books, 1967), pp. 257–58; Karl Marx and Frederick Engels, "Manifesto of the Communist Party," in *From Marx to Gramsci: A Reader in Revolutionary Marxist Politics*, ed. Paul Le Blanc (Amherst, NY: Humanity Books, 1996), pp. 136, 143, 144.

5. Lenin's comment on "tribune of the people," from *What Is to Be Done?* (1902), is provided in Paul Le Blanc, *Lenin and the Revolutionary Party* (Amherst, NY: Humanity Books, 1993), p. 67. His "whole their lives" comment is from the 1900 article "The Urgent Tasks of Our Movement," reprinted in Le Blanc, *From Marx to Gramsci*, pp. 201–205. Trotsky's comment on socialism is from a 1940 interview, "World Situation and Perspectives," in *Writings of Leon*

Trotsky (1939–40), ed. Naomi Allen and George Breitman (New York: Pathfinder Press, 1973), pp. 155–56.

6. "Questions for Communists," in *Writings of Leon Trotsky (1932)*, ed. George Breitman and Sarah Lovell (New York: Pathfinder Press, 1973), p. 326; Leon Trotsky, "The New Course," in *The Challenge of the Left Opposition (1923–25)*, ed. Naomi Allen (New York: Pathfinder Press, 1975), p. 127.

7. Allen and Lovell, *A Tribute to George Breitman*, pp. 70–71.

8. Steve Bloom to author, June 19, 2002. One might question whether "the *entire* Trotskyist movement" was able to accept Breitman's analyses of black nationalism and the youth radicalization of the 1960s, but there is no question about their being both original and influential.

9. Allen and Lovell, *A Tribute to George Breitman*, p. 157.

10. Breitman, "Answers to Questions," in *The Founding of the Socialist Workers Party: Minutes and Resolutions (1938–1939)*, ed. George Breitman (New York: Monad Press/Pathfinder Press, 1982), p. 18. Additional information on the history of US Trotskyism can be found in James P. Cannon, *History of American Trotskyism, Report of a Participant* (New York: Pathfinder Press, 1972); Robert J. Alexander, *International Trotskyism, 1929–1985: A Documented Analysis of the Movement* (Durham, NC: Duke University Press, 1991), pp. 461–952; George Breitman, Paul Le Blanc, and Alan Wald, *Trotskyism in the United States: Historical Essays and Reconsiderations* (Amherst, NY: Humanity Books, 1996). The broader context of US labor history is summarized in Paul Le Blanc, *A Short History of the U.S. Working Class: From Colonial Times to the Twenty-first Century* (Amherst, NY: Humanity Books, 1999).

11. Allen and Lovell, *A Tribute to George Breitman*, p. 19.

12. Ibid., pp. 15, 16.

13. Les Evans, ed., *Cannon as We Knew Him: By Thirty-three Comrades, Friends, and Relatives* (New York: Pathfinder Press, 1976), pp. 112, 125. An outstanding study of Cannon's rich experience from the early days of Debsian Socialism and the IWW through the first ten years of American Communism, down to the birth of US Trotskyism can be found in Bryan Palmer, *James P. Cannon and the Origins of the American Revolutionary Left: Labor Radicalism and the Uneasy Formative Years of United States Communism, 1890–1928* (Urbana: University of Illinois Press, forthcoming).

14. Allen and Lovell, *A Tribute to George Breitman*, p. 121.

15. Breitman, "Answers to Questions," p. 22.

16. Ibid., pp. 18, 27.

17. The Smith Act, passed in 1940, made it a crime to advocate the overthrow of the US government, and on the eve of US entry into World War II, it

was used against the Socialist Workers Party. The SWP was targeted, in part, for its charges of imperialist aims motivating US foreign policy. Eighteen prominent Trotskyists, headed by Cannon, were arrested in 1941, put on trial in 1943, and sent to prison for eighteen-month sentences in 1944–45. See Paul Le Blanc, "Smith Act Trial, 1943," in Buhle, Buhle, and Georgakas, *Encyclopedia of the American Left*, p. 706.

18. Allen and Lovell, *A Tribute to George Breitman*, pp. 38, 105.

19. Evans, *Cannon as We Knew Him*, p. 118.

20. Ibid., pp. 113, 116, 119, 120.

21. Ibid., 127.

22. Allen and Lovell, *A Tribute to George Breitman*, pp. 47–48, 106.

23. James P. Cannon, *Socialism on Trial* (New York: Pathfinder Press, 1973), pp. 48–52.

24. Allen and Lovell, *A Tribute to George Breitman*, p. 16.

25. Ibid., p. 71; Hedda Garza, "'Bring the Boys Home' Movement," in Buhle, Buhle, and Georgakas, *Encyclopedia of the American Left*, pp. 107–108; Alexander, *International Trotskyism, 1929–1985*, p. 305. On Morris Lewit, see Paul Le Blanc and Michael Steven Smith, "Morris Lewit, Pioneer Leader of American Trotskyism (1903–1998)," in *Revolutionary Labor Socialist: The Life, Ideas, and Comrades of Frank Lovell*, ed. Paul Le Blanc and Thomas Barrett (Union City, NJ: Smyrna Press, 2000), pp. 272–94.

26. On Weissman, see Editorial Board, "George Lavan Weissman (1916–85): 49 Years in the Struggle for Socialism," *Bulletin in Defense of Marxism* (May 1985): 15–16.

27. Allen and Lovell, *A Tribute to George Breitman*, p. 107. On Hansen, see George Novack, "Joseph Hansen, 1910–1979: Veteran Leader of Fourth International and SWP," *Intercontinental Press*, January 29, 1979, pp. 51–55; Susan Wald, "550 Attend U.S. Memorial Meeting for Joseph Hansen," *Intercontinental Press*, February 12, 1979, pp. 100–101.

28. Breitman's absorption of James's work is evident in George Breitman, ed., *Leon Trotsky on Black Nationalism and Self-Determination* (New York: Merit Publishers, 1967). More on James's Trotskyist years can be found in Scott McLemee and Paul Le Blanc, eds., *C. L. R. James and Revolutionary Marxism: Selected Writings (1939–1949)* (Amherst, NY: Humanity Books, 1993). Breitman's comment on Dunayevskaya's *Militant* contributions is quoted in Raya Dunayevskaya, "The Battle of Ideas: Philosophic-Theoretic Points of Departure as Political Tendencies Respond to the Objective Situation," in *The Power of Negativity: Selected Writings on the Dialectic in Hegel and Marx*, ed. Peter Hudis and Kevin B. Anderson (Lanham, MD: Lexington Books, 2002), p. 247.

29. Pierre Frank, *The Fourth International: The Long March of the Trotsky-ists* (London: Ink Links, 1977), p. 90.

30. James P. Cannon, *Speeches to the Party: The Revolutionary Perspective and the Revolutionary Party* (New York: Pathfinder Press, 1973), pp. 335, 347; Frank, *The Fourth International*, p. 93. The critique by Cochran and others can be found on pages 338–411 of the *Speeches*, with the remainder of the volume consisting of Cannon's countercritique. More on the Cochran group and its sub-sequent evolution can be found on a Web site devoted to it: http://marxists.org/history/etol/newspape/amersocialist/index.htm.

31. Allen and Lovell, *A Tribute to George Breitman*, p. 116. Breitman's cor-respondence with Ernest Mandel (Germain), vainly seeking "a meeting of minds," and with interesting commentary from Cannon, can be found in Fred Feldman, ed., *Towards a History of the Fouth International, Part 3: Struggle in the Fourth International: International Committee Documents, 1951–1954*, vol. 4 (New York: Pathfinder Press, 1974), pp. 196–220.

32. Tim Wohlforth, *The Prophet's Children: Travels on the American Left* (Amherst, NY: Humanity Books, 1994), p. 91.

33. Lewit quoted in Le Blanc and Smith, "Morris Lewit, Pioneer Leader of American Trotskyism (1903–1998)," p. 290. On the other hand, it is well worth examining Dobbs's invaluable four-volume series on the central involvement of Trotskyists in the Teamsters union: *Teamster Rebellion*, *Teamster Power*, *Team-ster Politics*, and *Teamster Bureaucracy* (New York: Monad Press/Pathfinder Press, 1972–77). These indicate some of the qualities that drew him into the top leadership of the SWP. Widely respected writer and translator George Shriver (in a May 13, 2002, communication) remembers Dobbs as "a very capable presiden-tial candidate from 1948 through the 1960 election," adding: "Farrell certainly influenced and helped educate me as a radical student at Harvard when he came through on his 1960 presidential campaign tour." Shriver recounts that "this was also true when I was working as a leader of the YSA in New York in 1962 and worked at 116 University Place [SWP national headquarters for many years], on the *Militant* staff, in 1963–64." Emphasizing the notion that the SWP leadership was a collective entity in which different strengths and weaknesses balanced each other, he concludes: "There was a team—Dobbs, Kerry, Hansen, Novack, Weissman, Breitman, Lovell, Ed Shaw, Fred Halstead, Dick Garza—each of them had strengths; and each contributed, in my experience, to the task of edu-cating and training a younger generation."

34. Wohlforth, *The Prophet's Children*, p. 83.

35. On Frank and Sarah Lovell, see Le Blanc and Barrett, *Revolutionary Labor Socialist*, pp. 12–96, 247–62.

36. Allen and Lovell, *A Tribute to George Breitman*, p. 22.

37. Wohlforth, *The Prophet's Children*, p. 271; Allen and Lovell, *A Tribute to George Breitman*, p. 137.

38. Allen and Lovell, *A Tribute to George Breitman*, pp. 22–23.

39. Ibid., p. 139; Wohlforth, *The Prophet's Children*, p. 111.

40. Allen and Lovell, *A Tribute to George Breitman*, p. 23.

41. Paul Lee, "Contributions of George Breitman," *Labor Standard*, 2002, http://www.laborstandard.org/Paul_Lee_on_MX/contributions_of_george _breitman.html.

42. Allen and Lovell, *A Tribute to George Breitman*, p. 50.

43. Ibid., p. 21.

44. Dan Georgakas, introduction to Michael Steven Smith, *Notebook of a Sixties Lawyer* (Brooklyn, NY: Smyrna Press, 1992), pp. xv–xvi.

45. Allen and Lovell, *A Tribute to George Breitman*, pp. 49, 71. See, for example, a letter from Breitman to SWP Political Committee, May 19, 1956, urging that "a review of the present situation be made, and consideration be given to adopting a more positive attitude toward continuing international discussion up to and including the possibility of a reunification congress," in *How Healy and Pablo Blocked Reunification (Documents, 1956–58)*, ed. Tim Wohlforth, vol. 3 of *The Struggle to Reunify the Fourth International (1954–63)* (New York: Pathfinder Press, 1978), p. 7.

46. Allen and Lovell, *A Tribute to George Breitman*, p. 20.

47. George Breitman, "The Current Radicalization Compared with Those of the Past," in *Towards an American Socialist Revolution: A Strategy for the 1970s*, ed. Jack Barnes et al. (New York: Pathfinder Press, 1970), pp. 83–84.

48. Ibid., p. 84.

49. Ibid., p. 85.

50. Ibid., p. 83.

51. Ibid., p. 88.

52. Ibid., pp. 88, 89, 90.

53. Ibid., pp. 91, 92, 93, 94.

54. Ibid., pp. 94, 95.

55. Ibid., p. 101.

56. Ibid., p. 102.

57. Ibid., pp. 102, 104, 105.

58. These issues were perceptively analyzed by Breitman's close friend and comrade Frank Lovell, in "The Socialist Purpose: To Educate the Working-Class," "The Cataclysm: World War II and the History of American Trotskyism," and "Toward and Understanding of Working Class Radicalization," in Le Blanc

and Barrett, *Revolutionary Labor Socialist*, pp. 127–61, 175–81. My own analysis, building on this, can be found in Breitman, Le Blanc, and Wald, *Trotskyism in the United States*, pp. 3–87, 161–233.

59. The Breitman quote and subsequent paragraph are drawn from my introduction in Breitman, Le Blanc, and Wald, *Trotskyism in the United States*, pp. xi–xii.

60. Lovell, "The Socialist Purpose," in Le Blanc and Barrett, *Revolutionary Labor Socialist*, p. 133.

61. John C. Leggett, *Class, Race, and Labor: Working-Class Consciousness in Detroit* (New York: Oxford University Press, 1968), pp. 52, 53; James Boggs, "The American Revolution: Pages from a Negro Worker's Notebook," *Monthly Review* (July–August 1963): 15, 16.

62. Stanley Aronowtiz, *False Promises: The Shaping of Working Class Consciousness* (New York: McGraw-Hill, 1973), p. 95; Donald Clark Hodges, "Cynicism in the Labor Movement," in *American Society, Inc.*, ed. Maurice Zeitlin (Chicago: Markham, 1970), p. 446.

63. *James P. Cannon, A Political Tribute, Including Five Interviews from the Last Year of His Life* (New York: Pathfinder Press, 1974), p. 34; this paragraph draws from Le Blanc, "Trotskyism in the United States: The First Fifty Years," in Breitman, Le Blanc, and Wald, *Trotskyism in the United States*, p. 69.

64. This is drawn from my essay "Leninism in the United States and the Decline of American Trotskyism," in Breitman, Le Blanc, and Wald, *Trotskyism in the United States*, pp. 192–94.

65. Allen and Lovell, *A Tribute to George Breitman*, pp. 39–40, 116.

66. On the SWP and the antiwar movement, see Fred Halstead, *Out Now! A Participant's Account of the American Movement against the Vietnam War* (New York: Monad Press/Pathfinder Press, 1978) and Nancy Zaroulis and Gerald Sullivan, *Who Spoke Up? American Protest against the War in Vietnam, 1963–1975* (New York: Holt, Rinehart and Winston, 1984). The general growth and dynamism of the SWP in this period is captured in Walter Schneir and Miriam Schneir, "The Socialist Workers Party: Square Target of the FBI," *Nation,* September 25, 1976, and in Smith, *Notebook of a Sixties Lawyer*, pp. 24–46. An excellent new source can be found in Barry Sheppard, *The Sixties*, vol. 1 of *The Party: A Political Memoir of the Socialist Workers Party, 1960–1988* (Melbourne, Australia: Resistance Books, 2005), available from Haymarket Books, www.haymarketbooks.com.

67. Smith, *Notebook of a Sixties Lawyer*, pp. 139–40.

68. Allen and Lovell, *A Tribute to George Breitman*, p. 108.

69. Evans, *Cannon as We Knew Him*, p. 127.

70. Wohlforth, *The Prophet's Children*, pp. 271–72.

71. Allen and Lovell, *A Tribute to George Breitman*, pp. 43, 53, 109.

72. A thorough documentation of these developments (328 pages and 412 pages, respectively) can be found in Sarah Lovell, ed., *The Struggle inside the Socialist Workers Party, 1979–1983* (New York: Fourth Internationalist Tendency, 1992) and Paul Le Blanc, ed., *Revolutionary Principles and Working-Class Democracy* (New York: Fourth Internationalist Tendency, 1992).

73. Breitman, Le Blanc, and Wald, *Trotskyism in the United States*, pp. 200–201.

74. Correspondence to author, February 21, February 27, and March 17, 1986; Allen and Lovell, *A Tribute to George Breitman*, p. 154.

75. Allen and Lovell, *A Tribute to George Breitman*, pp. 42, 44, 45.

76. Ibid., pp. 79, 91, 126, 127.

77. Ibid., pp. 57, 58.

78. Ibid., pp. 37, 61. Allen added: "He taught me to have confidence in my own ideas and to have the strength to fight for them." There were many who benefited from the kind of supportiveness she describes. George was responsible for some of my own early writing, particularly *Permanent Revolution in Nicaragua* (New York: Fourth Internationalist Tendency, 1984) and *Lenin and the Revolutionary Party* (Amherst, NY: Humanity Books, 1993). After expressing (in a letter of February 27, 1984) "admiration and enthusiasm" for the latter, he offered some criticism of its final chapters because they failed to deal sufficiently with struggles against Stalinism that resulted in the destruction of many of the revolution's finest—"hundreds of thousands died because they believed in the Leninist party." But he concluded: "It was a lot of hard work, but you should feel glad that you were able to do it and to do it so well." The critical thought and encouragement reflected here contributed significantly to my growth.

79. Allen and Lovell, *A Tribute to George Breitman*, p. 138.

BOOKS, PAMPHLETS, AND OTHER WRITINGS

WRITINGS BY GEORGE BREITMAN REPRINTED IN THIS VOLUME

Breitman, George

1936   *The Trenton Siege by the Army of Unoccupation*, Workers Alliance of America

1943   *Wartime Crimes of Big Business*, New York: Pioneer Publishers

1954   "Anti-Negro Prejudice: When It Began and When It Will End," *Fourth International*, Spring

1959   *Should Progressives Work in the Democratic Party?* Detroit: Friday Night Socialist Forum, June

1964   "How a Minority Can Change Society," *International Socialist Review*, Spring

1964   "Marxism and the Negro Struggle," *Militant* (in five parts) August and September

1964   "Malcolm X: The Man and His Ideas," *Militant*, March 22 and 29

1968   *The National Question and the Black Liberation Struggle in the United States*, New York: Merit Publishers

1969   "Is It Wrong for Revolutionaries to Fight for Reforms?" *Militant*, February 28

1975   "The Liberating Influence of the Transitional Program," *Socialist Workers Party Discussion Bulletin*, May

1979   "The Rocky Road to the Fourth International, 1933–38," *Education for Socialists Bulletin*

OTHER WRITINGS BY GEORGE BREITMAN

Pamphlets

The Workers Alliance vs. Mr. Mudd and the F.A.C., 1937
Workers Alliance N.J. Resolutions, 1937
The Fight against Hagueism, 1938
New Jersey in the 1940 Elections, Newark, NJ: Socialist Workers Party, 1940
Vote against Jim Crow, 1940
Defend the Philadelphia Sailors, New York: Pioneer Publishers, 1940
The Negro March on Washington, 1941
The March on Washington One Year After, New York: Pioneer Publishers, 1942
The Struggle for Negro Equality (with John Saunders), New York: Pioneer Publishers, 1943
Negroes in the Post-War World, New York: Pioneer Publishers, 1943
Jim Crow Murder of Mr. and Mrs. Harry T. Moore, New York: Pioneers Publishers, 1952
When Anti-Negro Prejudice Began, 1954 (with introduction and afterword, 1971)
Freedom Now: New Stage in the Struggle for Negro Emancipation, 1963
Myths about Malcolm X: Two Views (Rev. Albert Cleage and George Breitman), New York: Merit Publishers, 1968
Black Nationalism and Socialism (with George Novack), New York: Merit Publishers, 1968
The New Radicalization Compared with Those of the Past, 1970

Books on Malcolm X

The Last Year of Malcolm X: The Evolution of a Revolutionary, New York: Merit Publishers, 1967

Edited with Introductions by Breitman

Malcolm X Speaks: Selected Speeches and Statements, New York: Merit Publishers, 1965
Malcolm X on Afro-American History, New York: Merit Publishers, 1967
By Any Means Necessary: Speeches, Interviews, and a Letter, New York: Pathfinder Press, 1970
The Assassination of Malcolm X (collection of articles by George Breitman, Herman Porter, and Baxter Smith), New York: Pathfinder Press, 1976

Books on Leon Trotsky

Edited with Introductions by Breitman

Leon Trotsky on Black Nationalism and Self-Determination, New York: Merit Publishers, 1967
Military Writings, New York: Merit Publishers, 1969
Marxism in Our Time, New York: Pathfinder Press, 1970
Portraits: Political and Personal (with George Saunders), New York: Pathfinder Press, 1977
The Crisis of the French Section, 1935–36 (with Naomi Allen), New York: Pathfinder Press, 1977
Writings of Leon Trotsky (1929–1940), 14 volumes (edited with others), New York: Pathfinder Press, 1970–1979

OTHER WORKS BY GEORGE BREITMAN

"Remembering James P. Cannon," in *James P. Cannon As We Knew Him: By Thirty-three Comrades, Friends, and Relatives*, ed. Les Evans, New York: Pathfinder Press, 1976
Fighting Racism in World War II (collection of articles from the Socialist Appeal and the *Militant*, 1939–1945, by Breitman and others), New York: Monad Press, 1980
The Founding of the Socialist Workers Party: Minutes and Resolutions, 1938–39, New York: Monad Press, 1982

REISSUED WORKS

The Trenton Siege by the Army of Unoccupation, 1986
The Liberating Influence of the Transitional Program (three talks for an SWP educational conference), 1974
"The Rocky Road to the Fourth International" (a talk for an SWP educational conference), 1979
Don't Strangle the Party: Three Letters and a Talk by James P. Cannon (introduction by G. B.), New York: Fourth Internationalist Tendency Publications, 1985

OTHER NOTABLE
BIOGRAPHICAL INFORMATION

George Breitman's pen names were Albert Parker, Philip Blake, Anthony Massini, John F. Petrone, and Chester Hofla.

A listing by Breitman of his articles in the *Militant* for the years 1947 through 1955 showed a total of 515 articles.

Substantial material can also be found in the George Breitman Papers at the Tamiment Library/Robert F. Wagner Labor Archives, Elmer Holmes Bobst Library, 70 Washington Square South, New York, NY 10012.

INDEX